Henry Clay Frick
and the Golden Age
of Coal and Coke, 1870–1920

ALSO BY CASSANDRA VIVIAN

*Americans in Egypt, 1770–1915:
Explorers, Consuls, Travelers, Soldiers,
Missionaries, Writers and Scientists*
(McFarland, 2012)

Henry Clay Frick and the Golden Age of Coal and Coke, 1870–1920

CASSANDRA VIVIAN

McFarland & Company, Inc., Publishers
Jefferson, North Carolina

Library of Congress Cataloguing-in-Publication Data

Names: Vivian, Cassandra, author.
Title: Henry Clay Frick and the golden age of coal and coke, 1870–1920 / [by Cassandra Vivian].
Description: Jefferson, North Carolina : McFarland & Company, Inc., 2020 | Includes bibliographical references and index.
Identifiers: LCCN 2020008481 | ISBN 9781476681559 (paperback) ∞
ISBN 9781476639802 (ebook)
Subjects: LCSH: Frick, Henry Clay, 1849–1919. | Industrialists—United States—Biography. | Coke industry—United States—History—19th century. | Coke industry—United States—History—20th century.
Classification: LCC HD9559.C69 V58 2020 | DDC 338.7/66272092 [B]—dc23
LC record available at https://lccn.loc.gov/2020008481

British Library cataloguing data are available

ISBN (print) 978-1-4766-8155-9
ISBN (ebook) 978-1-4766-3980-2

© 2020 Cassandra Vivian. All rights reserved

No part of this book may be reproduced or transmitted in any form or by any means, electronic or mechanical, including photocopying or recording, or by any information storage and retrieval system, without permission in writing from the publisher.

On the cover: Henry Clay Frick (Carnegie Library of Pittsburgh); *background* Standard Mine was considered the biggest and best in the world and was the centerpiece of Henry Clay Frick's display at the Chicago World's Fair of 1893 (author collection)

Printed in the United States of America

McFarland & Company, Inc., Publishers
Box 611, Jefferson, North Carolina 28640
www.mcfarlandpub.com

Table of Contents

Acknowledgments	vi
Introductory Notes	vii
Preface	1
Introduction	5
One. Coal and Coke	9
Two. Henry Clay Frick	19
Three. The Workers and Their World	41
Four. Strikes from 1875 to 1886	63
Five. Strikes from 1887 to 1889	89
Six. Strike of 1891	102
Seven. Strike of 1894	121
Eight. Cleanup	132
Appendix: The Mines	141
Chapter Notes	179
Bibliography	197
Index	213

Acknowledgments

After more than eight years of work, you can be sure I will omit someone or some place. My apologies.

My grant partners: Jacobs Creek Watershed Association, Westmoreland-Fayette Historical Society, and Fayette County Cultural Trust. Without the trust of these three organizations who allowed me free reign to write the grant, research all the work, and submit the findings, this book would not be possible. I am grateful.

My assistants: Nick Weglowski, Aaron Hollis, Bobbi Kramer, and Eugene Kowalewski.

My main readers: Barbara Miller, Jeffrey Leech, Ronald A. Baraff.

Research organizations: Bureau of Mines, California, PA; Tony Graziani of RGGS; Mount Pleasant Library; Pennsylvania State Library; Helen C. Frick Archives, University of Pittsburgh; Coal & Coke Heritage Center; America's Industrial Heritage Project HABS/HAER–Special Collections and University Archives at Indiana University of Pennsylvania; Fayette County Cultural Trust; Pennsylvania Department of Conservation and Natural Resources; Rivers of Steel National Heritage Area; Braddock Trail Chapter of the DAR; Westmoreland Conservation District; Fayette Conservation District; Pennsylvania State Archives; Philadelphia Archives; Penn State University Archives; Pennsylvania Historical Society; Fayette and Westmoreland County Recorder of Deeds; Fayette and Westmoreland County Prothonotary; Fayette and Westmoreland County GIS; Abandoned Mine Reclamation; Westmoreland Conservancy; Coal & Coke Trail; and any other organization that I contacted and drove crazy with questions.

People who contributed: Galen S. Wagner, Robert Ferguson, Larry Hodge, Robert Hodge, George Wettgen, Joe Eckman, Mike Banaszak, Walter Brown, Duane Fuoss, Rich Rega, Harley N. Trice, Bill Hare, Bill Biller, Michael Mance, Peg Detling, Dale Basinger, Daniel Weinman, Andy McAllister, Bill Lessman, James Hart, Peter E. von Geis, Mary Lou Shick, Mary Kaufmann, Rosalind Ashmun, Connie Gore, Fred Lapisardi, Jim Steeley, Jeff Antol, David Grinnell, Harrison Wick, and all the good folks who attended the meetings at Mount Pleasant Library and the Canteen in Connellsville and participated in our interesting discussions. Nor can one investigate the coal mines and people of the region without referring to the extensive research done by Raymond A. Washlaski, whose web site is now gone.

This project was completed in partnership with the Rivers of Steel Heritage Area. Funding was provided in part by a grant from the Pennsylvania Department of Conservation and Natural Resources, Bureau of Recreation and Conservation, Environmental Stewardship Fund, administered by the Rivers of Steel Heritage Corp.

Introductory Notes

The name of Pittsburgh ended in an "h" when it was founded in the 1700s. It was taken away by the federal government in 1890 and remained that way until 1911, when the government gave in to protests. Since much of our research was within this time frame, throughout the text Pittsburgh has an "h," except in direct quotes.

There are several spellings of Broad Ford. The original name found on early maps is Broad Ford. Later the name was combined into a single word, Broadford. Both are correct. Broad Ford is the name given to the area by Native Americans, who identified it as a safe and good place to cross the Youghiogheny River: a broad ford. Many locals believe that Braddock's Army crossed the Youghiogheny at this place and not at Stewart's Crossing. It could have crossed in both places, with heavy equipment at Broadford. The spellings are used interchangeably.

The Connellsville newspaper, the *Courier*, has been called the *Weekly Courier*, the *Daily Courier*, the *Keystone Courier*, and for a short time the *Courier*. All are used.

The records of the Pinkerton Detective Agency are found in the Library of Congress. They cover 63,000 items in 183 containers plus 20 oversized, occupying 79 linear feet, and include three microfilm reels. The records include business and family correspondence, biographical and genealogical records, administrative records, and criminal case files. The documents span the years 1853–1999, with the bulk of the material dated 1880–1920.

The Heritage Documentation Program of the National Park Service has a number of programs to preserve America's physical history. Among them are two used in this study: the Historic American Building Survey (HABS) and the Historic American Engineering Record (HAER). Beginning in the 1980s, they did extensive work with America's Industrial Heritage Project of Pennsylvania. The project encompassed nine counties in Southwestern Pennsylvania researching steel, iron, coal and transportation history to create tourist venues of same. Their archives are at the Library of Congress and the Special Collection of Indiana University of Pennsylvania. I mention them here because I use one of their reports and prove much of it incorrect. The scope of their work is far significant beyond this single report.

Likewise, a second heritage project called the Rivers of Steel National Heritage Area, which provided three grants for this project, grew up in the Pittsburgh area to celebrate steel. It showcased the "artistry and innovation of southwestern Pennsylvania's industrial and cultural heritage by fostering dynamic initiatives and transformative experiences." It does this through tours, restoration, and more. It encompasses nine counties, too, but most of its records are found in Homestead. Fayette and Westmoreland counties belonged to both heritage areas.

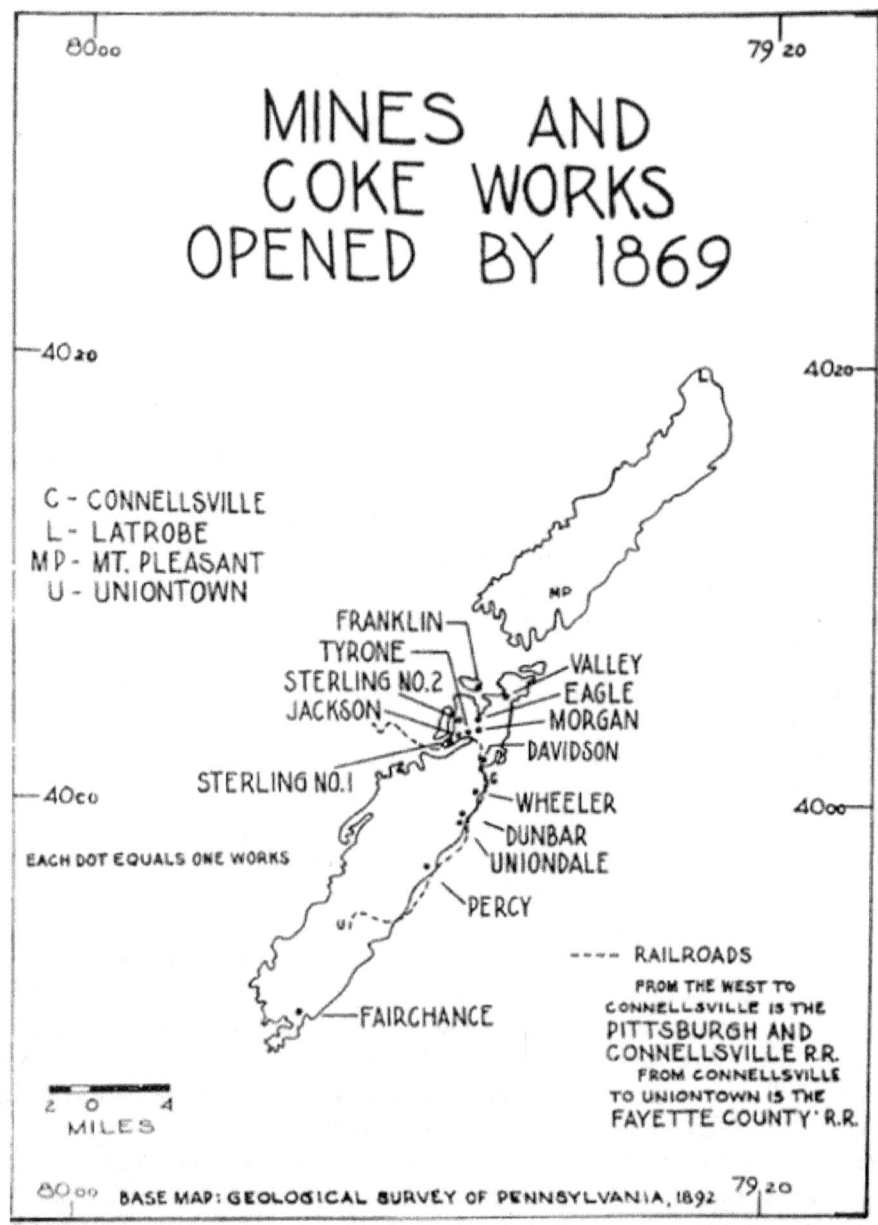

Above and opposite: Adapted from John Enman, *The Relationship of Coal Mining and Coke Making to the Distribution of Population Agglomerations in the Connellsville (Pennsylvania) Beehive Coke Region,* Unpublished Ph.D. Dissertation, Pittsburgh, PA: University of Pittsburgh, 1962, Coal and Coke Heritage Center at Penn State Fayette, The Eberly Campus.

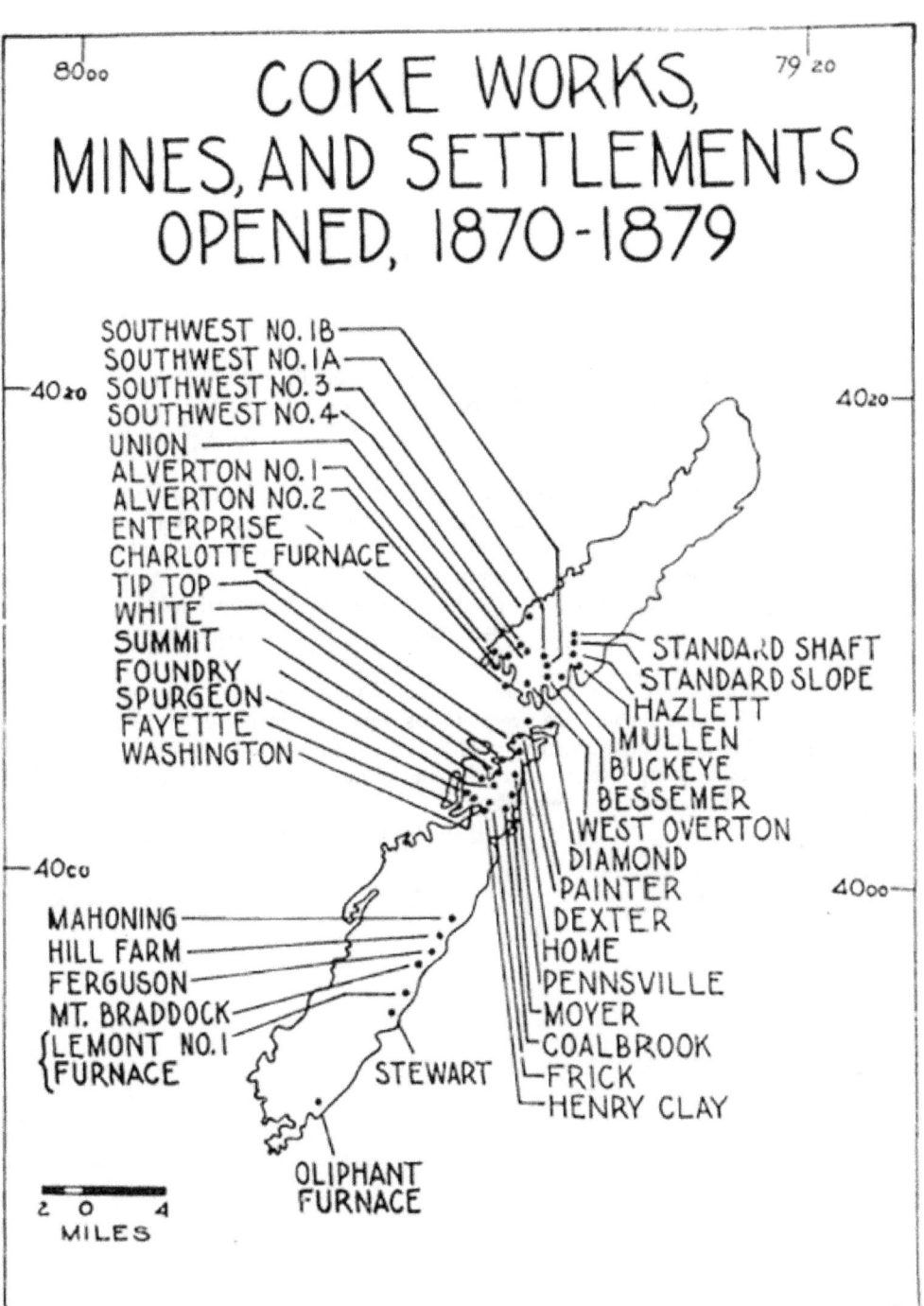

How interesting it would be if all these people could come to life and tell us what they know … if only they could talk.
— Henry Clay Frick

"If all the output in 1882 were put on one freight-haul traveling at the usual speed of 14 miles an hour, a man watching the train pull out at a given hour one morning would see coke cars passing in unbroken succession without a moment's pause or slackening for nine days and nights before he saw the tail light on the last car. By that time the engine would be 2,800 miles away."
—*Cloud by Day*, Muriel Earley Sheppard

"It is difficult, probably impossible, to find objective history. Historians rewrite the past in every age, seeing forces, values, or principles that were ignored or undervalued by their predecessors. The interpretation of events is affected by partisanship, either conscious or unrealized—nationalism or religious bias provide obvious examples."
—*Wealth, Waste, and Alienation*, Kenneth Warren

Preface

The main mission of this study is to present a readable, informative narrative of the events that formed the birth of the coal and coke industry in southwestern Pennsylvania using as many original sources as possible. This narrative is written in easy-to-read language and is geared not only to scholars but also to the general public and people whose ancestors lived the events described.

For a brief time in American history, the Connellsville Coke Region was the most important industrial center in the world. That history is seldom mentioned and often overshadowed by other industries that had less significance, especially in the very early eras. That needs to change. Modern families need to know the struggles their ancestors endured, not only as immigrants but as coal miners as well. What they know is mostly post–1920 myth, and unkind myth at that. In our text, names are named, events are described, and very little is judged. Mostly the events are presented so readers can form their own opinion. The people of the coke region generally have an image of Frick as an evil corrupt man. That image has been promoted and kept alive by the hundreds of articles and dozens of books that provide an image that is not just unkind but wrong. Hopefully the information provided in this book will create some doubt.

Of course, the book discusses Henry Clay Frick. A major mission of this book is to present a positive point of view about the man who practically built the bituminous industry in Fayette and Westmoreland counties by himself. But it also covers the miners—who they were, where they came from, how they lived and worked. That leads to a discussion of immigration, a discussion that exposes similar problems dealing with immigration today. And it covers unions and strikes. Violence shook the region. It was terrifying. Finally, the text presents a fresh perspective because it uses the sources of the day: regional newspapers like the *Mount Pleasant Dawn, Mount Pleasant Journal, Scottdale Independent,* and *Connellsville Courier* from 1870 to 1910, form the background of events as told and viewed by the people who lived it.

So what doesn't this book do? It is not balanced. When two points of view on a single subject are presented and discussed, there are moments when a point is argued, but it does not dominate the text. What the book does mostly is inform. It informs readers of often unknown facts found from original sources. There is no apology. For over a century the name Frick has been vilified. In this book he is acknowledged for the fair-minded genius he was.

Nor does it analyze. In presenting the long-overlooked voice of the original sources, it lets the reader read, compare, debate, accept or reject. The mission is to bring to the front what the original sources saw and reported. Their voices seem to have been lost far too long. One reason is that they are hard to find. The story of the immigrants, the forming of the syndicates, the beginnings of unionization, the battles through the various early strikes, the evolution of the patches and the company stores straight from the Middle Ages, are all told here via the written word of the day. Those words had their biases, their prejudices, and their fears, but they show life as it was lived, not as it has been analyzed and presented by people from a different century.

Why This Subject Is Important

It becomes obvious why the original voices are so important to any discussion of the coal and coke era in southwestern Pennsylvania. Too many errors have been introduced into history, not only by writers, but by family stories. Correcting these errors is an important aspect of this book. Often in discussions about the coal industry, people will tell a bad story and hold Frick responsible. Most of the time the event happened, but another coal baron was responsible, or the event took place in the 1930s, '40s, or '50s, long after Frick's death in 1919. One of the reasons for this is that the name Frick has become synonymous with the industry itself. One does not say "the Frick company," one simply says "Frick" for almost any coal company or the entire early industry.

How I Did My Research

I researched this subject in newspapers and journals of the day, in libraries and historical societies' archives, in personal papers and personal stories, in county records, in interviews, and on the Internet. Just as the coal and coke industry was beginning, so were many of the local newspapers. They were hard to find. When I discovered that the *Mount Pleasant Journal* had not been digitized, I got the job done, and it is now available on the website of state library of Pennsylvania. Of course, not the entire *Journal* is there. There are ownership restrictions. But from 1882 to 1922, with some gaps, it can be researched. It is an important document that reported day-by-day, event by event, the growth and early strikes in the southwestern Pennsylvania bituminous coal and coke region.

I traveled the district a hundred times looking for the specific mines in this study and what was left of their ovens. I visited the Frick archives at the University of Pittsburgh both personally and online. Their holdings are amazing, especially because the papers of other operators in the region are very difficult to find, if they exist at all. Then I went to the offices of RGGS, the company who bought the mineral rights from U.S. Steel.

I presented what I discovered in five open meetings at the Mount Pleasant Library and six at the Connellsville Canteen. Each event was a two-hour program with plenty of discussion and questions and answers. They were highly successful because I sent out press releases to ten different newspapers. At the first meeting in Mount Pleasant, one man was not happy that I saw Frick in a positive light. He never came back. At another meeting, Frick family members attended and were pleased to see an honest, open, balanced discussion about both Frick and the coal and coke industry. From the discussions I had and the reports I heard, I anticipate the book will be controversial and many will never forgive me for exploding the myth.

How This Book Is Organized

There are certain subjects that find their way into more than one chapter and seem to form a thread throughout the book: immigrants and immigration, company patches, company stores and, of course, Henry Clay Frick. The book covers the early mines in the Morgan Valley, a 9-mile-long ravine filled with coal mines, coke ovens and a stream. It marked the beginning of the growth of the industry in the region. It was where Frick built his first mines. Thus, Chapter One defines coal mining and its various jobs. Chapter Two introduces Henry Clay Frick. The next chapter is devoted to the immigrants: how they got here, where they lived in patches, their struggles to survive, and their dealings with the company stores. The next four chapters are devoted to the strikes in the region. The final chapter is on the cleanup. Coal mines and coke ovens were horrific polluters of streams. The stage of cleanup began in the 1920s and continues today with sporadic results. The appendix is devoted to the various mines in the valley and in our research. Each mine is discussed at length, including its development and demise, its role in strikes, and events that define it. These chapters include incidents and events that add color and detail. The mines stretched beyond the Morgan Valley as the Golden Age unfolded; the industry was growing, and all the mines around Mount Pleasant are included in this chapter. Much of what is found in these chapters will be new to most readers.

Introduction

Carmen Peter DiCiccio, in *Bituminous Coal and Coke Resources of Pennsylvania 1740–1945* for the National Register of Historic Places Continuation Sheet, defines the bituminous coal era in southwestern Pennsylvania into four distinct eras:

The Emergence of Coal in the Age of Wood (1740–1840)
Transportation, Iron and Railroad Revolution as Impetus for Expansion of the Coal and Coke Industry (1840–1880)
The Golden Era of King Coal, Queen Coke and Princess Steel (1880–1920)
Retrenchment, Decline and Mechanized Mines (1920–1945)[1]

These divisions are accurate. The assessments correct. Our project begins in 1870, as the Morgan Valley begins to develop a string of early mines, and concludes in 1920. The era is dominated by the man who opened his first mines in the Morgan Valley of Fayette County in 1871, steered the industry through early growth, and turned it into the most important industrial growth in America: Henry Clay Frick. Taking the lead from DiCiccio, we call this period the Golden Age. Thus our title: *Henry Clay Frick and the Golden Age of Coal and Coke: 1870 to 1920*.

The book is definitely about Frick. It portrays the side of Frick it seems few people know and acknowledge: the genius side that saw the potential, organized the operators, treated his men fairly, and guided the industry from infancy to maturity. But it is also about the people of the region: their hardships, their roles in the conflicts, and their joys. They are the people who lived the story. Yes, it is about the giants, the owners, and their attempts to understand the industry, to learn to control it, and to deal with the workers. But more important, it is about the workers too: the immigrants, the miners, the storekeepers, the ministers and even the children. It is their story to tell. What is most important is that the story is told using the sources of the day, the original source material from newspapers, government publications, and company records.

The first chapter takes us into the world of mining by discussing coal and its possibilities. The bituminous coal in Westmoreland and Fayette counties was the best in the world. This chapter tells why. It also explores the early development of coal mines in the Morgan Valley region, and why, how, and who converted coal to coke. The new industry needed services, so the new railways are discussed, as are the various shops needed to make cars, and the dangers of the industry including water and fire. How a mine was constructed, what it consisted of, what the uses of each department were, what kind of entrance it had, and all the various jobs in the mine are all defined. Next the narrative turns to the coke ovens. What a beehive is, how it operates, the process of converting coal to coke, and what a byproduct oven is, are all explained in detail.

The second chapter is about Henry Clay Frick. It begins with a short biography of Frick's early life as the grandson of a prominent Mennonite farmer and distiller at the southeastern edge of Westmoreland County, Pennsylvania. Frick's cousins became involved in the new industry of mining and coking, and he soon joined them, opening two mines in 1871. He met the Panic of 1873 head-on by using company scrip to keep his mines open, saving the newly constructed Mount Pleasant and Broadford Railroad from disaster, and buying properties as men failed in the business. These acts kept the industry alive. Soon he merged his company with that of Andrew Carnegie, and he did for Carnegie what he had done for himself: he organized, he consolidated, and he purchased subsidiary industries to their advantage. Carnegie, on the other hand, kept buying H.C. Frick Coke stock until he became the controlling partner, and then the trouble began. In the end Frick brokered a deal with a few New York men; they bought out Carnegie, and U.S. Steel was born. Frick was a part of that too.

The remainder of the lengthy chapter fights back against the horrific reputation of the man by quoting and disproving statement after statement related to Homestead, poor salaries of miners, safety in the mines, pensions, company stores, company patches, and Frick's philanthropy. These topics are dealt with in depth in further chapters too. The chapter also discusses the court case brought by Frick's daughter against a book that bought the hype and reported that Frick was evil. She lost the case because the judge did not respect Frick.

The third chapter does for the workers what the second did for Frick: it defines them. It begins by discussing the need for workers and how they were brought to this country: American Emigrant Company, Castle Garden men, and more. Then it defines each ethnic group, its customs, and its location within the bituminous region, showing us what in our culture today was given to us by these early immigrants. Then it turns to their lives and begins to blow away the false myths that so dominate beliefs today. The workers' housing was mostly good, as evidenced by the fact that many houses used by the miners are still standing and still occupied 150 years later. The mining patch in the Golden Age was not horrible. The miners were not forced to buy only in the company stores, they were not paid only in scrip, their wages were in keeping with the wages of other workers of the day, safety was a priority, and contrary to what is believed, they were compensated for injuries and death. All of these issues dominate the myths of the coal and coke industry, and through the use of original sources, they are examined and the truth is told. The narrative also proves that in the Golden Age, Frick led the way to do what was right for the miners and their families.

The chapter also covers the fact that immigrants were not welcome in America. They were accused of taking jobs away, sending their money back to the old country, and dozens of other claims that are used today to define new immigrants and keep the people fighting each other.

Chapters Four through Seven cover the various strikes from 1875 to 1894. Each strike is dealt with in depth, and the research was done, once again, using original sources. For the early mines, most of the sources were the newspapers of the day, as the government publications had not yet begun to publish, and the Frick correspondences often do not go back that far. The later strikes had more original sources to use, including government reports.

The first of these chapters begins by introducing the various unions trying to organize. Then it introduces the various enforcement agencies, like the Pinkertons and the Coal and Iron Police. The narrative describes the events of the day, including several panics, or depressions, and their effects on the mining world; the most important were the Panic of 1873 and the Panic of 1893. It becomes obvious that the mining world was divided into three groups: the operators, trying to understand a new industry, balance their costs to their income, and find markets for their products; the miners, looking for a fair wage and a good life; and the unions, fighting each other for dominance and fighting the companies in the name of the miners.

Each strike brought a new challenge. The very early strikes of the 1870s showed the miners that they had power. The strikes of 1875 to 1879 saw peaceful marches with bands and banners without damage or danger to the towns and the mines. The Strike of 1886 was violent, with much loss of property to mines and towns, and it also brought to light the growing immigration problem in the region. The Strike of 1887 was a battle between the emerging unions for domination, not only in the coal and coke region, but nationally as well. It also saw the intrusion of Andrew Carnegie into the coal fields. The Strike of 1889 saw the reemergence of the immigrants in a rampage that called for their deportation. The two worst strikes were the Strike of 1891, which saw the Morewood Massacre, and the Strike of 1894, which saw the murder of Mr. Paddock, the Frick company's chief engineer. Each of these strikes is described blow by blow with local newspapers filling their entire front page with the events.

All was enacted on the streets of Mount Pleasant and Scottdale and down the Morgan Valley. Massive marches, some 5,000 strong, roamed the streets with guns and clubs, terrorizing everyone. In the end the miners threw the unions out, and for decades afterward, there were no unions in the mining world.

The final chapter examines the problems that mining brought to the region. It involves the pollution and the cleanup. It began early and is still going on. It wasn't just mines that polluted. It was industry in general. The battle is still going on.

Finally, there is a lengthy appendix. It contains a section on each mine in the discussion, of which there are nearly twenty. They are arranged in chronological order from the day they were founded: Morgan, Eagle, Foundry, Valley, Frick, Henry Clay, Summit, White, Tip Top, and Rist were the original mines in the Morgan Valley. Only two were built by Frick, but he eventually owned all of them. As the research grew, the mines of the McClure Company, which Frick bought, began to play a role in the narrative: Star, Buckeye, Hazlett, Mullen, Bessemer, and Alverton. Then Frick began a second group of mines not affiliated with the H.C. Frick Coke Company. They were Morewood, Alice, and Standard. They are also part of the story.

Each of the mines is explored in depth. Each story begins with the founding of the mine, when Frick acquired it, how big it was, how many coke ovens it employed over the years, and what happened to it and to its workers through the years of growth, strikes, and demise. That includes floods, fires, strikes, and mining problems. By no means were these the only mines in the Connellsville region or the only ones owned by Frick. But they were the beginning and the most important to our narrative.

The importance of most of these mines is that they are forgotten. Few know where they were, how big they were, how many ovens they had, or what happened to them. Even fewer know that one of them was the biggest and best mine in the world, that another held the first coke ovens in Westmoreland County, or that a third has a large string of coke ovens still standing for all to see.

ONE

Coal and Coke

Coal is "the world's most valuable single mineral deposit."[1] It was formed 225 to 350 million years ago as the Carboniferous Period swamps turned into peat and the mud layers surrounding it turned to sandstone, shale, and limestone. It eventually hardened into the product we recognize today. It is so important to human evolution that an entire geological era is named in its honor. That era is called the Pennsylvanian Era (325–285 MYA) because the best coal deposits in the world are in Pennsylvania, especially in the southwest corner.

Pennsylvania has two kinds of coal: anthracite and bituminous. Anthracite, called clean coal, has far fewer impurities, which makes it produce a higher heat and burn cleaner. That coal is primarily used in smelting and in the metallurgical and chemical industries. The anthracite region is in central Pennsylvania. Bituminous, called soft coal, is converted into coke, which burns hotter than the coal it is derived from and is used for foundry and industrial applications such as steel production and, most recently, to produce electricity. The bituminous region in Pennsylvania is in the west, with the best bituminous coal found in the Connellsville Coal Basin in Fayette and Westmoreland counties. The *Engineering Magazine* of 1901 reported:

> The seam of Connellsville coal, which is the basis of all this wonderful progress and gratifying prosperity, is one of the most remarkable in the States, if not in the world. It is pre-eminently a coking coal. There is no other coal so regular in formation, so uniform in quality, of so convenient a thickness, or so easily mined. These are not mere statements, but facts—facts that have made Pittsburg the steel center of the world, and facts that in thirty years have been the means of bringing up the output of the blast furnaces of the United States from 30 tons per day to more than 700 tons per day.[2]

George Thurston, in his book *Pittsburgh and Allegheny in the Centennial Year*, called the coal in this region "The Great Seam."[3] The Great Seam is divided into the Old Basin and the Klondike. The Klondike came last and encompasses mostly western Fayette and Greene counties. The Old Basin covers northern Fayette County and passes into Westmoreland County, ending up around Latrobe. It is an area only 50 miles long and 2.5 miles wide.[4] Approximately twenty-one companies operated a series of mines in the Old Basin.[5]

This study is mostly about the earliest part of the Old Basin in Fayette and Westmoreland counties, covering about ten miles beginning at Broadford along the Youghiogheny and up a valley known as the Morgan Valley, crossing Jacobs Creek into Westmoreland County at Scottdale, and ending in a cluster of mines surrounding Mount Pleasant. The mines in the study include Henry Clay, Frick, Morgan, Rist, Foundry, White (Globe), Eagle, Summit, Tip Top, Valley, Buckeye, Star, Hazlett, Mullin, Bessemer, Union, Alverton (Donnelly and Mayfield), Morewood, Alice, and Standard (a few others are mentioned now and then). These mines began to operate in the late 1860s and were a major contribution to the beginning of coal mining as a major U.S. industry for several reasons. The best coal, in a formation called the Pittsburgh Seam, was easily found close to the surface in the area. Galley Run, the stream that flowed through the valley, and Jacobs Creek and its tributaries, surrounding Mount Pleasant, provided an abundance of water to quench the ovens. The streams had eroded the hillsides into a ravine so the coal was easily mined. Finally, and perhaps most important of all, turning the coal into coke using the beehive coke oven matured the industry.

Coal was not the first fuel for industry in the region. Wood was. But wood was limited, and soon it became obvious that the deposits of coal being used for small purposes could be the answer. Coal mining began as soon as people came into the region. The Native Americans used coal. So did the early travelers. The men of Braddock's army built campfires from coal. When George Washington passed the region in 1770, he noted in his journal: "October 14th. At Capt. Crawford's all day. Went to see a coal mine not far from his house on the bank of the river. The coal seemed to be of the very best kind burning freely and an abundance of it."[6]

As early as 1797, glassmaking began in New Geneva and used coal for its fire. So did distilleries, of which there were many. Boatbuilding was another major industry in the area that used coal. Boats were built along the Monongahela River in Brownsville, California, Fayette City, and Belle Vernon. They were sent all over the great Mississippi Watershed, expanding the country. It wasn't long before men began flatboating coal down the Ohio looking for customers. Once the Monongahela was dammed, steamboats replaced flatboats. In 1811, the *New Orleans*, the first steamboat to make its way to New Orleans, used local coal to build its steam.

Many small mining operations sprang up to fill local needs, including those of minor or small industries. Larger mines began to open along the Mon(ongahela) and the Yough(iogheny). Slowly the miners began to convert the coal to coke. They used various methods, and by 1855 there were twenty-six coke ovens around the Yough.[7] Converting the coal to coke was the key for the growth of the industry. Coke was pure carbon. It burned hotter and longer. Its use in industry began as early as 1817, when Isaac Meason used coke for his Plumstock Iron Works.[8] Nearly half a century later, the beehive coke oven was born. The beehive was crucial and its development made the region what it was. In the 1840s near the village of Dawson, 4 miles from Broadford, Provance McCormick, James Campbell, and John Taylor build this new style of coke oven. It converted coal to coke. In 1841 they took their product, launched a boat on the Yough, and headed to Cincinnati to market the coke. No one wanted it.[9] So they sold their mine and beehive ovens to Mordecai Cochran. Mordecai repeated the effort: he loaded coke on a boat he built, and tried to sell it to businesses along the Ohio River. His nephew James Cochran joined him on the river, and they sold the first coke for money to a company in Cincinnati in 1843. That company wanted more. That was the birth of an industry. In turn, other industries dependent upon coal or coke grew: iron, steel, zinc, salt, glass, and more. Thus, briefly stated, the industrial revolution of America began.

The Early Infrastructure

As the industry matured, it became obvious that getting the coal and coke to market was a major problem. Mines were developed in rural areas. Moving the coal and coke from the mines to customers required roads. The companies built the roads. Moving the coal and coke long distances required more than roads; it needed river transport and land transport. The biggest development on land was the coming of the railroads. That is an amazing story of intrigue and challenge. Each rail company wanted to control the region. The battle for coal country involved companies, states, and sabotage. As the mines from Broadford to Mount Pleasant grew, the need for transport became obvious. Two of the earliest and most important rail lines related to this study were the Mount Pleasant and Broad Ford Railroad and the Southwest Pennsylvania Railway Company.

In 1870 the Mount Pleasant and Broad Ford Railroad Company was incorporated by Daniel Shupe, C.S. Overholt, J.B. Jordan, William J. Hitchman, Joseph R. Stouffer (sic), A.O. Tinstman, Israel Painter, C.P. Markle, and James Neel, all local men whose last names still resonate in the region today. It was opened within a year and linked the mines to points south and east. Shortly thereafter, it was leased to the Pittsburgh and Connellsville Railroad Company, which in turn leased it to the Baltimore and Ohio Railroad Company, which still runs through the region today.[10]

The Southwest Pennsylvania Railway Company linked the region north through Westmoreland County. It was incorporated in 1871 by Israel Painter, Alpheus E. Willson, James E. Logan, Samuel Dellinger (sic), and Christopher Sherrick. The plan was to link to the Pennsylvania Railway, which was in a struggle with the Baltimore and Ohio for dominance in southwestern Pennsylvania. By 1875, not only did it link north, it also reached Uniontown in the south.[11] Ironically, today, the battle over modern-day trails have the same conflicts. Some want to journey north and link trails into and through Westmoreland County. Others want to travel down the Morgan Valley, past the ruins of the coal and coke era and the abandoned Overholt Distillery, to cross the Yough and link to the Great Allegheny Passage.

The mines and their owners so dominated the railroads that they built their own wooden cars to carry the coal and coke. "By 1889 there were about 4,000 private cars hauling coke out of the region, including 2,400 controlled by the H.C. Frick Coke Company, almost 1,000 controlled by the McClure Coke Company, and 200 owned by the W.J. Rainey Company."[12] They each built their own shops to build the cars: McClure at Lemont, Rainey at Mt. Braddock, and Frick at Morgan Station. The shops built the wooden wagons used by miners to mine the coal, and later built railroad cars to be used to haul the coke to market. In 1893, the *Mount Pleasant Journal* reported that the car shops at Morgan would soon be moved to Summit Mine.[13] The move was still underway in 1896, but instead of moving to Summit, the shops were moved to Everson (Summit is so near to Everson it may be considered the same place).[14] In *A History of Area Mines*, we probably have the definitive answer: The Frick company acquired the land for the Everson shops in 1895–6. In addition to the car shop, they established a pattern shop, foundry, machine shop, carpenter shop, and more. The workers also made major repairs to boilers, pumps, etc., for all Frick mines. By 1931 they added an electrical repair shop. The shops were dismantled and the land sold in 1940.[15]

So the development of the region was based on the needs of the industry. It needed transport and built roads and railroads. It needed workers and imported men. It needed housing, so the companies built villages. The workers and their families needed food and necessities, so the companies established stores within the towns. Some of these actions mimicked thousand-year-old worldwide industries and would bring long-lasting conflict.

Water and Fire

Water was a problem. As coal was removed, ground water often took its place, and had to be pumped out of the mine. A wall of coal could be holding back underground water, and once such a wall was breached, a flood began, sometimes closing the mine for good. Floods from rain could also close a mine. More than once, the entire region was out of work because of a storm. Storms create ground water, and it would flow into the mine via all of its openings (air vents, pit holes, shafts). A big flood accompanied an 18-hour deluge in August of 1888 and the entire Morgan Valley was closed.[16] In 1912, a storm trapped two miners at the White Mine. "Their lamps had been extinguished. The rescue party, led by Superintendent John Shields, waded into the mine and finally reached the two men."[17] Another flood hit in 1954. Accounts say it was 25 inches higher than a severe flood in 1936 and reached as far as Pittsburgh. At Broadford "a 60-foot span of the foot-bridge across the Yough between Adelaide and Broadford was carried away."[18] This type of storm continues to occur in the region. Connellsville was hit with a big storm in each of the winters of 2016, '17, '18, and '19, and the lower regions were decimated. All the abandoned mines had to receive some of this water too.

However, there were times when water was a blessing. In 1892–3, the Morgan Valley mines continued to operate while the rest of the region had to shut down for lack of water.[19] The mines had water partly because Henry Clay Frick had built a number of water companies in the region. They were used not only by the mines, but by the towns. The first was the Mount Pleasant Water Company, built along Jacob's Creek at Mount Pleasant. The second was the Youghiogheny Water Company, built at Broadford to supply water along the Morgan Valley. The final one was the Trotter Water Company above Connellsville.[20]

Fire was the second danger. It was among the most feared events in a mine. Coal burns. Once a fire began, it was almost impossible to extinguish permanently. The most famous mine fire is that of Centralia in Columbia County in central Pennsylvania, which has been burning for over 50 years and is estimated to burn for 250 more. Locally there were burning mines, too. Work crews building the new Route 119 accidentally opened two mines. The first caused a flood that had to be stopped. The second reignited a fire that had been burning for years but had been smothered by lack of air. Mines that burned or are burning in our study are discussed under the three mine chapters.

All the byproducts coal produced as it was mined also burned. There were gases underground that could ignite. Yet there had to be light in a mine. The first light was a flame worn on the helmet of the miner. If that flame entered a space where gases were intense, there could be an explosion. All the early mine disasters in the region were caused by explosions. The Hill Farm Mine fire of 1890 killed 31 (of 57 in the mine) and was caused by the lamp flame on a young miner's lamp coming into contact with gases rushing into the mine from a new bore hole. The Mammoth Mine disaster of 1891 killed 109 miners because of a firedamp explosion. As a result of the Mammoth disaster, the Frick company began a mine safety program that became the industry standard. The worst year in the area was 1907, and that year the worst mine disaster was at the Darr Mine along the Youghiogheny River near Van Meter, where 239 miners were killed. Again, an open-flame miner's lamp was probably to blame.

The Mine Itself

A typical early mine was a complex group of buildings and areas both above and below ground. It consisted of a mine office where the bosses worked and kept the mine records; an

Morewood Mine with a tipple, coke ovens, and various buildings. The building at the top center was the residence of the superintendent. It is still standing—all else is gone (postcard).

engine house, where the machines to run things like air fans operated; machine and repair shops, where coal cars were built and other items repaired; the wash house, where the miners showered and kept their personal items; a scale house, where the wagons of coal were weighed and the miners' wages assessed; a few sheds for various chores and supplies; and a tipple, where coal was moved from in the mine to the ovens and/or to the rails for transport.

The entrance to a mine was determined by the level of the coal seam to be mined. In the Connellsville district, the Pittsburgh Seam was mined. It was one of many different underground seams of coal packed one on top of the other. Each seam had a different name and a different value as to minable coal. The Pittsburgh Seam was considered to be among the best bituminous coal resources in the world, for it had a low sulfur content, roughly 1 to 2 percent, and a fixed carbon content after conversion that allowed it to be stable and provide the heat needed for burning. In the Connellsville district, on average, the seam was 9 feet thick and therefore very minable. Each seam was found at different heights depending on the terrain. Over the 300 million years it took to form, the earth went through upheavals, pushing and pulling the seam, so that it could be just below the surface or hundreds of feet below.[21]

If the seam was near the surface and one could walk into the mine and bring the coal out with little effort, the entrance was called a drift entrance. If the seam was a little deeper but the coal could still be hauled out easily, it was called a slope entrance. However, if the seam was hundreds of feet below the surface, a shaft had to be dug and an elevator system used. That was called a shaft mine. It was accepted in the industry that the deeper the Pittsburgh Seam in the ground and the thicker the seam, the purer the coal. Most of the mines in Morgan Valley and around Mount Pleasant were drift, and only a few were slope and shaft.

There may be more than one entrance to a mine, and in addition to entrances, there were a variety of shafts. Air shafts blew fresh air into the mine or allowed gases to escape. Underground tunnels led up and out of the mine or into various rooms. The rooms were once protected by thick walls of unmined coal that helped to keep the roof from falling. These were called pillars.

Each miner had wagons called larry cars that were used to haul the freshly mined coal. Once filled, the wagons were taken out of the mine—originally by mules, later by small locomotives. They were taken to a scale house where each load was weighed and credited to the miner, who was paid by the wagonload. If the coal was to be made into coke, it was taken in one direction and dropped into the coke ovens. If it was to be sold as coal, it was hoisted to the top of the tipple and dropped into awaiting railroad cars or river barges and shipped out.[22]

The Jobs

In addition to the men who mined the coal and fired the coke, there were a bevy of jobs that needed to be done: blacksmiths, carpenters, firemen, laborers, specialists such as engineers, and more. *Coal Mines & Coal Miners* lists over forty different positions in a coal mine. Each mine had a **superintendent** who was responsible for upholding the mining laws and seeing to supplies, safety, and general needs of the mine. Under him was the **mine boss**, who dealt with the everyday operations of the mine. He was responsible for the workers, their duties, and their adherence to rules of mining. He had to oversee the ventilation of the mine, the supplies, the way the coal was mined, the safety of the underground rooms, and the safety and maintenance of all the equipment, including safety lamps, which had to be secured and in good condition. The **outside foreman** did about the same things, only above ground. Next was the **fire boss**. It was his responsibility to see that the mine was safe from any dangerous gases. He preceded the men at the beginning of each shift to check for bad air or other dangers. He provided a written daily report related to any dangers and reported any violations of mining laws. **Engineers** were responsible for acquiring, maintaining, and inspecting all machinery, pumps, boilers, etc.

In addition to mining the coal, the **miner** checked his workplace each day, loosened and removed dangerous slate, confirmed the mine was secure before blasting, kept out of abandoned areas, and stayed informed of firedamp and other dangers. The **drivers** were responsible for the animals, their care, their food, and their security, along with the **barn boss**, who examined each animal daily and stopped any cruelty. **Trip riders** or **runners** were responsible to secure the equipment that hauled the coal out of the mine. The **weighmaster** was responsible to see that each load of coal was weighed correctly and each was credited to a miner.

There were children in the mines too. They worked specific jobs such as "runners, drivers, door boys, and couplers." Some simply were "employed with their fathers loading coal." Doctors would provide certificates stating they were "unable to attend school on account of physical disability" and then they would go directly into the mine.[23]

The Animals

Animals were a key component of mining. The smallest animal in the mines was the **canary**. The bird would be caged and hung in an area that could have gases and left there.

It was checked frequently, and if the canary died, the men exited the mine as quickly as possible, for deadly gases were in the air. Those gases could explode.

The hardest-working animals in the mine were the **mules** and **horses**. They were used to haul the coal up out of the mine, pull the larry cars over the coke ovens, and take the finished coke to the rail cars. It was dangerous and they were often involved in accidents. One accident reported in local papers happened at the Boyle & Hazlett coke works near Mount Pleasant. The cars were being hauled down into the pit and a rope gave way. There were two cars, and they zoomed down the incline picking up speed as they fell. A mule was in the way and was killed instantly.[24]

The animals had a miserable life. They were often purchased from nearby farms, but the Frick company had several stock farms to raise their animals. Their life expectancy in the mines was less than a decade, and then they were retired to the farms.

A local story relates to a mine mule called Rusty. When the horrific explosion happened at the Carpentertown Mine near Mount Pleasant in 1952, the cleanup took a few days. No one thought about the animals. As they looked for victims, they spotted Rusty standing in a side tunnel. He was never given hard labor again and became a local hero. Children of miners would beg to be placed on his back for a few moments.[25]

Folklore in the Mines

Mine workers developed their own folklore in their particular environment. "According to three of the five sources, there is a belief that no bananas can be eaten in the coal mine. George Monas and Nick Massini both recounted this belief. Richard Marcavitch also recounted this belief and provided suggestion that it is because they cause heartburn, but only underground."[26]

Another example: "Some miners believed that it was bad luck to have an alarm clock fall from a mantle. If this happened, the miner would not go to work for one day. Some miners would not go to work if they happened to put their shirts on inside out. Sometimes, if a woman crossed a miners [sic] path while he was on his way to work, he would go home and miss work that day."[27]

Types of Ovens

The Beehive Coke Oven

Once the coal was mined, it was heated in an oxygen-deprived environment to convert it into nearly pure carbon that burned hotter and longer than coal. Making coke was not new. In England they were doing it in the sixteenth century.[28] The challenge was to find the right method. After many trials and failures, the beehive coke oven was invented. It gave birth to the Connellsville coke region. The oven was built of special brick called firebrick to withstand the temperatures as high as 2000 degrees Fahrenheit. The oven stood inside a casing of cement to protect it and make it possible to drive larry cars loaded with coal over the top. Each oven had a hole in the top called the trunnel through which the coal was dropped. It had a door on the front from which the coke was drawn. There was a tax on each oven, so when an oven was no longer needed, the cement top was broken and then no tax was assessed.

Traditionally, companies made 48-hour and 72-hour coke. Each required a different load and burn time. The 48-hour needed 6½ to 7 tons of coal, which was burned for two days hours, while the 72-hour coke needed an 8-ton charge and was usually burned over a weekend. Each served a different purpose. After firing, each load of coke was quenched by water—850 gallons of it—which was poured back into the nearby stream. In 1888 the *Connellsville Courier* began to publish a weekly oven list, which named the mine, the owner, the number of ovens, and the number of ovens in blast. As the industry grew, the list was divided into merchant and furnace ovens. Merchant ovens made coke for general use, including foundries, while furnace ovens made coke exclusively for blast furnaces in steel mills. Each required a different firing.

Beehive coke ovens were erected in two ways: bank and block. The bank ovens were tucked into the bottom of a hill or along a stream in a single row, usually near the railroad track. The block ovens were stretched out in two rows, one behind the other. Both types were near water, as it was essential to quench the coke after firing.

The By-Product Oven

An improvement in the beehive oven was the by-product oven. The beehive polluted the air by belching out gases. The by-product, developed in Europe in the 1880s, caught the various gases once released into the air and made it possible to salvage them for use in other ways. Those gases included benzol, ammonia, naphtha, tar, and pitch. Although the by-product oven reached the United States in 1887, it was not produced for use until 1892, when twelve ovens were built and put into service at the Solvay Soda Ash Works in Syracuse, New York, by the Semet-Solvay Company. Two years later, in 1894, 50 ovens were constructed by the same company for the Dunbar Furnace Company of Connellsville in Dunbar, Fayette County, in the Connellsville bituminous region.[29]

The idea of using the gases for consumption is mentioned as early as 1881, when a company in Pittsburgh was trying to capture the gases "in a 24-inch main" and pipe them to Pittsburgh to "heat their residences and operate their puddling and heating furnaces."[30] In addition, these ovens were built to add heat from the outside of the ovens, enabling less consumption of the coal within, and therefore yielding a larger amount of coke. Finally, and perhaps most importantly, they could use an inferior coal and were not reliant solely on the Pittsburgh Seam.

The problem was that tens of thousands of beehives dominated the Connellsville district. Replacing them was a daunting task. In reality, the by-product oven put an end to the beehive and brought about the death of the early mines in our project. The Frick company was reluctant to abandon the beehive. It would be expensive to retool all the mines, especially since many would soon be depleted. But in 1918, U.S. Steel and its subsidiary, the H.C. Frick Coke Company, built a by-product plant at Clairton along the Monongahela River. That eventually ended industrial mining in the Connellsville region. The Clairton plant was still in operation in 2019 and under attack for its pollution.

The Rectangular Oven

In 1908, the rectangular oven was introduced to the region by Frick's main competitor W.J. Rainey at his Mount Braddock plant.[31] That oven, developed in Belgium, was in a single row, larger than a regular beehive, with two doors, one in front and one behind. When

Postcard showing the construction of a few of the 906 beehive coke ovens at Standard Mine outside of Mount Pleasant.

both doors were opened, the coke could be pushed out of the oven mechanically. Because the early mines were nearly depleted when the rectangular oven was created, it appears that none were constructed from Broadford to Mount Pleasant. However, John Enman, in a footnote, stated: "Frick experimented with 100 rectangular ovens at Broadford."[32] The claim has not been substantiated. Dunbar, a coal town south of Connellsville, and Carpentertown, a mine near Mount Pleasant, had rectangular ovens at a later date. In fact, "the H.C. Frick Coke Company's Phillips mine near Uniontown was the last beehive coke plant constructed in the Connellsville region in 1907 and from that year until 1910 rectangular ovens were the only coke ovens constructed in the district."[33]

In 1919, the H.C. Frick Coke Company shipped the last cars of coke from the Morgan Valley. They came from the White Mine. By 1921 there were more by-product ovens in operation than beehives. The number of beehives had decreased 73 percent over previous years.[34] The company ended all beehive operations in its coal mines in 1940.[35] The last beehive coke ovens in Fayette County were at Shoaf Mine, south of Uniontown, and were shut down for good in 1972. The last in Westmoreland County were at Alverton, near Mount Pleasant, and were shut down in 1982.[36] Both were closed by government decree. Thus ended the ovens that created the entire industry in the Connellsville region.

Creating the Infrastructure

Coal mines were created on farmland and wilderness. Coal companies would buy rights from the farmers: either surface and/or mineral rights. The meaning of surface rights is obvious, but mineral rights were the rights to mine underground. Sometimes the mine bought land from two or more farmers; these parcels were called tracts.

The mines and their miners needed services. Transportation was not only an issue for getting product to market; miners needed to get to work and find a place to live. Trains and trolleys would come later, but villages and company stores were a necessity. As stated earlier, the companies built the roads, created the rail system, and established villages, called coal patches, directly at the mines. Broadford existed prior to the mines, but it became a company town too. In the Morgan Valley, the villages of Morgan, Owensdale, and Everson emerged as a result of mines developing in their area, but they were not patches. In Westmoreland County, Scottdale and Mount Pleasant already existed, while Bridgeport and Alverton grew with the mines. Throughout the region, many of the small towns existing today were coal patches, and ruins of the industry can be found: ovens, company stores, patch houses, etc. The main point here is that not only did the companies build all these facilities, they maintained them, too, and they paid taxes. During the strike of 1894, Frick had the workers who were not on strike at Leith Mine fixing the roads of South Union Township to help pay off his road taxes.[37]

From Golden to Decline

It didn't last. For fifty years, from 1870 to 1920, the mining industry grew and thrived. The number of companies grew. The number and quality of mines increased. Immigrants from Europe came to America in search of a better life. Company towns were built. Housing improved. Company stores were created. They, too, got better. Unions were created and grew. Those were the Frick years, when from its infancy in the Morgan Valley, the Connellsville coke district grew into a bona fide industry that fueled the Industrial Revolution in America.

Then, for fifty more years, the coal and coke industry struggled in agony. The Depression was catastrophic, but the situation did not improve once the downturn was over. "The bituminous industry of the United States entered a period of decline following World War II that continued during the 1950s and 1960s. King Coal was soon replaced as the nation's principal source of energy—first by petroleum and then by natural gas...."[38] Experts give six main reasons for the decline: competition from southern fields, uses of other types of energy, more efficient burning techniques for coal, overdeveloped mine capacity, poor demand caused by the Depression, and lower production costs in southern fields.[39]

Decline was dramatic. Coke ovens numbered 15,333 in 1925, falling to 7,292 in 1930 and 4,355 in 1935. By 1929 the H.C. Frick Coke Company had only twenty-five beehive coke plants working. Part of the problem was that the government had instituted stringent air pollution controls and the beehive could not meet the standard.[40] Many of the mines closed, especially those in the Morgan Valley. The towns diminished. The company stores shut their doors. The miners had no work and suffered unimaginably. These were the bad years. Too often, these are the years that people recall when they make accusations against Henry Clay Frick, who died in 1919.

Two

Henry Clay Frick

The early life of Henry Clay Frick is fairly well known, and is well told in the book *Henry Clay Frick: The Man*, by George Harvey, his childhood friend. A more extensive biography reveals his private as well as public life in his great-granddaughter Martha Frick Symington Sanger's book *Henry Clay Frick: An Intimate Portrait*. This is an amazing chronicle of Frick's life, public and private, very well written and presented. Dozens of books evaluating and analyzing Frick as a professional have been written, each with a point of view about the man, many unkind.

Of all the capitalists of the day, Frick, his life, and his ethics dominate all discussions of coal and coke. In many instances, his achievement of guiding the development of the industry is ignored or barely acknowledged, while he is blamed for too many of the mistakes and flaws of the industry. This is especially true among the descendants of the miners in the region. Their hatred of Henry Clay Frick is astounding. Their belief that Frick was responsible for every mistake, every tragedy, every incident that happened to their ancestors, is shocking. Below, using the voices of the day, drawn from original sources, is a positive view of Henry Clay Frick, a view that challenges the negative myth.

Frick was born in 1849 in the Spring House of his grandfather Abraham Overholt's settlement between Scottdale and Mount Pleasant (Westmoreland County, Pennsylvania). This German-Mennonite family migrated to the region in the early 1800s and became famous as distillers of fine whiskey. After it had been abandoned for some time, Frick's daughter Helen Clay Frick purchased the languishing village for $14,000 in 1922,[1] created the Westmoreland and Fayette Historical Society in 1928, and completely restored the major buildings. It was named to the National Register of Historic Places in 1985.[2] Today the Overholt homestead is known as West Overton Village.

According to his great-granddaughter, Frick was a sickly youth, and a debilitating rheumatic condition would haunt him from his childhood. In 1875, while he was beginning to build his empire and struggle with the results of the Panic of 1873 in and around the Morgan Valley, he spent an entire year in bed, barely able to move.[3] There would be many such episodes. His education was sporadic, and he was fired from his Uncle Christian's store in Mount Pleasant in 1868.[4] It was co-owned by Lloyd Shallenberger, whose family still plays a role in mine properties today.[5] While working there, Henry Clay saw the need for books in the small borough library. He went door to door collecting books from people and delivered them to the library.[6] He moved on to work in his grandfather's second distillery at Broadford along the Youghiogheny River, walking daily from West Overton to Broadford, about six miles one way. Later he would often borrow a horse from Mr. Markle, and eventually, in 1876, the *Mount Pleasant Dawn* reported, "Mr. H. Clay Frick has purchased and had shipped to him at Broadford a very fine blooded Kentucky horse."[7] As he founded his coke company, his offices were in a supply store at Broadford that eventually became a hotel, now gone. Eventually he rented rooms from a man named George Washabaugh at Broadford.[8]

In the Beginning

Wood was the fuel of the nation before the emergence of coal. It was used for everything. However, its resources were limited, and its fire was not hot enough to fuel the emerging industries. Yet until the 1840s it was king. At that time two things happened: industrialization combined with transportation growth took place, and Henry Clay Frick was born. The two would create the Golden Age of Coal and Coke in the bituminous industry in Pennsylvania. But coal, mined since colonial times, first had to be converted to coke. After many trial-and-error efforts, the beehive coke oven emerged. That is when the industry began to grow. The fledgling coal and coke industry began to mature in the late 1860s and 1870s. Frick would be the catalyst.

Management, miners, and emerging unions were all trying to adapt and grow with the industry. It was complicated. Management had no training. It included anyone who could buy a piece of land, build a small mine, and hire a few workers. Its biggest economic problems were reaching the market and stabilizing the price of coke. Frick began to organize the owners into a syndicate that would work together. Not all the owners wanted to join. Some wanted to form a second organization to fill the needs of smaller companies. The miners wanted a good life for their families. But as the cost of coke rose and fell on the market, so did their wages. The miners were hampered by language problems, subject to rumors, and often confused. Just as Frick and the other owners formed a syndicate to deal with their problems, the miners would organize via unions. The problem was that there were too many budding unions trying to convince the miners their manifesto was the best. Not only did they fight the companies, they fought each other.

By the 1870s, mines were beginning to spring up along Galley Run through the Morgan Valley, and along Shupe Run, at Bridgeport, on the edge of Mount Pleasant. The first coal company Henry Clay Frick organized was Overholt, Frick & Co.[9] The partners in the firm were mostly related: A.O. Tinstman, J.S.R. Overholt, Joseph Rist, and Frick. Tinstman and

Frick's empire went through a number of transformations and corporate names. This is the earliest billhead and company name found. Note the original spelling of Broad Ford. (Broad Ford Mines Billhead 1870, Helen Clay Frick Foundation Archives [AIS 2002 06], Henry Clay Frick Business Records, 1862–1987, Box 523, Folder 1, Archives Service Center, University of Pittsburgh).

Rist originally bought the property in Morgan Valley, and it appears a portion was sold to the newly formed company in 1871. The two men had previously joined A.S.M. Morgan in Morgan & Company and created the Morgan Mine just up the valley from the Frick mines. Along with Frick, they were instrumental in the forming the Mount Pleasant and Broadford Railroad, which ran from Broadford through the Morgan Valley and up to Mount Pleasant.

It must be remembered that the region was farmland and wilderness. There were no roads by which the coal and coke could be transported. The companies built the roads. There were too few towns where the miners could live. The companies built the towns. Ditto for the railroads: too limited. The inroad for the railroads in the region was the coal and coke industry. As the mining industry grew, so did the railroad industry.

Frick capitalized on the location of the railroads around Broadford. He erected the coke ovens for his first mine, the Frick, along the Mount Pleasant Broadford Railroad, and he built his second mine, the Henry Clay, a short distance away, but along the Youghiogheny River and the B & O Railroad. These were brilliant moves as Frick could get the coke from either mine to market on either railroad.

The Overholt partnership did not last the year as Overholt's share was sold at a sheriff's sale and purchased by Frick on April 22, 1871.[10] Then Frick & Co. was born. It was a partnership between Tinstman, Rist, and Frick, and it would last, precariously, until the late 1870s, when the H.C. Frick Coke Company was created.[11] Two events in 1876 pushed the formation of the new company. Tinstman was going bankrupt. In March of 1876 he disposed of his shares of the Morgan and Co. for $60,000.[12] So was Rist who set off for Colorado to explore the silver and gold mines.

Many sources list different dates for the formation of the final entity, H.C. Frick Coke Company. An 1877 date is given in the *Connellsville Coke* booklet distributed by the Frick company.[13] The *Journal* of the company states on Friday, March 1, 1878, a capital investment of equal parts for a co-partnership of H.C. Frick and E.M. Ferguson was entered.[14] The pair became the partners of the H.C. Frick Coke Company. There are hundreds if not thousands of legal transactions including property transfers related to these events. This complex legal confusion dominated the world of mining, and probably other industries, and has proven difficult and time consuming to trace. Some of the problem is related to the fact that government records were either not kept at this time or have been lost. This confusion existed throughout this author's research at each mine.

The H.C. Frick Coke Company would remain throughout Frick's career, but ultimately not in his control, nor would it be his only coal and coke company. In 1883 he purchased the Standard mine near Mount Pleasant from A.A. Hutchison, and along with Morewood mine, he began to build another empire. Others included the Shaw Coal Company (1900), St. Paul Coal Company (1914), and his long and often complicated involvement with the Illinois Steel Company in all its different forms.[15]

Early Growth

As noted, Frick began his empire at Broadford, where he opened his first two mines: Frick and Henry Clay. After that, he seldom built a mine again. He invested in other mines and eventually bought out his partners. The worldwide economic downturn called the Panic of 1873 devastated the growing industries. Some of the small mines in the region could not withstand the financial issues. Frick found a way to buy them. In many instances he was purchasing the mine from a family member who was going broke. By 1879 he either owned or partially owned Broad Ford Mines (Frick and Henry Clay), Morgan, Tip Top, Valley, Anchor, Ferguson, Foundry, Fountain, and Sherrick Coal & Coke Company, all in Morgan Valley.[16] The mines around Mount Pleasant were not part of the Frick holdings at that time. The transfers ran the entire distance of the valley. They covered coal (including surface and mineral) and other rights to the sum of nearly $2 million.

In the late 1880s and early 1890s, many of the owners were fed up with all the strikes and problems in the mining industry, and Frick bought them out. They included his major competitors J.M. Schoonmaker (Jimtown, Sterling, Alice, Redstone) and Connellsville Coke and Iron's Leisenring (I, II, III). It was reported that at the same time he also bought out W.J. Rainey (Fort Hill, Grace, Paul), his most competitive operator, but that did not happen until Frick had moved on to U.S. Steel. In 1895 Frick bought all the mines from the McClure Coke Company, including Buckeye, Star, Hazlett, Mullin, Bessemer, and Alverton I, II, and III. None of this was ruthless. In most instances the purchase was after a major strike and months of conflict. The owners were either going broke or simply wanted out. Combined with the nearby Standard, Morewood, and Tarrs mines, Frick holdings now ringed the region where he grew up and went to school, and he dominated the coal fields in Connellsville.

As early as 1875, Frick rented rooms at the Monongahela House in Pittsburgh, where contacts could be made to find buyers. Many of the Connellsville coke owners did the same. Within a few years, Frick moved to Pittsburgh permanently, as did his corporate offices. First they were located at 104 Fifth Avenue, then in the Carnegie Building (opened 1895), and finally at 437 Grant Street in the Frick Building, which he built.[17] Thomas Lynch was the general superintendent. His staff included the treasurer Phillip Keller, and the general sales agent C.H. Spencer.[18] Of course, as noted above, Frick's first offices were at Broadford, and he kept offices in the region. In 1888, Frick moved the superintendent, engineers, and administrative offices from Broadford to Scottdale. Orran W. Kennedy was the general superintendent at Scottdale, W.H. Clingerman and Edward O'Toole were in the shipping department, and J.A. Barnhart was the chief clerk. In 1891 he sent his assistant S.L. Schoonmaker (not Colonel J.M. Schoonmaker) to New York to open an office there too.[19] The New York office was in the Trinity Building overlooking the Trinity Cemetery at 111 Broadway and across the street from the building that would eventually house United States Steel.[20]

In 1939, long after Frick was gone and U.S. Steel was in charge, the general superintendent announced that the local headquarters would be moved once again, this time from Scottdale to Uniontown.[21] At that time the general superintendent at H.C. Frick Coke Company was Harry M. Moses. They remained there until 2002, when U.S. Steel sold all of the H.C. Frick Company holdings to RGGS.

Frick and Carnegie

The most important merger in the steel and coal industry in the Pittsburgh region, if not the country, was the joining of forces by Henry Clay Frick and Andrew Carnegie. Frick controlled coal. Carnegie was dominant in steel. Carnegie needed coal. Frick bought up most of his competitors and built or bought his own supply companies. Carnegie did the same. Carnegie courted Frick until Frick joined him. Some consider this Frick's big mistake.

Frick's business sense and organizational skills did for Carnegie what he had done for the

COKÉ MEN CRUSHED.

Carnegie Thunders From His Castle in the Scottish Highlands.

HIS BOLT WRECKS THE SYNDICATE

Millionaire Operators Mourn and Hungry Hungarians Dance With Glee.

PRES'T FRICK OVERPOWERED RESIGNS.

An Electric Spark From Europe and the Message it Bore.

CAPITALISTS GET A BAD SHOCK.

Andrew Carnegie used his control of the Frick company to wield his power and, as claimed by the world of coke, interfere in the industry ("Coke Men Crushed," *Penny Press*, June 11, 1887, Scrapbook, March 22, 1884–August 18, 1887, Helen Clay Frick Foundation Archives [AIS 2002 06] Henry Clay Frick Business Records, 1862–1987, Box 488, Volume 1, Archives Service Center, University of Pittsburgh, p. 73).

Connellsville coke region: he created order out of chaos. But the two men had major differences. Carnegie needed Frick's coke. That meant the miners had to keep working. Frick needed to keep the men working too, but he needed to keep the salaries in balance with the market. The companies were joined, but they were still independently owned and managed. Carnegie kept buying stock in the H.C. Frick Coke Company until he owned the majority share. That put Frick in a bad position. In the 1887 coal strike, Frick stood his ground against the miners and unions, and the strikers were to return to work shortly. Carnegie stepped in and overruled him, not only forcing Frick to lose face, but nearly destroying the syndicate among operators that Frick had carefully nurtured. Frick resigned as head of the company he had founded. (See the chapter on the 1887 strike for full details).[22] He returned in 1888, but never had the power he formerly had.

Prior to Frick's arrival in his company, Carnegie had instituted something called the Iron Clad Agreement.

> Carnegie's weapon of choice was the "iron clad agreement." This was the brainchild of Carnegie's assistant Henry Phipps, and was drafted in 1877, shortly after the death of Tom Carnegie. It provided that a partner's share could be purchased at book value (far below the fair market value) from his estate with payments over time. This was designed to prevent a forced liquidation of the company. A second clause of particular importance to the Frick/Carnegie struggle provided that a partner could be forced to sell his shares back to the company at book value upon a 75 percent vote of the shareholders. Carnegie got the required signatures, and Frick was offered $5 million for his shares. On Carnegie's part it was an unconscionable act. Frick threatened to sue, making public the fantastic profitability of Carnegie Steel. The consequences could have been dire. With the intercession again of Phipps (who, to his credit, refused to vote with Carnegie) and other mutual friends, Carnegie backed down.[23]

Carnegie continued to aggravate Frick over many management details: he opposed the Mesabi ore purchase; he interfered with bidding on a contract and exposed the bid price to a competitor; he proved unsympathetic with the death of Mr. Paddock in the coal strike of 1894; and he tried to "merge the works of W.S. Rainey [sic] into H.C. Frick Coke. The last issue was the final straw. Frick was not consulted and resigned again in December of 1894." This, too, did not last. Then Carnegie began to interfere in the price of coke again. The price of coke was rising, but Carnegie insisted that Frick honor the $1.35 a ton price that had been set instead of the market value of $1.75. Frick refused. "On December 5, 1899, Carnegie called for Frick's resignation.... Without a fuss Frick resigned. But Carnegie was not through. Having stripped Frick of his power he attempted to deprive him of the better part of his wealth," through the Iron Clad. The Carnegie holdings were then restructured and named the Carnegie Company. Charles Schwab was the man in charge, not Frick.[24] Frick was out.

Frick struck back. Working with J.P. Morgan, he led the way for Morgan to buy out Carnegie and form U.S. Steel. Carnegie sold and left the world of business behind. Frick was appointed to the board of U.S. Steel, and for the next approximately seventeen years, he continued to be deeply involved in the world of steel and coke and the H.C. Frick Coke Company. The entire story is told in a myriad of publications by dozens of authors with many different points of view. In most instances, Carnegie is called out for the scheming, double-faced man that he was, and Frick is acknowledged as the brilliant brain behind one of the greatest industries of the era. This is contrary to the legacy in vogue today. These events are far more complicated, but this summary serves.

On Frick's retirement from Carnegie Steel, the *Connellsville Courier* wrote:

> Henry Clay Frick is a man of remarkable individuality. Pleasant and polished in his personal intercourse, broad-minded and liberal in his views of men and things; candid and straightforward, wasting no words in matters of business; keen and sagaelous [sic], active and alert, never failing to see an opportunity and to grasp it with a firm and confident hand.
> The Carnegie Steel Company will no doubt have able managers, but none better than the man who has just retired from the active direction of its vast and intricate interests.[25]

To clarify Frick's leadership years: In 1887, Frick resigned at the helm of his company because of his differences with Carnegie. A few months later, in 1888, he was back. In 1894, he resigned again when Carnegie tried to make a deal with Rainey without his input. Again, he was reinstated when one of the board members stated, "Mr. Frick is first and there's no second." His new title was chairman of the board of Carnegie Steel, while John Leishman became president, a newly created position. Leishman was replaced by Charles Schwab in

1897. In 1898, J.P. Morgan showed more than a fleeting interest in Carnegie Steel, H.C. Frick Coke, and all the combined holdings. Frick and Carnegie fought over the price Frick was charging Carnegie for his coke. In 1899, Carnegie asked for his resignation. He gave it. That was final. But in a long and complicated set of maneuvers, Carnegie Company was formed (April 1, 1900) with Charles Schwab as president and Frick as a member of the board (with the understanding Frick would not attend meetings). In 1901, Carnegie was bought out, and U.S. Steel, under the leadership of J.P. Morgan and Elbert H. Gary, was founded. Frick, who helped broker the deal, became more and more important to U.S. Steel. Although he was officially a member of the finance committee, they relied heavily on him to lead the company, which he often did.

Is the Homestead Strike Mainly Responsible for the Reputation?

Although probably beyond the scope of our study, the Homestead Strike of 1892 is definitely problematic in trying to understand Henry Clay Frick's reputation. One must begin with the strikes in the coal fields of Connellsville from 1875 to 1894 (and beyond). They were far more violent, far deadlier, far more incredible in their details. Thousands of men and women marched the ten miles from Broadford to Mount Pleasant, brandishing guns and destroying dozens of coke ovens and tipples. Their mission was to force the miners who were still working to come out on strike. Men were killed. Operator properties were destroyed.

During the nearly twenty years of struggle, companies began to organize among themselves, unions competed for dominance, and miners struggled for a decent life. It was several decades of chaos and anarchy. There were not enough law enforcement agencies in the region to deal with such an army of miners and to stop the destruction of both public and private property. The state refused to send in the Pennsylvania National Guard. The governors of Pennsylvania were firm that the National Guard would not be used to solve industrial issues. In the many decades of industrial struggles, the Guard was only used six times. The coal strike of 1891 and the steel strike at Homestead were two of those instances.

In order to protect their property from violence, the operators, including Frick, sent for the Pinkerton Detective Agency. That bears repeating: Frick was not the only operator who sent for the Pinkertons to protect his property during the decades of strikes in the Connellsville coke region. All the operators needed to protect their investments against violence. The towns and the counties did not have the manpower. The Pinkertons were there to create order. In the Golden Age of Coal and Coke (1870–1920), the Pinkertons' role had not broadened to daily monitoring the mines and the patches. Their horrific reputation was born after the Golden Age.

Nothing as long-lasting as the coal strikes would happen at Homestead, where there was only one company involved: Carnegie Steel. There was only one union involved: the Amalgamated. It created an atmosphere of siege and warfare. What Frick and Carnegie succeeded in doing at Homestead was to kill unions in the steel industry. In the Connellsville coal and coke district, it was the miners who threw the unions out. They had had enough of their dishonorable tactics and did not feel they represented the local men. Unlike Homestead, coal strikes continued, a number of unions continued to try to control the region, and the battles between operators, unions, and workers were continuous until the 1930s, when the government gave both steel and coal the right to unionize. At Homestead, violence did not span the decades beyond the 1892 steel conflict.

The Main Points

After well over a hundred years, here are bullet points of the main events at Homestead.

- On June 12, 1892, Henry Clay Frick build a 3-mile-long, 12-foot-high fence separating the Homestead Mill from the town in order to protect his property.
    - It had a barbed wire fence along the top and 3-inch holes in it at regular locations.
    - The media labeled it Fort Frick.
    - He then contacted the Pinkerton Detective Agency to send 300 guards to Homestead **to protect the mill**.
- On June 25, he posted that managers at the works would deal with employees on an individual basis.
- On June 30, Frick closed the plant and locked out 4,000 workers.
- On July 3, the Amalgamated union closed all but two bars in Homestead, while workers constructed bulwarks and guarded them to stop all entry into the mill.
    - An advisory committee created a 24-hour army of workers to guard entrances, the riverfront, water gate, pump house, railroad station and four gates.
    - A picket line was formed on the waterfront.
    - One thousand men patrolled the waterfront five miles on either side of Homestead.
    - A fleet was also launched on the Monongahela River.
    - Telegraph wires were erected at Amalgamated Headquarters.
    - An observatory was erected on top of the headquarters to view Fort Frick.
    - A steam whistle was installed to signal workers of events.
    - All roads into the town were blocked.
- On July 6, Frick announced he would restart the Homestead Works.
- The Pinkertons were placed on two barges and headed for Homestead.
    - They were discovered while two miles from Homestead.
    - The steam whistle blew.
    - Over 1,000 men and women came to the river armed with clubs, hoes, guns and more.
    - They tried to stop Pinkertons from landing.
    - Pinkerton's announced: "We were sent here to take possession of the property and to guard it for the company...."
    - Guns were fired.
    - Pinkertons declared strikers fired first.
    - Thirty strikers were hit.
    - Shots were fired by strikers from an old Civil War cannon.
    - Strikers lit a natural gas line near the pumping station and threw 4th of July rockets into it.
    - Strikers put oil on the Monongahela, setting it on fire.
    - The battle lasted 14 hours.
    - Pinkertons raised a white flag of surrender. The man who held it was shot.
    - One hundred strikers boarded the second barge.
    - They confiscated all the pistols and the uniform jackets of the Pinkertons and threw them into the river.

- The Pinkertons were taken to the skating rink instead of the jail.
- Women attacked the Pinkertons as they walked by, bludgeoning them with clubs.
- Sixty people were wounded.
* Carnegie cabled Frick on July 7. "All anxiety gone since know you stand firm. Never employ one of these rioters. Let grass grow over the works." Carnegie did not want any unions in his works.
* Frick announced to the press: "While nobody could regret the occurrences of the last few days more than myself, yet it is my duty as the executive head of the Carnegie Company to protect the interest of the association.... The matter is out of our hands now. We look to the sheriff to protect our property. The men upon our properties are not strikers, they are lawbreakers.... I will hold conferences with nobody ... the supremacy of the law is the only question involved."
* As of July 12, local police could not restore order.
  - Eighty-five-hundred Pennsylvania State Militia (National Guard) were sent to Homestead.
  - Four thousand were stationed in front of gates.
  - Office workers return to the Homestead Works.

The strike was certainly more complicated than this bulleted list, but essentially these were some major events. The unrest also continued beyond the confrontation, but never as threatening.[26]

Frick in Peril

On July 23, 1892, Alexander Berkman, a noted anarchist, shot Henry Clay Frick in Frick's Pittsburgh office. With a bullet in his neck, Frick fought back. He earned a bullet in his leg for his defiance. He refused treatment. The incident was even more incredible when one understood what was happening in Frick's personal life.

In August of 1891, while Frick was dealing with a major and deadly strike in the Connellsville coal fields that some scholars think was far more important than the Homestead strike, his beloved daughter Martha died. Her death was tragic and would never have happened today. She had been sick for several years and doctors could not discover the problem. Then a pus sac opened on her side, and amid the copious contents was a tiny pin. This was something an X-ray would have discovered, but X-ray machines were practically nonexistent. When they did become available, Frick bought them for hospitals.

Less than a year later, he was shot. In addition, the entire Frick family was ill. Then another tragedy happened: on August 3, ten days after Frick was shot, his newborn son died. Amid these tragedies, Frick had to try to keep the industry on a steady course. And as head of a vast coal and steel empire, he took most of the blame for the strike. The day his son died, the headlines in one of the papers read, "Mr. Frick to be Arrested." In fact, headline after headline in the newspapers of the Amalgamated and the Knights of Labor tore into Frick as the sole enemy of the workers. These are the words that would follow him all his life and beyond. In most instances, as the following chapters will show, it wasn't Frick at all, but more likely other owners like W.J. Rainey, the Cochrans, and Charles Armstrong, who were to blame for what had gone wrong.

Debunking the Bunk

Today in the Old Basin and throughout the former coal field, there are Frick schools, Frick streets, Frick parks, and even a Frick hospital, but few people have a decent word about the man who built an empire. It is time that one read some undoctored facts about Frick and his empire taken from original sources. Too many writers today, far removed from the actual events, accept the legend, which is mostly negative. In many instances, instead of stating "the company," meaning any company of the time, critics say "Frick," thereby blaming him instead of Rainey, Cochran, Moore, etc. Here is an Internet example:

> During the 1800s and till the mid–1900s, coal mining and the making of coke for the Pittsburgh steel mills, was the largest industry, next to farming, in Southwestern Pennsylvania. Coal mines largely company owned, and small private mines, abounded in this region. Many "patch towns" sprang up around these mines. "Patch towns" were a group of houses, built by the large coal companies, to house their workers. The H.C. Frick Coal Company, did not pay their workers in cash, but "script" that could only be used to pay rent for the "company house" and to buy groceries, clothing, and just about anything needed to buy for the household, at the "company store," owned by Frick. Not only did Henry Clay Frick rob his workers, by paying low wages, he also robbed them by forcing them to buy their food, clothes, and everything else needed for their families, at inflated prices at his "Company Store."[27]

There are many falsehoods in this quote. Almost all coal companies used scrip. Some few probably did not pay in cash, but Frick did. Some few probably forced their men to buy exclusively in their stores, but Frick did not. During slumps in the market, Frick continued to pay his men their agreed-upon salaries, whereas some owners did not pay their men for months at a time. All of these points are verified in the various chapters ahead.

As noted in the Introduction, Carmen Peter DiCiccio of the Pennsylvania Bureau of Historic Preservation defined the bituminous coke era by dividing the bituminous coal era in Pennsylvania into four distinct eras, the last two being important to our discussion. In fact, the title of this book is adapted from the third: *The Golden Era of King Coal, Queen Coke and Princess Steel, 1880–1920*. For our purposes, the era becomes an age, and the dates reflect the span of Henry Clay Frick in the industry. The fourth era is when most of the negative Frick reputation was born. It is titled Retrenchment, Decline and Mechanized Mine, 1920–1945. During that era there was a large depression, and the coal and coke industry did not fare well. The workers suffered. Truth is, by that time Henry Clay Frick was dead. The incidents attributed to him during this time belonged to someone else.[28]

In 1928, the United States Senate Committee on Interstate Commerce began an investigation of coal and coke, especially the Consolidation Coal Company. They send a subcommittee into the "strike torn mining communities," and documented the "dismal quality of daily life of miners and their families in western Pennsylvania." Journalist Lowell Limpus of the *New York Daily News* wrote:

> I have seen horrible things there: things which I almost hesitate to enumerate and describe.... We saw thousands of women and children, literally starving to death. We found hundreds of destitute families living in crudely constructed bare-board shacks. They had been evicted from their homes by the coal companies. We unearthed a system of despotic tyranny reminiscent of czar-ridden Siberia at its worst. We found police brutality and industrial slavery.... we unearthed evidence of terrorism and counter-terrorism; of mob beatings and near lynchings; of dishonesty, graft, and heartlessness....[29]

This quote resembles much of the hype of today. Blaming Frick is a mistake. Frick died in 1919, at the end of the Golden Age. This probe took place nine years later.

As one reads the chapters in this book, one will find Frick's company stores were fair and honest. His patches had the best houses, the best roads, and the best maintenance. During hard times, his company opened the Frick farms to anyone, employees and non-employees, to plant crops for themselves at no cost. Frick's company built reservoirs to provide water for his coke ovens, and he opened the reservoirs to the area towns. Likewise, when the company installed a whistle for the mines, it added weather info for the towns too: daily at 9 and 10, the whistle would sound 1 long whistle for attention, then: 3 short for snow; 1 short, 1 long for colder; 2 short, rain; 4 short, clear.[30] In the 1890s, the Frick company instituted the first safety programs in mining. Their mines were the safest, the cleanest, and had the best and most modern equipment. Yes, Frick was against the formation of unions, as was every business owner of the day (and perhaps today too). But he tried to avoid strikes by giving the miners salary increases before they struck. He was willing to negotiate, but with his own men, not outsiders. And there is more. He built hospitals, schools, and churches, and donated money, even giving it to municipalities in trouble.

Yet, who honors him? There is no statue in the Connellsville region in honor of Henry Clay Frick. The only permanent honor found locally is a plaque. In November of 1930, the Mount Pleasant Rotary Club dedicated a plaque commemorating young Henry Clay Frick's early job as a clerk in his uncle's store on Main Street in Mount Pleasant. The banquet at the National Hotel was attended by sixty people, including a bevy of Frick men. Erskine Ramsey, a longtime employee of Frick's, came home from Birmingham, Alabama, to give the keynote address. Other speakers included Walter H. Glasgow, State Secretary of Mines; James W. Anawait, president of the Uniontown [sic] Supply Company; Patrick J. Tormay, a Frick veteran; and John J. Murtha, a Frick pensioner.[31] The plaque still stands on the façade of 751 Main Street in Mount Pleasant.

The Miners and the Unions

The condemnation of Frick is not solely that conveyed by modern-day writers. Today families of former miners condemn Frick too. In an interview with the former mayor of Everson, such an event unfolded. The mayor reported that Frick killed his grandfather. When asked how, he said his grandfather was taking miners' ballots to Connellsville when he was ambushed and killed. When asked when this happened, it was deduced around 1930. As noted, Frick died in 1919 and had been dead for over ten years.[32] This claim is typical of many incidents falsely attributed to Frick.

What of the unions? In the Homestead Strike of 1892, the Amalgamated union turned the steelworkers into an army by setting up guards, a picket line, waterfront patrols, a river fleet, telegraph wires, an observatory, a signal system, rockets, and cannon. The mission of the Pinkertons was to guard the mill, not to attack the steelworkers. When the Pinkertons arrived, the steelworkers, like an army, attacked. In addition, the union bombarded its workers with propaganda against the owners. The union's conduct brought in the Pennsylvania National Guard. The Pinkertons were there because the governor had refused to bring in the Guard. They did not want the state involved in industrial matters. The action of the steelworkers at Homestead killed unions in the steel industry for over thirty years.

The unions did the same thing in the coal strikes of 1891 and 1894. Not by creating an army, but by organizing and supporting violence against operators and their property (and other miners). They spread false information. They accused Frick and the other operators of atrocities they did not commit.

In 1891, the *Connellsville Courier* stated, "We use the term incendiary speeches advisedly. The President of the United Mine Workers is quoted as saying that 'the strike must be won peaceably if possible, forcibly if necessary'; the Vice President, 'we will win by fair means or foul,' and the local officers talk in public about swooping down on the guards and the 'cowardly black-leg devils' and 'driving them to hell together.' Such expressions undoubtedly inflame the ignorant mind, and may have been one of underlying causes of the Morewood raid. Labor leaders carry a heavy responsibility, and they should guard carefully their tongues as well as their actions."[33]

During the same strike, Michael Barrett, a union leader, claimed Frick's "bosses and thugs" killed a man at Leisenring 3 just because "he laughed at them when they tried to get men to come to work." He accused Frick of offering bribes to get the men back to work. The biggest complaint was that they had driven the new men "into the mine and compelling them to work under a strong guard and not permitting them to come out at all," and that "several of these men so imprisoned had died, their bodies being buried in 'gob' piles." Some were said to be kept in chains. Evidently this final accusation had been passed among the citizens for some time, and finally someone reported it to the governor. This brought Adjunct General McClelland to the region to confirm if this was true. With him were union secretaries Parker and Barrett, Michael Disman, Antonio Palassio (the Italian interpreter), and all labor leaders.

Morris Ramsay, general manager at Morewood, was called to the meeting, where he heard the accusations and was told the committee intended to visit the mine without prior preparations. Ramsey said fine, and along with Superintendent Robert Ramsay of Standard and a company interpreter, they all went off to A shaft. The *Mount Pleasant Journal* reported:

> The investigation lasted four hours during which time the workings were gone over and the testimony of twelve men taken. Two of these were Italians from this place and the balance Hungarians from Pittsburg and vicinity. It was proven that nearly all were hired by Pontifrac, the purchasing agent of the Union Supply Company and were at present paid $2 by the day. One of them said the presence of the guards was good and made him sleep comfortably. When the tour had been made the members of the committee expressed themselves as gratified that there was no truth in the story that had led to the investigation.[34]

McClelland tried to conduct the same tour at Central Mine, but the superintendent refused because he did not have General Manager Schoonmaker's permission. McClelland then investigated on his own and came to the same conclusion. When he reported back to the governor, he said the troops were no longer needed in the region. The union was misrepresenting the facts. Yet this type of accusation by the unions reverberated throughout the district and was believed by the workers—and is still believed by their descendants.

Barrett was still at it during the strike of 1894: "It is given out by President Barrett's friends that he is actively engaged in reorganizing the strikers and that when he has everything in readiness, he will make an attack on all the plants in the region at the same time. This idea, they claim, will prevent the sheriffs from doing effective work for the protection of the men. Another of Barrett's plans is to meet the workingmen while on their way to work before they get on the company's property, and compel them to go home."[35]

In the end the miners had had enough. They did not want outsiders determining their fate. That was the Frick company's position too: willing to negotiate, but not with strangers. The miners destroyed the UMW in the region. They refused to join the union for a few decades. The union's conduct had an everlasting effect on the operators, especially Frick.

Houses were erected at Valley Works in the Morgan Valley. Six of them were burned in January of 1881. Four survived. There are up to ten houses still standing at Valley. Similar houses existed in all of Frick mines. Many still stand today, 150 years after they were built—one more piece of evidence that Frick did not build shoddy housing ("Surrounding Sections," *Weekly Courier*, January 21, 1881, p. 3).

Just the Facts!

In order to do justice to the image of Henry Clay Frick, one must have the positive as well as the negative. Below, the newspapers, the coal journals, and the mine inspectors of the day speak for Frick. Article after article on a number of topics related to Henry Clay Frick show the positive. A few have some introductory remarks, but most stand alone. They soften the concept that Frick was an evil man. Some samples are dated beyond Frick's death. But they reflect the policy that was instituted during his lifetime and his control or influence on the company, so they are valid reflections of his character.

Some contend Henry Clay Frick was not involved in the workings of the H.C. Frick Coke company in the 1890s, when there were upheavals in the Carnegie company. He was. Likewise, after he was appointed to the financial committee of U.S. Steel, the claim is made that his dealings with his own company were minimal. Again, the answer is yes, he was involved, highly involved, in the workings of the company he founded. When the *Mount Pleasant Journal* reported on the position of the operators and the unions during the strike of 1891, it was Henry Clay Frick who responded.[36]

It was also Henry Clay Frick who accused the union officials of being outsiders not caring for the miners at all.[37] In 1910, Frick met with Senator Boise Penrose, John Mitchell, former president of United Mine Workers, and others to try to end the current coal and steel strike.[38]

In 1914, Frick dominated the purchase of coal lands from J.V. Thompson of Uniontown. Thompson, who had considerable coal holdings in Greene County, flew to New York to meet Frick in the United States Steel offices. The book *Cloud by Day* reported that Thompson was disappointed that he met with Thomas Lynch and insisted on meeting Frick, who was listening in the next room. Sheppard, the author, does not provide an original source, nor, after investigation, was one found, so the claim cannot be confirmed.[39] However, the deal was concluded in Pittsburgh when Frick met with Thompson to sign the deal: "Henry C. Frick left Pittsburgh for the East last night with a consciousness that he had put in a busy and highly profitable afternoon. He had affixed his signature to a deal for the sale of the site of the proposed William Penn Hotel, and invested in some equally valuable Greene county coal lands. The purchase price of this property was not made public. Mr. Frick declined to disclose it, and the other principal to the transaction, J.V. Thompson of Uniontown, was just as reticent."[40] Yes, Frick continued to be highly involved until his death.

There are hundreds more examples, but the point is made. No one should throw to the curb a man of such wisdom and power.

Wages and Hours

During the strike of 1886, the Austro-Hungarian Consul from Pittsburgh wrote to Frick about the Hungarians in the coal fields. Frick's response shows that directing a note exclusively to him was wrong because he was not the only operator in the field. This is another big problem related to Frick's reputation. Many times, reports would use his name to represent the entire industry. That made him "guilty" of indiscretions done by other operators or incidents occurring in their mines, stores, and patches. Frick's reply shows his approach to a solution:

> Sir—I have your favor of to-day in relation to the strike by the Hungarians in the Connellsville coke region. As all the operators employ them in about equal proportion with ourselves we can speak as to those only who were lately in our employ. As to them I would say that they gave us no previous notice whatever of any demand, but abruptly severed their relations with us and united in a mob to destroy our property and terrorize and assail our peaceful employes who wanted to work. While they maintain this attitude of hostility they can claim no relationship to us which deserves consideration. Let them peaceable leave our employment and deliver up our property, if dissatisfied, or resume work. If they choose the latter course, it will then be time enough to treat with them for higher wages. If the coke business improves, as we hope it will in the near future, the price will advance, and we will then, as we have always said and intended, gladly share the benefit of it with our employes by advancing their wages. We appreciate your kind interest in this matter, and trust, understanding their language and enjoying their full and deserved confidence as you do, your intervention may avoid further trouble or misunderstanding between us.[41]

Further, in 1893 the *Scottdale Independent* wrote: "The H.C. Frick Coke Company, through the Union Supply company [sic], are providing for all the families in want at their idle plants. They have been very generous in supplying the wants of needy families."[42] In November of the same year, the *Scottdale Independent* continued:

> There has been considerable indignation throughout the region the last few days over the heavy reductions made in the wages of the coke workers at some of the plants. The H.C. Frick Coke company

continues to pay the rate of wages set out in their scale posted in 1891 and will do so until February 8, the date the scale expires; but some of the operators, particularly the Cochrans, are reported as paying a very much lower rate.... The Frick company has never missed a pay since the scale was posted, but some of the operators have practically abandoned payday, as the men at some of the plants have not been paid a cent in cash since the first of July, almost five months....[43]

These events were during the Panic of 1893, when industry nationwide was in a depression.

Thomas Lynch, Frick's superintendent, confirmed the company's support of its workers:

In March, 1891, the Connellsville coke operators, without exception, formulated a scale for the regulation of wages to be paid to their employes until February 1, 1894. This scale fixed the minimum wages on a basis of $1.75 per ton for furnace coke....

Today the Frick Coke Company, the Hostetter Connellsville Coke Company, which belongs to the estate of William Thaw, deceased, are the only firms in the whole region paying the prices and living up to that agreement. Before the agreement had run two years, some of the operators cut the market prices of coke, then cut the wages of their men to make themselves whole. That was the start. Down, down went the wages, one by one reduced, twice and even three times, regardless of the agreement, until now the Frick Coke Company are paying 40 per cent more wages for the same work than the Stewart Iron Company is paying at an adjoining works; 33½ per cent more than is being paid for the same work by James Cochran, Sons & Company; 22 per cent more than is being paid for the same work by W.J. Rainey; 15 per cent more than is being paid for the same work by the Oliver Coke and Furnace Company; 12½ per cent more than is being paid for the same work by the McClure Coke Company, 12½ per cent more than is being paid for the same work by Jones and Laughlin, 12½ per cent more than is being paid for the same work by the Cambria Iron Company, or an average of 25 percent more than the ruling rates of the region.

...[T]hese people have taken advantage of the condition of the times and unnecessarily reduced their men just because they could do so. Not satisfied with this, many of them, disregarding the laws of the State, abandoned payday in July last and did not pay their men 1 cent in cash for months. The Frick Coke Company is the only concern in the entire region which has done any business worth speaking of that has maintained its regular semi-monthly pay days.

...This is the third agreement or scale that we have made with our men in the last six years which proved to their advantage and to our disadvantage, but in every instance we have lived up to the agreement both in spirit and in letter. During our experience in the coke business, whether working under an agreement or not, we have invariably paid the highest wages, invariably the last to reduce and the first to increase.[44]

In 1894, as yet another strike occurred, Frick did it again:

The Frick Coke Company, according to an official, looks upon the organization movement of the miners of the Connellsville region with favor, for if [it is] successful, the other operators in the region will be compelled to pay as high wages as the Frick Company, which they do not do now. An official of the company said: "For several years the Frick Company has been paying wages higher than at competing ovens. The scale which expired in February was scrupulously lived up to, notwithstanding the fact that everywhere else in the region wages were lowered. The present scale is higher than is paid at two-thirds of the plants owned by others. The moment our scale was made known the smaller producer cut to a lower rate, and for this reason: The Frick Company and McClure Company have been trying to maintain a minimum price for coke at $1. In order to get what little outside business there is, the small producers cut this price 15 cents on the ton. To do this they had to slash wages severely; and knowing that under our agreement with our workers we would not do this, they are at an advantage."[45]

The subject of wages will be discussed again and again in the various chapters. One thing stands out in every instance: Frick paid higher wages than his competitors, and maintained his wages even under harsh circumstances.

Mines and Their Safety

In a 2007 interview for the *Greensburg Tribune Review*, the head of a regional heritage area was reported as calling Frick a "successful capitalist, a person who was unconcerned with the work-safety conditions and lives of people employed by him...."[46] Nothing in regional newspapers or other sources of the day supports such a claim. As early as 1890, the Frick company was concerned about safety. During that year, the Hill Farm Mine explosion killed thirty-one men. It was not owned by Frick, but by the Dunbar Furnace Company. Thomas Lynch, Frick's superintendent, wrote a letter to all the superintendents of Frick mines:

> The late disaster at the Hill Farm should serve as a reminder and a warning to us all, that we are liable to have accidents of the same kind, and we should spare neither time, labor, nor expense to guard against them. We should always keep the facts prominently in our mines that it is the desire of our company, and our duty as well, that we make the safety of the lives of our employes [sic] our first and most important Business.[47]

A year later, on January 27, 1891, Mammoth Mine, purchased by the H.C. Frick Company from the J.W. Moore Company in 1889,[48] had a massive mine explosion, killing over 100 miners. Immediately thereafter, the Frick Company stepped up its war for safety and instituted a series of changes in a program called *Safety is the First Consideration*, eventually simplified to *Safety First*.[49] The company created twenty-seven rules to govern safety throughout their mines and put them into a booklet for every miner.[50]

It must be said that Thomas Lynch was as much responsible for the good deeds of the company as was Frick, maybe more so. He is credited as the designer of the *Safety First* program. He was at the helm from the beginning and served as president and chair of the H.C. Frick Coke Company long after Frick had resigned and moved on to the board of U.S. Steel (where he still had input into the company he founded). The slogan and the movement became an industry standard and then a national standard, and many try to lay claim to its origin. Some credited it to U.S. Steel. It belongs to the H.C. Frick Coke Company: "In America the first notable effort to prevent accidents was under the United States Steel Corporation in 1907. At the time of its organization in 1900 it inherited from the H.C. Frick Coke Co. the slogan, 'Safety the first consideration,' which had been an operating rule of the Frick Co. for a score of years by order of its president, Thomas Lynch."[51]

That same year, 1891, the *Colliery Engineer* offered a sketch of Henry Clay Frick. On his mines they wrote: "The collieries are all supplied with the best obtainable machinery and appliances and each plant of the H.C. Frick Coke Company is a model one. Mechanical devices are used in every place where machinery can advantageously supersede man or animal power, and the inside haulage arrangements are particularly effective. There is no coal company in America that so extensively uses the most advanced systems of rope haulage."[52]

State reports consistently found the Frick company holdings superior to other companies in caring for the safety of the men and security of the mine. In 1912 a state report stated:

> In many of the [Frick] mines the requirements of the law are exceeded as regards safety; as for example, the use of locked safety-lamps in mines where fire-damp is not generated in sufficient quantities to be detected by the use of an ordinary safety-lamp, and the employment of competent shot firers in such

mines; the regular examination of mines by fire bosses in which fire-damp has not as yet been detected; the care in the use and handling of explosives; the clearance of three feet between the side of the wagon and the sideway of the rib throughout the mine, and not only at points where sprags or brakes are to be applied or removed, as the law provides; additional protection for the miners by increased supervision at the face of the workings, and the construction of comfortable travelling-ways wherever possible.[53]

One could cite dozens of additional references, including one from Ida Tarbell, the famous investigative reporter who brought down Standard Oil with her reporting. She stated before the United States Senate Commission on Industrial Relations subcommittee on Centralization of Industrial Control and Operation of Philanthropic Foundations that she was taken into the coal fields of the Connellsville region: "I should say that the attitude of Mr. Lynch, the head of the Frick Coke Co., toward labor was one of the most enlightened at the time that was in existence in the mines.... Fifteen or twenty years ago, in the Frick mines, you would find in half a dozen languages the slogan 'Safety, first consideration.' That was all over those mines.... I went over with labor people, and I remember distinctly an intelligent laboring man who said to me, 'If they would do in these mines as they do in the Frick Coal co., we would never have a bit of trouble.'"[54]

Nothing more need be said. Except: "A medal has been awarded the H.C. Frick Coke Co. for its specialized exhibit in accident prevention, industrial hygiene and mutuality at the International Exposition of Hygiene at Dresden, Germany. An additional honor was given their exhibit by making it a permanent part of the great Berlin Museum of Safety. The Frick exhibit is the first non–German exhibit ever established in the German Museum"[55]

Company Stores

When the Panic of 1873 began and Henry Clay Frick needed dollars to keep him afloat, he adopted scrip that his miners could use.[56] It allowed him to use his legal dollars to pay his bills and keep his company alive. It saved him, his partners, the mines, and the jobs of his miners. The scrip was used by every mining company thereafter, sometimes to cheat its miners by overcharging. The Frick company did not overcharge its miners. As one can see by the tables below, Frick's Union Supply Stores were competitive on the market with other outlets. Frick encouraged his miners to plant gardens, and he bought produce from them to sell in the stores. Not all owners did that. The story of scrip goes back to the Middle Ages and is told in the chapter on workers.

The bigger issue about company stores was that miners were cheated by the companies. The was true of some companies, but not of Frick's during the Golden Age. The accusations continue to this day with very little evidence to support the accusations.

During the strike of 1886, Thomas Lynch denied that Frick company stores overcharged their workers:

...I never heard any complaints about prices at our stores, and have always told our men to report any high charges to me. Every month, I have a man to go to the town stores and purchase a bill of goods, and then compare their prices with our own. I never find much difference, and when I do it is invariably on our side. Our goods are sold the cheapest. Why, our stores at Davidson and Trotter, which are closest to competition, sell far more goods than those at any of the others. Only a few weeks ago a Pittsburg wholesale grocer complained that we were hurting his trade in Connellsville. The small dealers couldn't be made to believe that he didn't sell goods to us cheaper. I have known men to strike for a company store. I see it stated that at our pay day on Saturday some men didn't draw a cent. That often happens. Some men are improvident. But for every such man, I will point you out two who don't buy a cent's worth, and who draw all their earnings on pay-day.[57]

And another. This one from a modern-day scholar who went back and consulted the original sources:

> John Enman completed a study in 1974 of prices charged by the Union Supply Company. Comparing prices at the company's Buffington store with those at independent stores in Washington, a comparably remote southwestern Pennsylvania community, and Pittsburgh, a large city, he found that the Buffington store's prices were about the same as those at Washington, but higher than prices in Pittsburgh. Noting that the Union Supply Company was the largest chain store in western Pennsylvania, Enman found that Union set its prices by what the market would bear. Thus, even though the Union Supply Company's bulk purchasing would likely have allowed it to retail at or below the prices charged in Pittsburgh, the company used prices which were competitive in the outlying areas its stores served. In this matter, company stores in larger communities in the Connellsville coke region actually drew customers from among residents who were not Frick employees. The Union Supply Company, Enman concluded, made its profits not by exploiting Frick employees but through the economies of scale possible when owning such a large chain of stores.[58]

When times were bad, the *Rural Free Press* of 1893 maintained:

> With all this fresh in the minds of the operators, when work closed down for want of orders and families became destitute of the necessaries of life, they came forward with one accord and furnished eatables and fuel to the needy. The store managers of the H.C. Frick company were ordered to see that none should suffer as did also the McClure and other companies. At Leisenring [which Frick owned] they allowed the men to go into the mines and dig their own coal. They gave them mules to haul it to the shaft and had their engineer to hoist it to the surface. They also gave them teams to haul it home. Moreover, the men at most places have been notified that no house rent will be charged during the time the works are standing idle.[59]

In addition, Frick company farmlands, which numbered in the thousands of acres, were thrown open for the public to use for planting.[60]

Company stores are a major subject when discussing miners and their world. It is a topic in a number of chapters because it is so important. In each instance there is enough sound, original source evidence to show that the Frick companies were fair and honest, as most companies were, and that a few companies and probably individual workers at the stores were problems. In some instances, they are called to task. The same can be said about the company towns. The Morgan Valley had few patches. Houses, yes, but not many patches. But as the industry grew, the patches, like the stores and the mining conditions, grew and got better. Remember, mines existed in rural areas with few towns, so houses and stores had to be created by the mining companies for the welfare of their workers. This, like scrip, is a long-standing tradition from the Middle Ages.

There is no doubt that life in the coal fields was difficult. Few people today would want to live with outhouses, clotheslines, transportation issues, and horrific working conditions. Why was Henry Clay Frick pointed out as the villain who made the lives of the miners miserable? Could it be because he stood at the top and the top man takes the hits? There is no doubt Henry Clay Frick was responsible for the growth of coal mining and coke making in the bituminous region of Pennsylvania and that the region dominated the industry. It was his sound management and good judgment that made it all work. He created and dominated the Golden Age of Coal and Coke from 1870 to 1920 and beyond. Much of the criticism leveled against him should be leveled at a different era. After the Golden Age was the slow demise of the industry, when there were horrific times, starvation, and more.

A portion of the Fowler map of Mount Pleasant showing Frick Park (also donated by Frick), with the observatory he donated to the town in 1894. Inside the observatory was a Brasher Refactor Telescope. The park still exists but the observatory and water tower are gone (Cassandra Vivian, "A Frick Observatory and a Brashear Telescope," *Hidden History of the Laurel Highlands*. Charleston: The History Press, 2014, pp. 107–09).

Philanthropy

When he died, Henry Clay Frick had approximately $145,000,000. He earned only a part of it in coal and coke. He kept $25,000,000 for his family and gave the rest away. His home in New York City was turned into a museum with a two-million-dollar trust to maintain it. According to an article in *Science Magazine*, he divided his bequests into 100 shares of $500,000 each. Princeton received 30 shares; Harvard 10; MIT 10; the Educational Fund Commission Pittsburgh 10; Mercy Hospital Pittsburgh 10. Helen Frick, in addition to her own endowment, received 13 shares to distribute at will. The following institutions related to our discussion received 1 share each, or $500,000: Uniontown Hospital; Cottage State Hospital in Connellsville; Westmoreland Hospital in Greenburg; and Mount Pleasant Memorial Hospital.[61] But he had been giving all his life.

In 1892, he gave part of the land at Frick Park in Mount Pleasant to be used as a school, probably where the Ramsey School now stands on Eagle Street. From the *Hidden History of the Laurel Highlands*:

> After his success, Frick began his philanthropy to Mount Pleasant. He gave the town a municipal building, then a park, which became Frick Park, and in the midst of the park he had an observatory built with a revolving roof. That wasn't all. Inside the observatory was an incredible telescope.

The telescope was a Brashear Refactor Telescope that was 12-foot-tall and 6-inches-in diameter. The telescope was created by another regional genius—John Brashear. Brashear, born in Brownsville, became one of the most successful producers of telescopes and precision scientific instruments in the world and was head of the Allegheny Observatory in Pittsburgh.[62]

In 1909, the *Courier* also commented on this largess:

> H.C. Frick has just added another donation to the many splendid gifts given to the town of Mt. Pleasant, the place of his birth. The United Presbyterian Church is the latest to benefit by his liberality. The pastor, Rev. Howard S. Wilson, received from Mr. Frick a few days ago, a check for a large sum....
>
> Mr. Frick recently gave a large tract of land in the center of Mt. Pleasant to be used as a park. It bears the name Frick Park and is being improved rapidly by the borough authorities. His first gift to the town was an observatory and telescope for use of the schools.[63]

And Pittsburgh Too!

Quentin Skrabec, Jr., in *The Life of the Perfect Capitalist*, sums up Henry Clay Frick's contributions to building Pittsburgh and making it an industrial capital:

> After the formation of United States Steel, Frick expanded into many commercial interests as well, such as banking and real estate. In 1900, Frick was one of the largest real estate owners in Pittsburgh and one of the wealthiest in the East End. In 1899, Frick purchased the old St. Peter's Episcopal church at the corner of Grant and Diamond streets in the city of Pittsburgh for $180,000. In late 1900, he launched the building of the future Frick Building. It would stand next to the Carnegie Building of 1893, which was known as the city's first skyscraper. Frick planned a 24-story skyscraper 265 feet tall to cast a shadow on Carnegie's 15-story building. The building was a steel frame with carved stone of classical Doric design. Each office had two 47-inch-by-62-inch mirror windows. The interior had rich Italian marble, Honduras mahogany, and bronze metalwork and doors. The primary tenant was to be Frick's Union Savings Bank. Another tenant was Equitable Life, of whose board Frick was a member. Frick maintained his own personal office there as well. The top floor was reserved for the Union Club, and the basement has the Union Restaurant, paneled in Flemish Renaissance oak.... The next year Frick planned a major hotel, which would be known as the William Penn Hotel. The William Penn was to be the second largest hotel in the United States at the time.... By 1904, Frick was the largest owner of real estate in the city of Pittsburgh....[64]

Along with the Mellons, Frick became heavily involved in banking. The Mellons and Frick "controlled a third of all the bank money in Pittsburgh in 1902." Out of their efforts such industries as ALCOA and Gulf Oil were born. "It is clearly overlooked that Henry Clay Frick, more than anyone else, built the city of Pittsburgh. Frick had deep roots in Pittsburgh banking, transportation, real estate, coal, steel, and manufacturing. More so than Carnegie, Frick was the builder of industrial Pittsburgh, and history shows he was the real force behind United States Steel Corporation."[65]

In Conclusion

Perhaps the saddest part of this story is what happened when Frick's daughter went to court to clear his name. In 1965, Helen Frick sued Sylvester K. Stevens, executive director of the Pennsylvania Historical and Museum Commission and author of *Pennsylvania: Birthplace of a Nation*, for his comments against her father.[66]

At page 226 of his book, defendant stated: "In the bituminous fields of western Pennsylvania Henry Clay Frick had built a similar monopoly of coal and coke production and was equally successful in beating down efforts at unionization. Frick also made extensive use of immigrant labor and cut wages to an average of about $1.60 a day while extracting the longest hours of work physically possible. Most mines of the time were without anything resembling modern safety appliances or practices and serious accidents were common.

"Still another abuse was the company town with its company store. The coal companies owned the houses, shoddy wooden shacks without sanitary facilities, which they rented at a high price to workers."

Just reading this chapter on Frick would challenge what the author wrote. But the court found them to be true:

23. On more than one occasion, Henry Clay Frick cut wages.
24. On February 1, 1894, Henry Clay Frick cut wages to his coke workers by 22 percent.
25. On February 1, 1894, Henry Clay Frick cut wages to an average of about $1.60 per day.
26. In 1886, average daily wages of miners had been $1.41 to $2.00 and were increased to an average of $1.75.
27. The Frick coke and coal employes worked a 10-hour day.
28. Ten hours a day were the longest working hours physically possible on a sustained basis in the coke and coal industry.
30. The Frick mines, as well as the other bituminous mines, were without anything resembling modern safety appliances or practices, and serious accidents were common.
33. The Frick company towns, as well as those of the other bituminous mine owners, were company owned houses that were shoddy wooden shacks without any sanitary facilities, which the operators rented at a high rate to the workers.
34. The Frick company stores, as well as those of the other bituminous mine owners, charged the workers higher prices than privately owned stores.
35. The Frick company, as well as the other coke and coal companies, issued paper scrip to their employes, so that they could see how much the employes were patronizing the company store.

And the court concluded:

88. Defendant's statements about Henry Clay Frick are not malicious.
89. Defendant's statements about Henry Clay Frick, if in error, were not made with knowledge of their falsity or with reckless disregard of whether false or not, but were based on reasonable investigation and research.

The suit continued for over two years. In the end, Helen lost her battle and Judge Clinton Weidner of Cumberland County, Pennsylvania, maintained the book protected by free speech.

He stated:

Simply, Miss Helen C. Frick seeks to enjoin publication and distribution of the book, "Pennsylvania: Birthplace of a Nation" in its present form because she does not believe certain statements about her father, Henry Clay Frick, in his business dealings. She admits she knows nothing of his business dealings, but claims they must be untrue because of the character of his personal relations with her as his daughter.

By analogy, Miss Frick might as well try to enjoin publication and distribution of the Holy Bible because, being a descendant of Eve, she does not believe that Eve gave Adam the forbidden fruit in the Garden of Eden, and because her senses are offended by such a statement about an ancestor of hers.[67]

Then he proclaimed the book "accurate and, in fact, too easy on the tycoon."[68]

Of all the operators in the Connellsville district, Frick was proclaimed the best, did more for the workers, and stood far and above the other owners in safety, housing, and more. The judge, at the head of one of the state's most prestigious organizations, did not honor that legacy. Page after page in this book will prove the judge wrong.

The above evidence that the court and the writers had to look deeper into the facts, and that public opinion is often built on misinformation or only knowing part of a story, is at the heart of what is wrong with the Frick reputation.

Three

The Workers and Their World

One of the greatest migrations of the modern world took place at the beginning of the Industrial Age. From 1880 to 1920, twenty-three million immigrants came to America, most from eastern and southern Europe. Their main destination was along the eastern coast, especially to Pennsylvania. In Pennsylvania, most came to coal country: anthracite and bituminous. Of those, a large number of new immigrants came to the southwestern counties of Fayette and Westmoreland.

Mines needed workers. The region did not have enough of them, so slowly, very slowly, immigrants began to migrate to the region. The first immigrants to work in the mines were German, Irish, Welsh, and Scottish. They mostly spoke or understood English and their traditions were similar to earlier colonial Americans. Most important of all, many were miners in their home country and were brought to the region specifically to mine coal. They began to arrive in the United States in the 1860s. It was a new industry and no one knew exactly how to hire them: "Each skilled miner was employed as an independent petty contractor who entered into a contract with the individual mine owner. Each contract stimulated rates of pay per bushel, ton, or car of mined coal delivered in the entry where it was collected by the 'mule skinners,' or trip ridders. As piece rate workers, they determined both the hours of their daily labor and the tempo of work at the face in the room where coal is extracted daily."[1] From that basic formula, the industry moved forward.

By the 1880s, Slovaks, Magyars, Poles, Croatians, and Italians joined the ever-growing number of immigrants. They, for the most part, were not miners. According to the *Weekly Courier*, Thomas Lynch, Frick's right-hand man, stated the first immigrants from central and southern Europe came to the region in 1870 and were sent to Morewood by the H.C. Frick Company.[2] According to the *Daily Courier* of 1910, the first foreigners in the Morgan Valley were sent to Eagle and White Mines.[3]

Life wasn't easy. The immigrants struggled. They had language barriers. They needed homes, jobs, and more. When the mines had orders, they worked. When the mines were down, there was no work. They were given homes where they paid rent and a company store where they could buy their groceries and equipment. Both became controversial through the decades. Some immigrants came to make money and then go home to a better life in the old country. Others came to stay and brought their families. The population of southwestern Pennsylvania today is peopled by their descendants.

Not Welcome

The biggest problem was that *foreigners were not welcome*. By 1884 the resentment by earlier immigrants was so intense, "An Appeal to American Working Men" was posted in the *Scottdale Independent* newspaper. It read:

American labor must be protected. There is a certain class of European Serfs amongst us, who are called Hungarians who are a curse to our Country and a disgrace to the civilized world. Wherever they are found these creatures live on the lowest kind of food, therefore they take away our labor, never becoming citizens, never invest their earnings in any way to make their homes here, but instead they send their earnings back to their native land, and thus make a continual drain on our country's money. Now we appeal to all American citizens to give us a helping hand, and protect us from this degrading evil. Signed Workingmen[4]

In 1885 the same paper lamented:

Foreign labors are being shipped to this region by the car load. On last Wednesday, a car load arrived; on Saturday, two car loads; and Monday morning one car load; in all between two and three persons [sic]. They are mostly composed of the lowest class of Hungarians, Sweeds, Poles, and Italians. These people can live on almost anything eatable. They have been known to eat carrion and the refuse of hog pens. They will be sent to the different coke works in this vicinity and put to such work as they know nothing about....[5]

Contract Labor and Other Laws

In 1885 the Contract Labor Law was enacted. It forbade American individuals or organizations from engaging in labor contracts with individuals prior to their immigration to the United States, and forbade ship captains from transporting immigrants under labor contracts. The law allowed private employers to recruit foreign workers and to pay their transportation expenses. In return for recruiting immigrants in foreign countries, these companies were paid fees by both the employers for whom they contracted workers and the steamship lines that transported the recruits from Europe.

In 1889 a bill was reintroduced in Harrisburg to assess the employer of a Hun fifteen cents a day in taxes to "protect American labor." It was called the Campbell Bill and was introduced by Representative George W. Campbell, a Republican of Fayette County. Campbell had originally introduced the bill at the beginning of February. It was designed for the "regulation of the employment of foreign born and unnaturalized persons, and providing a tax on the employers of such persons." The tax would be assessed on the company who employed foreigners from whatever nation. It was intended to "compel some sort of revenue from the Hungarians and Italians employed in the coke regions, who are not and do not intend becoming citizens, but still enjoy all the privileges of Americans." The bill was supported by Captain Dravo, a former coke operator, who said "it was a recognized fact, by the Republican party at least, that some restrictions should be placed on the flood of foreign immigration ... coming to amass ... wealth and had no intention of becoming citizens.... They crowded the local schools, receiving the same benefits as American citizens without paying a cent of tax."

It was opposed by Lytle of Huntingdon County, who said the bill was "foreign to the American principle of freedom." Adams of Bedford County was opposed too, but his focus was "to protect the interest of the farmer, who, if he were to employ a farm-hand temporarily" and did not pay the tax, would be liable to a fine. Deardon of Philadelphia County believed this was not a matter for the states to take up but the Congress of the United States.[6] The bill was passed on March 27 with an attachment that the assessment should not be deducted from laborer's wages.[7]

Pennsylvania was not the only state to enact such a law. In the 1850s the state of California did the same against Asians and Mexicans.[8] The issue festered for decades, with dozens of bills and dozens of vetoes enacted on the national level. It festers today.

In 1890, the 51st Congress House of Representatives held an investigation and found many issues. "The intent of our immigration laws is not to restrict immigration, but to shift it, to separate the desirable from the undesirable immigrants, and to permit only those to land on our shores who have certain physical and moral qualities" (p. II). They found that employers had found a way to circumvent the Contract Labor Law. "Employers interested in importing large bodies of men have devised other way to avoid the contract law. Agents are now sent to Europe who employ natives as assistant agents in districts where they decide to operate. They arouse an interest in America by circulating glowing descriptions of the development and prosperity of the new World ... fabulous fortunes ... promise of work ... and chartered ships" (p. V). Employers also advertised in newspapers abroad and with steamship companies that acted as subagents and solicitors (p. VI). Foreign workers also came to the United States through Canada (p. VII).[9]

In 1892 an official immigration custom was created at Ellis Island. By 1894, disgruntled Republican Bostonians created the Immigration Restriction League, trying to stop immigrants from entering the country. Republican Henry Cabot Lodge sponsored a bill in Congress in 1896 requiring immigrants to be able to read 40 words in any language. President Grover Cleveland, Democrat, vetoed the bill. He vetoed it again in 1897. In 1907, another attempt began to limit immigration. In 1913, President Taft, Republican, and in 1915 President Wilson, Democrat, vetoed such bills. It was brought up again in 1917 and passed as the Immigrant Act, requiring literacy tests and an Asian Barred Zone. Wilson again vetoed it, but the Congress, with a Republican majority, overrode his veto and passed the legislation.[10] Obviously the immigration issues sweeping the country in the early decades of the 21st century are not new.

How They Got Here

The importation of labor did not begin with the mining industry in Pennsylvania. During the Gold Rush, thousands of Chinese were imported in the West to work in the gold industry and to help build the railroad west. They suffered far beyond anything that happened in the coal and coke industry. But during the Civil War, immigration declined and labor was needed. In 1864 the Act to Encourage Immigration was passed by the Lincoln Administration, which also created the U.S. Emigration Office.[11]

The American Emigrant Company was chartered in 1863 "for the purpose of procuring and assisting emigrants from foreign countries to settle in the United States."[12] Foreigners were contacted to fill the request of American companies. Passage fees were advanced and had to be repaid. They were contracted to import as well as serve immigrants who made their own way to New York. The company's methods were clearly stated in their booklet *American Emigrant Company*:

> Parties desiring to import workmen through its agency are required to forward information as definite and explicit as possible, stating the exact qualifications of the men required; on receipt of this order, instructions will be sent to the proper agent located in the country where the men are to be obtained. This agent will have as careful a selection made as is practicable of the men needed, and will contract with them for their services for a certain time to be specified, undertaking to pay them the currencys in this country for such work, or to make such special rates as may be ordered.... where large numbers of men are required for one interest or one neighborhood, special agents are sent, upon reasonable terms, to conduct them the entire way ... across the ocean by the ordinary lines of passenger ships....[13]

To further clarify, in 1884 the *Scottdale Independent* had a column describing how immigrants were recruited:

> We stood in the lower part of Greenwich street…. Around the verdure-clad park could be seen Castle Garden…. The sidewalks were crowded with men and women of almost every European country. They were dissimilar in their stature and color, but all had a sameness of dirt and rags, and looked half-starved and dull-eyed.
>
> The man who answered the question was not one of these. He was well fed and well clad, displaying a large quantity of jewelry, and wearing a license badge which gave him the entrée to the "garden," where he could go and bargain for the herd he contracted to procure.
>
> "How many Hungarians did you say you want? … Yes, I can supply you with two hundred or more. Wages? Sometimes we furnish them for a dollar a day…."[14]

Not all coal companies imported labor. The smaller companies did not have the need or the funds. Nor were coal companies the only agencies importing labor to Pennsylvania. The Frick company did import labor.

Germans

Among the earliest immigrants to bituminous coal country were the Germans, and they were the largest group of immigrants in both Fayette and Westmoreland counties. The Mennonites dominated among the German immigrants. They arrived in the region in the 1700s, long before the Industrial Revolution arrived in the Mount Pleasant to Broadford district. They purchased farmland, and thus the coal that would make them rich lay beneath the corn, tomatoes, wheat, and rye. Among the Mennonites were the Overholt family, who would establish a homestead at a site now called West Overton. That family, in addition to farming, established two giant distilleries making rye whiskey, one at West Overton and another at Broadford. The Overholts were the ancestors of Henry Clay Frick, who, as noted before, was born at West Overton and worked for his grandfather at the Broadford distillery.

The names of the Overholt and the other Mennonite families became familiar to the bituminous coal and coke industry as they purchased land, built and invested in railroads, and owned and operated the early mines and ovens: Frick, Tinstman, Rist, Stauffer, and Sherrick, to name a few. All but Frick left the industry either through bankruptcy or frustration.

By the 1860s, the Germans had a second migration to the United States. And the Scots, English, and Welsh came with them. Many settled around Scottdale, where the Frick offices would eventually be established. Descendants can be found throughout the region including Broadford, Everson, and Mount Pleasant.

Irish

The Irish began migrating to America around 1840. Some sources say they migrated because the potato famine was devastating their homeland. Other sources maintain the famine had nothing to do with it. Their destination at the time was the anthracite region of Pennsylvania. In the 1860s, the number of miners in that region, far earlier than the bituminous region of southwestern Pennsylvania, rose from 25,000 to 53,000.[15] Among them was a secret organization called the Molly Maguires. They, too, came to the anthracite region and fought for Irish justice. Some consider them heroes, others terrorists.

During the bituminous boom in the 1870s and '80s, many Irish settled in Adelaide along the Youghiogheny near Connellsville and worked in the mine. Additional Irish worked in the mines around Everson, including Eagle. Among the places in the Connellsville coke region where they immigrated were Mammoth, Calumet, Fairchance, Edenborn, and Leisenring, where St. Vincent's Irish Catholic Church was established. Of course, larger communities like Connellsville, Mount Pleasant and Uniontown had their share of churches and clubs too.

Austro-Hungarians

The bulk of the new immigrants came from the Austro-Hungarian Empire. The once massive empire had conquered most of Europe and part of Asia, and thus the immigrants consisted of Hungarians, Slovaks, Poles, Ruthenians (Carpatho-Rusyns), Sebians, Croatians, Ukrainians, Slovenians and Romanians. They were Roman or Greek Catholic, Greek Orthodox, Jewish, and a variety of Protestant sects.[16] They were all known as Huns. Their ethnicity was often confused, and a nationality could be listed under several different names like the Ukrainians and the Carpatho-Rusyns.

By 1877, migration from the Austro-Hungarian Empire began. First the Ukrainians (Russniaks), then in the 1880s the Slovaks, in the 1890s the Polish, and after 1900 the Croatians, Lithuanians, and Ruthenians or Rusyns (Carpatho-Rusyns). Throughout Westmoreland and Fayette counties, their churches often tell us where they settled.

Ukrainians

Ukrainians arrived in Jamestown with John Smith in 1607. There may have been a few more over the years, but the big immigration began around the 1880s. They appear to be the smallest group of immigrants from the Empire. One of the reasons given for their immigration is that they were badly treated by the Empire. It is reported: "To pacify the Polish demands for independence [the Empire] gave the Poles full rein to exercise their domination over the Ukrainians. The Poles thereupon continued their centuries-old oppressive tactics over the Ukrainians, robbing them of all political, economic, and cultural rights...."[17] St. John the Baptist Byzantine Catholic Church, once on Porter Avenue in Scottdale, had a Ukrainian heritage.

Slovaks

The "Slavs" were considered to be in the majority, but the ancestry records do not seem to agree with this perception, and neither do other official records that suggest other groups were more dominant. Perhaps one of the reasons was that the term Slav was often used to represent a number of different ethnic groups from the Empire.

Many of the early Slav immigrants were employed at the Hazlett mine near Mount Pleasant, where two carloads were delivered in 1883. That meant there was a Slovak church

Ukrainian *pasanky* (sing. *pasanka*), decorated eggs in folklore patterns made during the Easter holidays are a gift of our Ukrainian people and all their Slavic neighbors as well. The eggs are believed to protect from the evil eye, promote fertility, bring a healthy and plentiful harvest, and protect the household from harm (author photo, 2002).

too, probably in Mount Pleasant. However, the first Slovak Catholic church in the Americas was erected in Hazleton, in the anthracite region of Pennsylvania.

The Slovak churches, many closed now, were in Connellsville (St. John's, St. Peter's Slovak Lutheran Church), Mount Pleasant (Church of God—East End Mission), Mammoth, Crabtree, Calumet, Wyano, Leith, Oliver, Lemont Furnace, Fairchance, Trauger (Forty Martyrs Church), United (St. Florin), and Yukon (Our Lady of Sorrows Slovak Church). In Mount Pleasant, three Slovak clubs still exist: Slovak Citizens, Slovak American Club, Kosciuszko Club.[18]

Polish

The Polish were "the largest single foreign-born group of miners numbering about 50,000 by 1920."[19] The *Daily Courier* reported that twenty-four Belgians and Poles arrived at Broadford for H.C. Frick Company on February 20, 1880.[20] Eventually they settled at Morewood, Alice, Standard, and Mount Pleasant, where a nearby Polish cemetery is located. In Everson, St. Joseph's Church still dominates the skyline. The Poles from Mount Pleasant also went to the Everson church, but in 1887 they founded their own church, the Parish of the Transfiguration.[21] When the Catholic Church began combining churches several decades ago, the parishioners of Transfiguration refused to join, and set up their own church. Polish clubs remain strong in the region. There is one in Mount Pleasant, another at Everson. Poles also settled in Mammoth (St. Stanislaus), Calumet, Crabtree, and Fairchance (Sts. Cyril and Methodius).

Croatians

In what was probably true of all the "birds of passage," when Croatians returned to their homeland, and 66 percent of them did, they brought the dream of freedom with them. "In 1906 Croatian writer Antun Matos wrote, 'America is presently the most important factor in the creation of Croatian democracy.'"[22] It appears that life in the coal patch offered them freedoms denied to them in their home country.

There are also Croatian clubs in the region. One, the Croatian Fraternal Union, Lodge 432, at Yukon, closed its doors for the last time in May of 2018.[23] Additional sites where Croatians worked the mines are Mammoth, Leith, Dunbar, and Fairchance.

Lithuanians

Three hundred thousand Lithuanians came to the United States. They were often called Russians, Poles, or Jews. Most settled in the anthracite region, especially Schuylkill County. That region became the center of Lithuanian immigration in America.[24] There are dozens of churches and clubs in that region and their traditions are well known throughout eastern Pennsylvania. Thirty percent of them returned to their homes in Europe and Russia.[25, 26]

In southwestern Pennsylvania in the Connellsville coal region, Lithuanians are few in number. A small number of Lithuanians were sent to the Orient Mine near the town of Cardale and Paradise Lake in the Klondike region of Fayette County. There, the Madonna of Czestochowa Catholic Church was built near the turn of the century on land donated by the Orient Coal Company owned by the Nobel family. It was mostly a Polish Catholic Church and served a number of small communities in the area. It was closed by the Catholic Church in recent years.[27]

Ruthenians or Rusyns (Carpatho-Rusyns)

The Carpatho-Rusyns had no country. They lived in a region that comprised a portion of three countries: Ukraine, Slovakia, and Poland. Two hundred twenty-five thousand Carpatho-Rusyns immigrated to the United States before 1914. Like other ethnic groups, many of them first settled in the anthracite coal region in eastern Pennsylvania. In southwest Pennsylvania they went more into the steel towns along the Monongahela River than into the coal mines.[28]

The other problem was their religion; they were Greek Catholics. In the eyes of the average person in the United States, they were neither Orthodox nor Catholic, and there was no such religion in the United States at the time. It became a battle with the Roman Catholic Church that would accept them on the condition the priests remained celibate. They refused and set up their church as a corporation.

> Monessen [along the Monongahela River in Westmoreland County] had one of the largest Greek Catholic communities in the United States and it became the epicenter for this problem. The controversy eventually pushed the congregation in two directions. A portion of the parishioners became Russian Orthodox and built their own church, Saint John the Divine Russian Orthodox Church. The remain-

der, wishing to remain Greek Catholic, but still not willing to give up their physical property, had to go to court to keep their identity as Greek Catholics....[29]

They did, and they won.

In the Connellsville region there was the Saint Stephen Byzantine Catholic Church at Leisenring as early as 1892. It had 1800 members and was the "first brick Greek Catholic church in the United States."[30] Additional churches and Carpatho-Rusyn communities existed at Scottdale (Swedetown), Trauger (St. Mary's Greek Catholic Church), and Uniontown (St. John the Baptist Byzantine Church).[31]

Hungarians

The Hungarians dominated the news in the region, primarily because the Austro-Hungarian immigrants were all called Huns. According to Thomas Lynch of the Frick company: "The first Hungarians were introduced in the region in 1870, but they weren't brought here to break a strike. We had just completed the Morewood works, Labor [sic] was scarce in the region, and we were obliged to look elsewhere for it. We sent to New York, and were supplied with Hungarians by one of the labor bureaus mentioned. They have since been writing to their friends and the region has gradually filled up with them."[32] Lynch went on to say: "Out of our 3,500 men, about 25 per cent. are Hungarians, Bohemians and Poles, mostly at Mt. Pleasant; 10 per cent. are Germans and Prussians, and the balance Irish and American, with a sprinkling of English, Welsh and Scotch."[33]

It was the Hungarian women who went into the coke oven area and helped their husbands so the family would have more money. It became a major issue as other workers were making less money. Some claim they created the Strike of 1886. They worked at Morewood, White, Eagle, and Calumet. The Russians settled in Smithton, Wyano, and Yukon.

Italians

Edwin Fenton, in *Italians in the Labor Movement*, makes an interesting assessment of the southern Italians who migrated to America. Most of the Italians who came to America were from the south. Fenton maintains they had three major characteristics: "[T]hey were provincial, trusting no one from outside the bounds of their village or at most their section of the peninsula; they were fatalistic, the result partly of centuries of oppression; and they were self-reliant, preferring to depend on their own strong backs and on their families."[34]

As early as 1874, Italians were brought into the Pittsburgh region by Charles Armstrong, owner of Westmoreland Coal and Coke Company in Westmoreland County. They were strikebreakers in an event that became known as the Buena Vista Affair. The mines in question were the Osceola and Armstrong Station southeast of Pittsburgh. Armstrong threw all his workers out and hired 173 Italians, equipping them with sixty "muskets and rented another sixty as well as revolvers and musket cartridges." It was a violent strike and a precursor of things to come.[35] Thereafter Italians were often used as strikebreakers. Armstrong and owners like him deserve most of the anger leveled against Frick.

Others

As for the "negros," as the African Americans were called, very few were in coal country. Occasionally they were brought in as strikebreakers, but they did not like it and no one liked them. So they left.

All these various nationalities mingled in many mines and their patches. They wore their ethnic clothes and cooked their ethnic meals. They shared their traditions at weddings, baptisms, and other celebrations. They shared their good times and bad. They learned to work with all the ethnic groups in the patches. What they gave us is our diversity: our halupki and our pizza, our sauerkraut and our salami, our *pasanka* and our sweet potato pie. How these immigrant women labored over coal stoves to make all the complicated ethnic recipes is a marvel. But they have handed them all down to us to make and to enjoy.

Where and How They Lived

"The word patch is from the German word spelled p-a-c-h-t, which means to rent or be a tenant. The word was anglicized by early English and Irish settlers to 'patch.'"[36] Mines existed in rural areas where there were few places for a worker to live. In Broadford, where Frick built his first mines, there was no patch. The patch as we know it never existed there or up the Morgan Valley, where the Frick Company built homes for their workers, but not in a controlled area in a specific pattern. Once the mines grew bigger, patches were built at Morewood, Standard, Alice, and throughout the Connellsville coke region and beyond.

They consisted of rows of houses set along streets in patterns that adjusted to the terrain. At one end of the patch was the company store, at the other end perhaps a small church. Most patches were well designed and houses were located close to the work area. As seen below, the Southwest and Frick company houses were built for two families side by side. Made of hemlock and painted, they consisted mostly of four rooms with an outhouse in the back yard. Superintendents, mine bosses and other men in authority often had single dwelling houses, some made of brick and often separated from the general patch. Eventually electricity would arrive, but during much of the Golden Age, the homes were lit by kerosene lanterns and heated by coal, maybe wood. Each home had a small garden. Rent varied over the years, but in 1888 each Frick family paid $6 a month rent, $1 for coal, and another dollar for the company doctor. The early homes still standing along the Morgan Valley mostly follow the same structure, some single dwellings, so it is doubtful that the Frick company built shanties from the beginning. The company may have absorbed shanties as they acquired properties, but those were replaced. As the industry grew and the Frick company began to create patches, they were often hailed as among the best.[37]

The bathrooms were outside. So, too, were the kitchens. It was in those kitchens that the immigrants made their traditional foods. It was where they learned that their neighbor from a different country ate the same food but called it a different name and had a different ingredient: a Croatian made and still makes a halupki with cabbage and pork and calls it *sarma*, a Pole uses rice or barley and calls it *golabki*, Ukrainians use sauerkraut and no meat, and the Hungarians use sour cream and paprika. The same was true of the Italians: a southern Italian made sauce without meat and added meatballs, a northern Italian had meat in the sauce and no meatballs. When they went looking for ricotta for their ravioli or lasagna and didn't find it, they substituted cottage cheese. And on it went through the dozens and dozens of nationalities that became part of the southwestern Pennsylvania landscape.

What is important here is that people from all over Europe were drawn together in patches and small steel towns. They mingled. They shared joys and they shared sorrows. When times were hard, they stood by each other regardless of nationality. They kept their traditions and adopted a few new ones from their neighbors.

Standard Mine, just outside Mount Pleasant, was not owned by the H.C. Frick Coke Company, but was part of the Frick holdings. The houses above were built at Standard Mine in the 1880s. The upper left image is as they stood on Low Street (Route 819) when they were first built. The larger image shows the same houses as they stand today, nearly 150 years later (author photo, 2012).

There is an interesting story about a draftee during World War II. He was being assessed with a group of men to determine what training they should receive. As the instructor asked them questions about Europe, the draftee had many answers. The instructor is reported to have said: "You must have traveled a lot to know so much about Europe." The draftee answered, "Yes, I went one block this way and another block that way." That is how we became Americans.

John Enman made an extensive study of the remaining patches in the 1950 and '60s. one must rely heavily on his work, as today much of that world is gone.

The Curse of Misinformation and Generalization

Today we make too many false statements about the coal and coke industry thinking they are fact. One such statement from a 1990s heritage project uses every cliché, rumor, and gross generalization to promote the false impression that is believed as truth today. It is an excellent example of what we call "fake news." In describing the control of the company over occupants of the patch, this source reported: "In an attempt to maximize profits, capitalists strove to run the company towns efficiently. Low wages, the use of scrip, company stores, and company houses all increased a company's earnings while minimizing not only the earnings and savings of laborers and their families, but also their freedom. The companies tried to control residents' lives through private police, religious establishments, leases, and, ultimately coercion."[38]

First, there is no time frame in this comment: was this true at the beginning of the industry, during the middle years, or throughout the 100+ years of the coal industry? When did these conditions exist? Certainly not the entire 100+ plus years. Second, not all the companies were guilty of such treatment, be it the beginning, the middle, or end of the in-

STATUS OF PATCHES 1959

PATCH	LOCATION	LAYOUT	CONDITION	HOUSES BLT	REMAIN 1959
Alverton No. 1 (Donnelly)	VALLEY	LINEAR	DEMOLISHED	10	0
Alverton No. 2 (Mayfield)	VALLEY	LINEAR	DEMOLISHED	57	12
Alverton No. 3					
Bessemer (Rising Sun	VALLEY	LINEAR	DEMOLISHED	58	0
Buckeye	VALLEY	LINEAR	DEMOLISHED	40	0
Eagle	HILLSIDE	LINEAR	DEMOLISHED	54	4
Foundry (Sumt 3)					
Franklin	HILLSIDE	LINEAR	DEMOLISHED		
Frick	HILLSIDE	LINEAR	DEMOLISHED		
Hazlett	VALLEY	LINEAR	DEMOLISHED	44	0
Henry Clay	HILLSIDE	LINEAR	DEMOLISHED	52	0
Morgan	HILLSIDE	LINEAR	LARGELY DEM	20	2
Mullen	VALLEY	LINEAR	DEMOLISHED	22	0
Rist					
Southwest No 1, Morewood	HILLSIDE	LINEAR	DEMOLISHED	179	10
Southwest No 2, Alice	HILLSIDE	SQUARE	DEMOLISHED	90	0
Standard Shaft	VALLEY	RECTANG	**COMPLETE**	134	98
Standard Slope	VALLEY	LINEAR	**COMPLETE**	182	150
Summit	HILLSIDE	LINEAR	DEMOLISHED	38	6
Tip Top	VALLEY	LINEAR	DEMOLISHED	4	0
Valley	VALLEY	LINEAR	DEMOLISHED	22	**0**
White, (Globe)	VALLEY	RECTANG	DEMOLISHED	28	0

ADAPTED FROM JOHN ENMAN, THE RELATIONSHIP OF COAL MINING AND COKE MAKING TO THE DISTRIBUTION OF POPULATION... PHD THESIS, 1962

What has happened to the communities built by various mining companies throughout the Connellsville region? This report answers many of those questions ("Status of Patches 1959," Adapted from Appendix D, pp. 442–448, John Enman, "The Relationship of Coal Mining and Coke Making to the Distribution of Population Agglomerations in the Connellsville (Pennsylvania) Beehive Coke Region," Ph.D. dissertation, University of Pittsburgh Library, 1962).

dustry. Copious sources have been cited throughout this research showing that not all mine operators tried to cheat their workers. Most pointed to the Frick company as outstanding when dealing with its workers. Yet in the 1990s we have researchers making these false and accusative statements more against Frick than anyone else.

In addition, a patch-type system was not a concept invented by mine operators to control their workers. A similar pattern existed as far back as the Middle Ages and probably beyond. This is a significant and important point. The new industry and its companies did not invent the patch. When they found they needed to create housing and other services, they looked to what had been done before and followed it while trying to find their way. An example of how it worked for hundreds of years is the *Mezzadria* serf system in Italy. It operated much like others throughout Europe. Peasants lived on land owned by a landed gentry, the *padrone*. He determined their lives. He encouraged breeding so he had more workers. They were forced to plant on a certain day, harvest on a certain day, to raise and slaughter animals following a specific system. The *padrone* had to approve marriages, and even the type of clothing the workers wore. All their movements were controlled by the *padrone* for centuries:

> The *padrone* system in Italy in the nineteenth century was a cruel one.... the *padrone* ... owned the land. They rented it out in a sharecropper system to a number of families. Each family lived on its own *podere*, or farm estate. Some *podere* held more than one family.... Each family, by contract to the *padrone*, had a fixed number of workers and each worker had a specific job. Everything was accountable to the *padrone* who got half of what the farm produced. If one member of the family died, or left for whatever reason, he or she had to be replaced by the farmer in order to meet his quota or his contract. If he did not have more family to put to work, he had to hire someone and that cut into the family profits.[39]

The early miners were well aware that they were not as controlled as they were in their home country. Remember the Croatians? They took the idea of freedom back to their homeland and fought for the freedom their relatives in the patch had. They had lived in the patch. They saw a freedom there they did not experience back home in Europe. Generalizations like the one quote above do not serve to paint a true picture of life in the patch. Unfortunately, they are believed.

The essay continues:

> Low-quality building materials and the bare necessities characterized the construction of workers' homes. The houses had no basements, foundations or insulation, and often clapboards were absent (Maclean 1909, 334). The houses were terribly cold and drafty in winter—weatherboards or clapboards, when installed, furnished the only protection from the weather. Heat from fireplaces and kitchen stoves was unsuccessful at warding off the cold. One former patch resident described trying to scrub the kitchen floor and seeing the water freeze before she could wipe it away [p 48].

Again, not everyone, not everywhere, not always. Granted, some owners allowed their workers to live in shacks. In 1879 a Senate committee came to the Connellsville coke region to see the conditions of the miners' homes of the Youghiogheny Mining Company at Wickhaven, the Banning mine of Morgan, Moore and Bain, and the Darr mine of Osborne & Saeger. "Banning is inhabited by Italians who work at Whitsett and Banning mines. The houses, if such, are built on stilts and one measured about 10 feet wide, 30 [illegible] feet long and 7 feet high. One row was occupied by thirteen people, and the cots were all placed side by side with no space between.... [The house] rented for $10 a month. The Italians said they could make 35 cents a day when working, but got work only from two and a half to three days a week."[40]

This type of disastrous living, per the quotes above, supposedly was found in the entire region. But the entire region was not like that. There are dozens and dozens of documents that contradict these general statements. The main one comes from John Enman. In his Ph.D. thesis, submitted in 1962, he did an extensive study of the housing in the patch towns in the Connellsville region:

> The frame houses of the older and smaller works were of cheap board-and-batten construction judging from those that remain.... Many of the frame houses seem to have been soundly, if somewhat unimaginatively, built. Those at Leisenring, now 80 years old, are substantial in appearance, thanks largely to a vigorous maintenance program carried on by Frick and the individuals who subsequently purchased them.
>
> Other materials used were stone and brick. Few houses in the settlements were made of stone, but it was a common foundation material. Blocks of sandstone or thin slabs of shale were locally available.... Sedimentary rock was common and seemingly each works had its own quarry ... so its use in house foundations is not surprising.[41]

Enman is a modern writer, and one of the best when discussing coal and coke in the Connellsville region. Golden Age writers agreed. Jett Lauck, in the article "The Bituminous

Coal Miner and Coke Worker of Western Pennsylvania," in *The Survey* of 1911, paints a dim view of the patches in general. He claims the houses are poorly constructed, have open drainage and rubbish in the gutters, with smoke from the ovens dominating the atmosphere. But then he goes on:

> One mining company in the coal and coke region affords a notable exception to the general conditions of affair and furnishes a striking object lesson as to what might be done. This company has entered into an extensive system of welfare work in order to develop a contented, stable, and efficient labor force. Its wage scale is twenty-five percent higher than that of its competitors. A company store is maintained but patronage is not compulsory and the competition of other stores and hucksters is permitted. Beer and whiskey peddlers and solicitors are excluded from the village and the consumption of alcoholic liquors is regulated by a committee of mine workers. Good dwellings are provided with comfortable porches, yards, shade trees, water in the houses, and electric lights. A deputy sheriff is employed to keep order and maintain the proper sanitary conditions. The fees for his arrests do not go into his pocket but are paid into a charitable fund. Children are required to attend either the public or parochial schools and if they are unable to secure books they are furnished by the company. The deputy sheriff enforces attendance. Pure milk at five cent a quart is supplied from inspected cows maintained by the company. In order to improve living conditions, the number of boarders which may be kept by a family is limited. The general results in better order and in housing and living conditions have been most gratifying. The policy has also paid the company in dollars and cents through increased efficiency and output.[42]

The name of the company is not given, but one can guess that it was U.S. Steel, which received its philosophy concerning workers from the ownership of the H.C. Frick Coke Company and Frick and Lynch.

More evidence: In 1912, the United States Steel Corporation was brought before a United States Senate committee to investigate the treatment of workers. It was a long hearing with many, many questions. Among the responses was a letter by Thomas Lynch outlining the history of the H.C. Frick Coke Company's treatment of workers and establishing that the company began early providing good lodging:

> As early as 1880 H.C. Frick & Co. commenced to tear down the shanties and poorer types of houses and replace them with a better type of house, built on stone foundations, plastered, larger and more conveniently arranged; planted shade trees and laid out gardens; also put water into the villages, locating hydrates along the streets, one for every three or four families; in fact, we had water in some of our mining villages before Greensburg, the county seat of Westmoreland, had a water system. There has been no radical change in the type of house up to this day, except variation in size and detail of arrangement to make them more convenient and to substitute slate for shingle roof, but the streets have been made wider, the gardens larger, water put into many of the houses, streets and alleys kept in better condition, gutters built along the principal streets and in some cases underground sewers installed. I think I can safely say that our new villages are clean, sanitary, and well kept. The houses are almost entirely frame; some two or three plants have some brick houses....[43]

The 1880 *Keystone Courier* said as much years earlier: "Messrs Frick & Co are building a number of new tenement houses. They have nine in course of erection at Broadford, four of which are under roof, ten at Morgan, seven of which are under roof, and three at Sherrick, under roof. There are also ten double tenements in course of erection at Summit mines."[44]

Let us be clear. Patches created before the 1880s did not have paved tree-lined streets and indoor plumbing. Many of the main roads leading from town to town were not paved; in fact, they had to be built by the companies. But as time moved on, there were major improvements. That can be interpreted to mean that as the industry grew, the miners' situation improved. Everything was better, from electricity in the mines to electricity in the homes.

What were the modern-day writers in the 1990s and the new century describing in their comments? The Depression years? The years when many of the mines were closing and men were out of work? That is era four of DiCiccio's division of the coal and coke industry: Retrenchment, Decline and Mechanized Mine, 1920–1945. Frick, as we have noted, was dead by then.

For the vast majority of miners, did the industry improve? For the most part, yes. But in the 2000s in West Virginia, some miners still live in shanties. The norm, for the average miner, was not what scholars and mining families were reporting. Because of them, the legend of mining is filled with fallacy and it must be reexamined through clear eyes. The mere mention of the name Henry Clay Frick sends elderly men into fits of anger. Most of them come from miner families. All of them express their anger vehemently. If one can calm them enough to get them to look at the facts, it becomes evident that neither the events they describe nor the anger they hold is related to Henry Clay Frick at all. Most of the events happened in the 1920s, '30s, and '40s, long after Frick was dead.

The Demise of the Patch

The patches existed as long as the mines were working. In the Morgan Valley and Mount Pleasant region, the mines began to close early; the last among this study shut down in the 1930s. When the mines closed, the workers had an option to buy their homes. Many did. Some miners were unemployed and stayed in their patch houses rent-free. But the patches changed. Some were demolished when the mines closed. Others were partially demolished, and others still stand and are occupied by people who bought the homes nearly a century ago. Enman, in the 1960s, reported that at least fifty-six patches were demolished, eleven mostly done, seventeen partly, and thirty-three left standing throughout the Connellsville region.[45]

Voices from the Patch

In modern time more and more miner families began recording life in the patches. Here are a few.

Helen Rollison recalls: "Yeah, they at that time, people was good neighbors. They was really good neighbors. If anything happened, your neighbor was right there. If anybody died, the neighbors was right there. Really, the patch people, patch hunkies we called it... [W]hen my dad got killed, every woman in that patch baked pies, baked bread, cooked soup, made chicken. Your name it, they brought it. Our house was just loaded...."[46]

Another remembers: "As children, my brother Bill and I would join many other children in the neighborhood and go down to the coal bank to pick coal for heating and cooking. This was quite a dangerous task, which we did not realize at the time. The large coal cars dumped coal and rock down a bank, and we scrambled around on the coal bank to

Opposite, top: High Street in Standard Coal Patch, taken by WPA Farm Security Administration photographer Walker Evans in 1935. **Bottom:** High Street, taken by HABS/HAER in 1991, showing very little change. The street remains the same today.

Three. The Workers and Their World

get the coal, crack it with a hammer into smaller size, put it into bags and take it home in a wheelbarrow."[47]

Here's a look at home life: "In addition to daily cleaning, special spring, fall, and Christmas house cleanings required especially vigorous efforts, for when these occurred, windows were removed from their sashes for washing and rugs were taken out to be beaten. In these days before vacuum sweepers, some housewives saved used tea leaves, dampened them, scattered them on their floors, and swept them up, leaving a clean floor behind...."[48]

Patch residents often relied on home remedies for illnesses:

> Occasionally, a parent brought a child to the company store for examination, which took place in a little hall outside the main room. Most mothers, however, practiced a little medicine on their own, and concocted some rather strange, though evidently harmless, remedies. One mother, upon hearing a case of diphtheria or scarlet fever in her locality, lined up her defenseless offspring and spooned into each a soup ladle full of castor oil containing nine drops of turpentine. After each child had visited the privy she considered her ounce of prevention well administered.
>
> For a cough, the housewife–general practitioner sliced onions, sprinkled them with sugar, baked them in the oven, and liberally doled out the resulting syrup. A case of croup was treated with nine drops of kerosene taken on a spoonful of sugar. A more serious cough required a chest plaster made of dried mustard, lard, and soda. For sore throats, a mother spooned honey and sulfur into the sufferer. Sauerkraut juice made a fine laxative, and every former coal town child remembers his dose of sulfur and molasses in the spring.[49]

The Company Store

Just as the concept of the patch was not new, so, too, the industrial store was an idea brought from Europe to America. Trunk stores existed in England earlier than the 15th century. In France the system was called the *economat* and "paralleled the growth of company stores in America." In Germany they were called *werkskonsumanstalten*.[50] In every instance they solved the problem of workers laboring in rural areas where there were limited resources. In every instance there were gross abuses that the government had to step in and correct.

The company store was the heartbeat of the patch. It was the gathering place where people would not only come to shop, but to hear the news, to share stories with friends, to bring in produce to sell and earn a little money. It took special orders. It delivered groceries. "The larger company stores operated ice cream parlors and soda fountains. Some larger company stores provided additional services including laundry, millinery, and gristmill."[51] There was a lot positive about the company store.

The company store in America, especially in the coal fields (they existed in other industries too), also became a symbol of corruption. The Frick company often took the blame. Why? Yes, he brought in company scrip. Yes, he had many company stores operating under the name Union Supply Company. All the records indicate that the Frick company did not cheat their miners. Each miner had an account at the store. He also had a small receipt book where all his purchases were listed. As he shopped in the store, his items were listed and the account was added. On payday, the clerks would deduct the expenses from the miners' pay and they would receive the remainder in cash. Eventually, if they spent more than what they earned, the law said they must receive at least one dollar in cash.

That was another fallacy. Critics maintain miners did not receive cash. Not true. The

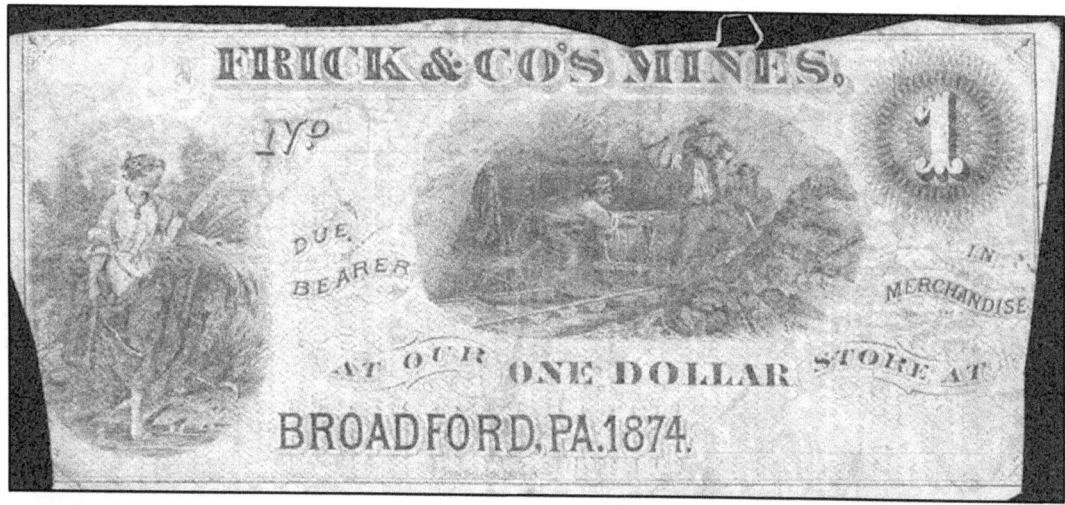

Frick's scrip, viewed today as a corrupt system, could be traded for cash throughout the Connellsville region in the Golden Age. Frick used it as one way of saving the fledgling coal and coke industry. He did not invent it. Scrip was used by land and industry owners in the Middle Ages (Frick & Co. Dollar Bill, Helen Clay Frick Foundation Archives [AIS 2002 06], Henry Clay Frick Business Records, 1862–1987, Box 523, Folder 1, Archives Service Center, University of Pittsburgh).

miners did receive cash. In discussing the coal patch isolation, *The Survey* of 1911 reported that miners left their patches on payday and headed to the nearby towns: "On Saturday or 'pay day' evenings the stores, amusement places, saloons and even the principal streets of the urban centers are filled with a heterogeneous collection of races and tongues. Each of the important centers in the coal and coke producing territories is indeed a diminutive Pittsburgh, and the Saturday and pay night scenes on its principal streets are a replica on a small scale of what may be observed on Fifth Avenue and other downtown sections of Pittsburgh proper."[52] As reported earlier, in 1884 a miner from Eagle mine had his pay stolen from his home. It was all cash! How is that possible if miners never received cash?[53] Simple contemporary observations, like "Lebanese settled in Uniontown and traveled as peddlers to the patches," show again and again that this belief is simply not true, at least not during the Golden Age.[54]

Of course, there were times when a man used most of his pay at the company store. And there were abuses. In 1881 the state of Pennsylvania, well aware of fraud in the stores, passed a law prohibiting company stores. It was ruled unconstitutional. It took another ten years for them to pass a new law that required the stores to be owned by a separate corporation. That is when the Frick company created the Union Supply Company.[55]

By 1891, Frick's Union Supply Company had 23 stores and served 9,000 miners in the Connellsville region.[56] That is the year it began its own butchering, and two slaughterhouses were created. The first was at Broadford, where the meat would supply the Morgan Valley and Adelaide stores. The second would be at the Old Ireland farm near Standard, and would service Standard, Morewood, Alice, and Tarrs. The animals did not come from the Frick company.

Voices from the Store

Among other goods, fabrics were available from the stores. "At the company store, mining town women bought bolts of the same coarse muslin used in the mines to block off dangerous or unused underground areas. From this material they made curtains, either on a treadle sewing machine or entirely by hand. The more imaginative housewives in town dyed their homemade products with coffee grounds. Called 'ecrue' curtains, these took on a dark beige color which lightened with each consecutive washing. During spring cleaning the curtains were dyed again."[57]

A contemporary source provides a look at the operation of the stores:

> This article comes from an American miner, resident all his life in the mining district of Pennsylvania. He has worked in the mines from his boyhood. His comparatively brief education in the public schools of the Commonwealth has been supplemented, like that of many other Americans in his walk of life, by a close reading of the daily papers, and particularly of those portions of the daily papers which bore directly upon his own interests. The facts which he gives about himself are true; the opinions he expresses are those which he, individually, has formed. By temperament he may be said to be conservative rather than radical; by habit he has always been a law-abiding citizen. He is, in effect, the typical American who is employed in the anthracite coal regions in the State of Pennsylvania—EDITOR. *The Independent*, 1902:
>
> > Company stores are of the time that has been. Their existence ended two years ago. But we've got a system growing up that threatens to be just as bad. Let me explain. Over a year ago I was given a breast to drive at one of our mines and was glad to get it. My wife took her cash and went around the different places to buy. When I went to the office for my first pay the "super" met me and asked me if I didn't know his wife's brother George kept a store. I answered, "Yes," and wanted to know what that had to do with it.
> >
> > "Nothing, only I thought I'd call your attention to it," he answered.
> >
> > No more was said then. But the next day I got a quiet tip that my breast was to be abandoned. This set me thinking. I went to the boss and, after a few words, told him my wife had found brother-in-law George's store and that she liked it much better than where she had bought before. I told him the other store didn't sell the right kind of silk waists, and their patent leather shoes were always black. Brother-in-law George had the right kind of stuff and, of course, we were willing to pay a few cents more to get just what we wanted.
> >
> > That was sarcastic, but it's the cash that has the influence. I have had work at that colliery ever since. I know my living costs me from 10 to 15 per cent extra. But I kept my job, which meant a good deal.[58]

To Conclude

To continue analyzing the article mentioned above, it is wrong for it to say, "you had to spend all your earnings at the store or you would lose your job."[59] It is simply not true as they wrote it. Obviously, it did happen. But it is the current belief around coal country that it always happened and that Henry Clay Frick condoned it.

John Enman concurs: "[A] second means of encouraging workers to trade at the company store was the threat of unemployment if a portion of wages earned was not spent there. The author has not discovered any written policy, but an unwritten one could have been effective."[60]

Enman cites Ole Johnson, who did the "first real analysis of the industrial store," and "concluded that some coal company stores charged about the same prices on similar items as neighboring independent stores."[61] Enman had discovered an old account book from the Union Supply Company store at Buffington. He concluded, as did Johnson, as told by

Lynch, and as agreed to by this author (as did Ida Tarbell, the investigative reporter who brought down Standard Oil and broke monopolies),[62] the majority of company stores did not overcharge.

Scrip, Again!

Next our article attacked Frick's use of company script. "H.C. Frick introduced the use of script [*sic*], the 'Frick Dollar,' in western Pennsylvania during the panic of 1873 both to free up capital for his continued expansion and to increase profits at his store."[63] Frick was losing his mines. So were all the other speculators in the Morgan Valley, many of them family members. The Panic was real. The problems were real. The newly built Mount Pleasant and Broadford Railroad was failing and up for sale. Scrip, which he adopted in 1874, was a stroke of genius. In fact, the Frick scrip became the legal tender for the district. Hard U.S. currency was hard to find, and Frick's solution fit the bill. His miners could shop at almost any place in the region and pay with his false money.[64] Not only did it save Frick, it saved his mines, it saved the Morgan Valley, it saved the merchants, and it saved the entire fledgling industry. And it wasn't a new concept. Like the company store, company scrip was an old idea used in Europe in remote regions where few services were available. In the U.S. it was also used in logging towns.

His other stroke of genius was brokering a deal to sell the failing railroad to the B&O (1875). That made him solvent. He did not buy a mine until three years later in 1878.[65] That was the Morgan Mine. So expansion was not on his mind at the time. It was not the reason for the scrip. His genius also saved many members of his family who were also involved in coal and coke.

Finally, and hopefully for the last time, Price V. Fishback, in his essay "Did Coal Miners 'Owe Their Souls to the Company Store'? Theory and Evidence from the Early 1900s," using the Coal Commission Report of 1922 (with no complete bibliography), and encompassing mining operations in eastern United States, concludes:

> Economic theory and empirical evidence offer several reasons to doubt labor historians' descriptions of monopolistic company stores. First, company stores faced competition not only from local stores but also from other mines to the extent that mine employers hired in a competitive labor market. In non-union areas like West Virginia, company-store prices were part of an employment package, including wages and housing, offered to mobile miners in a labor market with hundreds of mines. The theory of compensating differences suggests that the gain from charging high store prices would be offset by the higher wages the mine would be forced to offer to attract workers. Second, extension of this analysis suggests that the value of employment packages would have fluctuated cyclically within a long-term trend toward less opportunities for exploitation as information and transportation costs fell. Third, one reason company ownership of stores persisted was that it lowered transaction costs, reduced the costs of holding currency in isolated areas, lowering the risks of extending credit for store purchases, and preventing the costs of contracting to minimize opportunistic behavior. Fourth, comprehensive studies by the Immigration Commission in 1908 and the Coal Commission in 1922 show that prices at most company stores were similar to prices at nearby independent stores. Prices apparently were higher at isolated mines, in part due to higher transport costs, but scattered evidence suggests that higher prices were partially offset by higher wages. Finally, miners were typically not in debt to the stores nor paid entirely in scrip. Scrip was offered as an advance on payday, when miners, on average, received 30 to 80 percent of their earnings in cash after deductions of rent, fuel, doctors, and store purchases between paydays.[66]

The Wages

As pathetic as the wages were, they were on the same par as wages in other industries of the day. Miners' wages fluctuated during the years based on the market.

Based on the actual statistics, the average bituminous miner made $7.10 a week or $28.40 a month. The average coke charger made $24.16 a month. The mine boss made $48.00 a month. As for Frick, when his workers were making $30 to $50 a month in the 1870s, his account book recorded his monthly salary as $75.00 a month; in 1872 it was $83.33 a month. He was taking a salary approximately double that of his employees.[67] This was a legitimate and honorable compensation.

Turning to the entire scope of industry at the time, with the miners' salaries compared to bricklayers, carpenters, masons, and more, one finds the miners in last place.

Hours Per Week, Pay Per Week

Date	Bricklayers	Carpenters	Masons	Plumbers	Miners	Cokers
1871	60hr $4day	60hr $2.70	58hr $2.97	60hrs $3.02	?? $2.34	NO RECORD
1886	54hr $3.72	57hr $2.45	30hr $3.16	60hrs $2.81	60hrs $1.48	NO RECORD
1894	54hr $3.26	57hr $2.51	54hr $2.81	54hrs $3.06	(1891) $1.91[68]	NO RECORD

The pay of the miners got better as the industry grew. As for Frick, one must remember the Frick fortune was diverse. His incomes were not only from the coke world but from his various investments. Among the various companies where he served as a director were the Chicago and Northwestern Railway Company, City Deposit Bank, Mellon National Bank, National Union Fire Insurance Company, Pennsylvania Railroad Company, Philadelphia and Reading Coal and Iron Company, Philadelphia and Reading Railway Company, Reading Company, Union Insurance Company, Union Pacific Railroad Company, Union Trust Company of Pittsburgh, and the United States Steel Corporation.[69] This is a partial list.

Another point to be made is that capitalism was ruling in America. It is defined as "an economic and political system in which a country's trade and industry are controlled by private owners for profit, rather than by the state." Allowed to run without any controls or regulations, it "doesn't provide for those who lack competitive skills. This includes the elderly, children, the developmentally disabled, and caretakers. To keep society functioning, capitalism requires government policies that value the family unit."[70] In the Golden Era of Coal and Coke, that led to many of the problems. "By 1890 the richest 9 percent of Americans held nearly three-quarters of all wealth in the United States. By 1900, one American in eight (nearly 10 million people) lived below the poverty line."[71] If there is one single thing that caused all the hatred and resentment, this was it.

Benefits

The final inaccuracy in the essay states: "Before workmen's compensation was established, coal and coke companies did not reimburse laborers or their families for on-the-job injuries or death."[72] Wrong again! Workman's compensation began in Maryland in 1902. In 1915 Pennsylvania enacted the Pennsylvania Workmen's Compensation Act.[73] The Frick company, and surely others, beat the state by over five years. The program was organized in 1910 and put into effect in 1911. "For the loss of a hand or a leg, a year's wages will be allowed; 18 months for an arm, nine months for a foot and six months for an eye. In case of accidental death in the plant the victim's widow and children will receive a relief equal to 18 months' wages."[74]

And they were doing it long before 1910. In fact, as early as 1886: "The second annual statement of the relief fund of the H.C. Frick Coke Company's employes was issued last week. During the past year 274 persons have received benefits amounting to $6,087. The monthly assessments have been but 15 cents, but as the cash balance is but $208, an assessment of 25 cents will be laid this month to bring the balance up to $1,000, as is required by the rules...."[75] Evidently this was a miners' contribution project. But during the Mammoth Mine Disaster of 1891, the unions and the company pitched in. The Frick Company gave $25,000, would give more if necessary, and started a subscription to aid the families. The United Mine Workers and Knights of Labor unions drew funds from their relief resources.[76]

In addition to the established relief funds, there were also random acts of kindness: "Mrs. Andrjejewski, a widow, in Connellsville, was practically destroyed shortly after noon today by fire of unknown origin.—fire loss was about $500, partially covered by insurance, the premium being paid for a few days ago by Superintendent R.C. Beerbower, of the Davidson works of the HC. Frick Coke Company on orders from the company. Mr. Andrejejewski died about four months ago. He had been an employee of the Frick Company as a miner, more than 30 years...."[77] There are many incidents like this reported in the local papers.

Is this essay totally to be blamed for all these inaccuracies? No. The authors cite sources from which they got some of their information. Are the sources inaccurate, too, or did the authors pick what they wanted to prove their ideas? The problem was that they were prejudiced against the industry and had no business being called upon to report an accurate, fact-based account. They did not do the research. Most important of all, they did not look into original sources. They bought the rumor and allowed the myth to become the fact.

In Conclusion

The average miner and his family lived a hard life. So did the majority of workers in the United States at the time. Within the patch they had to struggle. Their 12-hour days left little time for entertainment, but when it came, it was in the form of weddings and other celebrations. They formed organizations that helped them in times of need, and the church not only provided religious support but also social and humanitarian support as well. By 1915, along with better housing, schools emerged, playgrounds began to appear, swimming pools too, and baseball teams were formed with well-managed fields and uniforms. There were even musical bands complete with instruments and uniforms. Medical help came and hospitals were established. All were encouraged by the companies and most financed by them too. But not everywhere and not for all.

Perhaps it is best summed up by an article on Ukrainians who came to Pennsylvania in 1877. It was written by Wasyl Halich in 1935.

It was then that an agent representing a coal company in Pennsylvania appeared in the western provinces of the [sic] Ukraine and began recruiting mine laborers. As an inducement he promised steady employment and high wages. A few daring men decided to go to America. Much excitement accompanied their departure; their relatives lamented they would never see them again. In the course of a few months letters came from America, and before long American dollars also. Because of the high exchange value of the dollar in Europe the American wages seemed almost fabulous and greatly stimulated emigration to America.[78]

Four

Strikes from 1875 to 1886

As reported and to be oft repeated, the battle in this developing industry was to create a proper balance between management, workers, and unions. To management, this was a new venture in a budding industry. Working independently to purchase the land, create the mine, build the coke ovens, mine the coal, turn it into coke, find the market, and deliver the product to market proved to be a struggle for individual owners. But by joining forces in a kind of union of their own, management could bring a semblance of order to the chaos. Joining forces was not an easy matter either and would take years to accomplish.

Workers wanted what everyone wants: a good life. They formed a formidable and mixed group of mostly immigrants trying to find a better life and a hope that a new country would offer them more than their native countries had done. With language barriers, 12-hour days, discrimination, and more, the new immigrants, now in the majority, were easy victims, but discovered a powerful voice when they joined together in protest. As the strikes continued, a new voice emerged among the immigrants: the voice of the women who stood beside their men and fought with them for their place in this new country.

Unions, to some, created more bedlam as they fought each other for power, and then fought management to meet their demands. Often the unions were a bigger problem than operators. For the unions, trying to organize workers who spoke dozens of different languages was yet another arduous barrier. The first American union created in the United States was the Noble Order of Knights of Labor of America, created in Philadelphia in 1869. It developed into an almost secret society steeped in ritual and was therefore not particularly desired by many workers. Yet, by 1879 it had twenty-three districts and thirteen hundred locals.[1] The main demands of this union included an eight-hour day, no convict labor, and equal pay.[2] The battle for the eight-hour day began just after the Civil War (and continues today). The Knights of Labor merged with the National Federation of Miners and Mine Laborers of the United States and Territories and became the first truly national union. Then in 1890 the United Mine Workers of America was founded "out of the National Trade Assembly No. 135 and the Knights of Labor and the National Progressive Union."[3]

The Amalgamated Association of Iron and Steel Workers was first organized in Pittsburgh in 1876 by consolidating yet another number of labor organizations: the United Sons of Vulcan; the Associated Brotherhood of Iron and Steel Heaters, Rollers, and Roughers of the United States; and the Iron and Steel Roll Hands Union. In 1867 the United Sons of Vulcan supported the concept of the sliding scale, whereby wages were based on the price of the product in the marketplace.[4] The Amalgamated added the name Tin Workers to its title in 1881, and by June of 1892 it had 292 lodges and 24,000 members in a number of states.[5] By the late 1880s it had changed its name to the Miners Progressive Union, and the *Coke Country Chronicle* was its official organ.[6] Both the Knights and the Amalgamated were active in the Connellsville region. At the end of the 1886 strike, they were trying to merge but faced significant differences.[7] It was the Amalgamated that fought for the workers in the coal strike of 1891 and in the Homestead Steel Strike of 1892. After these two events, its power began to diminish; and although it continued for a few more decades, it was disbanded in 1942.

All of the unions had dues. They also gave small benefits for sickness and death. Their struggle would continue decades beyond our study until the United Mine Workers became the primary union for miners. Its battle, and the battle of all unions in all industries, for the good life for the worker was finally realized in mid-century. After a hard-won struggle, life in the 1950s, '60s, and early '70s was good for the average coal and steel worker. A decent salary, an eight-hour day, a five-day work week, a home of his own, a family vacation once a year, and a college education for the kids was possible. There were even pensions!

Our effort is the early story of the struggle of these three entities to find the equilibrium in the Connellsville coke region. It is also the story of individuals. People gave their lives for this struggle, and whenever possible, the men and women involved are mentioned in the narrative. It begins in the 1870s and ends at 1900. The region suffered strikes in 1875–6, 1879, 1881, 1886, 1887, 1889, 1891, 1894, 1897, and long after the mines in our project were closed. Below is a synopsis taken from government records, newspapers of the day, and, when available, coal company records—in other words, original sources. The events are told by those who lived it as it happened.

Law Enforcement Agencies

Law and order in the coal fields fell to local authorities. That meant constables, county sheriffs and their deputies. When the great strikes came, these local officials were overwhelmed and tried to recruit deputies, even calling upon unemployed miners. It was not enough. Law enforcement on the county level was very much involved. In many instances their efforts were insufficient too. So they turned to the state. They were often refused. There was a Pennsylvania National Guard. It was created in Pennsylvania in 1870 from the remnants of the militia first established by Benjamin Franklin in 1747. But the state did not want the Guard to get into industrial matters. Things had to be desperate before the governors would call them out.

To maintain order and protect property land owners, local police, and occasionally unions called on private agencies. Foremost was the Pinkerton Detective Agency. This agency is the oldest private detective agency in the United States. Abraham Lincoln hired them to protect the Illinois Central Railroad as it was being built in the 1850s, and once he became president and the Civil War erupted, Lincoln and General George B. McClellan asked the Pinkerton agency to protect the president and seek military intelligence. They did extensive work in the anthracite and bituminous coal fields of Pennsylvania.[8]

Trained by the Pinkerton Detective Agency, the Coal and Iron Police were established in Pennsylvania as early as 1862. Their main objective was to serve at the county level and help local law enforcement protect the property of owners. They were a private police force. Their efforts in Pennsylvania began in Schuylkill County in the anthracite coal region. By 1886, perhaps earlier, they were involved in the Connellsville coke region.

During the Golden Age from 1870 to 1920, their reputation was not as outrageous as it would become. At this time, they protected the company property, evicted strikers from company housing, and hired additional help. As time went on, they were also used as strikebreakers, and the miners began to call them Yellow Dogs and Cossacks. Then they patrolled the patches on a daily basis, were feared by the miners and their families, and became far too violent. They were disbanded by state law in 1931.

The State Police was founded in 1905, well beyond the strikes discussed in this study, but its legacy maintains the state police became violent against miners.[9]

The Industrial World in 1873

The Panic of 1873 was a worldwide collapse. It began in Europe as a financial crisis. American banking systems began to feel the strain of the international collapse, and all the fledgling industries were affected. Wages plummeted. Companies failed. In 1877 the railroads fought a long and ugly strike. The Panic lasted from 1873 to 1879 and left its mark on the region.

The small village of Mount Pleasant began to thrive when the Mount Pleasant and Broad Ford Railroad was conceived in 1870. The 9.7-mile railroad was completed a year later and opened on February 18, 1871, after "being pushed with so much energy." It linked the Mount Pleasant region to Broadford and the main line railroads. It was created by a number of mostly local speculators involved in the mining business eager to find a way to get their product to market. They were C.S. Overholt, Joseph R. Stauffer, C.C. Markle, A.J. Crossland, Henry Clay Frick, B.F. Overholt, D.R. Davidson, Robert Pitcairn, Strickland Kneass, H.C. Marchand, J. M'Creighton, J.H. Clark, A.O. Tinstman, and Welty M'Cullough.

The small village of Mount Pleasant saw that the "opening of the immense coal fields along the line of the road and in the vicinity of town, gave to every interest of the place a

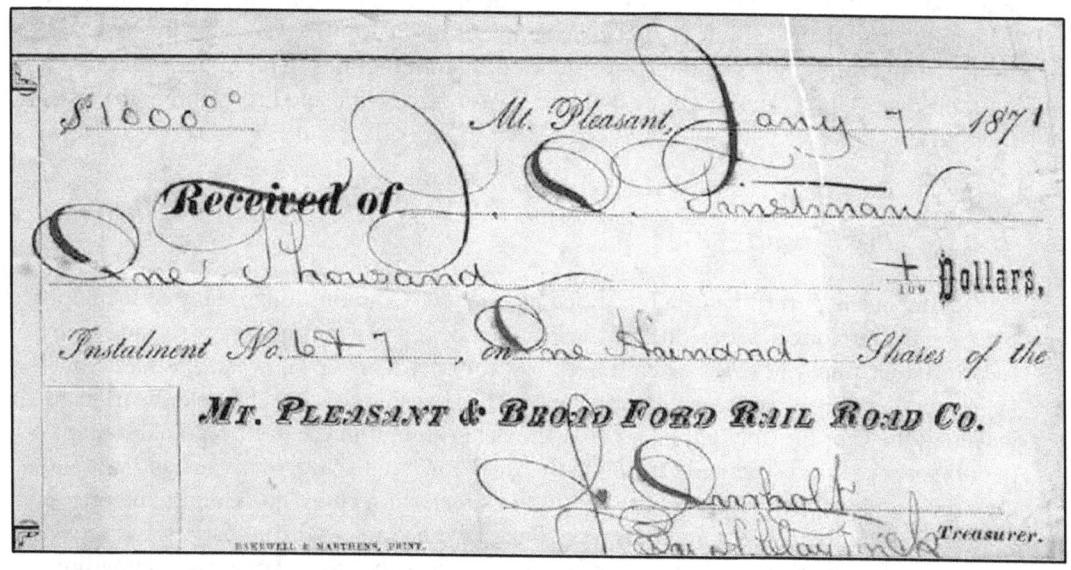

Bringing a railroad up the Morgan Valley to Mount Pleasant was a venture local people created, funded, and lost their shirts trying to accomplish. Among the leaders were the Tinstman brothers, Frick's cousins. This receipt is for 100 shares (Receipt of J.O. Tinstman, Westmoreland–Fayette Historical Society [Box 2 P16. Folder B10], West Overton Village and Museums, Scottdale, Pennsylvania).

new impetus. Many new buildings were erected and the population increased much more rapidly than ever before."[10] Then the Panic hit. In 1876, an essay on "The History of Mount Pleasant," published in the *Mount Pleasant Dawn*, described the devastation of the panic on the community: "The financial panic of '73, however, brought a reaction. A number of our business men failed. Many mechanics and others who came to the place but a few months before were compelled to leave and seak [sic] the means of living elsewhere. Houses but recently built were vacated, and others that were commenced were left unfinished...."[11] The effect spread all along the region, including the Morgan Valley.

It meant widespread bankruptcy. Too many of the region's speculators could not ride out the Panic and began to shut down their operations and count their losses. Henry Clay Frick, with two mines opened in 1871, did not panic. He saw an opportunity to buy up the failing properties. He did two things: he implemented the use of company scrip to free his limited cash, and went to visit his friends the Mellons in Pittsburgh to ask for a loan. Then he began to build his empire. His largest competitors would be Rainey, the Cochrans, Schoonmaker, and McClure.

The Strikes

The history of the strikes in the Connellsville district is not only an important history, but an amazing history as well. Each strike brought a new challenge. The very early strikes of the 1870s showed the miners that they had power. The strikes of 1875 to 1879 saw peaceful marches with bands and banners without damage or danger to the towns and the mines. The Strike of 1886 was violent, with much loss of property to mines and towns, and it also brought to light the growing immigration problem in the region. The Strike of 1887 was a battle between the emerging unions for domination, not only in the coal and coke region, but nationally as well. It also saw the intrusion of Andrew Carnegie into the coal fields. The Strike of 1889 saw the reemergence of the immigrants in a rampage that called for their deportation. The strikes of 1891 and 1894 were horrific and brought the unions to their knees.

The Research Resources

Many of the government publications had not started publishing. Many of the company records no longer exist. Most of the local police reports, coroner's reports, and court records either were not saved or have been lost to time. A few local newspapers were just beginning to publish. They are an important part of the story of coal and coke, as in many instances they are the only public record. The details found in the early regional newspapers expose the unprecedented turmoil in the small towns and rural roads as hundreds and then thousands of men and women took to the streets with clubs, guns, and dynamite to protest what they believed were injustices. Through the years, as the industry grew, so did the papers. Their articles, their points of view, leave us with a record of events, sometimes biased, sometimes angry, sometimes astounding, but definitely told as the events unfolded. Their coverage became copious. These papers are far more important to the narrative than the articles and books of historians who wrote about events in the bituminous coal fields decades later.

The *Connellsville Courier* did not begin publication until 1879. It went through several names: *Keystone Courier, Weekly Courier,* and *Daily Courier.* The earliest mention of the *Courier* in Newspapers.com is 1879, when the newspaper was called the *Keystone Courier.* It continued with that name until 1885. Then it operated under the banner of *Weekly Courier* until 1901. The *Daily Courier* began in 1902 and continues today. During the Golden Age, H.P. Snyder was the chief editor and eventual owner of the *Courier.* He was a Democrat and politically savvy. Under his leadership, the *Courier* became the organ of the coke era when he developed the weekly graphic called *Report on the Operation and Output of the Coke Ovens of the Connellsville Region.* It depicted the production of each mine in the district for the week and remains one of the most important records of the industry. The *Courier* has been digitized and can be found online in a number of newspaper archives.

Two other newspapers published in Connellsville were the *Fayette Monitor and Youghioghenian*, with D.P. Stentz as publisher, and the *Connellsville Tribune*, with S.J. Hayes as editor and publisher. The first was Democratic, the second Republican.[12]

The *Mount Pleasant Journal* began publication on October 19, 1872, as the *Mount Pleasant Independent.* It became the *Journal* the next year. It was a weekly then and is a weekly now. Through the early years it had a number of owners and editors. The founder and owner of the paper was W. Fox, and the first editor was E.B. Halsinger. The paper was purchased by A.C. Haverstick in 1874, then Mr. Cooper, and then Mr. Stevenson and Mr. McCurdy took the reins. It wasn't until 1882 that John L. Shields took over the paper as sole editor and owner. If there was a major bias in the *Journal,* its voice would have changed several times during the Golden Age. As for Shields, "The *Mount Pleasant Journal* is independent in politics although its proprietor is a strong Republican."[13]

Although the *Journal*'s editions from 1882 to the 1920s have now been digitized and can be found in the Pennsylvania State Library system, the very early editions have not. But there are hardcopies at a number of museums and libraries, including the Hillman Library at the University of Pittsburgh from the 1920s forward. Recently the West Overton Village and the Mount Pleasant Library gave their holdings to the Mount Pleasant Historical Society. The Braddock Road Chapter of the DAR in Mount Pleasant also holds newspaper collections on microfilm and hardcopy.

Another newspaper, the *Mount Pleasant Dawn,* operated from 1874 to 1881. Needless to say, it is elusive, too. The good news is that the Mount Pleasant Library has bound copies of the years 1875, 1876, and partial 1877. This newspaper claimed to be independent, with M.A. Cooper as editor and proprietor, and had a circulation of 800.[14] Cooper struck a nerve with the early miners on strike and did not stay long with the *Dawn.*

Likewise, Scottdale had several newspapers. The *Scottdale Independent* began publication in 1882 as the *Miner's Record*, which in eighteen months was converted to the *Independent.* It remained such until 1926 when it became the *Scottdale Independent Observer,* which still operates today. The first editor was J.R. Byrne, a coal operator, politician, and Republican. During the Golden Age, the *Independent* was hard on immigrants, a very Republican stance of the day. In 1885 Byrne took on W.N. Porter as his partner at the newspaper. The next year the two of them sold the paper to Hiram B. Strickler, who resold it "in 1887 to a joint stock company which employed Mr. Byrne as editor." He moved on to the *Tribune Press* in Scottdale in 1889, "a republican paper."[15] Byrne was the first Republican from Fayette County elected to the state assembly. Other papers once operating in Scottdale were the *Scottdale Tribune,* which began publishing in 1880, the *Scottdale Rural Free Press,* and the *Scottdale Herald.*[16] None of the Scottdale newspapers have been digitized. Most of the research done in the Scottdale papers was found in the online scrapbooks of the Frick archives at the University of Pittsburgh.

Overall one must say that most of the reporting in the various newspapers was exceptionally good and the bias, if any, was not overwhelming.

The Mines and the Syndicate

At this early date, only a few mines existed. Those that did were only a few years old. The industry was in confusion. The concept of a coke syndicate was formed by the owners with the mission of joining together to stabilize the price of coke on the market and deal with the miners collectively. Historians claim that the syndicate was actually founded in 1884, but the *Mount Pleasant Dawn* reported on meetings held by the coke manufacturers as early as August 12, 1875.[17]

It was obvious that there was a need to present a united front in regards to setting the price of coke in the marketplace and paying their workers. It would take a lot of ups and downs before organization became finalized: "In 1884 the four largest producers, H.C. Frick and Co., McClure Coke, Schoonmaker, and Connellsville Coke and Iron formed the so-called Coke Syndicate, controlling about half of the ovens in the district. Eighteen other firms with about one-seventh of the ovens were linked in the Connellsville Coke Producers Association, three independents had a further 9 percent, and the remainder were controlled by companies having their own blast furnaces."[18]

The sliding scale did not yet exist in the region. The scale was designed in England and was created to match the wages of miners to the price of coke on the market. The price of coke on the market rose and fell, so the wages should do the same. This was a major factor in establishing wages for workers that would rise and fall with the price of coke; thus, the name sliding scale. It was also a big problem that took several decades to realize. Of course, things were far more complicated than this simple explanation.

Strike of 1875

In the mid–1870s the region was just emerging from the sluggish market created by the Panic of 1873. The price of coke was rising. The *Mount Pleasant Dawn* acknowledged the trauma of the marketplace and criticized the miners for aggravating the problem through striking: "Just when the people throughout this part of the coal and coke region were beginning to have reasons for believing that the season of activity would be experienced during the coming Summer, they are called upon to again endure a season of business prostration, this time, through the agency of striking miners."[19] The article continues to show the plight of the owners:

> It is scarcely necessary to refer to the state of trade, during the past winter, everybody being familiar with the fact that the proprietors made no money, although paying but twenty-five cents per wagon for digging. With Spring, came a starting up of furnaces in different parts of the country, and consequently a corresponding brightening up of the coke business, so much so, that on the 1st of April the proprietors advanced the wages of their men 20 per cent, this was done at all of the works along the Mount Pleasant and Broad Ford Railroad, those on the Uniontown branch remaining at 25 cts per wagon. Now the miners at the works on the former road demand 33 cts per wagon for "digging, and, judging by the past, where is this thing to end" [p. 1].

The H.C. Frick Coke Company complied with the advance in wages. Boyle & Hazlett, owners of the Hazlett Mine, eager to get back to work before they lost contracts, also offered the 33 cents if men would begin work immediately (p. 3). Others refused. Sherrick and Markle, owners of the Eagle Mine, posted a notice: "We will positively not pay more than 30 cents per wagon for mining, and, unless our men go to work before we lose some of our contracts, we will then pay only such prices, and run so much of our works as may be convenient." Similar notices were posted by other operators.

The *Dawn* had an opinion. "The average miner can make at the present wages $80 per month, some make more, some less. It is hard and disagreeable work, they have a perfect right to say what they won't work for; but when they fail to get what they think their labor is worth, they should exercise the privilege of going somewhere else and not bring the condemnation of the public upon them by preventing those who are willing to work, from doing so" (p. 1). The *Dawn*'s position would not go unnoticed by the miners. It would have long-lasting results.

By mid–May of 1875, some of the miners held a demonstration in Mount Pleasant. They were asking a raise of "one cent per bushel for mining and seventy-five cents per oven for drawing." Men from all the region from Broadford to Mount Pleasant attended:

The delegation from Mt. Pleasant, one hundred strong, arrived first. Soon far down the line beyond Valley Station toward Porter's Gap, was seen coming "with measured steps and slow," those from "below." They met each other with three cheers and a tiger at the railroad crossing—the scene of one of the bloodless battles of nearly three years ago between the Pennsylvania Railroad and the Baltimore & Ohio Railroad. They fused the delegations into one long procession and started on foot to Stonerville [Alverton] to compel certain non-striking men there to cease work. Your correspondent stood on the porch of Brown & Co.'s store and saw them go through Scottdale. And this is the way they marched:

First came their leader or captain, in his hand a steel cutlass, its bright blade held perpendicularly. He was followed by a man carrying the American flag, the sun shining down upon its golden stars through the black-blue dusky atmosphere that forever hangs over the valley of Jacob's Creek. A square white muslin banner bore the inscription: "Bridgeport Delegation; Boyle & Hazlett, Mullin and J.T. Stouffer, are paying one cent per bushel for mining and seventy-five cents for drawing." Another in the shape of an ellipse, decked with evergreens and entwined with ribbons of many colors, was inscribed in argent [silver] on one side: "State Rights and National Union," and on the other: "All shall be represented." It was evidently a Democratic banner of the year 1859. One huge Hibernian bore aloft a very large vert Irish flag, said to be one that was carried to Canada during one of the Fenian raids of 1866. One side was pictured in gold the harp of Erin entwined with a shamrock, all resting on the back of the Irish mastiff couchant; and on the other was the sun rising from the curling waves.

The most fearful object in the procession was a scaffold, borne by three white men and one negro. From it hangled [sic] by a hangman's rope a fiendish figure, a representation of a human being, labeled on breast and back, "Black Leg," meaning one who refuses to strike with the rest. Instead of a mustache the paddy had a living, biting, wriggling serpent fastened to its upper lip. A single look at it was calculated to cause the beholder to tremble and his blood to run cold.

Strains of martial music, two fifes and three drums, filled the smoky air and reminded many a surprised inhabitant of the town, of the dark days of the great rebellion. Two by two, quietly and orderly, came and went those hundreds of hard fisted working men between the blast furnace and the rolling mill, up the cindery pavement of Pittsburgh street, out Eagle street passed the Trinity Church and on to Stonerville. From the vest of the last man in the procession as it passed the writer, stuck the butt of a huge revolver.[20]

This appeared to be a well-organized, peaceful demonstration by the miners asking for what they believed to be theirs: decent wages. It was the first of many to come during the coming years, some not so peaceful. The miners paused in front of the *Dawn*'s office, took out the paper with the article "Strike Among the Miners," burned it, and voted not to subscribe to the *Dawn* for its transgression. They threatened to burn the editor too.

Editor Cooper responded:

> We are in favor of our miners receiving a fair compensation for their labor, and if the operators are not willing to remunerate them sufficiently they should quit work and go where they can pay higher wages; but in no case have they a right to compel those who are willing to work at the present prices to come out on strike. We had an interview with a number of miners on the Southwest R.R. on Tuesday, and they informed us that they could make good wages at 30 cents per car, and were willing to work. It seems hard when men who have large families dependent upon them for support, are compelled to quit work because another class of men demand higher wages. Where this state of affairs will end no one is able to predict, but it is to be hoped that those who have been engaged in making public demonstrations will have discretion enough not to persist in their present course until the strong arm of the law is applied to them.[21]

M.A. Cooper must have taken this threat seriously, for very little about the coke region miners and their strikes appeared in the *Dawn* during the rest of his leadership. No editorials. No judgments. No reports of miner strikes or marches. There was an occasional short statement on happenings related to additions and more at the various local mines. That is all. One wonders if the threats became a reality. Nothing could be found to indicate that. In mid–1877, Cooper was no longer the editor. He was replaced by John Stevenson.[22]

The strike continued, but the miners began to weaken. On May 20, the miners of Boyle and Hazlett went to work at 30 cents.[23] When the strike ended sometime in June, Frick & Co. reported it would "not employ any of the men who were engaged in the strike. Mr. Frick is now operating with German workmen from New York."[24] He also pushed for the quick formation of the syndicate so that the companies could join forces just as the men had done to present a united front.

On August 28, the Executive Committee of the Coke manufactures met at Scottdale House in Scottdale. They elected officers: Col. Lake, chairman; D.L. Dillinger and H. Clay Frick, secretaries. They appointed a committee of seven members chaired by Lake to draw up a plan for uniform pricing. The next meeting was set for September 4. Also attending: Peter Sherrick, John F. Cochran, John D. Boyle, Solomon Keister, J. Laughrey, Samuel Warden, J.A. Strickler, W.W. Mullin, A.O. Tinstman, I.F. Overholt, B.F. Overholt, Mr. Stant, Mr. Orr, A.J. Crossland, W.A. Kefer, Jos. R. Stauffer, Samuel Dillinger, and A.H. Sherrick.[25]

Nothing of significance was settled during the Strike of 1875. Eventually the men went back to work.

Strike of 1876

By May of 1876, the miners were on strike again. Limited information can be found, but some of the owners were cruel. When their men returned to work at the same rate as before the strike of 1875, Boyle & Hazlett "compelled their men to dig four wagons free to recompense them for the expense incurred by the strike." Worse, in 1875 the miners were earning 30 to 33 cents. Now, according to the *Dawn*, they were only getting 25.[26]

Mr. Cooper gave the coke business one more hit. Not the miners; he let them alone. This time it was the effects of the coke industry on the towns and villages. One continuously reads about the strikers and the operators, but little seems to be said about the effect of these businesses and the uproar they caused to the towns and villages themselves. Cooper spoke out:

> The coke business thus having swallowed up much of the available capital of the community, withdrew its patronage from the town, and somewhat selfishly retained all its profits in its own pockets. No

interest was ever received on the money invested in the railroad, and some six months ago much of the stock was sold at half the original cost. Many of those parties who had borrowed largely in the community, were not only not able to pay the high rates of interest promised, but in a of number [sic] cases failed entirely, and principal and interest were lost. And thus we find ourselves, having partly neglected the agricultural interest for some years, thrown back upon it for support, after our time was wasted, our energies exhausted and our money swallowed up by that which failed in the end to yield the anticipated rewards of wealth....[27]

Obviously, the coal and coke industry was proving a disappointment and a financial burden to the banks, the investors, and the people in general. Some of the good folks in town did invest in the Mount Pleasant and Broad Ford Railroad. Those shares, as noted by Cooper, were not yielding positive results. There were few mines in existence along its route, so the railroad was struggling. The Panic of 1873 only contributed to the railroad's woes. Several major stockholders were to declare bankruptcy in the months to come. One of the most prominent was A.O. Tinstman, stockholder and board member. He was the man who speculated in the Morgan Valley and the railroad and pushed his cousin Henry Clay Frick into the coal and coke business. In May of 1875, the *Mount Pleasant Dawn* reported that the railroad "will be offered at sheriff's sale at the depot in this place on the 5th of June,"[28] only to be rescinded in the next edition: "The claim against the Mount Pleasant and Broad Ford Railroad was satisfied on Wednesday last by the stockholders, and consequently the sale, as noted in our last issue, will not take place."[29] Henry Clay Frick saved the railroad and its investors, and then put a nice piece of change into his own pocket by selling it to the B&O.

So Cooper was not wrong. Everyone was struggling: the operators, the miners, the subsidiary industries, the investors, the average town folks. As Morgan Valley grew and the number of mines increased, the tracks served their purpose, though too late for Mount Pleasant investors. Today those tracks are still operating.

Strike of 1879

The miners, via the National Progressive Union, had issued an ultimatum to the operators to present a "uniform sliding scale" and were awaiting an answer. They were willing to have a conference to discuss the matter or a strike would occur. They voiced their views in their official organ, the *Coke Country Chronicle*:

> The coke workers are about tired of enduring the present system of inequality in wages. That the trouble can be averted is plain. The power of so doing is in the hands of the operators and as a consequence upon them rests the responsibility. If they meet the committee and endeavor squarely to do what is right and fair among themselves as competitors and justice to their employes we believe it will be better for all concerned. If this is not done the indications are at present that a strike will be in progress within the next few days. The demands made are fair and reasonable in every respect and will no doubt receive the individual support of the men in an effort to receive justice.[30]

Some of the operators commented on the union's position. Schoonmaker believed there would not be a strike. Gilbert Rafferty, president of McClure Coke Company, was blunt and put the blame on Frick. The *Courier* stated:

> We must not advance the scale in any event because there is not enough in coke at $1.25 to allow it. We are just in that position that we don't care whether they strike or not. I think Frick is at the bottom of the whole thing. His company is paying the men 6½ per cent more than other operators and I believe he wants the other cokers to strike while his men will stay at work. So far as I know the reason why

Frick can pay more is because he has some high priced contracts. But you may rest assured that we will not sign his scale.

As for the unions, the Progressive Union invited the Knights to join them. The Knights, after holding their own meeting, issued a joint resolution condemning the Progressive and asking all miners to abandon them and join the Knights. The Progressives maintained all the effort to create a scale was done by them, and that "there never would be a scale in the coke regions" if left to the Knights. The battling unions would continue such avarice for decades to come. In answer to all of this, Superintendent Lynch of the Frick Company commented that the current scale with the Frick company would expire today and despite the rumors otherwise, "his company would sign any scale that the other operators would."[31]

Up to this point there had been no violence in the coke region. Marching, yes, but no violence. The strike of 1879 began on March 17 when twenty-five miners from the Fountain Mine in the Morgan Valley, then owned by W.H. Blake & Co., and seventy-five miners at the Tip Top and Valley mines of the Frick company laid down their tools and walked out. By Thursday of the same week, twenty men at the Home Mine did the same. On Friday the miners of Brown and Cochran quit, and the following Monday, one hundred twenty-five Dravo men and thirty from West Overton joined. On March 25, the miners at Morgan, Foundry, Henry Clay, and Eagle, all Frick mines, walked off too.[32]

Gone was the thirty-cent wage. They were now getting only twenty-five cents and had been getting it since November 1875. "At that time coke was selling for fifteen or twenty cents a ton more than it is now, and the employers have not only kept up the wages but have been giving them steady employment all through the year."[33] The cokers did not come out.

By April 9 some of the miners were back at work and others had just gone out. Uniontown region went out and Mt. Pleasant went back to work. April 11 reports from the *Pittsburgh Dispatch* maintained the strike was still in full swing. Only the works of W.H. Brown (run by his son-in-law Col. Schoonmaker) and Cochran were at work. Coke stockpiles were running low. The operators did not want to increase the price of coke on the market to accommodate the advance the miners wanted.

So four hundred to five hundred miners met at Everson. The population of the town was only around eight hundred, so the gathering of that size had to be intimidating to the residents. Then the reporter dropped a bomb: "At Frick's mines a number of Germans brought from New York, were at work a few days ago at the old wages. Sixteen of the Germans were imported, but at latest account the strikers had persuaded six of them to leave. John White, superintendent at Frick's works, was charged with assault by a German, who alleges that he (White) threatened his life with a revolver. White gave bail for his appearance at court. Thomas Lynch is also under bail on a charge of illegal arrest."[34]

Confirmation came a day later when a reporter from the *Pittsburgh Commercial Gazette* traveled to the Connellsville region to talk to the operators. It was pointed out that 1,800 miners were in the Connellsville district. Diggers were offered twenty-five cents and they wanted thirty. So 1,200 men went on strike, pulling out others who were willing to work, bringing the total to 2,400. Without divulging who he was interviewing, the reporter asked many questions, the answers to which explained the situation to the readers. Then he asked:

> **Reporter:** What are the prospects in regard to a resumption of operations at the suspended mines?
>
> **Operator:** The outlook at present is very gloomy. The operators held a meeting recently and resolved to refuse the demand of the strikers and they mean to stick together. If the miners hold

out as firmly as we intend to it will be some time before there will be much done in the way of manufacturing coke in the Youghiogheny district. One large firm has been importing German emigrants, securing them through an agent at Castle Garden, New York City. The movement has caused considerable ill-feeling among the strikers, who will refuse to work as long as the "German blacklegs," as they term them, are employed.[35]

So the beginning of the immigrant issues that would haunt the mining industry through the next decades, and the country through the next century, raised its head in the Connellsville coke district. And it was Germans, not Huns, who had been imported. This may not have been the first time, either. This is not the last time we will hear of this issue. It will dominate the issues in strikes yet to come.

By the following week, things began to look better. Boyle and Hazlett met with their men to explain they could not give them a raise but "agreed to adopt a sliding scale," which did not happen for over a decade. They did not go back to work. Frick's men were working.[36]

In the end, all the men went back to work without a resolution. The unions continued to fight for dominance. The companies continued to organize. Chaos continued to exist in the region.

Strike of 1881

The coal strike of 1881 was bigger than previous strikes. It occupied more time and involved more mines as the industry, though in chaos, continued to grow. By this time, events in the Connellsville district were so important to the national stability that newspapers around the country announced the coming strike. The *Nashville Tennessean* stated: "The miners of the Connellsville coke regions struck yesterday for an advance of five cents per wagon for mining coal and ten cents for drawing coke. The strike is quite extensive, affecting several thousand men. Nearly all of the works have suspended."[37]

The region had also changed. Mines in the region had spread far beyond the Morgan Valley, south past Connellsville into the Uniontown area, and north beyond Mount Pleasant far into Westmoreland County. The newer mines were larger, employed more men, built company towns, and were more proactive in the strikes. As the Morgan Valley mines diminished, the new mines grew in prominence, but the early Frick mines remained very much involved in the events throughout the decades.

On May 16 and 28, the miners met at the small village of Everson, in the Morgan Valley northeast of Connellsville, to plan a united front. They issued their circular on June 2 with an order and a series of resolves. It demanded an increase in salary, and if operators would not comply by June 4, the men would "resign their positions."[38] The men wanted an increase of a penny for each bushel mined and ten cents for each oven drawn. They posted their demands on walls around the district on June 1. The operators maintained the market was sluggish, and summer was coming, when demand for coke would fall. The men did not agree.[39] The strike was on.

On June 5, only one-fourth of the men came out on strike. Men from the larger companies did not strike. Most important, the iron companies were in a glut. All seven of the Frick mines "from Broad Ford to Summit" continued to work. On June 9, men began to return to work. The *Weekly Courier* reported twenty-three mines working and twenty-three mines idle, which translated into 3,200 ovens working and 2,600 idle.[40] By mid-month, "out of forty-eight works in the regions forty are entirely idle, and at four or five of those that are running the increase wages demanded are paid."[41]

Things began to turn violent. J. Need of the Miners' Association threatened to shoot a German interpreter at Broadford and was arrested.[42] Five hundred men from the various Frick mines camped at Morgan Station, held a meeting, decided to join the other miners already on strike, and refused to go to work.[43] Austro-Hungarian immigrants were imported to Frick's Morewood mine, but once they discovered they were replacing striking miners, they refused to work. J.M. White, the Broadford Superintendent, and James Jackson, the pit boss at Valley mine, were arrested for attacking striking miners.[44]

And there were evictions. The position of the operators was that they provided housing for their workers. If the workers refused to work, then they had to leave to make room for the new men who would work. All the regional mines above Summit were idle by June 27. Tip Top and Valley had been working, but they were visited by striking miners and joined them. It was mass confusion with people running all over the place trying to discover what was happening.

At the end of June, it appeared that the strike was over. The men began to return to work. Then they began to organize. By July 1, nearly all men were back at work.[45] Then, in mid-July the miners of the Connellsville region officially organized at a meeting held at Miners' Hall in Everson. Peter Wise was president. John Needhum was vice president. They picked the newspaper *Miner's Record* of Scottdale as their official organ. There were, confusingly, two additional unions vying for support in the region: the Amalgamated and the Knights of Labor.[46] This effort was for the Knights of Labor. They issued a resolution:

> Resolved, that this convention being duly called, deem it beneficial to the welfare of the miners and coke drawers of the Connellsville coke district to come under the general direction of General Secretary D.R. Jones. Mr. Jones will therefore proceed to organize the district and will work in person or by deputy. It was also resolved that the *Miners Record*, of Scottdale, be made the official organ of the miners of the region, and a vote of thanks was given the editor and publisher for his labors during the late strike.[47]

Some of the miners wanted to continue the strike. The resolution did not pass at the time, but the men believed that once the union was fully organized, it was not out of the question. The issue of the size of the wagons was discussed at length. They planned to meet again the following Saturday. By the time it was over, nothing had been settled.

All of the strikes to this point were a prelude. Although there was already anger and confusion among the miners, what was to come was cataclysmic by comparison. It took eleven years for the industry to explode.

Strike of 1886

The strike of 1886 was much bigger and much more organized than any previous strike in the Connellsville region. This was ultimately not only a strike against management, but developed into a strike against immigrants, their women, their place in the regional mining industry, and, perhaps, in America as well. It also began the violence that would rock the region for the next decades.

By this time Henry Clay Frick had expanded his properties throughout the Connellsville region. In addition, he had created a new company around Mount Pleasant that

The strike of 1886 continued to draw national attention. *Frank Leslie's Illustrated Newspaper* had a feature on February 6, 1886, with these stunning illustrations of the events. Panel one is titled "Mount Pleasant During the Strike," and is probably Washington Street. Panel two, "Storming the Coke Ovens," is probably at Morewood. Panel three, "Homes of the Hungarians," is also probably at Morewood (*Frank Leslie's Illustrated Newspaper* 21 (January to June 1886): p. 408).

incorporated the large and important mines of Morewood, Alice, and Standard. Much of the activity of this strike took place at these sites.

The local papers, the *Mount Pleasant Journal*, the *Connellsville Weekly Courier* and the *Scottdale Independent*, were up and running and tell the story in graphic detail day by day, event by event, a far cry from the minimal reporting of the earlier strikes. Their reporting and points of view are as much a part of the story of coal and coke as were the unions. It shows how important coke had become to the region, how terrorizing the marches and protests had become, and the effect the industry had on all the people of the region. It is firsthand coverage. It reports events as they unfolded.

Mount Pleasant Journal

Under the headline "Hordes of Huns," the 1886 *Journal* began its report of the weekly events of January 13–18, filling almost the entire front page. It explained that miners at Morewood protested to the company Southwest Coal and Coke, partially owned by Henry Clay Frick, that their coke haulers were not making the same wages as the coke haulers at Standard mine, also owned by Frick.[48] The discrepancy was corrected so both mines paid the same wage. But the diggers at Morewood, all Hungarian immigrants, misunderstood the transaction and went out on strike. This action would create months of discord and riots.

The editorial in the same *Mount Pleasant Journal* was a balanced view of the position of both companies and workers: "The working men of the coke region labor hard, are poorly paid and suffer grievances which have been very patiently borne.... The present trouble, however, is with men with whom it is very difficult to reason.... However unpopular a corporation may be, it has the right to the peaceful possession of its property, and it is the duty of the Commonwealth to see that its rights are not interfered with...." The latter point being one that would haunt the coal and the steel industry for decades without resolution.

On the March

The *Journal*'s words had little effect on the rioting miners. On Thursday the 14th, the Hungarians at Standard joined the Morewood Hungarians in protest. One hundred and fifty men from Morewood and one hundred and ten men from Standard paraded around Mount Pleasant on the morning of Friday 15th, and then held a meeting at the Morewood company store. At that meeting the strikers decided to raid Standard and get the coke drawers to come out. The organized march was led by boys carrying United States flags and a banner "MOREWOOD: OUR CAUSE IS JUST." As the *Pittsburgh Daily Post* recounted this event, it claimed "two broad-shouldered" Hungarian women headed the parade.[49] When they arrived at Standard, the miners headed for the slope. The police stopped them. They did not resist. They left Standard and marched through Mount Pleasant, on to Scottdale, across Jacobs Creek, and through Everson, to the Frick-owned Valley Works in Morgan Valley.

Some striking miners remained behind at Standard and Morewood and became violent. While officers Kelley and Keister guarded the company store at Morewood, they noted that men began to congregate. They notified Superintendent Ramsey that trouble was coming. As they tried to arrest a rioter, they were surrounded by strikers carrying clubs. Things escalated and became dangerous: "[T]he mob then retreated to the railroad, firing pistols, shouting and making other demonstrations to terrorize those who were willing to work." Violence had now become a part of the protests.

The company store at Morewood became a gathering point for miners throughout many of the difficult strikes in the region ("Morewood Company Store," Eureka Fuel Company, Fayette County, Pennsylvania, and the South-West Connellsville Coke Company, Westmoreland County, Pennsylvania, June 1901).

The ovens at Morewood had to be guarded, for drawers were beginning to tear the doors off the ovens.

Marches and Arrests

The *Journal* continued its front-page news. On Saturday the 16th, the police began to question miners including John Kitchman, A. Hansil, M. Garshbar, A. Polko, P. Kowalshik, and John Kowalshik. They were arrested, tied together with ropes, and marched to jail by policeman Ben May, "a regular Hercules in strength," and Officer Cooper of the Mount Pleasant borough police force. One hundred and fifty strikers followed. This had to be quite a terrifying scene in a community of around five hundred people (borough, 534; township, 2,578).[50] At Shupe's mill, on Main Street, the mob overcame the officers "while several Hun women rushed in with knives and severed the bond of the prisoners...." Polko got away.

The mob headed for Standard again. Polko was recaptured, and as Superintendent Slater, Al Slater, Joe Breiner and Armel Keister took him to the station, they were accosted near the lime kilns near Shupe's mill by "a big German named Mike Gotler" who put a gun to Superintendent Slater's heart, saying "me shoot you." Luckily the gun misfired.

The mob now gathered at the railroad station. Joe Breiner found Gotler, grabbed him and whirled him around, and Keister tripped him. Before he could shout, Gotler was flat on the waiting room floor with big Ben May on top of him. "Ben seized him, lifted him to his feet without exertion, and jammed him down on a seat with a force that made the windows rattle." Station master John Hartigan assisted in getting the men on the train.

It was not over. The miners tried one more time to free Polko. They left Mount Pleasant for Stonerville (Alverton) to catch the train as it was headed to Greensburg with the prisoners on board. They tried to board the train and attempted to attack the officers, but they failed to free their friend, who was taken to Greensburg.

THE STRIKE EXPANDS

The strike began to spread. More men at Morewood walked out. Drawers at "the Boyle works" (Hazlett) quit on Friday the 15th, and tried to get the Alice miners to come out. Then they attended a union meeting on Saturday the 16th. On Monday the 18th, Stefan (Steve) Stannix was charged with trying to stop a worker at the point of a gun. Westmoreland County Sheriff Stewart, along with Officer May, engineer Ramsay and pit boss Menoher went to Stannix's house to arrest him, but he refused to go. He was guarded by twenty Huns: "As soon as his approach was heralded by a sentinel, the alarm cry brought the Huns from their houses, the men armed with clubs and the women brandishing knives." The sheriff left. He contacted the Frick directors.

Frick responded: "The men at our Standard, Morewood, and Valley works are out, but we don't know what their demands are for they have not made any yet. We have not received any communication from the committee appointed by the convention on Saturday and no conference has yet been held." Charles Donnelly of McClure & Company also responded: "Until the last few months we were running only 40 per cent of our ovens and could not make any money at that. We are making very little now, and certainly cannot afford to pay an advance at present."[51]

THE MINERS MEET

The Knights of Labor met at Scottdale to form a plan. They only had 1,500 members in the Connellsville district, as opposed to the 8,000 men throughout the region. That included assemblies in Mount Pleasant, Stonerville, Scottdale, Connellsville, and Uniontown. Their position was that coke was getting a good price on the market, and their salaries needed to reflect the prosperity. More important, the biggest concern of the membership was not salary, but the fear that if they went out on strike, more Hungarians would be called in to replace them. An attempt had been made to bring the current Hungarians into the union in 1884, but: "They stood by us as long as we fed them, but when the funds ran out they immediately started work."[52]

Their answer to Frick: "What is confidently expected to be the greatest strike in the history of the coke trade was formally ordered at an adjourned convention of delegates from the various mines, held in this town this afternoon." Peter Wise was elected president.[53] The miners claimed that the operators never answered their many telegrams asking for a conference. The strike was on. Two thousand men were idled at Standard, Morewood, McClure & Co. at Bridgeport, Overton, and Valley. "What the workmen want is 30 cents a car for mining and 60 cents an oven for drawing. 7,000 should be out by end of week." One must recall that in former strikes, the men were calling for a raise from thirty cents to thirty-three cents, and again from twenty-five cents to thirty cents, so obviously there had been no major increase since 1875.

HOSTILE HUNS

The January 26 *Journal*, under the headline "Hostile Huns," continued its detailed reporting, again giving three-fourths of its front page to the events around Mount Pleasant for a single week.⁵⁴ On Tuesday the 19th, guards were driven from Morewood. On Wednesday:

> Headed by banners and enlivened by music furnished by a fiddler and a man drumming on a tin boiler, the line of march was taken up for Alice mines, where a few of the braver men, although besought not to do so by their wives and children, were at work drawing their ovens. When the advance column of Hungarian army swept into view, there was a general stampede among the drawers. A Bohemian, who was unable to get away, was knocked over the head with a club in the hands of one of the charging Huns. Oven fronts were driven in, hoses cut and the tipple, used in transferring coal from the wagons to the bin, was turned completely over.

Leaving Alice for Stonerville, the men formed "two columns and marched by the right and left flank on the Southwest Company." The few men working fled. The men marched through Stonerville, on to Mayfield, at the mine owned by the McClure company. There they found a 15-year-old boy named Mentzer and beat him with clubs while his mother and sisters were crying in protest. Then on to Donnelly, the second McClure plant (the two became Alverton). The miners fled. John McCabe, the yard boss, was beaten. There they smashed eighty-four oven fronts, broke tools, and held a meeting. Then on to Scottdale.

An observer reported:

> At noon Wednesday about 1,000 Hungarians came marching into the town, carrying weapons of all descriptions, led by a violin and bass viol. They carried fence rails, clubs, pick-handles, crow-bars, gas-pipe, and, in fact, any conceivable form of bludgeon. They visited the saloons and got a quantity of Liquor, and all along the line men were seen drinking out of bottles. They remained here about an hour and then left for other works. They terrorized the whole village while here, but did no damage.

Scottdale, founded in 1872, had a population of only around 1,300 in 1886. To say the village was also terrorized is an understatement. Children in schools, merchants and customers in their shops, wives at home who worried about their families, could not continue business as usual. Everything shut down as the miners rioted. These details are often overlooked when reporting events in coal and coke history. But it is these details that explain the era, that help people understand that the battle was long and gory.

Nor were the rioters finished. They moved on to McClure's Painter works, where they smashed sixty-five ovens, broke wheelbarrows, and shattered all the windows in a house. "A negro, who had fired at a Hungarian, but missed, and then took refuge in his house, was dragged out and terribly beaten by the infuriated Huns." Then they returned to Morewood and Sheriff Stewart, who was waiting for them. He had arranged for a special car of twenty Pittsburgh policemen to come by train the night before. Detective Dick Brophy of the Frick Southwest Company was sworn in by Sheriff Stewart. The major confrontation was about to begin.

Captain Schoonmaker, not Colonel Schoonmaker, and superintendents Robert and Morris Ramsay awaited at the Morewood company store for the striking rioters to arrive. The store became their headquarters. They had contacted Father Lambling, a priest from Scottdale, to join them in the hopes that he could stop the miners from rioting. The mob arrived before Lambling did. The strikers took possession of the shaft and lined up along their homes on what was called Hungary Row. The police formed a line: first the twenty Pittsburgh police, then the fourteen special officers. They faced 250 miners. The hilltop surrounding the event, called Fort Defiance, was filled with spectators.⁵⁵ They stood on roofs and oven tops. Sheriff Stewart stepped forward, along with Policeman Loar, and announced to the miners "that their deeds of the past few days were entirely beyond the limits of the law and that the Commonwealth was forced to compel acquiescence in its laws." Warrants would be issued. As the police advanced, the strikers began to disperse, running in all directions. There was no battle. Ben May of the Coal and Iron Police caught a running rioter. Steve Stannix fired at a deputy and ran up the hill trying to gather his forces. He failed and disappeared over the rim. "Martin Gankey [sic], when captured, was embraced by his wife and the couple had to be taken off together, the officers not being able to separate them."

The officers, confident now that the miners had dispersed, began to go through the homes, arresting strikers and putting them in the rail car for transport to jail in Greensburg. Among the prisoners were 4 Stannix men (Steve, his sons George and Andy, and his father), Jake Johnston, Martin Ganskey, Charles Dorsett, John Tuzak, George Slangina, and N. Shulak. They were taken to jail in Greensburg. (Stannix would escape and go to the Hocking Valley in Ohio to avoid punishment, but returned to the district at the end of June.[56] He was reinstated to his old job at Morewood, partly in fear of another strike.[57] He became a union leader and in 1890 was appointed the Hungarian organizer.[58])

Father Lambling, who had arrived too late to stop the confrontation, was seen in his buggy atop Fort Defiance above Alice Mine. He came down to the sheriff and lamented: "The coke operators brought these men into the region as a preventative of strikes and now you are hunting them down like dogs. You sent for me to intercede with them, and, after receiving an affirmative answer from me, you would not even await my arrival, but have brought about all this trouble. Much if not all of it might have been averted had you done as you said you would."

On Thursday, Peter Wise chaired another meeting of the Knights of Labor. There were 600 delegates. The strike was to continue. Resolutions were passed. They would meet again on Saturday the 23rd. It must be remembered that the strike was not just located around Mount Pleasant and Scottdale. It ran the entire length of the area through the Morgan Valley to Broadford. Unfortunately, the newspapers recorded little of events in the entire area.

In fact, there were three meetings that Saturday. In the morning the men marched to Bowers' store, where W.F. Barkley, a merchant, and Joseph Rooks, "a prominent labor agitator," spoke. John McClain, the chairman, adjourned until three in the afternoon. At the 3 o'clock meeting, McClain was elected chairman. There were 500 in attendance. Father Lambling spoke, assuring the miners they had a right to good pay and to organize, but should *be careful to stay within the law*. Joseph Rooks spoke too, in Hungarian and in German. Even Sheriff Stewart spoke. He told them to keep the peace. As the train with the prisoners went by, the crowd became agitated.

That night a meeting was held at Bunker Hill schoolhouse in Mount Pleasant, presided by John McClain again. Attempts were made to organize. Did the men want to belong to the Knights of Labor or the Amalgamated? They chose the Amalgamated. A Connellsville meeting was also held. Other meetings would be held at Trotter and Leisenring to continue the organizing.

The Austro-Hungarian Consul Gets Involved

On Monday, Consul Max Schamberg, the Austro-Hungarian consul at Pittsburgh, came to Mount Pleasant to see what was happening to the Hungarians. A thousand men met him at the depot and relayed their story. He promised to investigate and selected six men to form a committee. They met with Consul Schamberg at the National Hotel. The topics were the company stores, pit regulations, the check system, the docking of wages for minor reasons, and evictions. He went to visit their homes and listened to their issues.[59] Prior to his visit, and noted above, he had sent a letter to the H.C. Frick Coke Company.

They were read to the six men, who felt the letters showed promise. They brought them to a meeting of the rest of the men, who rejected the offers. The letters were translated into the various languages and distributed in anticipation of the meeting to be held the following Wednesday in Scottdale. The consul asked for assurance that there would be no more violence, adding that "if it was true that they struck without notification to their employees of their demands, they had acted wrongly and he would give his support to no evil-doers."[60]

These were the activities of a single week in the strike mostly reported by the *Mount Pleasant Journal*.

Connellsville Weekly Courier

During that same week, the *Weekly Courier* summed up the events as their staff saw them. In practically a full-page story titled "The Harrowing Hun," they added details to the events of the month. The article began by creating a fair assessment of the situation. It is more an editorial than a news story and allows more insight into the tone of the region during the strike.

> A bitter and unreasonable spirit of resentment against the operators seems to tinge every act and utterance of the strikers. They refused to pull the ovens and save the coke therein from burning up; they refused to permit enough coal to be dug to run the pumps at some of the mines, though they knew refusal meant that the mines would be flooded. The operators, on their part, treated the demands of the strikers with contempt. With such a feeling of hatred and distrust existing between them there is poor prospect of the two parties coming together.
>
> It is merely a question of endurance on either side, with all the advantages in favor of the operators. His contracts are stayed by strike or accident, and he is not liable for any loss or damage from that source. His only loss is from the natural rust of idleness and the interest on idle capital. The miner has his all at stake. When his scant wages have been expended for food, his only source of existence is the charity of the public, a most uncertain income. Encouragement has been received from farmers and merchants, but it takes money to feed 10,000 miners and their families; and the sympathy that is offered on the impulse of the moment, or for the mere purpose of effect, has no more substantial character than the four winds of heaven. Men cannot live on this kind of sympathy any more than they can live on air. If the men can hold out several weeks, there may be prospects of success, but we can offer them no encouragement in this direction. The operators are as stiff-necked as the miners are stubborn, but unbiased observers unite in the opinion that if the latter return to work, public feeling will compel the former to grant the advance asked and remedy the abuses complained of—abuses that even the operators admit do exist.

And on it continues. It commends the miners for trying to organize, and finally it calls for arbitration to end the differences. The *Courier* barely mentioned the marches, the riots, or the violence. Instead it focused more on interviews with key men.

In reporting on the meeting at the skating rink, the *Courier* stated that three companies had granted the advance and were working: "The Moyer works of W.J. Rainey and Company; the Percy works of the Percy Mining Company, and the Mammoth works of J.W. Moore in the Pleasant Unity district." None were part of the syndicate or the producers. It repeated the Consul's letter to Frick and Frick's reply. It then discussed the meeting, calling it the "largest mass meeting ... ever held in the region." At that meeting, William Mullin spoke about destroying the company store: "Let the workingmen of the region now call on the retail dealers in such towns as Mt. Pleasant, Scottdale, Connellsville, Dunbar and Uniontown and ask them for goods in this their hour of need. Those who favor the workingmen now can expect to receive their favors when work is resumed.—Then, by honesty and fair dealing with the town merchants, all will prosper and the company store will die a natural death." Which seems to further acknowledge that miners were not required to buy all their needs at the company store, and that they were paid in cash. It also indicates their displeasure with the company store.

Thomas Lynch Speaks

The speakers and the resolutions are given ample space, but the *Courier* does something else: it presents the operator's side by interviewing superintendent Thomas Lynch, Frick's right-hand man.

Lynch conceded there were grievances: "We employ 3,500. It would be strange if out of that number there would be none to complain." He goes on: "But there is no general complaint or widespread dissatisfaction, as the newspapers report. I had a full and accurate report of the delegate meeting at Scottdale that ordered this strike. But 3 of our 18 works were represented, and not one of the delegates from those three works were in favor of this strike, but they acquiesced with its conclusion. The convention was dominated by men who don't work at the coke works at all." This is a very important point, a position that would be repeated again and again by the Frick forces. They wanted to negotiate with their miners, not outsiders.

Then the reporter asked Lynch if importing the Hungarians was a mistake. "I think not," was the reply.

> But it's too late to speak of that now. I can say, however, that there is a popular error aboard about them. They are not brought hither as contract labor from the old country. There is not a Hun in the coke region that has been "imported" here. They are sent here, as a rule, by New York employment agents, who make a business of supplying men to contractors, mines, furnaces, mills, etc. The employer pays the agent a fee of so much per head, and sometimes advances the car fare. The agent sees about their transportation and usually sends a man with them to their destination.
>
> The first Hungarians were introduced in the region in 1870, but they weren't brought here to break a strike. We had just completed the Morewood works, Labor [sic] was scarce in the region, and we were obliged to look elsewhere for it. We sent to New York, and were supplied with Hungarians by one of the labor bureaus mentioned. They have since been writing to their friends and the region has gradually filled up with them. The talk about bringing these people in to reduce the price of labor is all bosh. There has been but one reduction of wages since 1880, and the Huns have always been paid as much as any other labor. You must take into consideration the fact that the coke business has increased 300 per cent, since 1878; instead of 3,600, there are now 10,800 ovens in the coke region. This has created a demand for labor that couldn't be supplied here at home and this was the sole cause of the introduction of Hungarian labor.

When asked how many Huns the Frick company employed, Lynch answered:

> Out of our 3,500 men, about 25 per cent. are Hungarians, Bohemians and Poles, mostly at Mt. Pleasant; 10 per cent. are Germans and Prussians, and the balance Irish and American, with a sprinkling of English, Welsh and Scotch. But we have always given American and English-speaking labor the preference, as the files of the newspapers will prove. During the past two years, when trade was flat, it was the Huns who were discharged, and whose passage home the papers recorded. At many of our works lots of the company houses were idle all summer, when natives, who lived in their own houses were retained in our employ.

Lynch also defended against the allegation that the company would let diggers dig only three wagons a day. The accusation was that the company was imposing the limit "in order to make more for the company store." Lynch denied the accusation:

> In one sense it is [true] and in another it isn't. It is true that during the past summer, when but 42 per cent of the ovens were in blast, that often the pits were crowded and didn't average more than three or

four wagons. But the object wasn't to make money for the company stores. It was to give employment to as many men as possible. Times were hard and work scarce. It was certainly better to divide our pay roll among all than to give it to a few and let the others starve. But now it is different. With 95 per cent. of the ovens in, there is plenty of work for everybody; in fact, during the past couple of months we couldn't get diggers enough to supply our quota of ovens with coal.

Our men average now from $35 to $70 per month. The price paid varies all the way from 27 to 48 cents per wagon. At the Standard works the price is 32 cents. This is on account of the varying size of the wagons, which run from 30 to 50 bushels, the nature of the coal, the pit, etc.

Many modern-day myths are blown by the following Lynch comments on the "pluck-me" or company stores:

In 1876, 1877, 1878 and, I believe, part of 1879, it was the custom among operators to employ men with the understanding that they take $20 of their wages out of the store. This was during the panic times, when only two-thirds of the 3,600 ovens were in operation. When times got better and the boom came and big works were built, like Morewood and Standard, this requirement to deal at the store was abandoned; and it has never been resumed since at any of our works. During the dull times of the past summer we discharged the Huns and single men and kept the men with families. This was done for a double purpose. First, because such men would be better customers, of course, and second, because they could least afford to be out of work.

Lynch had addressed this issue before back in 1880–81 and created a chart comparing company store prices of the H.C. Frick Coke Company with general grocers in the region. The topic is addressed in several chapters of this book.

On the subject of the advance, he emphatically stated, "The advance will not be given." He maintained that the advance would have been granted in a few months, but now the companies had to be strong against the men. And then he turned to the Hungarians:

The advance won't be granted. We saw this strike coming and prepared for it. Had the men continued work the wages of 1884 would have been restored in a few months without asking. But the operators won't give in to the strikers now, and it is only a question of time until the latter will be forced to go back to work. Though this is the most general lockout we ever had in the coke region, there are a large proportion of the men who don't want to strike—whose hearts are not in the movement—and when the break comes the movement will crumble all at once. The only strange thing about the present strike is the active part being taken by the Hungarians, heretofore quiet and docile people. They seem to be the most fierce and belligerent now. Yet they are not suffering. I am told they have $25,000 to $30,000 on deposit in the First National Bank, of Connellsville, alone.

Miners Respond

After Lynch's comments, the *Courier* turned to the strikers and their list of complaints. The reporter wanted to talk to Peter Wise, but there was a warrant out for his arrest. So an unnamed miner was questioned. He blamed the problems on the formation of the syndicate:

The operators resolved to restrict the supply, so that a strong demand would enable them to raise the selling price. To do this they formed a combination. The more extensive operators formed the syndicate and all the coke produced in the coke region, with the exception of a few independent operators and iron operators' production, is sold by them. The less extensive ones formed the pool. Commissioning the syndicate to sell their coke and paying them a certain percentage for it; and all acting conjointly in producing an amount of coke in proportion to the ovens they owned. This was the beginning of hard times.

He explained:

Twenty-five per cent of the ovens were left out and a great many men discharged. The people live in houses owned by the operators and to discharge a householder would curtail the profits of the operators about $6 per month, therefore the single men were discharged. Labor was a drug in the market and the operators took advantage of the situation by enlarging the wagons and compelling the diggers to heap coal on them, until at present there is scarcely a wagon in the coke region that carries less than 10 bushels. Another percentage of the ovens were left out and more men discharged. The mines were run only 4 days per week, and instead of 3 wagons of coal per oven, 4 and 4½ were put in, and the coke drawer got no more for pulling it out. The digger had to put as much coal on four wagons as he did formally [sic] on five wagons for the same wages. Dread of poverty compelled the workmen to accede to every arbitrary demand, and when, in December, 1884, a reduction of 10 per cent was imposed upon them it was accepted without a murmur.

He went on to explain how the companies were "dodging the checkweightman law."

In June, 1883, a law was passed by the legislature calling on all operators of mines to have their wagons built to a uniform capacity, or have weigh-scales to weight the coal sent out by the miners; and furthermore, giving the miners power to select a competent person as checkweightman or check measurer, as the case might require, who should have permission to be present at all times when coal is being weighed or measured, the price to be paid that which was agreed upon between employer and employe before the passage of this act. A proviso in the law gave power to operators and workmen to contract out of it if they agreed to do so. Every man was promptly called up to the office and ordered to sign a printed contract agreeing to load wagons full and round to the top, no matter what their capacity, for 27 cents. Refusal to sign meant discharge, and discharge meant starvation. They signed, of course. The thought of a hungry wife and family outweighed the spirit of resentment, and intent of the checkweighman act was thus frustrated.

Then there was an accounting of how the companies were making money off the miners:

Just before the strike began I made the following account at a certain works: Diggers, 400 wagons of coal at 27¢ per wagon, $108.00; coke drawers, 120 ovens at 55¢ per oven, $66.00; wages of 30 laborers, including officials at an average pay of $2 per day, $60.00; cost of feeding 18 mules at 25¢ each, $4.50; other expenses $10.00. Total $248.50. Output of coke, 400 tons at $1.25 per ton, $500.00. Expenses deducted $251.50, net profit for one day's work. An estimate of the profits of store and income from house rent would be at least $50, making in all upwards of $300 profit for one day's work alone.

As can be seen, it was complicated. One can see the point of view of the owners, but one can also understand the point of view of the workers. The same incident can be interpreted a number of ways depending on the needs of the observer.

Finally, the *Courier* gave W.J. Rainey a voice. Rainey was a coal operator from Ohio who began speculating in the Morgan Valley and vicinity around 1877. He remained independent. He refused to join the syndicate and refused to allow his miners to join the union. He kept his men working when others went out on strike by, in this instance, giving them the advance. At this point he was Frick's biggest competitor.

I think the operators made a mistake in not giving the men five per cent advance now and another advance later on.... It would have had a tendency to have kept the men contentedly at work. I know that Schoonmaker has contracts with Belmont and Benwood mills at Wheeling to furnish coke till April at $1.20 a ton, and the Carrie furnace in this city at the same price, while Frick has the Top mill at Wheeling at the same price. The men should have been given a better chance under these circumstances. I think the producers will ultimately win, but I am not certain that the fruits of the victory will be of a permanent character. Coke is becoming scarce in all localities, and many furnaces will have to be banked until the issue of the strike shall have been determined.

It's the Women

Finally, a member of the coke syndicate put the blame of the strike exactly where they thought it should go: not on the companies, not on the miners, but on the women. "'The

Hungarian women were almost the sole cause of the strike in the coke region,' said a prominent member of the coke syndicate, yesterday. 'The entire subject of dispute between ourselves and our employees has been much misrepresented day after day. The cause of the strike has never been fairly put before the public.'"

The *Courier* wanted to know why:

> Well, until a recent law they daily assisted their husbands in the yards. As a rule they are superior to the men in manual labor, and as a result the wages of the men were greatly increased. When the enactment forbidding women to labor in the yard went into operation last summer they naturally thought that the employers were to blame. These women cannot talk English and when our officials ordered them from the premises discontent began to prevail at once. Consequently the monthly wages of the men became less and they claimed that they should have as much for themselves as when assisted by their wives. This was the foundation of the present strike.

For the first time in the local reporting, the Hungarian women were blamed for the strike. The topic would continue through various sources. The fact of the matter was that the Hungarian women did work at the coke ovens. They snuck into the area each day and helped their husbands pull the coke and load it. That meant twice the effort on an oven and it was unloaded twice as fast. When the yard boss found them, he would force them to leave. As soon as he was gone, they came right back in and started again.

George Dallas Albert, in the *History of the County of Westmoreland*, had a lot to say:

> Among the miners underground Hungarian men are plenty enough. Above surface their wives and daughters share their labor with the men. Broad backed and brawny, the women handle the long, heavy iron scraper at the hot mouth of the oven, and their burly, dumpy figures are seen between the handles of the big wheelbarrows as they trot from the oven to the car with five or six bushels of coke, weighing from two hundred to two hundred and forty pounds. Their principal employment, however, is forking coke in the cars. They all wear boots; that is for a few months in the winter. In the summer they go barefoot, and even this early are found the strong imprint of plenty of pink toes in the yellow mud. Their skirts are scant, and leave room for about two feet of sunburn below. A distinctive feature of their costume is their head-dress, which usually consists of a shawl, not wrapped turban fashion, but pinned under the chin. Men and women are alike short, almost squat in stature, but broad and strongly built.... The women are accustomed to hard work in their own country, and the men seem to be willing to let them do it.[61]

In October of 1886 the state released its official report. It agreed that women were working in the coke yards. It further agreed that the management knew the women were working. It dismissed the assertion that the women were officially employed by the companies. The report was published in the *Weekly Courier*. It was, however, based on observations and events in 1885, the year before the strike. The 1887 *Annual Report* has proved to be elusive. It should have a summary of the events in the Connellsville coke region in 1886. The report that does exist is for the anthracite region only.[62]

Scottdale Independent

The final local paper of which we could find information was the *Scottdale Independent*. In addition to summarizing events around Mount Pleasant, this newspaper turned its eyes south through the Morgan Valley and reported events at and near Broadford.

On January 13 it reported:

> A large procession was on its way here from Connellsville, and on passing the slope at the Henry Clay mines near Broad Ford, they were accosted by a French-Canadian who, in response to their yells opened fire with a 38-calibre revolver and brought down an Italian named Michael Saggie who was the

last man in the procession. The men had all deserted their posts upon the appearance of the army of strikers and much excitement prevailed. It is impossible to know just what followed for the next few moments, but in a short time the entire tipple was ablaze. An eye witness, who is noted for his veracity, says that a trip of wagons was being hoisted and the engineer having deserted his post a total wreck occurred on the tipple, upsetting the stove, and the structure being saturated with oil, burned rapidly. The Canadian escaped but the Italian was borne upon the arms of his associates to the office of Dr. Reagan, a short distance from the place where he fell. Dr. Reagan probed four inches but failed to find the ball. It having entered beneath the edge of the shoulder blade. He will likely die.[63]

That event occurred in early January, while the Hungarians were rebelling at Morewood on their first attacks. Events were also unfolding near Connellsville. The January 23 edition of the *Scottdale Independent* had a story headlined "The Great Strike" that also filled its front page.[64] It called the workers: "Fiery Huns, Furious Bohemians, and Frantic Poles." It was not sympathetic:

> The present strike in the coke region has taught the operators several important lessons. It is abundantly proven that cheap Hungarian labor has been a curse to the coke region. Socially they are worse than nobody; morally they are below the lowest American standard; in a business way they are of as little use to the country as any class of men could be. They take the places which by right belong to native born citizens—men who read, reflect, study and advance in mental power. Laborers who support the press, the pulpit, the school, and the lecture are driven out and their places filled by those who benefit none but the bar-keeper.

On January 30, the editorial on page two only confirmed the opinion that the *Independent* had been voicing:

> In his recent message to Max Schamberg, Austro-Hungarian Consul at this place Wednesday, the H.C. Frick coke company expressed a desire to have the Slavs quietly removed from the company's premises offering to pay the fares of those who are not able to pay for themselves. It is a case in which the bear is easily caught, but hard to let go of, for the miners have resolved to keep them here so long as they are useful to them in helping carry on the strike.
>
> That message should have read, "We were instrumental in bringing these men here for the purpose of breaking up strikes and of lowering the standard of the laboring man's wages. Now that they themselves inaugurate strikes and show themselves to be as persistent in their demands for high wages as any other class, we would be glad to have you quietly lead them back to their own country, give us porsession [sic] of our property and we will fill their places with men who are not so hard to manage when their demands are not met. Probably John Chinaman might answer their purpose for a year or two, or perhaps longer."[65]

In the February 27 edition the headline read "The Strikers Win."

> The news was received with favor by all the English speaking laborers and everybody not intimately connected with the coke industry. But the Hungarians—the "fiery Huns"—were not satisfied. They could not return to their work so long as their countrymen languished in the jails. They felt that their harps must hang upon the weeping willow so long as the captivity of their brothers continued. All day Sunday bands of angry Slavs paraded the vicinity of Mt. Pleasant breathing threats and uttering expressions of dissatisfaction. At some of the mines the men were afraid to go to work lest their lives would be in danger from the angry Huns. Tuesday, however, the Huns began to weaken and decided to go to work with the understanding that if the prisoners were not released after five days they would again quit work, and many of them crowded around the shafts at Morewood seeking admission to the mines but the superintendent explained to the men that ... [illegible]
>
> The Huns having been informed that their countrymen could not be gotten out, except on bail, have been trying to secure bail and are, apparently better satisfied.
>
> The strike is virtually over. There are numerous little local difficulties yet to be settled but it is not likely there will be general lay off again for some time.
>
> The Hungarians might be released from jail upon a *nolle pros* as the law has several times been strained in favor of the operators.

The cost of the strike to the operators and employes is estimated at seven hundred thousand dollars. The coke trade has been injured for months to come. Anthracite furnaces that have been using coke have contracted for coal and orders come in slowly. The syndicate will not be able to run ninety-five per cent of their ovens even if the men were all willing to go to work, but the cessation in the production of coke has had the effect of stiffening the prices of iron and may have a beneficial effect upon the industry.

Evictions

Just how and when the miners were evicted from their homes is not clear in the local papers. It was a dirty business. The owners' position was clear: they had orders to fill, the miners walked off the job, they would lose everything if they did not fill their orders, that meant the miners would permanently be out of a job. They had to find new workers. The strikers were living in company homes. They needed homes for the new workers. So, go to work or get out!

The *Independent* reported:

> The work of evicting the striking miners was begun this week in a very cautious manner by the sheriff of Fayette county at the instance of the H.C. Frick Coke Company. But a few of the men were evicted at each works. These were the leaders in the strike. The evictions did not provoke resistance much less riot. This was due to the fact that they were isolated cases and were handled judiciously. Otherwise, trouble would have certainly ensued. Notice has been given all the strikers to leave the houses to-day or return to work. The strikers will do neither. Owing to the severity of the weather it is not thought the operators will insist upon the evictions. They decline to say anything about the matter, and it is fair to presume that they are in a quandary about it. They recognize that eviction is the first step toward breaking the strike, yet their humanity revolts against the harshness of the method.[66]

In fact, the *Philadelphia Inquirer* reported that Sheriff Stewart of Westmoreland County refused to evict miners because the weather was too harsh.[67]

Nonetheless, the evictions became a reality. They began at Valley Mine at the top of the Morgan Valley. One family's goods were set out along the road. A second family had a sick member and was not evicted. These evictions were done by Sheriff Sterling and his deputies. At Broadford, four families "were set out in the snow." At Summit, two more families were evicted. The evictions continued in other areas, and then the sheriff warned the miners to return to work or more evictions would occur. There were more a few days later: Five families at Leith, notices posted at Trotter that evictions would begin on Friday, and "A German miner, who was evicted at Broadford yesterday, was here to-day, accompanied by a number of his countrymen. Their object, as stated to a Justice of the Peace, was to enter suit against the H.C. Frick Coke company for ten thousand dollars damages. Another evicted miner from the Cochran Works was here to bring suit against his late employer for the full amount of his wages, less cash received."[68]

Then the strikebreakers arrived. Ninety-six Hungarians were brought into the district. Sixteen were sent to Summit, sixteen to Valley, and sixty-four were taken to Mount Pleasant. Twenty of those:

> were lowered into a shaft at 4 o'clock. They were all supplied with lamps, picks, and shovels by the Company. They worked until 10 o'clock when they all threw down their tools and forced the bosses to have them hoisted to the surface. In 15 minutes afterwards they were all received with open arms by their striking countrymen. The Huns had a regular jubilee over the summary way in which they knocked out the operators, and Hungary Row presented a sort of a Fourth of July appearance for the balance of the day. It appears the new arrivals all found relatives either at Morewood, Bessemer or Standard, and there they are yet. All efforts to persuade them to return to work have been failures.[69]

On came the socialists. While 1,000 men gathered at Morgan Station to discuss the events at Broadford the day before, another meeting took place at Mount Pleasant with the Hungarians of Morewood. Newspapers reported that "Socialistic agitators from Chicago and New York" were recruiting members among the foreigners and they were bringing weapons and ammunition into the region.[70] Things were getting out of hand. Companies had to become alarmed. So, too, the police. So, too, the general public: all were affected by the violence among them.

Syndicate, Producers and Amalgamated Meet

On February 26 the *Connellsville Courier* announced "The Strike Settled." The Amalgamated had called for a meeting, which was granted. The men included Joseph Welsh, Herman Stickleback, Michael Dismen (?), George Thompson, and Patrick McKenna. The syndicate in the form of H.C. Frick, Thomas Lynch, Colonel J.M. Schoonmaker, B.F. Rafferty, Charles Donnelly, and J.K. Taggart, took the train from Pittsburgh; and the Connellsville Coke Producers' Association, in the form of D.L. Dillinger, Colonel J.M. Reid, A.W. Bliss, R.L. Martin, A.H. Sherrick, Joseph R. Stauffer, B.F. Keister, J.A. Strickler, B.F. Overhold, John S. Newmyer, and A.C. Cochran, joined them at Schoonmaker's office in Everson.

There were now two organizations for the companies: the larger companies were in the syndicate, and the smaller in the producers' association. There were even operators who would not join either organization, such as Rainey. The men appointed Charles Donnelly and Joseph R. Stauffer, one from each organization, to meet with the miners' committee. The meeting was held at Frick's offices in Scottdale. The miners talked only of an advance from 27 to 30 cents a wagon and 55 to 60 cents per oven drawing.

The miners made a good case for giving the advance now instead of waiting until April 1. Then George or William Thompson (the newspaper uses both names for the same man) spoke:

> Colonel Schoonmaker, he observed, had said that he would not knowingly do an injustice to any man who had slept with him on the tented field and with him faced the bullets of the enemy. The speaker himself, and many of those for whom he spoke had served in the army, and he asked that justice be accorded all. He thought that if the syndicate could accede to the demands of the men April 1st, they could do so now, even if they had to run their works at a loss until that time. They would then lose no contracts.[71]

The owners went back to Everson, where all were waiting. The companies agreed to the advance. How much Colonel Schoonmaker's views swayed the syndicate we do not know. Just a week before he was quoted as saying he would never, no never, grant the advance until the miners resumed work; that they would not even entertain anything propositioned looking forward, such as an advance before April 1. The Hungarians were not happy. They wanted some men who were arrested freed. But within days they settled too. The strike was over. The *Scottdale Independent* concluded that the strike cost $700,000.[72]

Aftermath

The strike of 1886 had a number of important achievements. Yes, it created a great divide among immigrants and former immigrants, which would continue through decades if not centuries. It also focused on the rights of women in the workforce. And it strengthened the operators into a firm syndicate and organized the men into struggling unions. It also saw the true beginning of violence in the strikes.

Five

Strikes from 1887 to 1889

By 1887 the Connellsville coke region had spread further beyond the Morgan Valley. The new mines were bigger, had complete company towns or patches, and hundreds of coke ovens. There were more voices describing events in the region, including official government records. The Frick company continued to absorb new mines into their holdings.

In 1887 there was a continuation of the unrest of 1886. "To-day the ovens from Fairchance [south of Uniontown in Fayette County] to Greensburg [middle of Westmoreland County] are idle. 12,000 men are out of employment, $80,000 worth of coke is burning up and at some of the works the pumps have stopped and the mines are slowly being flooded."[1] Everyone was losing. By midyear, Andrew Carnegie threw a wrench into the situation and created even more bedlam. His meddling collapsed the syndicate, nearly destroyed Henry Clay Frick, and aggravated the efforts of the two unions for domination in the Connellsville district.

The early part of the year was more a battle of unions than anything else. In January the Knights reorganized their unions in fourteen states and five territories into a single union.[2] Then Thomas P. James of the National Board, and John Costello, the general organizer, came to Scottdale and offered Amalgamated District Three a chance to change affiliation to a sub-district of the Knights. They met informally with Amalgamated President Trimbath, the Hungarian organizer John Yochman, and A.P. Frazier. The offer was refused, with the Amalgamated representatives pointing out that the focus of the two organizations was not the same, and that the secret portion of the Knights' mission was unacceptable.[3]

This prompted a *Journal* editorial to exclaim: "If the leaders of the Knights of Labor and the Amalgamated Association allow these two organizations to become involved in a quarrel the officers are bigger fools than *THE JOURNAL* would take them to be."[4] It did not take long before the Knights and the Amalgamated confirmed the *Journal*'s fears. Once again, the issues were at Morewood, where the haulers refused to work because they were being forced to work overtime. They wanted the company to pay them for a full day's work if they reported to work, and for the day to be from 6 in the morning to 4 in the afternoon, a total of ten hours. The company said no. The miners struck. The Amalgamated agreed that the company should discharge nine of the strikers, mostly members of the Knights. They were fired. The Knights, who it seems were not permitted to offer an idea, objected, and the diggers now refused to work.[5] In March the two unions met with Mr. Frick and created a resolve to meet in every works in the region and vote to strike or not. The ballots would then go to the executive committee. Until the committee tallies were completed: "All works to stop on Tuesday, pending an answer from the Executive Committee."[6]

The miners at Standard were well prepared for the strike. "At nearly all their houses can be found from 100 to 150 bushels of coal, every pound of which has been carried by their wives from the tipple or taken from out the ovens just after the charge is made."[7]

In February, the federal government passed an interstate commerce bill, which could have created far-reaching problems for the coal and coke industry. The new law placed federal regulation on the railroads and created the Interstate Commerce Commission. This act was in answer to public concern about how railroads charged rates and made decisions. It brought a strong reaction in the Connellsville district. Col. J.M. Schoonmaker, owner of a number of mines in the Morgan Valley–Mount Pleasant area, was deeply concerned as to how it would affect shipping the coal and coke to market.[8]

The syndicate, with the agreement of the producers, advanced the price of coke on the market to $2.00.[9] That was a 50-cent raise from the former rate. Some thought the amount was too high and could be the product of the new interstate commerce law. No raise was offered to the miners.[10] That prompted a meeting with the miners. The miners wanted a general advance of 20 percent, but the operators only offered 5. The meeting included the syndicate, the producers, the Knights and the Amalgamated, and took place in Pittsburgh at the syndicate's offices. Everyone of any importance was there, including Frick. When the owners refused, the miners requested arbitration. The meeting concluded without an agreement, but with a promise by the operators that one would be forthcoming shortly.[11]

By March 15 the arbitration was underway. The Knights and the syndicate were ready, awaiting the Amalgamated. The Amalgamated decided to have its own vote. This time they did not limit it to its members, but threw it open to all miners, asking them to elect arbitrators, and suggesting John McBride of Columbus, Ohio, and William Mullen of Scottdale. The men were getting weary of the struggle between the unions and were ready to strike.[12] By the 22nd, the Knights wanted to act without the Amalgamated. They had selected their arbitrator and were waiting for the Amalgamated to select theirs. Instead it appeared as if the Amalgamated was trying to get only their reps on as arbitrators. The case went before attorney John Jarrett in Fayette County for a decision.[13] It took until April for the issue to be resolved and arbitration to begin. They agreed to increase the size of the arbitration board to seven instead of five: McBride and Mullen for Amalgamated; John R. Bryne for the Knights; James M. Bailey, Oliver P. Scaife, and A.W. Bliss for the operators. The meeting was to take place in Pittsburgh. Also present were President Harris of the Pennsylvania Miners' Association; Superintendent Lynch of the Frick Coke Works; Col. J.M. Schoonmaker, S.L. Schoonmaker, B.H. Rubie and J.K. Taggart. It took two hours to agree to an umpire. John B. Jackson was suggested as the umpire and could have been considered the eighth person. Items under discussion included actual contract price of coke, the average wage, and coke wages compared to other industries.[14]

Finally, after every effort, however chaotic, the arbitration failed. In early May, the men throughout the district put down their tools and walked away. The strike was on.

Conflict Continues

Despite the strike, the Amalgamated met in their hall at Everson that Saturday with thirty-three delegates from their thirty-six lodges. They reported that they had been instructed by the national committee to accept Umpire Jackson's award "under protest." Regardless, they issued a demand of an advance between 10 and 27 percent be granted within three to six days or they would strike. At that same meeting, John Yochman asked to resign as Hungarian organizer, but his request was refused. The appeal for a 12-percent advance was refused by the syndicate as they met in Pittsburgh. On Tuesday, the Amalgamated met again in Everson and the Knights in Scottdale. They agreed (quite an achievement) that during the strike the "pumps at the pits and shafts be allowed to run and other work done necessary to keep the pits in order, providing that the men thus employed be paid the advance demanded." It was contingent upon allowing the striking miners to remain in their homes and be furnished coal for their heat. If the operators denied these concessions, then the pits would not be cared for.[15] It was all becoming terribly complicated as each organization was trying to find its way. The operators were pretty firm. The unions were in confusion. The miners were in limbo. Mines were beginning to close: Buckeye idle; Standard idle; Hazlett at a standstill except the pumps, which furnished water for the boilers. The regular pumper refused to work, so a yard boss took the job.[16] So far it was a calm strike.

By the next week, the *Courier* announced "No Break in the Strike." No evictions. No imported miners. The men were fairly peaceful. In fact, they were visiting various mines, not to compel the men and beat them, but to help them get ready for the strike. But then, at the end of the week, the Knights "decided that the strikers were in the wrong and ordered them back to work."[17] This demand must have come from the national organization, for the *Courier* reported, "The local assemblies of the Knights were more violent in demanding a strike than were their brethren of the Amalgamated association, and it is freely predicted that, rather than back down now, they will withdraw from the order and unite forces with the Amalgamated. They freely declare that they have inaugurated this strike on their own account and are abundantly able to take care of themselves without assistance from the general executive board."[18] As predicted by the paper, the local district ignored the national Knights' views. These events were appreciated by Henry Clay Frick, who strongly felt that outsiders should not intervene in the problems of the Connellsville coke region.

In the meantime, the factories in Shenango Valley, Cleveland, and Chicago that needed coke to continue production were beginning to feel the pinch of the strike in the Connellsville district. Rumors began to circulate that the men themselves wanted to return to work. Two hundred men from the Leisenring works were among them. Another large group of Huns returned to their homeland, having had enough of coal mines, unions, and operators. Another group headed to Morgantown to work on the railroad. They were fed up with the chaos and the uncertainty.

Events intensified. A.C. Cochran & Co. granted the advance to their men at the Buckeye and Star mines. Both immediately began working. Cochran was not a member of the syndicate, but his decision affected his fellow operators. In his view, his obligations to his customers, mainly the Bellair Nail Works, were more important.[19] The *Scottdale Independent* clarified some of the situation: "The works in and about Bridgeport are still idle, except Buckeye which resumed operations on Tuesday at the advance demanded—12½ per cent— also the blacksmith, who has been working by contract for 2 per day, was raised to $2.25, the advance additional, and the chargers who work at the Star ovens had only been getting $1.10 per day for charging 20, was raised to $1.50 per day and the advance additional."[20]

Some of the miners found part-time work elsewhere. Some did odd jobs; others were put to work by the operators. Frick had his men fixing the roads, which helped him cut down on the road taxes and also provided them with a paycheck.

Violence Begins

In the third week of the strike, the *Journal* headline read "Coke Strike Continues." Advances had been granted to many of the nonaligned companies. The strikers considered stopping the pumps that kept the water out of the mines. The Knights were considering abandoning the advice of their national leaders and sending the men back to work. Alice strikers were angry because the operators deducted rent from their May checks. And at a meeting at Greenlick Junction, the Amalgamated addressed eight hundred miners, giving them courage. "A resolution to boycott certain papers that were thought to incline too much to the side of the operators was withdrawn as it savored too much of conspiracy to suit the cooler heads present. A motion was then made and carried to denounce these gazettes, and to demand the name of a Scottdale correspondent to the *Labor Tribune*, who claimed that the majority of the strikers were in favor of returning to work."[21]

Then the *Journal* article turned to the events at Jimtown, just outside the Morgan Valley. The mine there was one of the oldest in the region and was now owned by Schoonmaker. Only sixteen men, nine of them Hungarians, were still working the Friday before when three hundred armed miners believed to be from the Trotter, Wheeler, and Leisenring mines attacked. The workers were pulling coke from the ovens before it was completely burned up. The mob smashed the barrows and broke their tools, and then attacked the men, especially Michael Biasco, a longtime miner who refused to join the union. The *Journal* continued to report that they broke both of his arms and "beat him into insensibility." Also beaten were Michael Truca, Bon Jac [Andrew Benjoe], John Helm, Andrew Walker [yard boss at Sterling], and William Laxsell [farm boss]. Once done there, the mob intended to visit another mine nearby, but the workers fled before they got there. The action was blamed on the unions who had met the day before.

J.M. Schoonmaker was livid. Still on the front page, the *Journal* reported him saying:

> Immediately on hearing of the injury to our workmen instructions were sent to have every possible care taken of them at our expense. Neither time nor expense will be spared to arrest and convict all the parties to the outrage. The injured men were all at work of their own free will, no effort having been made to resume work at the mines. Nearly all the men were old and reliable employes and never were members of either labor organization. The feeling against the outrage at Jimtown is intensified from the close relations of these men to their fellow workmen, none of whom, it is believed, were engaged in the assault, and who are loud in their denunciation of the outrage. This procedure will change the whole course of action on the part of the operators, who now have nothing to expect but violations of contracts on the part of the labor organizations and outrages on the part of their members, and we will make immediate preparations to replace them with other laborers.

The chief of the Coal and Iron Police, named William Kelley, was brought onto the case. Within a day or two he had some of the names. Twenty to twenty-five men were named, including a "prominent member of the Amalgamated Association." It was John McSloy of Trotter, and he was immediately arrested. Then Rainey granted the advance, and his Fort Hill and Moyer works would soon be back at work.

By week four of the strike, the *Journal* reported the annual convention of the Amalgamated was held in Scottdale with local and national dignitaries and thousands of men present. They appointed solicitors throughout the regions, including in West Virginia and Maryland. Among their tasks was acquiring help and provisions for the miners.

By the end of May, hearings began related to the Jimtown affair. John McSloy was called before Justice Lytle and proclaimed his innocence. The courtroom was filled with company, union, and mine men. McSloy was held over for trial, bonded by Barney Logan of Connellsville, and released. Additional men, including two young boys, were also held for court. They included: William Bellstein of the Association board, Joseph Neuner, Thomas Price, John Cook, Martin McDonnell, Julius Lydon, Karl Komm, Mike Magyar, Frank Basco, Viq John, and Jim Balogh.[22]

Then the focus turned back to W.J. Rainey. The syndicate believed he was harming all the operators by allowing the advance and having his men start work. Col. Schoonmaker stated:

> Mr. Rainey is wildcatting the market. He can afford to pay the advanced wages for the reason that he is receiving a big price for his coke. There are firms that only use about two cars of coke a month. They can afford to pay $5 a ton for it. There are a great many firms like this, and Rainey can make money. If the strike is lost, and the old wages are paid, he can easily drop the wages of his men and resume his old trade. Now he is getting all the business. If the syndicate pays the advance he can keep on as usual. He can't lose anything, and while the operators are idle he is making money. There is nothing to present the members of the syndicate from starting their works, except honor. I could start up to-day if I desire, but I would be breaking faith with the other members of the syndicate.[23]

Soon it was June, and the strike was still raging. The operators wanted the men back at work. Most of the men wanted to be back at work. The unions were still vying for position and varying in their messages from week to week, which prolonged everything.[24] Both unions met on a Saturday. The Amalgamated was against the report by the national Knights that called the strike illegal; the local Knights told them to "keep their hands off," and made another resolution to oppose the return to work. They went against the national wishes. Mullen of the Amalgamated responded. And on it went. All they were doing was delaying, creating confusion, dividing the miners, and prolonging the strike.[25]

Enter Carnegie

Carnegie Intervened: Newspapers Went Wild

Local Weekly Papers Filled Full Pages:
"Carnegie's Cablegram," *Mt. Pleasant Journal*, June 14
"A Break in the Strike," *Weekly Courier*, June 17
"The H.C. Frick Coke Co Conceded the Demands," *Scottdale Independent*, June 17

Regional Papers Too:
"The Strike Broken," *Pittsburgh Dispatch*, June 11
"The Cokers Win," *Pittsburgh Post*, June 11
"Big Point for Cokers," *Pittsburgh Times*, June 11
"The Coke Strike: Steel Makers Cause a Change," *Commercial Telegraph*, June 11
"Coke Men Crushed," *Penny Press*, June 11.

In mid-June, Andrew Carnegie, partner of Henry Clay Frick, stepped into the coal and coke strike and created more chaos. This chaos was deadlier and more far-reaching than anything that had come before. As related in an earlier chapter, Frick had joined his H.C. Frick Coke Company to the Carnegie, Phipps & Co. of Andrew Carnegie. By 1886–7 Frick's partners E.M. and Walter Ferguson sold their shares in the H.C. Frick Coke Company and Carnegie bought most of them. That made Carnegie the controlling partner of the H.C. Frick Coke Company. He had done to Frick what Frick had done to some of the coal operators in the Connellsville district.[26]

The reason Carnegie wooed Frick is obvious. Carnegie wanted a guaranteed stream of coke for his steel mills. By investing in a coke company, he made this arrangement possible. Frick wanted a solid customer for his coke, so the deal was perfect for him too. Frick's

Southwest Coal and Coke Company was created with similar ideas in mind. They sold exclusively to another Frick investment, the Illinois Steel Company; they were not linked to the H.C. Frick Coke Company, and were therefore out of the hands of Carnegie.

For Frick, Carnegie's takeover was a near death blow. He had lost control of the company he had nurtured since 1871, carefully building it and the region into a national powerhouse. Now he had to answer to someone else.

Despite the dramas of the unions, the strike was nearing an end. The syndicate would soon have the men returning to work. The two unions were squabbling to see which of them would call an end to the strike. But Carnegie would not wait. He wanted his coke and he wanted it at a price that was to his advantage. He was also adamantly against unions, didn't want any in his steel mills, and obviously not in his coke company either.

The newspapers would not report events until mid–June, but on May 13, Henry Clay Frick tendered his resignation as president of the H.C. Frick Coke Company, his own company. The letter was handwritten and addressed to Henry Phipps, Jr., a Carnegie partner, and John Walker, an industrialist and lifelong friend who would support Frick against Carnegie:

> I cannot honorably carry out your policy in regard to this company and beg to tender my resignation as President.
> Having temporized with our employes and made concession after concession to satisfy them and largely in your interest, and against the interest and judgment of all other coke producers, and finally prevailing on them to agree to arbitration and decision having been rendered in our favor, I think that cost what it may we should abide by it, and not start our works until our employes resume work at the old wages, but in as much as you have large interests depending on our works being operated I do not feel like standing in the way of you managing the property as your judgment and interests dictate.
>
> Very respectfully,
> H.C. Frick

Evidently things festered for some time. Finally, Carnegie issued his decree. On June 7, Frick dictated another resignation, this one accepted and final:

> To the Board of Directors of the H.C. Frick Coke Company
> Gentlemen:
> I beg to resign as President of this Company to take effect at once; and would ask that the letters herewith, addressed to Messrs. Henry Phipps, Jr., John Walker, et al. dated May 13rd [sic] 1887 and this date be spread upon the minutes.
>
> Respectfully,
> H.C. Frick

Frick accompanied his resignation with a letter explaining his decision:

> But I accompany it with this my serious protest against the course you propose to take regarding the pending strike. I am satisfied that it must occasion heavy loss to the Coke Company. Besides the loss occasioned by granting the men's present unreasonable demands, it will only lead to still more unreasonable demands in the near future. The loss to the Coke Company may be far more than made up. So far as you are concerned, by gains in your Steel interests, but I object to so manifest a prostitution of the Coke Company's interests in order to promote your steel interests. Whilst a majority of the stock entitles you to control, I deny that it confers the right to manage so as to benefit your interests in other concerns at the loss and injury of the Coke company in which I am interested.
>
> Very respectfully yours,
> H.C. Frick[27]

A cable was sent from Scotland by Andrew Carnegie to General Superintendent Lynch at the H.C. Frick Coke Company. Lynch had to honor Carnegie's wish as Carnegie was the controlling partner. These must have been very trying times for the men who built the Frick company.

As shown in the illustration above, the newspapers went wild. That was just the first day. National papers too spoke out. These events were so astounding that national labor magazines had something to say, and it wasn't in Carnegie's favor. In the June 1887 issue, the *American Manufacturer* wrote:

> The action of the H.C. Frick Coke company in agreeing to pay the advance demanded by the men, coming at the moment it did, was exceedingly unfortunate. There is no question but that the men were on the point of resuming work under the arbitrator's award. The Executive Committee of the Knights of Labor had advocated it, the leaders of both unions were urging it, and it was but a question of time, and a very short time at that—possibly of hours and not of days—when the strike would have been ended…. It also looks as if the effect of this action would be, in the long run, injurious to the men. If it results in the disruption of the syndicate and a return to the conditions that existed before its formation, viz. unrestricted competition and ruinous prices, the men would be compelled to accept rates of wages much below those ruling before the strike….[28]

In the July edition of the same magazine there was more:

> The great strike in the Connellsville coke region is about entering upon its third month. At the present writing some 3500 out of 12,500 coke ovens in the region are in operation most of them at the 12.5 per cent advance demanded by the workers at the beginning of the strike. In this number are included what may now be called the Carnegie ovens of the H.C. Frick Coke company, but none of the ovens controlled by Mr. Frick personally, he still standing with the members of the syndicate in favor of the umpire's award and against granting the advance….
>
> This has been in many respects a most notable strike, and furnishes opportunity to study certain phases of the labor question that are rarely brought together in the same strike. To begin with, there is the effect of the antagonism and the struggle for supremacy of two opposing labor unions. It is nothing unusual for strikes to be precipitated and continued as the result of the personal ambition of opposing labor leaders, but it has been only very recently, in this country at least, that the effect of a struggle for supremacy on the part of two labor organizations in the same industry and interested in the settlement of the same question could be studied. It is clearly evident from a study of the Connellsville coke strike that while there may be some apparent advantage both to manufacturers and to workmen in rival unions in the same industry and at the same place, yet the effect upon both of such unions is injurious and ultimately disastrous.
>
> A second circumstance that is notable in this strike is the bad faith on the part of the unions…. In this connection is a third circumstance that is notable, and that is the impotency of the General Executive Board of the K. of L. to compel obedience to its orders…. A fourth interesting circumstance in connection with the strike is the slight effect the defection of the member of the syndicate operating the largest number of ovens had upon the remaining members of the syndicate and the other coke operators who had refused to pay the demand….
>
> The coke strikers have torn down better than they knew. They have disrupted the coke syndicate, the very agent that kept up prices and wages. If the syndicate should go to pieces entirely, who can tell how low prices and wages will fall within a very short time.[29]

The importance of what happened here cannot be denied. From mid–June to early July, everyone was trying to find the balance once again. It was one failure after another. The miners struck and refused to go to work.

Call in the Pinkertons

On July 7, the Pinkerton Detective Agency arrived in the Connellsville region. The Pinkertons had been contacted much earlier when the operators applied to Governor James

Beaver to send one hundred men to keep the peace in the coke region. The governor—who, as noted before, did not want the state to get involved in industrial matters—kept it under consideration and sent Adj. Gen. Hastings to assess the situation. He agreed that help was needed. After the debacle of Carnegie, the operators called in the Pinkertons. They believed they needed the Pinkertons to protect their property. About 150 arrived (some papers said 160). "They went up to the region in a special car on the Pittsburgh, Virginia and Charleston railway, Redstone branch, and in a baggage-car attached to the special were a number of boxes containing ammunition and arms. One smaller box contained handcuffs."[30] They were sworn in as Coal and Iron Police and sent to Leisenring. They wore uniforms and carried Winchester rifles. They were commanded by Captain Linden. The operators alleged that they did not ask for the Pinkertons, but that they had been requested by Sheriff Miller of Fayette County.[31]

The operators decided to break the strike by calling in new workers. Notices were posted around the region:

> From McClure & Co
> NOTICE
> TO ALL EMPLOYEES!
> Work will be resumed at these works on Wednesday morning July 6th at the same wages as paid before the present strike.
> Our old employees will be given the preference.
>
> Donneley(?) & Dillinger
> J P Brennen Genl. Supt.[32]

Miners were afraid they would soon be evicted. Trying to get the men back to work was difficult. Alice, Morewood, and Hazlett refused to go to work. At Leisenring only thirteen men were working, and that included the superintendent, the bosses, and the store clerks.[33]

The role of the Pinkerton was explained in the *Journal*:

> It is understood that these men have been sworn in as special officers, whose duty it is to do nothing but keep the peace and afford protection to men who want to work. They are not to aid in any other way in starting up the mines and ovens, but it can be asserted as fact that they are all selected men who have faced death many times before and are as well drilled to their duty as regulars in the army. They never fire to scare, and never fire till commanded; but once they receive the command they shoot to kill.[34]

Not everyone saw the Pinkertons in that light. Master Workman Powderly of the national headquarters of the Knights, an Irishman, came from Eastern Pennsylvania, where he was mayor of Scranton for some time. He became a member of the Knights of Labor in 1874, becoming Grand Master Workman in 1879.[35] He stated:

> The men who make up the Pinkerton army are gathered in from the brothels, gambling dens and slums of our large cities, composed of creatures who are outcasts from decent society. Their introduction for the purpose of settling disputes through force of arms is an insult to society everywhere. The employer of labor who calls to his aid a body of hired assassins, and the Pinkerton Thugs can be called by no more appropriate name, must have a poor estimate of his own abilities and intelligence when it lets such delicate and important work as the regulation of his business with his employees out to a human brute.[36]

From comments like these, the reputation of the Pinkerton Agency among the miners and steelworkers began to grow. Was it earned? In the Golden Age, probably not. Unraveling truth under these circumstances is not easy.

Once the Pinkertons arrived, the Amalgamated met and resolved to go back to work.

They visited various mine communities. The West Leisenring meeting was in the woods. They refused to return to work. Another meeting was near West Overton with men from Morewood, Alice, Bessemer and other works around Mount Pleasant. They, as probably all of the meetings, were addressed in various languages. At the Mount Pleasant meeting, Michael O'Neil of Bridgeport spoke in English; Joseph Dungler in Bohemian; Michael Sheiebell in Slavic. The Knights did the same. They, too, were rejected "To the bitter end." Those who did get back to work were the Leisenrings, Redstone, Fairchance, Oliphant, Donnelly, Mayfield, Jimtown and a few others in the Morgan Valley.[37]

By July 22 the Knights declared the strike over and ordered the men back to work.[38] Then more mines went back to work. On July 29 the *Scottdale Independent* reported that J.R. Stauffer and Dexter would start on Monday. West Overton would not start. McClure and Company works were in full operation with original miners. At Alice, Morewood, and Standard no discrimination was enacted against the employees, and all returned to work. Frick mines were operating on the advance, as were the mines of Rainey. By the end of July, the strike was over.[39]

The Outcome

When the men went back to work, the syndicate was in shambles, the unions were feuding, there was no scale yet, and only a part of the Pinkertons were gone. These issues went on for the rest of the year. Things remained in chaos. Each operator was trying to get the best advantage. Charles Armstrong's Westmoreland Coal and Coke Company was out to stop all the chaos. They wanted their men to sign an ironclad agreement. It was intense. First and foremost, the miners had to agree that there would be no union or combination of unions. In addition, the miners must perform a full day's work; would be suspended for holding meetings; would not deal with leagues or organizations; would not make any grievances to mine bosses; if they left work, they would get all arrears pay; no one would be permitted to interfere with hiring or discharging or disciplining; no one could work in their place them (such as women); payday would be once a month; everything must be kept clean and in good order; if a miner left for no reason, he would not be paid.[40] Charles Armstrong was continuing his harsh demands noted in the Buena Vista Affair of the 1870s.

The Scale

The scale continued to be discussed. The sliding scale was a process that began in England back in the 1840s. The concept was that a wage earner should earn a salary based on the going rate of the product on the market. If the market was good, the wages would rise with the price of the product on the market, and if the market was sluggish, the wages would fall as the product price fell. The concept had a lot of problems, and the sliding scale vanished after World War II.[41]

On August 19, 1887, the Frick company signed a scale with its workers. It was for a fixed market amount and would be a minimum scale. The agreement also stated that the company could employ anyone they wanted; the men were forbidden to strike unless there was a six-day notice; the men had to furnish their own oil and attend to their lamps themselves; and they would be paid semi-monthly.[42]

In early September the syndicate and the producers also offered a scale.[43] It was described in detail in all the local papers and brought on the usual meetings and discussions. What was left of the syndicate gave the workers a scale to discuss at a meeting with the syndicate, producers, Knights, and Amalgamated. They rejected it and asked for a scale similar to the one the Frick company accepted.[44] A group took the scale to Philadelphia and Master Workman Powderly. No results there, either.[45]

As late as December there was no scale and no syndicate. Of the latter, efforts were being made at meeting with the producers. A lot of talking and manipulating were detailed in the local papers, but no progress.[46]

Strike of 1889

In 1889 there was yet another strike. Again, the matter was wages, a permanent sliding scale, and an advance. The long and agonizing road to unionization and stability continued. The Huns took center stage again and violence continued. It had been fourteen years since the first strike in 1875.

The H.C. Frick Coke Company renewed its scale until January of 1890. Individual mines went out on strike for various reasons: Mammoth went out; Schoonmaker laid off men in some of its works; McClure and Frick's Southwest did the same. These were mines where the Amalgamated was in the majority. The Knights brought their men back to work. The outcome was that the men at Standard not only lost four days' wages, but the company forced them to repay "50 cents each, or $485, for coke that was destroyed by being left in the ovens when the strike began."[47]

Throughout March the battle continued. The Knights ordered a strike. The unions continued to fight. At the end of March, the workers were to receive yet another reduction in wages. The scale was discussed again. The syndicate was still stressed from Carnegie's blow. The H.C. Frick Coke Company was no longer a member of the syndicate. The operators, unions, and miners were struggling for a sliding scale.

By early August, the strike had spread throughout the district, including north far into Westmoreland County. Miners who had walked out were from Buckeye, Charlotte, Clinton, Central, Davidson, Dexter, Eagle, Foundry, Henry Clay, Frick, Home, Lemont, Leith, Morgan, Stewart, Summit, Tip Top, Valley, Uniondale, White, Youngstown, Morrell, and Wheeler.[48] A few days later, Standard, Morewood, Alice and Tarrs joined them. When a few of the men at Morewood refused to strike, they were attacked. The *Journal* continued:

> There were about two hundred men in the crowd which visited Morewood, although it is said no employes of the Southwest company were with them. They started from the Central works very early in the morning and marched, by way of Tarrs, to Donnelly and Mayfield. Thence they went to Union and back to Stonerville and then across the hill to Alice, where men, many of them against their will, were compelled to join in the procession that moved across old "Fort Defiance" to Morewood, passing down by the Hungarian Row to the Pennsylvania track and moving up along it to the Stonerville road. Here they were addressed by one of their number and before day they dispersed.

Men from Alice and Morewood, four hundred in number, paraded through Mount Pleasant. Among them the *Journal* named Steve Stannix, who had been deeply involved in the strike of 1886.

By mid-August it looked as if the strike was coming to an end. Once again, as in 1887, an event turned everything around. In 1887 it was Carnegie; in this instance, the Huns went on a raid. Calling them "The Horrible Huns," the *Weekly Courier* reported that they raided seven coke plants before they stopped their rampage.

Once again it started at Morewood, now called Southwest No. 1. It all started with a lie. An interpreter told the Hungarians at Morewood that the operators were offering bribes to get the men back to work. They had to stop the men from going back to work. First stop, as usual, was Alice, or Southwest No. 2. The miners at Alice were at work because they had been notified that the advance had been granted. Six hundred strong, the rioters began their carnage. Coal cars were pushed down Fort Defiance, larry cars were thrown over and destroyed, wheelbarrows broken, oven fronts smashed, houses stoned, windows broken, and occupants of the houses were forced to run away. J.M. Dayton, Worthy Foreman of the District Assembly No. 11 of the Knights of Labor, tried to stop the slaughter, but he was heartlessly beaten.

The Huns marched on to Bessemer:

> After doing all possible damage at Alice the mob, armed with clubs, coke forks, revolvers, etc., marched to Bessemer, two miles distant where they continued their fiendish work only to a greater extent. Here the officials were panic stricken and men, women and children fled for their lives. The men then raided the house of a miner named Gilhooly, an old man of 80 years of age, and brutally assaulted him and insulted and terrified his daughters, who tried to defend him. Gilhooly was beaten because one of the bosses had taken refuge in his house. The old man's injuries are such that he will hardly recover. His daughter Mrs. Farley, who is in a delicate condition, was kicked out in the middle of the road when she attempted to protect her father. The mob then attacked a young man named Thomas Love and beat him unmercifully, breaking his right arm above the elbow and otherwise injuring him. The company store was then attacked, the windows broken, goods carried out and the mob was about to set fire to it when Secretary Watchorn and James Keegan, who had received word of the riot at this place, drove into the midst of the crowd in a buggy.[49]

Watchorn mounted on a buggy and told the men to stop and put down their weapons before he spoke. He told them the scale had been signed, and instead of receiving 88 cents they would be receiving a dollar.

That stopped the terror at Morewood and Alice, but throughout the region, riots were in action. Coalbrook of McClure was at work under the advance, and according to the *Courier*, Huns from Moyer came after them:

> The Huns caught Joseph Harshman, a drawer, and beat him in a terrible manner and dragged him over the hills to Morgan in an insensible condition. Here others joined the Huns, and the mob dragged Harshman back to Moyer, leaving him at his own door. Harshman's life was despaired of for a time, but he is now much better and will recover. Ever since the strike was inaugurated deputies have been guarding the Coalbrook ovens. When the assault upon Harshman was committed, the guards, Squire A.C. Duncan, Burgess of Dunbar, and Constable Scott Franks of the same place, issued warrants for the arrest of fifteen of the assailants, and on Saturday morning, with the assistance of Constable William Shrum of New Haven, went to Moyer to make the arrests.
>
> The officers arrested three of the Huns and were proceeding to the office of Squire A.S. Murphy at Pennsville with the prisoners, when, at a short distance below W.J. Rainey's store, a mob of 75 Huns attached the officers to rescue their comrades. Two of the officers escaped unhurt, Franks by running and Shrum by hiding in a culvert under the railroad. Duncan had no time to get away before the Huns were upon him. He was struck in the face several times with stones and his leg bruised by being struck with a club, but he was not seriously hurt. Sheriff Miller was telegraphed for, and went to the scene of disorder at once, but discovered that without a posse he could do nothing. Returning to Uniontown he deputized about twenty-five men to assist him. This number was reinforced at Connellsville, New Haven and Moyer, making in all a force of about 75 men. When Moyer was reached not a Hun was in sight. The sheriff was informed that two of the rioters were concealed in the hollow. These were arrested and put under guard in Squire Murphy's office. Two more were arrested on the hill. In the

meantime part of the posse, led by Constable Frank Campbell of Connellsville, were on the way to Morgan Station, where, it was reported the main body of the Huns were stationed. About halfway between Moyer and Morgan the officers discovered the Huns hiding behind a stone fence. They were armed with clubs, knives and revolvers. A shot was fired to warn the remainder of the posse, and the Huns, thinking the shot was aimed at them, returned the fire, then broke and ran. More shots were exchanged, and when the other officers came up, the posse went on to Morgan in hot pursuit of the Huns. When they Huns reached Morgan they took refuge in the "soup-house."

Sheriff Miller tried to get the Huns to surrender. Shots were fired. Officers entered the soup house. They captured 21 of the rioters. As noted, they were "hidden in every conceivable place: some under the beds and in cupboards, and two were found in a chimney." They were taken to the railroad and sent to Uniontown. There, if there had not been strong guards, more trouble would have erupted. In all the *Courier* listed twenty-three as arrested: Steve Piteur, John Woshuck, John Fairdull, Andy Shosky, John Struckey, Mike Muscovit, Stany Smith, Mike Mutchko, Joe Prebula, John Tomosko, Steve Lesko, John Patroski, John Smithley, Peter Mencovish, Mike Pigots, John Marenko, Vint Wetherell, Frank Incox, Jo Gregor, Mike Eastman, Steve Commer, John Yusco, and Andy Musco.

Then the rioting moved to central Westmoreland County. Two hundred Hungarians from Calumet joined 230 or 250 more from Mammoth and they descended on United. They moved on to Hecla.

More armed men arrived the following Monday. Captain William Kelley, chief of the Coal and Iron Police, was sent to guard Southwest No. 1. On Wednesday, 556 more officers were sworn in at Mount Pleasant. The violence was coming to an end and the other miners were swift to condemn the Huns and their violence. The men at Standard held a meeting and condemned the actions of the Huns at Alice and Bessemer. All was according to the same *Courier* article called "The Horrible Huns" of August 16.

It is hard to imagine that such events took place in the peaceful region of today. It is unfathomable that the people of the region and of southwestern Pennsylvania know very little of the details of what transpired in their region during the emergence of coal and coke. Everyone was terrorized, from children to grandparents. Everyone feared they would be next, or a loved one would be assaulted. There are no markers to tell of the event. There are few books that give the details and tell of the people.

The Poor Huns

The next week the *Weekly Courier* showed some sympathy for the Huns:

The reports of the Hungarian terrorization of different parts of the coke region are perhaps a little exaggerated, but they are in the main true enough to call for grave consideration. The lawless raids of this foreign element, call it by what name you please, is fast creating an antipathy for all such emigrants that might all too soon end in the bloody race war predicted. This conclusion may seem far-fetched, but it is based upon information that appears to be terribly reliable.

So far as our observation goes, the Hun is a quiet and peaceable citizen when in a state of sobriety and prosperity; but bad times and bad whisky made a wild demon of him, especially when he is in a crowd. The strike is practically settled now, and an early repetition of his disorders is not at all likely. The raids of last week, according to the very plausible explanation offered by an operator, were not, as is generally supposed, lacking in motive, purely wanton and malicious; on the contrary, they were directed against men whom they conceived had enveigled [sic] them into a strike against their will and then basely deserted them.

The popular idea that the remedy for the situation lies in some vague legislative cure-all is altogether erroneous. The remedy lies in the enforcing the laws that now exist. The Huns must be taught that the Law is not a myth, and that its infraction will be followed by swift and sure punishment. Coke operators should not be compelled to hire Pinkerton detectives to protect their property from incendiarism and pillage and their employes from assault and perhaps murder. Under the plain compact of society the government is bound to do this; and if the local government did its duty in this behalf the moral effect would be most salutary. The great body of taxpayers, who now look upon such outrages with mere passing disapproval, would be aroused to greater activity in maintaining peace and order if they saw the cost of doing it come right out of their own pockets.[50]

The violence in the Connellsville coke region had been going on for well over a decade. Ten-plus years of fear, of unrest, of shopkeepers guarding their property, of women afraid to walk the streets, of guns, and clubs, and sticks and stones. And there were anarchists. The *Journal* reported that during the Hun riots, anarchists took part, especially to the north in Westmoreland County. The ringleaders were named as Jacob Otto and Christ Body, both former miners who had been discharged. The damage these voices inflicted on the immigrants would not heal in a hundred years. The false accusations were similar to the those inflicted on Henry Clay Frick.

Getting Out and Consolidating

By the end of August, some of the operators seem to have had enough of all the drama. Moore and Schoonmaker both sold their operations to Frick. The *Mount Pleasant Journal* called it "The Biggest Sale in the History of the Region."[51] The J.W. Moore & Co., never a part of the syndicate, owned the Mammoth Mine with 509 ovens, and the Wynn Mine with 70 ovens. Schoonmaker owned four plants: Alice, Redstone, Jimtown, and Sterling, with a combined 1,504 ovens. The *Journal* felt that Carnegie had his hands in the deal.

The *Weekly Courier* called Frick "The Great Gobbler," and stated that he had finally cornered the coke business. It also called Frick the "Napoleon of Cokedom." It provided a statement by the Schoonmakers that announced the sale:

> We beg to announce that we have sold the entire property of this company to the H.C. Frick Coke Company. No change will occur in the management or business of the company; and in all respects its affairs will be conducted in the future as in the past.
>
> We ask our friends and the trade a continuance to the new owners in the future of the support that have been so generously extended us in the past.[52]

The Schoonmakers in the coke business consisted of Colonel J.M. Schoonmaker, the owner of the J.M. Schoonmaker Coke Company; S.L. Schoonmaker, secretary and treasurer of the same; and J.S. Schoonmaker, who became general manager of Frick's Southwest Coal and Coke Company. What the two newspapers do not answer is how the Schoonmaker holdings remained separate from the H.C. Frick Coke Company. It seems logical that Frick wanted to keep the new mines out of Carnegie's control. It must be noted that although Schoonmaker sold his properties, during the future strike of 1891, a Schoonmaker continued to participate in discussions with unions. The only major Frick competitors remaining in the region were McClure and Rainey.

Six

Strike of 1891

Kenneth Warren, in *Wealth, Waste, and Alienation: Growth and Decline in the Connellsville Coke Industry*, stated: "The 1891 conflict highlighted the intensity of violence that could occur even in this country district. In fact, it achieved an intensity as great as that of the Homestead strike of the following year without receiving anywhere near a comparable stature in the collective memory of working people or the same prominence in labor history."[1]

In 1890 the United Mine Workers became a player not only in the Connellsville region and Pennsylvania, but in West Virginia, Ohio, and beyond. The industry continued to grow and expand. By 1891 the latest agreement between the miners and the operators was due to expire, and miners were ready to strike again. The industry was not working in a vacuum. When the mines closed, so too did the industries dependent upon them. The local railroads were being built mainly to transport coal and coke out of the region to destinations around the United States. The railroad workers were already on strike in 1891, asking for higher wages and an 8-hour day.

This strike was huge. The men wanted a scale for weighing on the tipples, a sliding scale for wages, an 8-hour day, and a 15 percent wage increase.[2] On January 4, the miners and the owners met in conference. Attending for the operators were Lynch, Brennan, and J.S. Schoonmaker (for Frick), McClure and J.M. Schoonmaker for their companies, and Rae, Kerfoot, and Parker for the workers. (J.M. Schoonmaker had sold his company to Frick a few years before, but obviously still had a voice.) They adjourned without settling anything.

The annual convention of the United Mine Workers met in Scottdale the next week with seventy-five delegates in attendance. Present from the national organization were Robert Watchorn, the secretary, and R. McBryde of the General Executive Board.[3] They held elections, and the current Master Workman Kerfoot was replaced by Peter Wise; C.M. Parker became District Secretary; and Executive Board members were James McBride, John McNulty, Mike Disman, James McGuire, W.T. Humphries, James Crow, H.L. Ball, and William Hay. Kerfoot would remain to assist Wise in dealing with the operators. Then the men turned to the problem at hand: "It was decided to serve a notice on the operators this week that they must meet them by February 2, to confer on the wage differences else a strike will be declared on February 10, to involve the whole region."[4]

They met on February 2, again reaching no agreement, but things looked hopeful.[5] The miners offered yet another proposal to work at the old rates until March 1 while negotiating. It was rejected. The smaller operators leaned toward agreeing to it. Since the operators seemed divided, the miners resolved to offer no special considerations to any operators. That included the Rainey works, whose miners were not on strike and were non-union members. The H.C. Frick Coke Company posted a notice at all of its mines for the men: "As the present wage scale will expire on Tuesday, the 10th day of February, and no arrangement for regulation of wages after that date has been made with our representatives, we have decided to draw out the ovens on Monday and Tuesday next and remain idle until some arrangement for regulation of wages is made. This should not be considered as a lock out nor a strike—merely a suspension of work pending the adjustment of wages; and we want it distinctly understood that we will be ready at all times in the future, as in the past, to take up the wage question with you or your representatives."[6]

In the same edition of the *Journal*, an editorial showed the paper's position: "The present disagreement between coke operators and their employes on the question of wages is called a simple suspension of operations, but unless THE JOURNAL is greatly mistaken, both sides are determined in the stand each has taken and a long strike must be expected. The Connellsville region's system has, however, been out of fix for some time and needs a dose of medicine, which the sooner taken will the sooner restore the patient to its wonted healthy condition."[7]

Strike Begins

On February 10 the strike was called, and 10–13,000 miners were affected. This is an astounding number of men in a mainly rural area of small towns and hamlets and attests to the growth of the industry in the past decades. The Frick company simply closed. Rainey kept his regional mines open. It became important that the non-union Rainey miners join the strikers. The United Mine Workers sent the miners to Dawson to Rainey's Fort Hill and Paul works to draw the men out. This was definitely a union maneuver. On February 23, newspapers reported that over 4,000 armed Hungarian, Slav, Italian, German, and American miners descended on Dawson at Rainey's Paul Mine. The Paul miners ran. The Pinkertons did nothing except guard the facility, as was their job. The invaders were to pitch tents and remain at Paul until the Rainey men came out.[8] They still resisted. It must be pointed out that the small hamlet of Dawson had a population of roughly 600. An invasion of 4,000 was terrifying.

The next meeting of the miners was at Scottdale on March 2. Most of the operators were there: Lynch for Frick, J.M. Schoonmaker, Ramsay, Hostetter, Stauffer, and Overholt. Missing were Rainey and Brennen of McClure. No progress was made.[9] The union now renamed the suspension as a strike. Yet another invasion of the Paul and Fort Hill mines took place. The sheriff called for help, but by the time Sheriff McCormick arrived, things had calmed down. Strikers rented a house in the area, which meant they were not going away. Warrants were issued against strike leaders, including John Fisher and Lawrence Kline from Leisenring No. 2 and Harry Dellegati from Nellie. Rainey filed suit too, this time in Pittsburgh against John McSloy, John McBryde, Peter Wise, C.M. Parker, Mike Disman, R.D. Kerfoot, Frank DeHaven, and J.B. Rae, all officers of the United Mine Workers.[10]

Rainey's injunctions were upheld by the court and the union men were forbidden to gather near any of his properties or interfere with his works or his men. Other operators would soon follow his lead.

The Sliding Scale Offered

During every strike, the miners would eventually march through Mount Pleasant. At the end of March, 1,000 men did it again. They issued a resolution: "Resolved, that we, the workingmen assembled, will stand out until our demands are granted, as they are just. All we ask is our share of the profits which we produce."[11]

A major event in the strike came on March 25 when the United Mine Workers declared they could hold out until August. The McClure Coke Company, which Frick would eventually buy out, took action, posting a notice at their plants that they would "resume immediately on a three-year sliding scale" that began with a 7 percent reduction in current wages. Once coke prices rose on the market to $2.15, the former rate would be restored.[12] The Frick company created their own scale and told the men to come back to work. It was posted at all Frick plants except Kyle, Wynn, Oliphant, Eagle, Foundry, Tip Top, Valley, and Mammoth. No explanation has been found for the exceptions.[13]

The strikers met at the Grand Opera House. Master Workman Wise and men of the United Mine Workers presented the offer to the men, who "unanimously adopted a resolution which declared that the scale presented by the operators was an insult to labor, that it was preposterous and that they would remain out a whole year before they would accept such terms."[14] The meeting was repeated at Fairchance, Scottdale, Uniontown, Connellsville and Dawson. Some men began slowly reporting to work. In the Morgan Valley, the return appeared to be much slower than elsewhere: Broadford, Morgan, and Valley, zero returns; White, only two men went back to work.[15] Most of the miners remained firm. The operators began preparing for violence.

From Morewood to Jimtown Violence Erupts

Morewood was firing up to begin work. The managers at Morewood began making preparations: they clogged the entrances near A shaft, filled the railroad tracks with empty cars, and asked Sheriff Clawson for help. He swore in twenty men as deputies. The next move created a great deal of anxiety among the miners. They heard that "Company E, of the Pennsylvania National Guard, was to be called into service by the sheriff." Indeed, Captain Loar did look into the matter, and twenty-one members of the local National Guard had been sworn in in Greensburg. "Labor officials were much wrought up over the move, ... telegraphing Governor [Robert] Patterson [sic; Pattison] to prevent the taking of state arms and equipment from the armory."[16] It must be remembered that the state did not want the Guard to be embroiled in industrial matters. As expected, the strikers marched to Morewood, as reported in the same *Journal* article:

> Shortly after midnight the Standard cornet band made a round of that plant and in the course of an hour was at the head of a procession of some three hundred men who marched by North Diamond [819], Main [31], Eagle, West Washington and South Quarry streets [in Mount Pleasant] to the Morewood works [981], where they arrived shortly after 2 o'clock, and were joined by 1,000 or more men from Bessemer, Alice, Tarrs, and Central. One of the worse features of the whole affair was the shock it occasioned to General Manager Ramsay's invalid wife. The excitement rendered the lady unconscious and her condition is still alarming....
>
> The deputies on guard about the plant were powerless as they had strict orders from the sheriff not to shoot. The strikers were soon in possession and they celebrated their easily won victory by tearing to pieces the new fence about the store. The larry tracks leading from A shaft to the ovens were torn up, fronts of burning ovens knocked in and a lot of wheelbarrows burned. The building in which the larries are kept was riddled with stones and as a parting defiance the rioters smashed in some of the store windows with stones. The mob held full sway for almost two hours.

The sheer numbers of miners were alarming. As they were gathering, Ramsey, Clawson, and the deputies went to Standard, where Josef Yenrack hit Ramsey in the nose, drawing blood. Ramsey held him until deputies arrested him and took him to Greensburg. Clawson telegraphed Governor Pattison for help. It was refused. Master Workman Wise wrote to the operators: "You ask honest workingmen to dig and load a ton of coal for less than you would pay a common tramp for shoveling a ton of coal into your cellar, and then ask them to suffer a reduction of 10 per cent, and because of their refusal every effort is being made to turn public opinion against them. We are quite willing that an impartial public, with those facts before it, shall be judge between us."[17] That's where things stood.

Around the District

Morewood dominated the news. But the violence was everywhere. The last days of March, 300 men marched on Jimtown, near Dawson, to stop workers and bring them out on strike. Warned of the impending danger, Superintendent Rosser and six deputies were waiting. Although an attack took place, the mob left. At the same time, Hungarian women attacked the Leith mine. The *Weekly Courier* claimed they were "inflamed by liquor and encouraged by the men, who stood discreetly behind." They attacked with yells and stones. "Superintendent Whyel and Bookkeeper Taylor, who were at breakfast, hearing the noise ran out, and Whyel drew a revolver [and] frighten back the women. But on they come [sic]. Yard Boss O'Connell was struck in the face with a piece of coke. Pit Boss Hooper received a blow on the head with an iron bar. A coke drawer named Stuch had his head cut by a piece of flying coke. The men seeing that resistance was useless dropped their tools and fled."[18] The women came again the next day. This time the men came too. They were met by officers Wilson Collins, Chick [sic] and General Manager Thomas Lynch, Harry Whyel and Yard Boss O'Connell. They could not hold the gigantic group. "Stones, coke coal clubs [sic] and everything they could lay their hands upon were used to put the men to flight.... General Manager Lynch advised the men working to withdraw which they did in good order. Deputy Collins captured a rioter Steve Butcher whom he lodged in jail."[19]

Following the Rainey lead, the Frick company now asked for an injunction to "restrain all men not in their employ at their works from assembling on their grounds congregating in the vicinity of their works, intimidating or interfering with their men at work, or going to and from work making threats against the lives of the men or the company's property and restraining them from any acts of violence or interfering in any way with the operation of their works." It was granted.[20]

The Morewood Massacre

On April 2, another battle took place at Morewood.[21] This was the battle that would define the strike of 1891. At 11 o'clock at night, men from Alice, Stonerville, Mayfield, Tarrs, Central and Donnelly marched through Mount Pleasant to Standard and held a meeting. They broke into two groups, and three hours later marched back through Mount Pleasant, clubs in hand. The second group was led by a band. It was the middle of the night.[22]

Waiting for them at Morewood were about sixty deputies carrying Winchesters divided into two groups. Under Deputy McConnell, a group stood to the east side of the

THE FIGHT WITH THE MOB.

Scene of the Morewood Massacre. *1 and 2:* Houses fronting on street called Willow Row *3:* The company's barns enclosed by high board fence. *4:* The high board fence. *5* is near the gate where the shooting took place. *6:* A company dwelling house. *7:* Company store. *8:* Fence by the Stonerville road, along which the mob marched. *9:* The dead strikers, several of the bodies lying on a bridge that crosses a run at that point. *10:* About 45 sheriff's deputies armed with rifles ("The Fight with the Mob," *Commercial Gazette*, April 3, 1891, p. 1).

company store; the other group under Captain Loar stood to the west side of the same building. The April 7 *Mount Pleasant Journal* reported:

> When the strikers reached that point they are said to have stoned the store and fired off pistols so that Deputy McConnell had difficulty in keeping his men from returning the fire. He got in front of his men and commanded them not to shoot. It seems the order was not to fire unless attacked or in case a command to halt was disobeyed.
>
> The strikers passed down the road to the gate leading to the works near the company stables to which Captain Loar moved his party. The stories from this point widely differ. One is that the strikers although commanded to halt in both English and Hungarian terms attacked the gate, tearing it down with the intention of throwing oil on and burning the stables and were then fired upon by Captain Loar's deputies. Another account has it that the strikers were peacefully returning to their homes at Stonerville and Donnelly and were the attacked party.
>
> … 12 rifles were leveled at the mob and 12 balls plowed their way through its ranks. The rioters were instantly repulsed, but in the heat of the skirmish the firing continued and three or four volleys were rapidly poured into the crowd. The ranks of the attacking party were broken, and leaving the road the men broke over the barbed wire fence and through the fields to the north of the works and only a few of them remained to send a parting shot at the deputies not one of whom was harmed….
>
> The road along and in front of the line of fire was covered with clubs dropped by the mob, and among the other articles picked up after daylight were no less than one hundred and five men's hats.

Some of them were good ones and not a few had bullet holes through them. A very long handled hatchet was found in the hands of one dead man, while a revolver was taken from another.

Two Huns, both from Donnelly, were arrested soon after the shooting by deputies and sent to jail at Greensburg. One of them had been shot in the leg. The other was not injured at all although it was at first supposed he was dead. He was found lying under a dead man and when the body was picked up the live man jumped up and started to run. He was captured after he had run into a neighboring house.

Eleven dead bodies were found all without the big gates of which so much is being said. Four lay on the bridge which crosses from the public road to the company's property line; two were picked up in the road, while the seventh was found some distance out in the field through which the strikers scattered.[23]

The *Journal* continued its lengthy report. When the second group of strikers arrived, they demanded the bodies of the dead. They were refused. They were not happy. They went away, but came back again and were refused again. The bodies were brought back to Mount Pleasant and placed in the care of Undertaker Zimmerman. The town was extremely agitated. Businesses closed. Captain Loar was condemned, and was threatened with lynching and the burning of his home on College Avenue. Peter Wise and other union officials came to Mount Pleasant and all day tried to keep the strikers at bay. Then they filed suit with Squire J.D. McCaleb against the deputies, claiming their attack was unwarranted: "J.A. Loar and deputies Richard Burns, J.A. Zundle, L.S. Davis, Harry Wilson, Norman Brown, George Carbaugh, Harry Berger, Elmer Nichol, Edward Seeman, Miles Hann and Harry Gilbert were charged with felonious shooting. General Managers Morris Ramsay, of The Southwest Coal & Coke Company, and Thomas Lynch, of the H.C. Frick Coke Company, were charged with being accessories before the killing."

TYPES OF HUNS AND COKE WORKERS.

The many hats and nationalities of the miners ("Bayonet Rule for Slav and Hun," *New York Herald*, May 3, 1891, p. 13).

A very thorough government report on the strike of 1891 called it "the most disastrous strike of the year." It consisted of twelve pages of detailed information of the strike. After the Morewood Massacre, as the event would come to be called, the report assessed the situation in Mount Pleasant:

> The sun rose on a troubled community at Mt. Pleasant on the morning of the riot, but few had slept during the night and the quiet citizens assembled at the street corners and with anxiety discussed the

terrible affair of the early morning. Business was practically at a standstill and the most exaggerated rumors were flying about, and grave fears were expressed that the killing of the strikers was only the forerunner of further and more serious trouble. It was at first reported, and generally believed, that at least forty men had been killed, and that the strikers would exact a terrible revenge for the killing of their friends generally conceded, unless prompt measures were taken by the state authorities, and the rumor that prevailed later in the day that the state troops had been ordered out, did not tend to decrease the feeling of anxiety among the people. All the morning the arriving trains brought numbers of the friends of the strikers from all parts of the coke region and by noon the streets of Mt. Pleasant were crowded with coke workers who surged about from one place to another, seemingly unmindful of the cold drizzling rain that had commenced to fall. They seemed to grow more restless as the day wore on, and their manner, seemed to indicate that there was further trouble ahead; but the day ended quietly....[24]

The Funerals

Although the newspapers reported eleven dead, on Saturday, April 4, a funeral was held for seven of the victims. It is unclear from conflicting reports how many actually died. The *Weekly Courier* of Connellsville reported the event in detail:

> The funeral of the seven victims of the Morewood riot was held at Scottdale on Saturday afternoon. Thousands of cokers flocked to that place, and while the scenes enacted were remarkable in many ways they were entirely free from disorderly demonstrations which had been expected. This was largely due to the influence exercised over the multitude by Fathers Lambing and Smeigle, who conducted the exercises.
>
> The train bearing the bodies, consisting of six coaches and a baggage car, arrived at the station over the Southwest road and stopped in front of the depot. The latter car contained the bodies, and was attached to the rear of the train. The coaches were packed to suffocation with friends of the dead men. When the work of removing the caskets from the train was begun there was a mad rush and crush on all sides by those anxious to view the dead. Master Workman Wise and Undertaker Zimmerman finally succeeded in clearing a passage way, and the line of march to the Catholic cemetery, two miles away, was formed. Six of the caskets were entrusted to pall-bearers and the seventh was conveyed in a hearse. The Standard and Scottdale band headed the line of procession and when they struck up the funeral dirges many of the mourners were deeply moved with grief. Flags and banners of many nationalities floated over the procession and although the roads were almost ankle deep in mud, the procession grew in numbers until the cemetery was reached.
>
> The grave consisted of a trench 16 feet long, 7 feet wide and 5 feet deep. The coffins were ranged along its brink, but one of them being opened. A distressing scene followed this, for no sooner was the lid removed than an aged lady, whose face bore traces of unutterable grief, threw herself at the foot of the casket, and with hands uplifted and streaming eyes implored the blessing of God upon her dead. After the bodies had been lowered to their final rest Father Lambing celebrated the dead service and sprinkled the coffins with holy water. Rev. Smeigle conducted services in the Polish and Slavish [sic] tongues, the foreign element largely predominating. He cautioned them to be law-abiding, to follow peaceful methods, to avoid saloons and to shun intoxicating drink. His words had a marked effect for good upon his bearers.[25]

The cemetery was St. John the Baptist Roman Catholic Cemetery in Scottdale.

Two more men died of their wounds: Paul Salinski of Donnelly and Joseph Kleaman of Mullen. That brought the total dead at Morewood to nine.

Aftermath

Westmoreland County Sheriff Clawson sent for state help. Finally, the governor contacted Colonel A.L. Hawkins of the Tenth Regiment, Second Brigade, Pennsylvania National

Guard: "Put your regiment under arms and move at once, with ammunition, to the support of the Sheriff of Westmoreland county at Mt. Pleasant. Maintain the peace, protect all persons in their rights under the Constitution and laws of the state. Communicate with me." The 18th Regiment was also ordered to proceed to Mt. Pleasant. When they arrived, they were mustered on Main Street near Church. "Companies E and K were left at the armory as a guard to the town, while B, D, H, and I were moved on out to Morewood and placed in position to guard the entire plant...."[26]

Then the coroner held the inquest into the events, and the same issue of the *Courier* reported: His jury: Robert Lamb, foreman, with J.J. Hitchman, M.S. Brinker, David Shupe, William Barkley, and A.B. Kantz. Witnesses included Mrs. Mary McIndoe, Robert Weddell, Daniel Shrader, James Jordan, and John McIndoe. The inquest continued on Friday, and John Rowbaker, Albert Holly, George Taylor, Joseph Angus, Peter Buskey, Mrs. Buskey, William Dorm, Marshal Busko, Grant Baer, John Hardy, and William Hanney, all gave testimony. The voices of these witnesses are all recorded in the same issue of the *Journal*. The inquest was adjourned until the following week.

The Problems as Seen by Watchorn and Frick

Needless to say, the operators and the union men saw the events differently. Which points of view were truthful? Which were designed to provoke? Which formed the formula for confrontation between workers and employers for the century ahead? The *Journal* recorded the comments by Robert Watchorn, former Secretary of the United Mine Workers, and Henry Clay Frick, who was having severe problems with Andrew Carnegie, but seemed to be still the voice of the H.C. Frick Coke Company.

First, Watchorn:

> From what I can understand the shooting of the strikers was an unprovoked murder. I have received a report this morning that three of the deputy sheriffs under Capt Loar themselves broke down the fence and then shot the men. It certainly is not reasonable to suppose that 500 men armed with guns and 500 with other weapons would deliberately plan an attack and then be driven away by 13 men without shooting one of the latter. The people in the coke regions are not such cowards as that.
>
> The Hungarians, or Slavs, in the coke regions have always been grossly imposed upon. They were induced to settle in the coke regions under misrepresentations, and constantly ground down. Then, if they strike, the operators employ some of the brighter men at big salaries to go around among the others and try to induce them to return to work.
>
> In this the Frick Coke Company has always been especially forward. The result of this course is to divide the Hungarians among themselves and to cause ever increasing bitterness. The coke workers all hate Capt. Loar, for there has not been a strike in years in which he has not petitioned the Sheriff of Westmoreland county to swear in his company of guards as deputy sheriffs so that they can have an opportunity of shooting some Hungarians. Capt. Loar has frequently made that statement. We can bring many witnesses to prove it.

Frick first stated that his "company had [n]ever imported labor under contract." There is a difference from bringing men into the area from New York, Philadelphia, or other towns in and around the region, and going overseas and recruiting men from towns and villages in Europe. His position here is that his company did not do the latter. He further responded:

> Although the violence committed in the vicinity of our works has been mainly by foreigners, the public knows that these people are simply the tools working out the plans and designs of others. The plan now adopted of using these men to accomplish their work of violence is but a repitition [sic] of

former acts. In every strike in the coke region these are the men who have been used and found to be pliant tools whenever violence is to be done. The public should not allow itself to be blinded to the real authors of the present trouble. The controversy is now not one between our company and its empolyes [sic], but is between the lawful authorities of our Commonwealth and a mob of irresponsible men in the hands of cunning demagogues.

It needs no argument to show that this violence is the result of such acts, and the public press, and the lawful authority of our state, should fix on them the responsibility rather than upon the poor deluded foreigners. The sentiment of the people and the established civil authority of our state should see to it that these men do not escape the odium resting upon them, which is due to their acts and conduct.

Finding we were not able to pursue our business peaceably, we handed over our works to the civil authorities of the state. Let the labor leaders, if they can, show how it came that these men, belonging to their union, and whom they claim to represent, came in conflict with the authority of the state. Let them explain why these rioters were marched around our works with drums and firearms at 3 o'clock in the morning. Why did the sheriff deem it necessary at all to have deputies to preserve the public peace? If these men were law-abiding men, as the leader would have you believe they are? It is a significant fact that not a single employe of the Morewood coke works, where the riot took place, is found among either the killed or wounded.

The statement made by Mr. Watchorn that we were trying to compel our men to go to work is false. We simply offered to put our works in operation again and to employ such men as wished to go to work upon a sliding scale proposed by our company, based on the selling price of coke. Many of our men accepted this proposal, and were glad to do so, and it is to prevent these men, willing and anxious to work, from doing so that violence has been resorted to.[27]

It looked like the battle was between the operators and the unions, with the men in the middle! Frick was clear. He was not against his men organizing and his negotiating with them. He was against outsiders coming in and forcing the men to obey them and expecting him to negotiate with them. He never wavered from this position through all the strikes.

Watchorn could not allow Frick's statement to stand and in a lengthy response took on the issues. He offered proof that Frick's company did indeed import workers. The first was evidence from 1887 when a man named Daniel Collins "claims that while in England … he was offered, by a man named Hargraves, $2.00 per day and passage free to come to work in Connellsville coke region mines. He declined but his brother and eight others accepted the offer, came to Scottdale and were put to work at the Frick company's Valley works." This would be an ongoing debate.

On April 14, the *Journal* continued reporting on events surrounding Morewood, with lengthy comments by Thomas Lynch, but the front page of the *Journal* is torn and not legible, and additional copies could not be found.

More on the Inquest

Week by week the newspapers reported the events as they unfolded. The coroner continued his inquest. He called additional witnesses including John Sheebock, a Morewood stable boy; Thomas Shirer from Stonerville; W.J. Cunningham, a driver; Mrs. Agnes Baughman; Mrs. Nora Ringler; John Collins; and Thomas Fietcher. They all gave contradictory stories about the shooting. Here are three of the many depositions that were reported in the *Mount Pleasant Journal*:

John Sheebock said: "I went with the men from Morewood to Standard and returned with them about 3 o'clock. Somebody at Standard said that everybody must attend the meeting, but I did not know where the meeting was to be held. When we reached Morewood we stopped at the company's store. On our way there somebody shot three or four times, but after we left the store no one fired. We stopped at the bridge and some man said, 'Checki! Checki!' then they fired. When the shooting took place I crawled under the bridge and stayed there in the water four hours. Then a man came and said, "You fellows come to the company store." I did not go.

Thomas Shirer said: "I live at Stonerville and am a coal miner. I was in Mt. Pleasant the night of the shooting, and was returning home after the shooting. I met a deputy after it was over and he told me that it was dangerous to pass, as the strikers were massed on the hill and might fire. I saw no firing, [illegible] was in the crowd. The dead men were found on the bridge leading to the stable."

John Collins said: "I was at Morewood. I stopped before the shooting just beyond the bridge. We stood awhile there talking, and soon they fired on us. I did not see any arms in the crowd, and I did not hear any one say 'checki.' I did not have any idea why the men went to Morewood. I saw no carbon oil cans in the crowd."[28]

Held for Murder

As an outcome of the inquest, the men who were believed to have done the shooting at Morewood were held for court. They included Captain Loar, Dick Burns, Elmer Nichols, Harry Wilson, Lewis Davis, Carey Brown, Jacob Zundell, Orrin Reese, Miley Hann, and Steve Carnes. The local justices refused to serve the warrants, and it fell to Justice Eicher of Scottdale. He gave the warrants to Constable Gay, who served them. They all appeared in court the following Friday with Judge Reyburn of Kittanning presiding. They were prosecuted by James S. Beacom and were defended by Messrs. Moorhead and Head. Sheriff Clawson was also arrested, and he was defended by H.W. Wilkinshaw.

Mr. Moorhead made the opening address, reviewing the Morewood troubles and asking that the court release the prisoners on a reasonable amount of bail. As District Attorney Gregg had nothing to say, Mr. Beacom followed. He said that he had heard all the evidence offered so far before the Coroner's jury and that there was nothing in the testimony which were to show that the defendants were justified in shooting. He, however, said that the matter of bail rested entirely with the court. Mr. Head then closed the arguments with a strong plea for the defendants. He argued that the defendants were acting as officers of the law while the killing was done, and claimed that the circumstances justified the deed.

Judge Reyburn then ruled that the defendants were at Morewood as officers to protect the property of the Southwest Coal and Coke Company, and there was no evidence produced, as yet to convict them of murder in the first degree, they be admitted to bail in the amount of $3,000 each for their appearance in the May term of court. Mr. Moorhead at once arose and said that the [?]wing [illegible] known gentlemen would [illegible] on the bond: J.W. Moore, H.J. Bru[illegible] E.M. Gross, John M. Stewart, M S. [?]bury [illegible], W.J. Hitchman, and others [?] [illegible] the bonds were duly filed and the defendants discharged George Carbaugh, H. Berger and Edward Seeman who had been similarly indicted, went to Greensburg later in the day and entered [illegible] each in the same sum....[29]

Nine more men were charged with riot and riotous destruction of property, most of them members of the brass band. They were brought before Squire McCaleb and given bail of $500 each. They included Harry Buckley, James Baldwin, James Agan, Robert Nix [?] [illegible], James Lane, Patrick McDonon [?], [illegible] William, and Mart Rinehart and Michael Barrett.

The trial would continue at the end of May.

Evictions

Then the evictions began. The company leases were clear: a miner had to work to stay in a company house. If he did not, he had ten days to vacate. On April 8, the eviction notices were to go to the constables for delivery.[30] It started at Morewood. On April 9, the following notice was posted on homes:

> Name: You are hereby notified to quit and give up peaceable possession of the house and lot you now occupy and known and numbered as No. __ at Morewood mines, East Huntington Township, Westmoreland County, PA., on or before April 19th, as per terms of the lease under which you now hold, as we wish to have and repossess the same. Signed: The Southwest Coal and Coke Co.[31]

Once again, the people chosen to be evicted were those the company considered troublemakers. A company spokesman stated:

> These people are continually infusing the striking workers with anarchistic notions and urging them to commit deeds of violence, and: [illegible]. Propose to get rid of them if possible. They refuse to pay rent and will not vacate our houses peaceable. No attempt will be made to throw them out unless every possible hope of a settlement of the difficulties vanishes. Several hundred men and their families are living in our houses at Morewood and there are many good men among them.[32]

Those who received notices at Morewood were Michael Barrett, John Welsh, Steve Promuka, Martin Winjeuski, Peter Skera, August Bentz, Henry Howard, John Campbell, John Dank, Daniel Shrader, Jerry Barrett, Mike Lindway, Elizabeth Murphy, and T.S. Grimm.[33]

When the ten-day notice expired at Morewood, Sheriff Clawson did not move to vacate the houses. More notices were sent to Standard works. Among those evicted there were M [illegible] Disman, a labor leader who left peacefully and went to what was known as the East End House.[34]

The evictions did not occur at Morewood until the end of the month. When they did, the *Journal* claimed they were the first such events in Westmoreland County. The first person to be evicted was Mrs. Elizabeth Murphy. The others, as named above, followed. It was peaceful. One man, William Schrader, removed his goods from the house before the sheriff came. But at the house of the Polish family of Martin Weigenski and his wife, things changed: "Mrs. Martin is a big woman and don't know what fear is. One of the deputies started with a bucket and shovel to go upstairs and remove the fire from a coking stove when she snatched the shovel and proceeded to lay it over his head. The pair clinched and it was two to one on Poland until the officer's companions rallied to his assistance." The deputies jumped into action. So did the crowd. So did her husband: "Suddenly Martin Weigenski, the husband of the woman, out of breath and crazed with excitement, attempted to run past Deputy Leinsen." He didn't succeed. His wife escaped from her captors and ran toward him and hugged him. Then Captain Loar and his men arrived and things calmed down. Mrs. Weigenski remained in her home.

The next day the following were also evicted: John Pramiki George Meiliga, Mike Sligra, Frank Eckles, John Paratic, Frank Sen, John Schrader and John Brendlinger.[35]

Coroner's Final Report

The coroner resumed his hearings and more men and women testified as to what they saw. They included George Keller, a watchman at Shupe's Mill in Mount Pleasant; Mathias King from Central works, who reported the strikers came to his house to attack him and his son; C.H. [illegible]; J.T. Anderson, a mine boss from Central; Jesse Rock, the yard boss at Central, who maintained the rioters were shooting and threatening, pounding on houses to get men to join them; Mrs. Jerry Stoner from Redtop, who closed the door when men tried to recruit her husband, after which they stoned the house; Mrs. Shawley, also from Redtop, who confirmed the men were bound for Morewood; Morris Pigman, manager of Standard store, who reported that the Huns tore down the telephone wires so no one could notify Morewood they were coming.

James Shorthill reported: "I am stable boss at Morewood; heard the rioters shooting and daring the deputies to come out of the store and shoot; also saw them tear the company's fence down, and heard them threaten to burn his [witness's] house, because he boarded the deputies; in the morning the store floor was covered with clubs, stones and revolvers, and all the windows were broken; the nearest dead striker was within six or eight feet of the gate." John Hart corroborated Morris Pigman's report "and said he examined a club which one of the strikers carried; it seemed to be a table leg; the striker remarked with a grin that if he should hit one deputy the rest would all run; tried to persuade a Hun not to go to Morewood; the Hun replied: 'Me no go Morewood, all men fixie me.'"[36]

It appears not all the rioters were there because they wanted to be. They, too, were fearful.

The testimony of the men and women was followed by the testimony of Sheriff Clawson:

> I was called to Morewood March 29; took 22 deputies with me, and saw a crowd of 400 or 500 men howling and shooting; the crowd tore up the track, smashed windows, set fire to wheelbarrows and destroyed tools; arrested two of the band and found revolvers on them; heard about 1,000 shots fired. I stationed deputies there and instructed them to protect property, and if they saw any one destroying property to put a bullet through them. I instructed the men, however, to use all due caution, and only resort to extreme measures when necessary. I deputized Captain Loar and his men....

Deputy McConnell followed:

> We concentrated our force at the store when the strikers closed in; 400 to 500 men come from the direction of Mt. Pleasant. The deputies were divided into two squads, one under myself and the other under command of Capt. Loar; from 200 to 250 shots were fired before General Manager Ramsey's house; the crowd then came on down shooting and howling; then one of them made a speech in a foreign language, the mob then fired a few shots and came as far as the bridge; then I heard the fence being torn down; eight or nine shots were fired at Captain Loar's men and then the deputies returned the fire which lasted about 8 or 9 seconds.

Finally, Captain Loar had his chance to speak:

> I live at Mt. Pleasant; went to Morewood with 10 deputies in citizens' clothes; found from 50 to 60 others there; Sheriff McConnell gave us arms, Winchester and Springfield Rifles; we were ordered to halt a mob, should any come on the company's property, and if any refused to halt, we were to fire and aim to hit; several crowds passed in an orderly manner; at 3 o'clock word came that a mob was approaching from Mt. Pleasant; the mob fired about 200 shots at Ramsey's house by word of command; the strikers marched in a solid column and halted before the store when a speech was made and a bullet fired at one of my men which tore up the earth beside him. McConnell then ordered 20 of us to the stables; the crowd began to break down the fences; I called "halt" twice, then said "checki"; one of the strikers then said "checki --- --- ---; deputy sheriff no shoot"; they advanced, and some one behind me said "Let them have it," at the same time discharging his piece; I was thrown down by the concussion; the strikers fired many shots at us; I stopped the firing as soon as possible. There was no command given to fire; the mob began firing as soon as they began tearing through the fence; I fired twice when I recovered from the shock of the discharge back of me; I did not tender my company's service to the Governor; the sheriff asked for my men to be sworn in at [illegible] Greensburg; many strikers were through the gate and over the fence before my men fired; the hat of Deputy J.A. Zundel had a bullet hole through the crown.

A few more men testified, including Deputy Jacob Zundell, who supported Captain Loar's testimony. Then lawyer Moorhead for the defense addressed the jury, reminding them that the deputies were honor-bound to defend the property of the Southwest Coal & Coke Company and that the mob fired first. Attorney Beacom responded for the prosecution.

The following Monday the coroner returned a verdict from the National Hotel in Mount Pleasant: "That the deceased came to his death at Morewood, East Huntingdon township, Westmoreland county, on the morning of April 2, 1891, about [illegible] o'clock, by a bullet discharged from a gun or revolver in the hands of deputies of the Sheriff of Westmoreland county." The labor leaders present said they "will prosecute Captain Loar and his men for all that is out."[37]

More Evictions

By May 5 the strike was in its twelfth week. The evictions were in full force. Sheriff Clawson headed to Standard mines with twenty deputies and Company E under Captain Loar. Six miners were evicted at Standard Shaft. The next day, twelve more Morewood families were thrown out. "The first place visited was No. 43, occupied by Martin Weigenski and wife. The latter had managed to hold the fort on two former calls by the sheriff and came very nearly scoring a third victory. Her husband met the visitors at the door with a doctor's certificate which stated that the madam wasn't able to move out. One of the deputies who had seen her over at Standard Friday grew inquisitive and examined the little piece of paper, discovering that the date was April 23. The sheriff rubbed his glasses and found this was correct and the Weigenski household goods soon lined the road."[38]

Thirty-seven families were evicted by Sheriff Clawson at Central, and then his men moved on to Alice. By this time, he had evicted 100 families and had writs for 400. Sheriff McCormick had evicted 200 families and writs for more. Some of the evicted families found empty houses, moved in with other miners who owned their own homes, or set up tents. The labor leaders provided the tents and one large one was erected at the J.H. Rumbaugh field near Standard.[39]

Honoring Morewood

On Friday, September 29, 2000, 109 years after the massacre at Morewood, the Commonwealth of Pennsylvania erected a historic roadside marker along Morewood Road, aka Route 981, just after it crosses route 119. At that time nearly all evidence of the mighty mine had been obliterated: no ovens, no tipple, no gob pile, nothing. The superintendent's home still stands and, of course, the coal and the remnants of underground mining are there.

There are several other markers in the region, mostly about mining disasters. In the anthracite region, riots are recorded on Pennsylvania markers. A marker in downtown Scranton reads: "A riot occurred here on August 1, 1877, in which armed citizens fired upon strikers, killing four. Many were injured, including Scranton's mayor. As in numerous U.S. cities, this labor unrest was a result of the U.S. depression of 1873 and a nationwide railroad strike of 1877." How many more markers should there be in the Connellsville coke region?

Beyond Morewood

In Fayette, County Sheriff McCormick had also asked the governor for the Pennsylvania National Guard. "Affairs have assumed such a shape here that I am unable to execute legal process and preserve the peace in this county, so as to further protect the property at the several coke works in said county, owning to the violence and unlawful acts of the former employes of said companies." As was the case with Westmoreland County, the governor hesitated. McCormick was requested to send details: 300 miners stopped him from executing a writ at Trotter; men blew up the water tank at Kyle; 250 strikers freed a prisoner from deputies at Leith; 300 strikers tried to stop 150 workers from working at Leisenring. Company E, already deployed to Captain Loar, was to prepare to move and assist Uniontown's Company C, led by Captain Frasher. Frasher was asked to "place your company under arms and report to Sheriff McCormick...."[40]

Through all of this, the Morgan Valley miners participated in the strike. A meeting was held at Morgan, and at the same time, miners at Morgan were thrown out into the street. The Ager (Eggers) and McEnery families found their furniture piled on the road while strikers watched. When the deputies left, they put their furniture back inside.[41] Evictions

Images like this one filled newspapers in Pittsburgh and beyond, showing the public the suffering of miners (Summit Evicted Miners. *Pittsburgh Times*. Scrapbook, April 18–May 20, 1891. Helen Clay Frick Foundation Archives [AIS 2002 06]. Henry Clay Frick Business Records, 1862–1987. Box 497. Vol. 10: 1891, p. 123).

also took place at Summit Mine and Adelaide Mine, all owned by Frick. The *Reading Times* reported: "Managers of the great Frick firms say that the strikers cannot live in company's houses."[42] Throughout the region, 471 eviction writs (out of 500) were prepared by H.C. Frick Coke Company alone.[43]

The miners were facing confusing choices. The companies wanted them back to work at the old rate. The unions wanted them to hold out for more and better wages.

Importing Labor and More Violence

By mid–April the companies were desperate to fill new orders and began looking elsewhere to find labor. All the people who had been or were being evicted were considered troublemakers and would not be invited back to work. So the importation of laborers became more intense. When the five families were evicted by deputies at Morgan and Summit, the Frick company tried to start the Summit Mine.[44] Only twenty-eight men reported for work, so twenty-six Italians were sent to work at Summit. More were shipped to Whitney outside of the Morgan Valley.[45]

Things appeared to be settling, so the 10th Regiment, having been sent to the region by the Pennsylvania governor, was recalled, leaving a gap in security. Adjunct General William McClelland sent a telegram to Sheriff Clawson of Westmoreland County: "Your telegram to the Governor received. He directs me to say if order is restored there is no necessity for the further presence of the troops. In the event of any disturbance of the peace which the local authorities cannot quell, the military will be ordered to your support at once."[46] The next day all except for Company E, the local company, left.

The evening before the soldiers left, a mass meeting was held at Summit. It was about the Italian imports. The men were trying to get them to leave or join the strike. It did not work, and the Italians were placed under guard to protect them. The Italians told the miners via letter that they were from New York and thought they would be working on a pipeline, not breaking a strike. Frick's office denied this, maintaining they were not from New York but were miners from the anthracite region, and they came to work in the local mines.[47] Very confusing.

The next day brought more evictions. At Broadford, eighty notices were given, allowing the families ten days to vacate. More were served at Leisenring No. 2 south of the Morgan Valley. The miners began to fight back, turning to the law. A Slavic woman from Summit, whose family had been evicted the day before, filed a legal suit against deputy John Kyle for drawing a revolver on her. He was to be arrested.[48] Violence began again. One hundred strikers attacked Leisenring. Guns were involved.[49]

Then some miners, in desperation, turned to dynamite. The night of April 17, explosions occurred throughout the region, including at Frick's Kyle plant near Fairchance, where the water tank was blown up to stop production.[50] At Leisenring "about 300 of the strikers gathered on the hill tops above the Leisenring plants, where they formed a line and began firing and throwing the bombs. They secured beer kegs, placed the bombs in them, and fired them off. Over thirty of these bombs were discharged and for a time it seemed as if the strikers were determined to destroy the works. Not a soul was injured, however, and the only objective of the strikers was to warn a few black sheep that they had better quit work."[51] Twenty-six men were arrested and put aboard the train to Uniontown. However, friends and families joined the men and tried to board the train. They all refused to pay, and the conductor put the train on the side-track, where it remained. The sheriff, engineer, and a few of the strikers moved on to Uniontown, leaving the train and families behind.[52]

The next day, riots began at Adelaide, across the river from the Morgan Valley and linked to Broadford by bridges. Deputies arrived to serve eviction notices and were stoned and driven away. The sheriff called in Company C from Fayette County and they arrived at Adelaide by train to calm things.[53] The Morgan Valley, closed and on strike since the beginning, was in turmoil. Sheriff McCormick asked for the militia to return. They did.

Then the Pinkertons returned, over one hundred of them. This time it wasn't Rainey who called them. It was Frick. They headed to Leisenring. Frick was clear, and he would not budge. Men who disobeyed would not be rehired. The terms would stand.[54]

Sheriff McCormick went to Leisenring No. 3 to evict fifteen families. Andy Blashko and his wife were not going easily.

> They occupied a part of the house, but not the part which the sheriff had taken possession of. The sheriff was standing on the top step at the kitchen door when Mrs. Blashko mounted the steps and made an attempt to gain admission to the house. The sheriff ordered her to leave, but she refused and tried to gain an entrance by force. She was then pushed down the steps by the sheriff. This was repeated several times. The woman's husband went to aid her. The sheriff was then compelled to use force to keep the angry pair at bay. Finally, the woman uttered a wild peculiar yell. A crowd of her countrymen immediately came to her assistance. The sheriff drew his revolver and ordered the mob to halt. They were deaf to his command and pressed on. Realizing that words were useless, the sheriff opened fire upon the mob. They fled in all directions.[55]

But it wasn't over. The women returned and attacked the sheriff. Then some of the men returned carrying guns and bats. The sheriff and his deputies opened fire and Andy Blashko was shot in the leg by his own wife:

> In the meantime the attack had been renewed with more vigor than ever. Some of the mob has secured revolvers, Mrs. Blashko among the rest. Revolver in hand, she headed the crowd in the next attack. As she approached the steps she opened fire on the Sheriff. The latter was surrounded on all sides and in the fracas he received a bullet in the ankle from the revolver in the hands of Mrs. Blashko, who marched defiantly on until she received a bullet in the thigh....
>
> The wounded woman fell to the ground in an unconscious condition, where she lay for fifteen minutes or more, her three little children sitting beside her crying in a pitiful manner. Finally some of her friends carried her home and put her in bed. She lay apparently unmindful of her surroundings until Sheriff McCormick entered the room for the purpose of learning the nature of her injuries. At the sight of the Sheriff she sprang from her bed like an enraged tigress and attacked him again. It was with difficulty that Lieutenant Wakefield succeeded in holding her until the Sheriff could get out of her sight. After evicting one more family the Sheriff and the militia withdrew from the scene of action and proceeded to Trotter.[56]

The Socialists Speak

Wherever there is unrest, groups arrive to encourage the disenfranchised to join their cause. On came the Socialists. Under the leadership of Deieber and Jonas of New York, they issued a circular and distributed it all over the Connellsville coke region:

> The ranks of cheap labor will ever continue to receive accessions through the tide of immigration, and in a course of a few years, sooner or later, according to circumstances, the time will come when the supply of the commodity of labor will exceed the demand; when again will begin that pernicious turmoil which must end with a crash and with the loss of innumerable lives. This is what must come to pass—that is, if nothing occurs to prevent it. But revoluize [sic] the affairs of today. This is the true way, and the only way to bring relief, genuine and lasting relief to the working people!

Are you ready; foreward [sic] then; we are with you. Where is the coward that would draw back? Battallion [sic], to arms. Have you not weapons enough? There are the arsenals of the counter jumper militia stocked with military stores, repeating rifles and ammunition. Fling the police in the gutter, the militia in the river; drag the venal politician and corrupt judges from their seats; chase the capitalistic hyena from the town, the priest from the churches; take rifle in hand and range your forces from town to town. Take possession of the land that belongs to you, and of the factories and machinery that you erect, and of the houses that you build. Who can withstand you, thousands and millions? Into the street! Forward! forward! *Allons enfants de la patria.*[57]

The socialists were at it again at a meeting in Scottdale. The speaker was Professor DeLeon of New York. Founder of the Socialist Labor Party of America, he called President Cleveland a "stuffed prophet," and Father Lambling as Frick's spokesman. Labor leaders did not attend.[58]

The Miners Speak

The position of the H.C. Frick Company was clearly stated and clear in meaning: they would not recognize the union. The position of the other operators was not stated. Some of them had already settled with their miners, giving them concessions. The local union position was also clear. They would fight on to the end, believing their position was just. The national position was filled with words like "mercenary reporters, capitalistic inclined editors, malicious and vindictive deputies."

Very important to the discussion is the question that something was missing here. Where was the voice of the miners themselves? How were they dealing with the bombardment of different voices? Perhaps the answer lies in the comments made during the week of April 17. The first inklings that the miners were unhappy with both the company and the unions came at a meeting in Scottdale during that week: "The first kick came from John McClan, of the Whitney worky [sic], John Welsh, Valley works, Owen Denk, Morgan, and Robert Sweeney. The latter was Secretary of the old National Progressive Union, and the others representatives of that branch. They kicked and fought all afternoon with the managers of the strike. They pronounced the strike management a failure...."[59]

Another miner was recorded to have said to the union reps: "You people have deceived us in leading us into this fight. You did not do it through ignorance, and I warn you that if this condition is not changed soon, some one will be made to answer. I know men who will sacrifice their lives before they will blackleg, but before they and their children die from hunger you people will be made to pay a heavy penalty."[60]

Final Morewood Trials Get Underway

The first case to get underway in the Westmoreland court under Judge Reyburn was held at McCausland's Hall. The prosecuting attorneys were Messrs. "Morehead" [sic] & Head, and for the defense were Messrs. Beacom, Eicher and Speigle. The accused were Michael Barrett, union secretary; William Coleman, an official of the Knights of Labor at Morewood; Charles Frey, James Lane, Mike Phillippi, Steve Sclava, Alex Metz, Michael and Pat McDonough, John Hailes, John McCarthy, William and Ward Rinehart, Henry Buckley, James Baldwin and Robert Nixon. The jury deliberated for five hours and "found Barrett and Coleman guilty of riot and assault and Henry Buckley, James Baldwin, Robert Nixon,

Pat McDonough, John Hailes, John McCarthy, Ward and William Rinehart, all members of the Standard band, guilty of riot but recommended to the extreme mercy of the court."[61]

John and Harry Shrader and Robert Weddell were then tried for the second riot at Morewood on April 2. The verdict was sealed. All the other men who had been arrested were fined, sent to jail for thirty days to six months, or, if underage, sent to Huntingdon Reformatory, an institution for first-time offenders ages 15 to 25.[62] The trial of Captain Loar and the deputies started the same day.[63]

Judge Doty presided over the trial of Captain Loar and his deputies at the Greensburg court house. Tom Marshall, an attorney from Pittsburgh, was brought in to assist the prosecuting attorneys District Attorney Gregg and Hon. J.S. Beacom, his assistant. For the defense were Messrs. Moorhead and Head. The men charged with murder included: J.A. Loar, Harry Wilson, Richard Burns, Lewis Davis, Carey Brown, Orrin Reese, Jacob Zundel, Harry Gilbert, Miles Hann, Elmer Nichols, and Jesse Berger. The jury was S.B. Fry, Latrobe; John E. Eisaman, Hempfield township; David Reed, Jr., Allegheny township; John Harbaugh, Latrobe; Robert Shrum, Ligonier township; Josiah Hunter, Cook township; Wm. Ulery, Donegal township; J.R. Steel, Unity township; Lew K. Hawk, Greensburg; Wm. M. Larimer, Bell township; and John Kerr, Hempfield township.[64] The leaders of the coal strike brought the charges: Messrs Wise, Barrett, McBride and Disman. Scores of witnesses were called. The *Journal* wrote:

> The prosecution rested at noon Wednesday after having made a very weak case. The strikers had claimed all along that it was not a riot, but simply men going peacefully to their Stonerville, Tarrs and Central homes after having attended a meeting at the Standard works; that they committed no overt act at Morewood that morning and that the shooting of seven of their number was murder. They failed, however, to prove that they did not shoot off pistols and break down the gates to the company's property before they were fired upon. With the exception of Loar, Burns and Zundel the deputies were not identified by witnesses for the prosecution. Nor was it explained, if the prosecution's claim was right, and the strikers were simply walking down the public road, how it came that all the dead were shot in the head and front parts of the body and that three of those killed were Standard men.
>
> For the defense it was clearly proven how strikers left Tarrs, Central and Stonerville the evening before for the avowed purpose of making a second attack on Morewood; how these men gathered at Standard and broke in the doors in order to compel the Hungarian occupants to go along; how the mob fired pistols before and after the Morewood store was reached; how the crowd tore down one gate and opened the other and refused to halt before the deputies opened fire. A few of the clubs, a revolver and two oil cans picked up on the battlefield were produced in evidence as were a section of the gate post and a fencing board that showed, by a bullet hole through both that the gate was open at the time the shooting was done.[65]

On Friday, Loar and Zundel were questioned. After dinner the final arguments were made. The *Journal* called them masterpieces but did not print them. It took the jury five hours, having had four ballots, to find all NOT GUILTY.[66]

The End

On May 26 the *Mount Pleasant Journal* declared the strike over. In a subheading it stated: "The Scottdale Convention Votes to Continue the Struggle, but the Rank and File Rush Back to Work."[67] The miners finally had a voice. They had been bombarded with propaganda by the unions and the socialists and they had had enough. In the editorial John Shields, editor and proprietor of the *Journal*, stated:

> After fifteen weeks of the bitterest struggle in the history of organized labor the great coke strike in the Connellsville region has ended in the defeat of the men who have been compelled to accept of the [sic] operators' wage scale and return to work. The long fight has cost both sides dear, particularly so the vanquished who have lost almost four months' wages, brought much suffering upon themselves and families, crippled general business over a large section of the country and destroyed, for a long time to come at least, their organization as a body of workers. Theirs has proven a truly bitter experience, but one whose lesson should not be forgotten....[68]

By the end of the month, all the soldiers had left the area. In the end, after nearly fifteen weeks of riots, marches, evictions, the Pennsylvania National Guard, fires at the Rainey plants, the socialists introducing the red flag of anarchy, and men killed at Morewood Mine, the miners rushed back to work. Instead of receiving an 8-hour day and wage increases, they were facing lower wages and more imported labor to replace them. They were beaten.

Seven

Strike of 1894

Where Kenneth Warren felt the strike of 1891 in the coke region deserved more attention than the Homestead Strike of 1892, Muriel Earley Sheppard, in the classic coke book *Cloud by Day*, stated: "The Region has always considered the industrial conflicts that shake it from time to time as private fights and discouraged news coverage. Thus, while nearly everyone knows about the Homestead Steel strike, the coke strike of 1894, which involved more operators, lasted longer, and cost the lives of more people, is hardly known outside the district. In this chapter therefore, I have continued to use eye-witness accounts as far as possible, supplemented by local newspaper articles."[1]

By 1894 there were more sources of information available. Newspapers had developed from the early years of the 1870s when many were originally founded. Government agencies had been created to supervise and oversee industries. They began publishing monthly and yearly reports. Industrial magazines also appeared that educated, reported, and editorialized. Thus, for Sheppard and for us, there was and is more original information to consult.

The industry also developed. All phases of industry were widespread. In addition to the mines in Pennsylvania, there were mines throughout the country mining iron ore, silver, and gold. The 1894 strike went far beyond the Connellsville region. It affected states as far away as Colorado. It was led by the United Mine Workers, which was a union that was trying to grow despite a lack of funds. They called the strike on April 11 and 200,000 bituminous miners around the country went out on strike.[2] The Connellsville region was already on strike. The Connellsville strike began the first week of April.

Panic of 1893

The events of the strikes of 1894 came after a year of drought, lack of mine cars, poor business, and hard times. It was called the Panic of 1893. For a good part of 1893, the ovens were banked and work was hard to find. The nationwide Panic lasted through 1897. Wikipedia reports that 500 banks and 15,000 companies failed. Unemployment reached nearly 25 percent in Pennsylvania.[3] Thousands of immigrant workers began to leave the area, some to go back to Europe, others to find work further west in the USA. Among them were 300 Slovak miners from the Connellsville region who were helped by the Slovak Colonization Society.[4]

Come September, the Frick company tried to start up a few ovens. The company had to cut prices because of stockpiles of coke. This was a problem, for they had a scale with the workers and it would not hold.[5] Throughout September the effort to keep the ovens working was difficult. Fewer and fewer miners were working. The Union Supply Company stores were ordered to take care of their miners' needs so families would not starve.[6] By November it was worse. Not only did some of the companies allow the miners to continue to receive food at the company stores, the Frick holdings stopped charging rent and allowed the miners to dig coal for their homes and use the mine mules to haul it out of the mine.[7] As late as November, the Frick company maintained the scale agreed upon in the final 1891 strike agreement. That agreement was valid until February 8, 1894, so the few miners who were working would receive the agreed-upon scale wage. The rate was $1.75 for coke, $1.00 per hundred for mining, and $1.95 for hauling. Other operators had reduced their rate considerably due to low demand.[8] The situation was becoming grave. The *Scottdale Independent* clearly stated that most of the operators had not paid their men a cent for over five months, while the Frick company maintained its scale.[9]

As mentioned in an earlier chapter and worth repeating, the *Courier* quoted Thomas Lynch: "Frick company are paying 40 per cent more wages for the same work than the Stewart Iron Company is paying in an adjoining works; 33½ per cent more than is being paid for the same work by James Cochran, Sons & Company; 22 percent more than … W.J. Rainey; 15 per cent more than Oliver Coke & Furnace Company; 12½ per cent more than … the McClure Coke Company…. Jones & Laughlin and Cambria Iron Company…"[10]

The stage was set for a strike similar to that of 1891. As the new year dawned and little improvement was made, it became every company for itself in a struggle for survival. Coke went down to 90 cents and some of the operators began to shut down.[11] The 1891 scale was due to expire at the end of January. In mid–January the Frick company posted its new scale. It reduced the 1891 rate by 10 to 20 per cent with a base of $1.15 instead of $1.75. It was higher than other operators. The *Courier* announced the new Frick company scale on January 19. They didn't announce much because the various provisions were not made public. But the minimum price that determined wages, as stated, was lowered from $1.75 to $1.15. Thus wages would be "greater than the average of the other operators, with the important additional advantage that any subsequent advances in the price of coke above the minimum will carry with them an advance in wages, an assurance which the employes of operators not working under a sliding scale do not have."[12] The Frick company miners signed the scale, which would commence the beginning of February. Other miners were not hopeful, as the last scale had been broken by most operators and they felt this one would be broken too.[13] The newspapers seldom reported the situation with the other operators. They focused on the Frick Company and never seemed to mention Frick's Southwest Company. In fact, the local papers were extremely difficult to find for the year 1894: the *Mount Pleasant Journal* was missing in action; and the *Connellsville Courier*, for the month of April when the strike began, had only one date available, April 13, and it was mostly illegible.

The *Courier*'s weekly report found that as of January 6, 8,396 ovens were active and 9,117 ovens were idle.[14] By February 2 the *Courier* made an assessment of life in the Connellsville coke region because of the rise of the industry:

> What the Connellsville region most needs to insure a reasonably prosperous condition of trade, steady employment and fair wages is that the coke industry be brought under the control of one concern. The field is limited and thus far the only persons who have derived any benefit from it have been the farmers who originally owned the coal. Every person residing in the field, from Latrobe to Fairchance should be receiving some benefit from this vast deposit of mineral wealth. The coke operator has received but little out of it, and the same is true of the miner. The merchant, the mechanic and those of other industries should, along with the miner and operator, receive their portion. If some person, by intelligent direction, could bring about a consolidation of the coke manufacturing interests into a single concern, much benefit would accrue to the region and all dependent upon it. Such a combination

would render impossible the repeated and often unwarranted reduction of wages, and steady employment would be assured.[15]

The paper wasn't wrong. It was the same message sent by the editor of the *Mount Pleasant Dawn* in 1875, nearly twenty years earlier. And it is exactly what Henry Clay Frick had been doing for twenty years. His employees were faring better than the rest. Frick was not the evil operator. He was the man who was building the industry and bringing it together. This was a rough time in the region: plenty of pain, plenty of violence, plenty of insecurity and plenty of fear. And there seemed to be no end in sight.

At the end of May, E.F. Duffy of the *Pittsburgh Daily Post* visited the coke region and in a lengthy front-page article reported what he saw and heard. Among the many items was a condemnation of Rainey:

> A Slav who worked at the W.J. Rainey works at Moyer, Fayette county, told the writer that he had not received as much as 1 cent in cash for eight months before the strike and that he did not know of a man who did. He told me that a surplus force of men is kept at the works, and the work is so distributed that each man is permitted to work enough to pay his store bill and no more. He illustrated this by saying he was a driver and his wages were $1.20 a day but that two men had to work at one job; that he was given 2 days in one week and three in the next; that the other man had to work the same way, making five days in the week for the two men, and making their joint earnings $6 a week.[16]

The story made Rainey look evil. However, if he was doing what Frick had been doing, keeping as many men working as possible so no one would do without completely, the story does its readers a disservice.

Union Holds Secret Meetings

Enter the unions, again! In mid–March the United Mine Workers, making a concerted effort to unite the region under their banner, held a meeting at Scottdale's Byrnes Hall, and the Connellsville area formally joined the now national union. They elected L.R. Davis of Uniontown as president of the local order and Daniel Darby as its secretary. A foreign miner, Michael Disman, was elected as vice president. Then they created committees including a wage scale committee.[17] The committee presented the following wage scale, which was approved: "The scale calls for 90 cents for mining room coal, 48 cents from drawing coke, $1.80 for inside labor, drift mines, and $1.85 for shafts and slopes. The balance of the scale is based on the Frick company sliding scale with a level advance of 12½ per cent all around. The scale does not have any sliding features...."[18]

A letter was sent to the operators: "The oppression that has existed for some time, together with the lack of co-operation between operators and miners of the region, has demoralized trade and has made business unprofitable to you and has kept your workmen in a state of starvation. To remedy existing evils as much as possible we think this can best be accomplished by the equalization of mining rates and conditions. We respectfully ask you to meet representatives of miners in Scottdale on Monday, March 26."[19]

The Frick company supported the effort because it had maintained its scale while other operators did not, putting it at a disadvantage: "A uniform rate of wages if maintained by the workmen throughout the coke region, would place all producers upon an equality and would certainly be advantageous to the workmen. The organization of coke-workers must be strong enough to maintain its agreements or else it will collapse as the former Miner's union did."[20] The remainder of the operators were against the idea. They accused the Frick company of manipulating the union. Rainey maintained he kept the same scale as the Frick company. Others claimed the Frick company intended to monopolize the coke trade and force them out of business. They made it clear that if their men joined the union they would be dismissed and replaced.[21] The Frick company's scale had a similar clause. If the miners signed its scale, they were not permitted to strike. No operators appeared at the March 26 meeting.

The Frick company made it clear that they wanted to negotiate with local men and workers and not outsiders. Men from Leisenring attended a mass meeting at Trotter. The next day twelve of those men were fired. The same at Leith. "[P]reparations are being made to close down tight as a drum all those works at which the greatest unrest as to present conditions of wages and labor have been manifest by the men. Orders were issued today to close down Leisenring work No. 1 in the morning. The tools and mules are being taken from the pit, and this is an absolute sign that the duration of operations is not to be of a few days' duration, but if need be for an indefinite period." In retaliation, the men refused to draw the coke ovens.[22]

One of the Frick company's constant themes was that the union men were foreign to the Connellsville region. It was reiterated again: "At the Scottdale meeting the other day it was reported that fifty-six delegates were present. By actual count there were twenty-one, only four of whom are engaged in work about the coke works. John McSloy, who figures as a leader in the movement for a strike, is at present engaged as barkeeper. The occupation of many other delegates and leaders bears even a more remote relation to the labor of coke making."[23]

The Strike

The strike was called for April 2.[24] On that day the McClure plants of Donnelly, Mayfield, Bessemer, Rising Sun, Mullen, Painter, Buckeye, Star, and Pennsville were working. Most of the Frick holdings went to work, but Standard, Morewood, Alice, Trotter, Nellie, and Stonerville were out, and some men from the Leisenring plants too.[25] It did not take long before guns, clubs, dynamite, and intimidation were employed by strikers to force the workers out. The very next day, 400 deputies were in the region protecting mines. A new six-month reign of terror began and violence led to death.

Death of Frick Engineer

It was during this strike that J.H. Paddock, the chief engineer of the H.C. Frick Coke Company, was beaten to death at Davidson Mine, a few miles from Broadford at the edge of Route 119. It happened on April 4 following several days of rioting.

The *Scottdale Independent* reported it this way:

A band of five hundred strikers marched to the Davidson plant of the H.C. Frick Coke company near Connellsville about three o'clock yesterday afternoon and clubbed Chief Engineer of the Frick Coke company J.H. Paddock, to death. Hugh Call [sic; Coll], superintendent of the Water company was assaulted at the same ... time and badly beaten.

The band formed somewhere near Vanderbilt early in the day and marched to the Adelaide plant of the Frick company and forced the men to quit their work, from Adelaide they marched to Broadford

Seven. Strike of 1894

THE MURDER OF ENGINEER PADDOCK.

This illustration appeared in the *Pittsburgh Press*, picturing the death of engineer John H. Paddock. He grew up near Philadelphia in a ministerial family, lived in Connellsville, served as vestryman at the Episcopal church, and was a member of the town council. Many of the achievements of the H.C. Frick Coke Company were due to his hard work and inspired creativity ("The Murder of Engineer Paddock," *Pittsburg Press*, April 5, 1894, p. 1).

but by the time they reached there the men had finished their work and gone home. The band then took up the line of march and went to the Davidson plant to intimidate the men working there, when near the plant they overtook Chief Engineer Paddock and Superintendent of Water Work, Hugh Call [Coll]. Mr. Call [Coll] ordered them to get off the ground of the Frick Coke company and they obeyed his order and retreated a couple of hundred feet. When that distance away they hesitated for a moment and turned about and started to pursue Paddock and Call [Coll]. The two men took to their feet and ran for the office, but before they could reach the office both were overtaken, knocked down with stones and clubbed. Paddock was beaten to death in a half minute's time and Call [Coll] was badly used up. After the assault the raiders retraced their steps and returned to Vanderbilt by way of Broadford.

Sheriff Wilhelm was in the vicinity at the time and at once raised a posse of men to follow the rioters and arrest as many as possible. Up to 10 o'clock last night 105 had been placed under arrest and taken to jail at Uniontown. In capturing a number of the raiders crossing the railroad bridge at Broadford, the posse was compelled to open fire, and one of the raiders fell dead. The region is in a fever of excitement.[26]

A coroner's jury was immediately impaneled under Squire James Eckard. The jury viewed Paddock's remains and found: "a bullet hole just back of the left ear and two horrible scalp cuts on the back of his head. The bullet was evidently from a revolver of large caliber, and the cuts were made by stones. His face was not mutilated, and his death is supposed to have been instantaneous."[27]

Master Mechanic Hugh Coll added more details:

Mr. Paddock and I had gone up to the works not expecting any trouble. While we were there a crowd of fully 500 to 600 Hungarians and Slavs came up and gathered in front of the houses owned by the company and occupied chiefly by foreign workmen and we saw them arguing with our people. So Mr. Paddock and I walked over and told the leaders that they were trespassing on property of the company and ordered them off.

They grumbled awhile, but at last started off. Mr. Paddock and I then walked toward the shaft…. stones commenced to fly…. I was struck in the back twice and was nearly knocked down the second time. Then I drew my revolver and fired five shots into the crowd…. Mr. Paddock was then about 20 yards ahead of me and running toward the engine house….

When I turned I saw somebody whom I supposed to be Paddock throw up his hands in the midst of the crowd. I started back. The crowd came toward me, and when I stopped they stopped. We kept this up for five minutes until the crowd turned and ran, and I then went up to Mr. Paddock, who was lying on the ground. He was dead.[28]

Paddock was the man who created the amazing Frick map for the Chicago World's Fair, which is still used today by local companies. The map took three years to make and cost $15,000 in 1893. It shows the topography of the area from Latrobe to Smithfield.[29] Engineer Kenneth Allen did the surveying. Then they had to establish levels throughout the region. They also marked "Every farm, farm house, and outbuilding with the owner's name. Every stream, large or small, can be traced from its source to its mouth. Swamps and woods are noted with the area they cover. The railroads, sidings and spurs; the coke plants and villages; the towns in the region, with their streets and alleys; and, in fact, everything has its proper place on this paper."[30] Unfortunately it was revised in 1915 and much of the early info was removed. Needless to say, it is huge.

Arrests and Trial

By midnight 94 rioters were jailed in Uniontown. As an aftermath to the murder, events unfolded at Broadford as the miners fled from the scene. An elaboration of the events at Broadford was given by the *Commercial Gazette*:

Not a shot was fired by the pursuers until the Pittsburg, McKeesport and Youghiogheny bridge at Broadford was reached. At this point the remainder of the fleeing Hungarians, numbering about 300, stopped momentarily, delayed by the necessity of narrowing their ranks in order to cross the bridge.

This was the deputies' opportunity. They called upon the Huns to surrender, but the order received no attention. The deputies fired and their shots told, as several of the rioters were seen to stumble and to clap their hands to various parts of their bodies. Another volley was fired, and one of the pursued was seen to drop.

Here the deputies witnessed a scene creditable to one of the rioters. A Hun looked around as his companion fell, stopped and attempted to pick up the body. Bullets flew about him thick and fast, but, nothing daunted, he stopped long enough to pull a red bandana handkerchief from his pocket and lay it on the face of the corpse. Then he sped away and rejoined his fleeing companions.

The dead rioter was lying across the railroad track. When the deputies came up the body was kicked aside to prevent it being run over by a train. Through Broadford pursuers and pursued ran below the village. The rioters slackened their pace for a second, and then, apparently by preconcerted signal, scattered in squads in all directions. Here the deputies also parted, seventeen following a crowd of fifty-two.

Two miles below Broadford the seventeen deputies came up with their prey. Both sides were exhausted by their forced march, and the rioters stopped to parley. Unconditional surrender was demanded, and, like lambs, the Hungarians were marched down the road. They were taken to Dawson and there guarded by the deputies until the train that leaves Pittsburgh at 5:50 P.M. arrived.

Though fully 1,000 people gathered at the station to see the prisoners, there were no violent demonstrations, and the captives were placed on the train.[31]

But the riots were not over. Twelve hundred men were on their way to Rainey's Moyer Mine. Rainey's men were waiting for them with over 150 deputies. Rainey closed his works and intended to stand and fight. His deputies arrested thirty strikers and sent them off to jail. Mr. Coll identified them as the men who had assaulted and killed Paddock. President Davis of the Mine Workers Association was also arrested.[32]

John Paddock's funeral was held in Connellsville. Most of the dignitaries of the region attended, including Henry Clay Frick. The streets of the region were quiet. No riots took place. Frick called off all work at his mines in honor of Paddock. After the funeral, Paddock's remains were taken to Cooperstown, New York, for burial.

The Trial

The trial did not take place until June. At that time the *Pittsburgh Press* reported another eyewitness account of the murder. This time the events varied from those described by Coll and others.

> In the Paddock murder case the first witness called this morning was Annie Nogel, an 18-year-old German girl, who proved to be a very baffling and shrewd witness. She lived on "Nigger hill," above Davidson, and saw Paddock the day he was killed. The strikers told the officials they wanted to hold a meeting. When Hugh Coll told them to keep off the company's ground they said they were going to do no harm.
>
> She said positively the mob was starting to leave the grounds when Coll started to shoot, and that Paddock also fired. They then ran, Coll over the hill and Paddock into the tipple, and she said she saw him jump from the window to the ovens beneath and lying on his back at the base of the tipple with his feet toward the sun. She said after Paddock jumped from the window she heard a striker exclaim: "Oh, there is a man has killed himself." She swore that she saw several strikers fire in the air, but none at Paddock.
>
> Other witnesses testified in the same strain, the drift of it all going to establish that the company officials fired first, and that Mr. Paddock in trying to escape, ran into the tipple, and, being hotly pursued, jumped from the window, 40 feet above the ovens, and that the fall killed him.[33]

A man named John Hussar was accused of being the leader and probably the shooter.[34] John McSloy and Mike Furen were also among those arrested. Hussar was tried first. It did not take long for the verdict. John Hussar was found guilty of involuntary manslaughter: "The verdict is a compromise one, three jurors favoring first degree murder and a few acquittals. The defense is satisfied with the verdict, and say that it does not follow that all the other defendants will be convicted."[35] The trial of Mike Furen, who worked at Rainey's Fort Hill works, followed. He was found guilty of second-degree murder. "It is said that on the first ballot the jury stood eight for second degree, one for first, two for manslaughter and one for acquittal.... The penalty for second degree murder is twenty years in the penitentiary."[36] All the other men arrested and held for trail were acquitted in late June:

> The speeches to the jury were made Friday night. Thomas M. Marshall and Frank A. Ammon, of Pittsburgh each spoke for a Slav defendant. D.W. McDonald defended Samuel Mason, the only English speaking defendant, and Ira E. Partridge spoke for the other 24 defendants. R.H. Lindsay addressed the jury for the Commonwealth. The case went to the jury at 11 o'clock and at the opening of court, Saturday morning, a verdict of not guilty as to the whole 27 defendants was returned.
>
> After the announcement of the verdict Judge Ewing called John Hussar and Mike Furin, two Paddock defendants who were convicted of manslaughter and second degree murder, respectively, for sentence. Each of these men demanded separate trials and were accordingly convicted. Their counsel asked for a new trial, but the motion was overruled. There is no doubt that if all had been tried together before the jury in the last cases that all would have gone free. Judge Ewing sentence Furin and Hussar to 12 years in the penitentiary.[37]

Violence Continues

The turmoil, however, continued throughout the region. The pattern remained as it was nearly ten years earlier in 1886: strikers roamed the region looking for miners still working and attempted to drive them from the field. It was not peaceful. Clubs, guns, and bombs were part of the drama. The unions encouraged the action. All the newspapers carried the details. As noted, the *Mount Pleasant Journal* for the year cannot be found. Only a few editions of the *Connellsville Courier* can be found. Much of the blow-by-blow descriptions are lost.

In the early April *Dispatch*, events were recorded:

> Late to-night 700 strikers from the Leisenring district are camped in the commons east of Scottdale. They marched to the Grace plant to-day to force the men out, but were met at the entrance to the plant by a large force of deputies armed with Winchester rifles. When the leaders confronted the rifles, carrying bayonets, the mob marched along, passing the plant without a stop. This force reached Scottdale at 6 o'clock, led by President Davis, who is wanted on a warrant.
>
> The line of march will be taken up by this mob in the morning, and trouble is almost certain. The Painter plant of the McClure Company and the famous Morewood plant will be visited. At both plants a large force of guards are on duty, and if an attempt is made to force an entrance blood will be shed that will break all former records.

> ...Yesterday the superintendents of the work not operating under the Frick scale called meetings of their workmen and begged of them to remain at work until the Frick men came out first. They claimed that they were paying more than the Frick Company and were not opposed to their striking for better wages and better conditions, provided the Frick men took the initiative.[38]

The latter statement was not true, and even the president of the union spoke against it. But as one can see, no one—management, miner, or union—was above lying and misrepresenting in order to advance their issues. On April 6, the Frick company mines began to close down as rioters gathered at Mount Pleasant, and it was feared they would once again, as they did in the strike of 1891, head for Morewood or Standard. At Mount Pleasant, "Many had lunches with them. They went wherever they could sit down, and ate dinner with their clubs and pistols lying beside them. There was no attempt at concealment of the weapons." Another group of 600 camped at Scottdale.[39] These are staggering figures. The mere mass caused trauma in the small towns. No one was safe.

> The meeting held in Scottdale Sunday resulted in bringing out a part of the men at the Standard and Valley plants. There were forty-five delegates present at the meeting Monday and they voted unanimously to continue the strike. By resolution passed the Connellsville region was formally put under the national strike, and the men made part of it. The district management was taken out of the hands of Acting President Barrett and vested in the executive board. Although the convention was largely attended and the delegates enthusiastic for continuing the strike, the resolutions are looked upon as not being representative, from the fact that the large majority of the delegates were not coke workers.
>
> Monday noon a delegation of men called on the general superintendent of The Southwest Coke Company and asked to have the No. 3 plant, now idle, started up. They offered to sign the Frick scale and agree to work against all objections. At the same time a delegation visited the superintendent of the Central plant of the United Coal and Coke Company and made the same proposition. The company agreed to start the plants, and at the latter place fifty-three men signed the Frick agreement within an hour. At the Southwest plant eighty diggers signed to go to work Monday morning. These plants have been idle since last July. The men are in very poor circumstances, and they say that no inducement can be offered to get them to come out now.
>
> Tuesday morning the Valley men assembled and marched to Mt. Pleasant where they were joined by the Standard and Buckeye strikers. They paraded near the plants, were peaceable and offered no interference. They marched back to Scottdale, arriving about 1:30 P.M. There were then about 1,200 men in line.
>
> They were joined along the march by the men from Rainey and Bessemer plants and also small delegations from some other works. They marched from Scottdale at 2 P.M. holding meetings at Summit, Morgan, Broadford and Adelaide. In the evening the return march was made, the men dropping out as they reached their respective homes. At Morgan 18 armed deputies fell in line and followed the men until they reached the County line at Everson.
>
> Wednesday found nearly all the works in the north end of the district out. All the plants from Broadford to Everson except Valley and Summit, which are badly crippled, were out solid and everything on the Mt. Pleasant branch of the B.&O. from Everson to Mt. Pleasant were also out…. The Valley and Summit plants were working but with a short supply of men. Nearly all those at work at the Frick plants are English speaking men, who have signed the agreement and as they feel bound by it, they are the only obstacle in the way of a general strike. As it is, two thirds of the men employed at all the works are out, and 8,000 of the 12,000 active ovens are idle.[40]

Evictions Begin

Once again, as in previous strikes, evictions of the strikers to make room for new workers began. By the end of May over 150,000 miners from all over the country were on strike. As in our region of interest, there were riots and murders, and violence everywhere. Negroes, convict labor and more were brought into the various regions to work in the mines. Regular miners were starving. Their families were in the worst poverty. The effects were widespread throughout industry. Railroads weren't running. Steel mills had to close. Shopkeepers had no business. The Pennsylvania governor, who had not sent the National Guard into the region as he had done in 1891, threatened to settle the strike himself. He was joined by five other governors who asked for national help in bringing an end to the strike that was crippling the nation. The nation was in peril.

Then the evictions became more intense. Oliver, Mammoth, and Smithton were among the first patches for evictions in the Connellsville region. At Oliver, the miners and their goods were dumped along the road. They simply set up housekeeping there. In Smithton, the workers at the Port Royal Mine moved their cow sheds into the woods and moved into them.[41] The Frick company also began to evict the miners from their homes. Up and down the Morgan Valley, families were thrown into the streets.

Slav and Hun agitators were thrown out of the Frick mines for good. They were not allowed to go back to work for the Frick company. To replace them, the Frick company contracted for more Italians. They came but soon left, claiming they were not hired to work the mines. They were afraid of the atmosphere in the region.

Details of the evictions began to emerge in the various papers. The focus shifted to the plight of the miners and their families once they were thrown out of their homes. A miner told John B. Baskin of the *Post* about the camp at Adelaide, across the river from Broadford:

> The Slavonic camp I spoke of is situated on the south bank of the Youghiogheny, a short distance from Broadford, but on the opposite side of the stream. It is near the little mining village of Adelaide, and is perhaps three miles west of Connellsville. I walked down there yesterday, and finally made an inspection of the camp, for it can be called nothing else. Three weeks ago 60 families were evicted from the company houses at Adelaide, and their household goods were hauled to the plateau by the river where they are now located. About 40 families are there, I was told.... The habitations are of the rudest and most primitive description. They are a conglomeration of green thatching boughs, canvas, bedquilts and planks. The quarters are necessarily contracted, and the housewives are no doubt worried to keep their houses in order. But, nevertheless, as at the village at Leisenring No. 2, everything was clean, and the women made the best of their hard surroundings. The cooking stoves were nearly all out in the open....
>
> Many of the Slavs have, I am informed, received assistance from friends at home in the Austro-Hungarian empire, and this has no doubt proved of material assistance in many instances. A gentleman in a position to know told me last week no less an amount than 12,000 florins, or nearly $5,000, was received by some of the striking Slavs, and that more will probably follow.
>
> Numerous strikers are doing what they can to turn an honest penny. Just now the blackberry crop is ripening, and many of them are industriously engaged in picking berries and taking them to market. They will walk four or five miles to Connellsville, or seven or eight miles to Uniontown, as the case may be. A clean and neatly-dressed woman, with a kerchiefed head, will walk for miles under a broiling sun on a dusty highway to sell a bucket of berries and add a mite to the common family fund.[42]

Baskin came back a few days later and reported more pathos. This time he began at Standard Mine.

> At Standard I saw a very strange and pathetic sight, and one which will not soon be forgotten. After making my way through long streets of company houses, now tenanted by imported negro workers, I came, at the end of the village, to a little schoolhouse, over which the Stars and Stripes were hanging languidly under the hot August sun.
>
> A board fence enclosed the ground about the schoolhouse on both sides and built against the inside of the fence was a conglomeration of the most miserable apologies for dwellings that it is possible to imagine. I have seen the dugouts and sod shanties of the west, but for comfort, convenience and all the essentials of a home they were far ahead of these abodes, if such they can be called. Everything that could be utilized in the way of old lumber, broken boards, planks, etc., had been gathered up and put together in the hope of effecting some protection against the sun and rain. There many of the evicted Slavs lived their daily lives. Not many of the men were present. A number of the patient-faced women and pale-faced children were about, however.
>
> But it was in the schoolhouse that the strangest sight was to be seen. There, under the flag supposed to float alike for both poor and rich, were the household goods of a number of the evicted families. Beds were given the preference, and the two ordinary sized rooms were crowded with them. There must have been a dozen in all. The reason there are so many beds is to enable as many persons as

possible to have the protection of a roof. There were tables, chairs, stools, etc. In those two rooms, the blackboards of which still bore the figures of sums worked out by pupils, 34 families slept nightly, I was told. Everything was cleanly for these Slavish people are a cleanly, industrious race. One mother was washing her little one's legs and feet, and another was holding in her arms a child suffering from whooping cough.

The women admitted they had a pretty hard time of it, and one of the few men present asked me in a wistful voice when I thought the strike would be over. But there was no thought or intention of giving in. They expressed themselves against that....

From Standard I walked to Scottdale, as I wanted to see some of the evicted families at Morewood. A colony of them, the principal one, I believe, had moved into a neck of woods a considerable distance from the road, and I did not visit them. Other families were scattered about in various places....

Before closing, however, I wish to say a few words about the coming exodus of coke workers and miners from this region. The movement is on in earnest, and it seems to be only a question of whether those who wish to leave can secure a sufficient amount of money to enable them to do so. A meeting of Germans was held here yesterday in the German Lutheran church and was presided over by Rev. Lambertin [Lambling?], the well-known friend of the strikers. Three questions were proposed: Shall we emigrate? If so, when and where? It was decided to emigrate, and the other questions will be decided later....

There is no question but a large number will decide to emigrate, and it is probable they will go to a point in Wisconsin where they will be given an opportunity to purchase homes and be assured of enough work to secure a living the coming fall and winter. A large number of Slavs and Italians have already called on Mr. Lambertin to inquire about the matter.[43]

By the end of June, almost all workers were back at work. By the end of July, everyone had a gun. The sheriff, the companies, and some union officials worked to disarm the men and persuade them to leave the guns behind. It worked. By August and September, many of the workers begged to go back to work. The Negroes began to leave and go back home. In March of the next year, the miners received a "voluntary" increase in pay from 78 cents to 90 cents.[44]

The Historic American Engineering Record, a secondary source, reported: "From 1894 until 1922, the Connellsville coke region was virtually free of strikes, and labor organizations were unsuccessful in recruiting members.... In 1899 and again in 1904, the Pittsburgh District of the UMW mounted unsuccessful organizing drives in the Connellsville region."[45] The companies did not want them, but neither did the miners.

Epilogue

The story of these events has been recorded in this chapter from the media of the day as they occurred. The voices are of the people who lived through this horrific time in America. These sources provide the small details of what transpired on our streets and in our neighborhoods. Is there bias? Yes. Is there dishonesty? Yes. But by hearing these voices, one can feel the events, speak of the average person involved, and evaluate the events from the perspective of the people who lived them.

These strikes put the entire region into turmoil. Each was a national event with far-reaching consequences. Each was an incident in the industry that built a nation on the backbone of its immigrants. Most far outweigh the occurrences of the Homestead Strike of 1892. Yet the Homestead Strike has a voice. It has a foundation. It has books. The coal strikes from 1875 through 1894 have very little in the way of a record. They deserve more. The entire population lived in terror for decades.

Eight

Cleanup

Mine pollution comes in the form of air, water, and fire. Without air in a mine, the miners could not operate. But with air there was danger of explosions, fires, and bad water. Miners needed light to see. In early mining, they wore light in the form of a flammable substance and a wick on their helmets and lit them when they entered the mine. If they entered a gaseous area, an explosion would occur.

Water in a mine was and is a constant problem. There is natural water underground, and if a miner opened a new wall, a ton of water could have descended upon him. Water also entered the mine especially after a hard rain. Rainwater that flooded a mine was acidic from the contents of the mine. That created more problems as all the fixtures in the mine corroded and had to be replaced, including the pumps that pumped the bad water out of the mine. In addition, enormous quantities of water were necessary to quench the coke after it had been fired. That water was the worst, filled with the debris of the coke ovens. Both the mine water and the quenching water made their way into streams, polluting them. When air, water, and iron pyrite (a shiny yellow mineral) merged, they created acid mine water. That is the orange-colored water one sees coming out of a mine.

Fire could close a mine for good. There were dozens of ways a fire could start: the flame from the helmet light was the first. Natural gases could explode. Then there was spontaneous combustion: a fire just started on its own. Once a fire started it was almost impossible to put out. Once put out, it could start up again at any time. Some mine fires have been burning for decades. The long-believed solution to these problems was to cut the air. Solving the problems all these elements created has taken over a hundred years and the issue still persists.

By the late 1860s, the bituminous coal district of southwestern Pennsylvania became the center of coke production in the United States. That meant its runoff was becoming visible in the small streams that led to the rivers. Fish were dying, and that became an issue for the fish and wildlife organizations. In 1875, Senator George H. Anderson of Allegheny County introduced a bill in the Pennsylvania Senate against the pollution of streams that would affect the fish. It did not pass, but a little later a new game law was brought up and it included Anderson's bill. That passed. Because of ongoing concerns, new legislation was passed in 1876 that demanded that all polluted water from industry be contained in tanks.[1] All of this was done to save the fish. No one was concerned about other pollutants. No one foresaw the incredible aftermath of mining.

As mines began to close, new problems arose. There were no laws determining just how an abandoned mine should be shut down. Therefore, companies just walked away. They left mines to gravity for drainage of water, and they did not close interconnections between mines, entrances, or other openings. All would be left open.[2] In 1905, still in the

Sealing a mine is a difficult job. Keeping it sealed is even more difficult. This image is of a seal at the Henry Clay Mine at Broadford, taken in 2017. The water is orange from the sulfur escaping the mine. That sulfur flows into streams, in this instance the Youghiogheny, and causes the massive pollution (author photo).

Golden Age of mining, the state passed the Purity of Waters Act. But it did not apply to the growing industries, including mining. So it did not help.[3] It was becoming obvious that the industries of mining, tanning, and others had influence with government.

Sanitary Water Board

In 1915 the state thought they had solved the pollution problem by neutralizing water via chemicals. By this time, it was acknowledged that mines were polluters, but they were not the only polluters: "acid factories and chemical works, paper and pulp mills, tanneries and indeed all forms of industries" were polluting the streams. The authorities performed many tests, finding limestone to be the solution to the pollution, but in the end, this too did not work.[4] It took the railroad to find the beginning of the solution. They could not get enough clear water to run their trains. They sued eighteen coal companies and the battle was on. Lower courts sided with the companies. The Pennsylvania Supreme Court overturned the decision and supported the railroad claims. The United States Supreme Court refused to hear the case, so the railroad won. The mining companies were forced to deal with the issue.[5] That was a monumental victory and a monumental task.

To help with the task, Governor Gifford Pinchot created the Sanitary Water Board. It was designed to supervise all the streams in the state and work toward cleanup, especially from acid mine drainage (AMD). But unfortunately, it exempted mines, which reduced its effectiveness again.[6]

The original Sanitary Water Board consisted of five state cabinet officers, including the Attorney General, Public Service and Fisheries Commissioners, and the Secretaries of Wealth and Forest and Waters. In 1927, three citizens at large joined the board. The legislative intent was for the board to focus on sewage disposal practices, to develop a permanent system for such discharges, and work with neighboring states on common water problems (129).

The Sanitary Water Board divided Pennsylvania streams into three categories: Class A: fairly clear streams; Class B: polluted streams that could be cleared; and Class C: streams that were too badly polluted and could not be saved (131–32). Through the years the board joined forces with various organizations and worked toward maintaining clear streams.

By 1924 little had been accomplished, so another major effort was tried. The State Supreme Court prohibited mines from draining water into creeks.[7] That did not work either, for once again, polluting industries were not policed. Fayette County forbade discharge of AMD as of January 29, 1925. No one listened. In 1926 Andrew Crichton presented a paper before the American Mining Congress titled *Mine Drainage Stream Pollution*. His conclusion was to stop mining in rural areas.[8] Most mining was only done in rural areas. so this was not going to work either.

During the same period the Sanitary Water Board formed boards with various polluters: Tannery Waste Disposal Committee of Pennsylvania; Pulp and Paper Mills; and finally, the Bituminous Coal Mine Drainage Board (138–39).

Sealing Begins

In 1927, the state passed the Goehring Bill, which was to seal all abandoned mines in Pennsylvania. Sealing a mine was a way to contain fires by cutting off the oxygen, to stop anything from coming out of the mine carrying pollutants, and hopefully to guarantee better water. By 1930 an experiment was carried out to see if a mine could be sealed. The Bureau of Mines conducted a series of experiments in several mines. By sealing off sections, they discovered that sealing could help solve the problem.[9] There were thousands of mines in Pennsylvania. Each mine had many holes: entrances, air vents, caved-in areas, and more. Sealing all of them was a monumental task. And an expensive one.

Enter the Depression

During the Depression, the National Industrial Recovery Act was passed. It had two main sections: Title I for Industrial Recovery and Title II for the Public Works Administration. The second helped clean up the mines.[10] By 1934 the first survey of abandoned bituminous coal mines in Pennsylvania was conducted. They used mainly unemployed miners and intended to hire 160 men in southwestern Pennsylvania. Their task was to map and chart the abandoned mines. Men were paid $30 a week. In Westmoreland County, fifty men worked out of Latrobe under Leo T. Gibson.[11] It took until 1936 for the project to reach

Fayette County. There the project was supervised by Thomas McGinty of Uniontown. Almost 400 men were employed to close "all abandoned openings with concrete and earth."[12]

In early May, Dr. Edith MacBride-Dexter, Pennsylvania Secretary of Health, announced that across the state, "3,595 mine drifts, shafts and cave holes, in addition to 9,374 feet of crevices, have been sealed since the start of work on January 1." A force of 1,238 laborers, ten storekeepers, and twenty-two supervisors were employed. In all there were 2,282 known abandoned bituminous mines. They created nine million pounds of sulfuric acid.[13]

In and around Mount Pleasant in Westmoreland County, they were faced with an additional problem. It seems the sewage of that community, as well as others in the region, was being thrown into the acidic streams. The acid would previously take care of the sewage. With the seals, the acid was gone or minimal, and that created a sewage disposal problem.[14]

These early seals consisted of dams constructed at the entrances to hold back the water. Sometimes the water broke through. Another type was a "curtain wall ... extending from the roof of the mine to within a short distance of the ground. A second wall is built up from the ground back of the first wall and well above the bottom opening of the curtain wall. The outer curtain completes the seal closing the opening, except for a weh, a quick coupling used to measure the water movement. The effect is like the ordinary sewer trap in a kitchen sink."[15]

In 1937 the Clean Streams Law was enacted. (It has been amended eight times, the latest in 2006.) Also passed was Pamphlet Law 2787, which made mine owners responsible for what we call mine subsidence today. It meant that if a cave-in occurred in a mine under a building, street, bridge, and even a cemetery, the mine owner was responsible for the repairs.[16] Today owners who know their structures are over an old mine are expected to take out insurance. There is even a web site that has maps showing where potential subsidence may occur.

On August 30, 1937, the *Connellsville Daily Courier* reported there were 3,464 abandoned mines in Western Pennsylvania, 1,003 idle mines, and 2,130 working mines, and all had acid mine drainage.[17] To this point the WPA had sealed 400 openings in the area and filled 60,000 cave-ins. The estimate for completion of the job was ten years.

By 1946 the Sanitary Board of the Department of Health partnered with the Mellon Institute for Industrial Research. The study of mine sealing and acid mine drainage lasted until 1962. It concluded that mine sealing *did not work*.[18] Before that conclusion, in 1947 mine sealing had become a state law. By that law, operators were required to seal their abandoned mines within 60 days.[19]

1948, Sealing Began Again

In 1948 a new round of sealing began in Pennsylvania. As did all the attempts, it began with a survey. In Westmoreland County, John Y. Woods of the Greensburg office was in charge, and the main aim was Jacobs Creek between Mount Pleasant and Scottdale. "The crew of three mining engineers, eight handymen and 35 laborers, aided by heavy machinery, have been in the Scottdale-Mount Pleasant area since May. Five seals have been made at Bessemer. The workers are backfilling, including that at Morewood and three others. Sherrick's run [sic] is the tributary in that district which empties into Jacobs creek [sic] and it in turn goes into the Youghiogheny."[20] The state would do the work on mines abandoned six months before passage of the law; all others must be done by owners.[21]

By July of 1949, mine sealing moved into Fayette County. Again, it was administered from a Uniontown office, and this time the division engineer was Thomas W. Keighley. The head of the mine sealing program was W.O. Vancourt of Ebensburg. The "objective is to get to the headwaters of a stream and work downward, stating that the work will be concentrated on tributaries of the Youghiogheny River and thus eventually clean up the principal stream."[22] They planned on using both dry and wet seals but needed help to find all the mine openings. They would "pump out and filter the existing water, then construct a stone wall to prevent air from getting to the remaining Sulphur."[23] They expected to take 25 to 30 years to complete the project. In 1950 the two shafts at Morewood (A and B) were sealed, as were an old shaft at Rainey works.[24]

Into the 1970s

By the 1970s, more sophisticated methods of sealing were being used. For water, there were subsidence seals, borehole seals, and surface seals. Of the three, surface seals are "airtight plugs constructed in dry drift openings, air shafts, boreholes to prevent air and water going into the mine workings." For the mine itself, there were dry seals, air seals, and hydraulic seals.[25] Hydraulic seals "are water tight plugs constructed in mine openings to flood reactive deposits and reduce formation of pollutants."[26] Fire issues were another question. Municipalities were dumping their garbage into abandoned mines. Almost forty mine fires existed in Fayette County: twenty-five had been extinguished, but by July 1970, eighteen were still burning.[27]

The work was still going on in 1971. Along Galley Run, six hydraulic seals and backfill were put in place. Adelaide mine, a short distance from Henry Clay (across the Yough), received two.

Operation Scarlift 1977

An extensive survey was conducted in 1977 throughout the bituminous region. Related to our discussion were the findings along Galley Run and Jacobs Creek. At the time of the study, after all the attempts at stopping the pollution, Galley Run, Stauffer Run, and Sherrick Run each had two miles of acid, iron, and sulfate pollution.[28] The mines along Galley Run were Henry Clay (M20, M56), Tip Top (M58, M59), and Rist (M57; also Adelaide outside our study) (V-10). Along Jacobs Creek were two at the Alvertons (V-11). Galley Run mines received four hydraulic seals, backfill subsidence, and grout curtain. Along Stauffer Run, which merges into Jacobs Creek, six hydraulic seals and four surface seals were installed.[29]

In addition to the Youghiogheny River report, there was also a Redstone Creek Watershed report during Operation Scarlift. It was primarily concerned with the Monongahela River, but there was a section on the Yough that included Galley Run. The mandate of this report was to place hydraulic seals in deep mine workings, restore strip mines and subsidence areas, construct barriers in deep mines, dispose of fly ash in abandoned mines, and lower the ground water table.[30]

This report called Galley Run Work Area 2 found thirty-eight acid mine drainage sources along its length. The waterway received 2,277 pounds of acidity daily, caused by acid mine drainage. Their conclusion was to treat the region with chemical treatment, "the only technically feasible and practical method of abatement."

In a much-appreciated summary, the report listed each mine in our survey that was affecting the small stream. This comprehensive detail was not found in the other surveys.

> White Mine called US-46 had seepage.
> Foundry Mine called US-47 had a collapsed drift entry.
> Henry Clay Mine called US-48 had seepage caused by highway construction breaking through the mine.
> Unnamed mine (could be Frick) called US-49 seepage.
> Morgan Mine called US-50 had a collapsed drift entry.
> Unnamed (also could be Frick) called US-51 had a collapsed drift entry.
> Morgan Mine, again called US-58, had seepage from collapsed or backfilled drift entry.
> White Mine called US-60 had a collapsed drift entry.[31]

Conservation Coalitions

In 1982 yet another new approach was tried. The state began to look to the population, and the people were given a chance to get involved in the cleanup of water pollution. The

Henry Clay Mine along Galley Run. The water coming from the interior of the mine along the far bank is orange, a continuous stream of pollutants flowing into the Youghiogheny River less than 100 yards away (author, 2017).

Western Pennsylvania Coalition for Abandoned Mine Reclamation was begun, forming six conservation districts in Western Pennsylvania. The same was done in Eastern Pennsylvania in 1996. Today in our region, the Jacobs Creek Watershed Association, the Mountain Watershed Association, plus dozens of others work hard, get grants, and try to help clean up the region. Today twenty-four counties in Pennsylvania have conservation districts.[32]

In 1998 Pennsylvania's *Comprehensive Plan for Abandoned Mine Reclamation* reported: "There are over 250,000 acres of abandoned surface mine with dangerous highwalls and water filled pits. About 2,400 miles of streams do not meet water quality standards because of drainage from abandoned mines."[33] It continues.

In 1998, Carnegie Mellon University located AMD at the Henry Clay shaft, which they called the B1. They noted the mine was flooded.

In 2002, 5,172 abandoned mines covering 184,431 acres with impaired water covering 3,239 miles and an estimated 50 years to solve. In Westmoreland County, there are 228 Abandoned Mine Land (AML) Sites with 887 unreclaimed AML features covering 4,862 acres. In Fayette, 226 sites, 1,058 features and 5,482 acres.[34]

Trying Again

By the 21st century, there were new ways of dealing with water treatment. In an article titled "Researchers team up to tackle state's acid mine drainage problem," a Penn State team discussed the new methods of cleaning up acid mine drainage: active and passive mitigation. "Active treatment, where drainage is collected and then chemically treated, is expensive and labor intensive. Passive treatment, where drainage is exposed to wetlands or limestone beds, is less costly, and is more commonly used to treat AMD, especially because Pennsylvania has so many points of pollution."[35] They further found that Mother Nature can do the work for us, and that setting up treatment systems within what they call the "kill zone" is a mistake. That area needed to remain because it helped clean up the pollution.

Such a system already existed. It began back in 1994 when a group of scientists, artists, and humanists got together and formed *AMD and Art*. Through hard work and an enormous number of grants, they put together a program that restored the Ghost Town Trail and restored and celebrated the Vintondale Mine in Cambria County. One of the features was an Acid Mine Drainage Treatment System devised to clean up the pollution from Vintondale.

The project built a series of pools that would be used to clean the AMD of the Vintondale Mine. The first pool is called the acid pool, and the AMD from the mine is drained into this pool. The next three pools are wetland treatment cells that have plants and compost to "slow the water and promote biological activity, making the water less acidic, allowing the metals to settle out." They remove metals. Pool five is a Vertical Flow Pond. At the bottom of the pool is "a thick layer of organic material and then about four feet of limestone." Drainage pipes line the bottom. As the AMD passes through the layers, it loses oxygen and the limestone raises its pH. At pool 6, the water is free and can be discharged into the stream again.[36] This, too, was not the solution to AMD.

In the meantime, projects continue. In May of 2018, the state under Growing Greener Plus allocated $20 million to improve its water. These grants were to be given to municipalities and nonprofits. It was a small portion of the $300 million already given to 2,100 projects throughout the state.[37] Every month or so a new idea appears in the newspapers to try to put a halt to the acid mine drainage. This brief summary does not do justice to all the efforts that have existed through the years, but it shows the depth of the problem.

Appendix: The Mines

The establishment of coal mines and coke ovens in the Morgan Valley began the great industrialization of the region, which led to the industrial growth of America. The first successful regional beehive coke oven was not created in Morgan Valley, but nearby, near Hickman Run and the town of Dawson. Its invention enabled the industry. The development, through the establishment of a series of mines, was in the valley that stretched from Broadford on the Youghiogheny through Everson and Scottdale to the mines surrounding Mount Pleasant. That is where the bituminous industry began to thrive. Why? Because a nine-foot wall of the Pittsburgh Seam coal bed was just below the surface.

The *Connellsville Weekly Courier* began recording mine statistics in 1888 with a chart titled *Report on the Operation and Output of the Coke Ovens of the Connellsville Region*. It lasted for well over fifty years, with several format changes through the years. The original format, which lasted through most of the Golden Age, gave the name of the mine, the owner, the number of ovens, the number of ovens in blast, the number out of blast, the number of days the mine was worked that week, and the estimated output. When sales were good, the ovens were fired. When sales were bad, they stood idle and the men were often out of work or forced to take a pay cut.

The Frick company kept a detailed and extremely complicated system of records of who owned what in each mine. These records, called *Property Records*, began at the very beginning of Frick ownership and have been maintained until today. Dozens of people sold portions of their property to mining companies. Their names remained on the property and it was called a tract. Further, they sold the property to the mining company as either surface or mineral rights, sometimes both. Surface rights gave the mining company ownership of the property above the ground. It did not provide mineral rights. Mineral rights gave the mining company ownership of the property below the surface, or underground, where the coal or other types of minerals were to be found. Each tract had dozens of transactions through the years.

Trying to research such mines is confusing and frustrating. To substantiate information, one must wade through hundreds of documents and spend years deciphering the material. In most instances, county and state records did not begin until later. Deeds and transfers of property numbering in the hundreds for a single tract of land were common. Even the Bureau of Mines and all its subsidiary and related organizations cannot provide exact information. They maintain they do not have it, at least not for this very early history. Consulting a single source when delving into mining history is a mistake. To substantiate, John Enman, a modern-day scholar, wrote: "The Frick Division maintained records only for those mines and coke plants over which it had control. The records of other concerns have long since disappeared along with the companies. The Department of Mines, Harrisburg, has never maintained a file on individual mines which indicates their opening and closing dates."[1]

The mines in this study are presented in chronological order, maybe. Historians, even of the day, and company records seldom agree on details. Every attempt has been made to produce an accurate brief history of the mine and its environment: its foundation, its development, its transition from industrial to domestic use, to the aftermath and cleanup. Each mine has a few small incidents and events that add details about the people who worked in the mines. The H.C. Frick Coke Company went from Frick to Carnegie to U.S. Steel. U.S. Steel sold all to RGGS in 2003, so that is the bottom line of all the entries below.

For well over a century, the industry in its various forms, dominated the region. But its greatest era was from 1871 to 1920, the Golden Age of Coal and Coke.

Morgan Mine

The Morgan Mine was believed to be the first mine built in the valley; thus the name Morgan Valley. However, if some of the dates are to be believed, one or two mines in the valley were begun before Morgan. It was a small mine with only twenty acres of coal land.[2] Its original entrance was a drift. Eventually it had two drift openings called Upper and Lower. The Lower linked to the Frick Mine south of it. The mine entrance was located on the northwest side of the valley, about ¼ of a mile from the beginning of the Broadford Road. Traveling up the valley on the current Broadford Road, one must look to the hillside on the left to see the location. The entire mine is beyond the railroad tracks to the south of Dry Run Road (the name changes to Narrows Road as it crosses Broadford Road).

The village around the mine was originally known as Sherrick Station, but became known as Morgan Station after the mine was built. It had ten tenements to begin with and various shops for building cars, wagons, and wheelbarrows.[3] To the north of Dry Run Road were a string of tenement houses along the edge of the railroad tracks. Today the village is called Morgan.

The Panic of 1873 took its toll on the valley, and portions of Morgan Mine were up for sale. On December 14, 1877, Frick reported in his journal that T. Mellon & Sons loaned the Clay Coke Co. $8,450 "in order to start their business properly at Morgan mines."[4] (Additional references to the Clay Coke Company have not been found.) The *Industrial Statistics* of 1878 said that Frick was leasing the Morgan Mine by 1877.[5] Frick continued his quest for ownership of the Morgan Mine on June 15, 1878, when he and E.M. Ferguson (surely as the H.C. Frick Coke Company) invested ¼ interest each in Morgan Mines.

1865 "[Tintsman] and Joseph Rist bought six hundred acres of coking coal land at Broad Ford."[6]
1866 Franklin Ellis maintained Morgan and Co. was founded this year.[7]
1868 G.D. Albert maintained Col. A.S.M. Morgan founded this mine.[8]
1869 Modern-day researcher John Enman fixes the founding date as 1869.[9]
1874 Morgan Mine shipped west, including the state of California. During anthracite strike it shipped "east to the Susquehanna and Lehigh valleys."[10]
1875 Morgan Mine had 111, 11' × 6' bank beehive coke ovens, each charged with 110 bushels of coal for 4 days to produce 48-hour coke and 125 bushels on weekends to produce 72-hour coke.[11]

The Mines

- 1876 Morgan sold his interest in the mine to Col. Daniel Davidson (built Pittsburgh & Connellsville RR, first RR in area) and Albert Patterson for $60,000.[12]
- 1876 The mine employed 74: 30 miners, 32 outside laborers, 2 inside laborers, 1 outside mechanic, 2 inside mechanics, 1 outside mule driver, 4 inside mule drivers, 1 weigh master, and 1 mining overseer.[13]
- 1878 The firm was sold to the H.C. Frick Coke Company.[14] It may have been Frick's first purchase.
- 1878 Consisted of the Rist Coal Tract of c. 217 acres, the Newcomer Coal Tract of c. 60 acres, and the Old Morgan Tract of c. 150 acres. It also included a house, a storehouse, car shop, stables, one-half interest in two houses at Morgan Station, 111 coke ovens, 111 railroad cars, pit wagons, larries, wheelbarrows, tools, mules, horses, and cart: a complete mine.[15]
- 1880 Company had 120 men[16] at Morgan and built 50 new ovens. That brought the total to 161, but records of the Connellsville oven reports over years list 165, so 4 more were added at some point.
- 1881 500 miners camped at Morgan Station while trying to get other men to come out on strike.[17]
- 1889 Headquarters for the strikers were at Morgan Station.
- 1895 Morgan Mine, whose mine boss at the time was Thomas Coulehan, operated only 96 days.[18]
- 1897 All that remained in the mine was ribs and stumps. The mine boss then was Daniel Alsop.[19]
- 1910 Union Supply Company store was closed and workers had to use the one at Broadford (Matthew Gault manager of both stores).[20]
- 1917 Frick company papers list Morgan as closed.
- 1921 On April 21, 1921, the unsold interests of the Morgan Mine were conveyed to Samuel Wiggins, as was the Frick Mine property.
- 1921 Corrado-Schenck owned Morgan. Most likely they leased Morgan. They invested a great deal of money, but by 1922 they only had 16 ovens working.[21]
- 1930 Morgan Mine abandoned on January 1, 1930.
- 1954 Coal was still being mined. Called house coal, delivered to homes to fire furnaces.[22] Miner was Gould Coal Company. Uncovered the coke ovens.[23]
- 1977 Morgan Mine called U.S.-50 had a collapsed drift entry causing seepage.[24]
- 2016 At some point the slag dump from Morgan was taken to Ohio for roadwork.[25]

Incidents and Events

"In 1886 a Frenchman named Kaiser [French Canadian named Joseph Case] who worked as a coke drawer at Morgan Station refused to go out on strike. He received several threatening notices beginning with the words 'Death to Traitors.'" Finally, fourteen strikers beat him with clubs. "Sheriff Sterling was notified, and on a special train soon arrived at the scene of the assault before noon. The assailants all lived in a row of houses which the deputies surrounded, and after a fight which lasted an hour, the eleven men were captured and handcuffed together. Several had to be knocked down before they could be landed on the car. They are now securely locked up in the Uniontown jail to await the result of the Frenchman's injuries. Not one of the arrested men are Hungarians."[26] Case identified the men and they were "held for trial."[27]

During the many strikes it would become common for miners to gather at Morgan Station as it was a midway point. The strike of 1889 began near Mount Pleasant at Schoonmaker's Alice Works, on the hill above Morewood. Six hundred Huns did not want a new agreement, so they cut six coal cars from the pit mouth and they ran downhill and crashed. A larry car, used to carry coal, was thrown off the top of the ovens, some wheelbarrows were broken until they were only splinters, and an oven front was smashed. Then the Huns from Alice marched on to Bessemer Mine armed with clubs, coke forks, and guns. There they continued to riot. They assaulted people, then raided the company store and almost set it on fire. They did the same at Coalbrook Mine. They beat a man named Joseph Harshman, a drawer, and dragged him down the valley to Morgan Station, where they set up their headquarters. Just outside of Morgan Station they encountered a posse and there was a shootout. They took refuge in a place called the Soup House, the former company multi-resident house of Sherrick (the former name for Morgan Station). The posse raided the Soup House and captured 21 of them. They found them under beds, in cupboards, and everyplace else. The remainder marched to Connellsville and continued their battle at Calumet, Mammoth, Hecla, and Stonerville (Alverton) patches. Eventually all became calm with nothing settled.[28]

"On last Tuesday evening Charles Stillwagon and Joseph Robbins got a buggy and drove down to Morgan Station to get their truant wives, who had gone off on a visit without the consent of their liege lords. Robbins located his runaway wife and commenced to beat her in a brutal manner with the butt end of a buggy whip. At that stage of the proceedings Stillwagon interfered in behalf of the woman. This angered Robbins still more, and he drew a knife and commenced cutting Stillwagon. Before the latter could recover from his surprise he was bleeding from numerous wounds in his side and back. He will recover."[29]

The strike of 1891 was even more intense and troubling at Morgan. Thousands would descend on Morgan for meetings. By April, when the strike looked hopeless, the companies, in order to find homes for the new workers they were bringing in, began to evict the strikers throughout the region. The *Post* reported: "The eviction of strikers from the houses of the companies has begun. Two families were forcible ejected from their homes at the Morgan mines this afternoon. Their furniture was thrown into the road, while a large crowd stood by and watched the work of the deputy sheriffs. By May, things were no better. This time a reporter for the *Pittsburg Times* took a ride through the valley. "Yesterday a representative of THE TIMES traversed the coke region between Broadford and Mount Pleasant. In this strip there are dozens of families living in stables and outhouses. Among the evicted at Morgan is M.T. McInerney. He has a wife and children. At present this entire family is living in a cow-house, about 10 feet long, 8 feet wide and with holes for chimney and windows. Mr. McInerney said: 'Although these quarters are uncomfortable we are willing to put up with them. Our people try to help each other out in their distress. I lived in a tent for a few days after they evicted me, but gave it up to a family that was without any shelter.'"[30]

"Early this morning coke workers along the Morgan yard of the plant of the H.C. Frick Coke Company saw standing on the edge of the coke ovens a tall and haggard man. As the workers gazed, he deliberately walked to the red rim of the trunnel head, looked in, and with a last gesture of farewell, directed as to heaven, brushed back his hat from his forehead and leaped into the coke oven. A flame of unusual brilliancy and length shot up through the trunnel opening, and the workmen ran to the oven. Tearing down the clay and brick doors they could see the body within the glowing furnace, writhing and seething. When the body was taken out it was unrecognizable. So far there has been no identification."[31]

Eagle Mine (Sherrick)

A dirt road leads to Eagle Mine from the left side of Broadford Road. It is blocked by a gate. The mine is a good mile back from the turn. Nothing is left, as it appears to have been strip mined and landscaped. In 1876, still under its original owner, the Eagle Mine had two drift entrances, both running southwest. There were 80 coke ovens and a 100-foot ventilation shaft that made the mine reportedly "one of the best ventilated in coke region."[32] The owners actually worked in the mine. Mr. Sherrick was described by the *Pittsburgh Post* as "a great, tall, gaunt looking coal miner, his lamp in front of his cap—the grease trickling down over his forehead, and his clothes hanging in ribbons...."[33]

Like Foundry, Eagle was a small mine. The *Annual Report of Industrial Statistics of 1879-80* reported there were only 50 acres of coal land at Eagle Mine.[34] It had 80 beehive coke ovens throughout its existence and it was seldom that all of them were in blast at the same time.

The land where this mine stood is now part of Connellsville Auto Sales. The grounds near the railroad tracks where the ovens stood are strewn with automobiles and either they are covered or were torn out. Not a trace of this mine can be found above ground. It was probably strip mined, for the land is all flat and contoured. No information about strip mining has been found.

- 1868 Franklin Ellis lists Markle, Sherrick & Co. as founders.[35]
- 1870 HAER and the inhouse H.C. Frick Coke Company record state it was founded in 1870.[36]
- 1878 Frick & Co began buying an interest in the Eagle Mine.[37]
- 1879 H.C. Frick & Co. had one-half interest in the Eagle; the other half was owned by John and J.L.B. Sherrick.
- 1880 Bad pillars created carbonic acid gas, so Frick organization built a new shaft and ventilating furnaces.[38]
- 1887 Eagle was connected underground to Foundry.[39]
- 1889 Along with Tiptop and White, Eagle was shut down due to lack of orders.[40]
- 1891 Eagle Mine name was changed to Summit 1 and 2.[41]
- 1894 Still under the name Eagle, eighteen families were evicted.[42]
- 1909 Foreman of the Summit Mine reopens the Eagle, putting 20–30 ovens in operation.[43]
- 1910 There were 132 people living at Eagle. By 1960, none.[44]
- 1917 Frick marked Eagle as closed and James Wardlaw was superintendent and part owner of Eagle Mine.[45]
- 1918 Corrado Coal Company or the Corrado Schenck Coal Company leased Eagle Mine from Frick.[46]
- 1970s Eagle Mine discharged acid mine drainage into Galley Run as late as the 1970s.[47]

Incidents and Events

"John Sable of Morgan, an employe of the Eagle mine, has broken his own record for coal mining the latter part of July. In two weeks he earned $146.20 or $73.13 a week. Working straight time, Sable loaded 215 34-bushel wagons. His previous record was 170 34-bushel wagons. His best previous pay was $122 for two weeks."[48]

James Wardlaw, superintendent at Eagle in 1917, was an educator who published educational books on mining for miners, offered citizenship classes, and eventually had a mining school.[49] His two important publications were *Mining in a Nutshell* and *Mining Mathematics Simplified*. He held classes at Mount Pleasant Township High School twice a week for men trying to obtain foreman and fire boss certificates.

Corrado Coal Company or the Corrado Schenck Coal Company, with offices in Connellsville, consisted of Gaetano Corrado, F.B. Donnelly, H.E. Schenck, and W.P. Schenck. The Corrado Company immediately opened a new pit at Eagle, increased the railroad siding, build a new tipple, and got underway.[50] In 1926, the Corrado Company was still in operation and had 14 plants in the region.[51] Corrado continued to work in the region as late as 1933, when they leased the Lemont Mine from the Frick holdings. It had been idle for six years. He would employ 200 miners.[52] Ownership, however, remained in the hands of U.S. Steel.

Foundry Mine

The Foundry Mine is directly across the ravine from the White Mine. Its ovens are beyond the railroad track and its tipple and entry were in the hillside beyond that.

1869 Franklin Ellis reported Foundry Mine established in 1869 by Strickler and Lane.[53]
1870 HAER, relying on the *Historical Data H.C. Frick Coke Company Plants*, says it was founded in 1870.[54]
1875 There were 44 beehive bank ovens sized 11½' × 6' to make 48-hour and 72-hour coke. They shipped 28 cars of coke each week and 30 men were employed.[55]
1876 Frick purchased ⅔rd interest of C.P. Markle and Sons in "Foundry Mine Property."[56]
1880 30 new coke ovens and 50 men worked there.[57]
1881 Reported to state for lack of air by Mine Inspectors. Mining boss John Minert.[58] Total coal acres 40.[59]
1887 Connected underground with the Eagle Mine, just northeast of it up the valley.[60]
1890 One of three mines merged into the name Summit: 1, 2, and 3. Foundry was number 3.[61]
1891 Mines shared the same ventilation system and the mining boss was Edward Mooney.[62]
1896 Mine foreman James Connor. Idle part of year.[63]
1897 Summit and Eagle always have good ventilation and drainage. Mine Foreman is John Nolan.[64]

1905   All the 97 ovens out of blast.⁶⁵
1912   Coke ovens remained on the Connellsville list through 1912.
1920   Area occupied by the plant was 1.544 acres.

Incidents and Events

"Just after the convention closed two deputies from Summit, McDonald and Dickson, got into an altercation with the crowd of strikers who gave the officers both a bad beating. Then a negro cook from the Valley works named St. Clair came along and the excitement was increased when he fired his pistol putting a bullet through the shoulder of an Alice Hun named Peter Ghost. The angry crowd was dispersed when treated to a bath from the hose of the local fire company that had been called out."⁶⁶

Valley Mine

Perhaps the best of all the Frick company mines in Morgan Valley, the Valley Mine had the most ovens for the most years and often was the only mine working in the area. It had a total of 200 acres of coal land.⁶⁷ As with all mines in the region, Valley was mining the

Some of the many beehive oven ruins at Valley Mine in the Morgan Valley run in a continuous line along the dirt road leading to a farm area. Some of the ovens were buried, as were those at Star, but others simply had the protective fronts broken off when the ovens were no longer in use, as seen here (author photo, 2016).

Pittsburgh Seam, considered the best in the world, but unlike most, Valley's seam was not the normal 9 feet, but rather, an 11-foot wall of coal.[68]

In 1882 Thomas Lynch was appointed general superintendent of all of the Frick company operations. Also in 1882 and 1883, the H.C. Frick Company concluded two important consolidation events in connection to the Valley Mine. First, it bought the Pennsville Mine and then it purchased the farm adjacent to the Valley works. The Pennsville Mine was owned by Wilson, Boyle, Playford and Ewing and the purchase was called "One of the largest coal sales ever made in the coke region" by the *Mount Pleasant Journal*. It consisted of 400 acres and sold for $190,600. It joined the Valley works on the southeastern side.[69] The farm adjacent to the Valley works was purchased by the Frick company for $32,000.[70] What was unique about this farm is that it linked Valley Mine to two rail lines just as Frick had done with his first two mines at Broadford: the Southwest and the B&O. It remained a Frick company farm for a long time and still serves as farmland.

Valley Mine had a drift opening, double main-headings, and five single cross-headings at 1180 yards apart. A small furnace was used for ventilation and sixty men were employed.[71] There were 102 ovens, and the coke was being shipped over the B&O (former Mount Pleasant and Broadford RR). The mine had been divided into three sections, the first having three openings. The second section was called the southwest section and the interior was redesigned. The coal was hauled out of the mine by a stationary engine and steel wire rope, as opposed to mules and wagons.

- 1869 HAER reported Wilson, Boyle & Playford mine founded in 1869.
- 1870 Ellis stated the mine was opened by Wilson, Boyle & Playford and puts the date *around* 1870.[72]
- 1873 The state *Annual Report* of 1878 put the founding of Valley at yet another date: 1873.[73]
- 1875 Coal fed into 102 bank ovens each charged by 3½ to 4 wagons of coal and produced 11 cars of coke daily. That coke was shipped "both east and west." 80 men working.[74]
- 1877 Frick company leased the idle Valley Mine for $650 a month.[75] Thomas Lynch as superintendent and James Jackson as mine boss.
- 1878 60 acres of coal had already been mined and approximately 340 acres remained.[76]
- 1879 The strike began on March 17 when twenty-five miners from the Fountain mines then owned by the W.H. Blake & Co. and seventy-five miners at the Tip Top and Valley mines of the Frick company laid down their tools and walked out.
- 1880 Frick company had bought the mine outright and built a crusher at Valley Mine.[77]
- 1880 Frick company built a block of sixteen or eighteen new two-story houses[78] Some still standing in 2019.
- 1881 In this strike, pit boss James Jackson was arrested for attacking miners.[79]
- 1882 Installed a new tipple for the Valley Mine.[80]
- 1885 57 men and 5 boys working at the mine. It had 9 mules, 16 day persons inside, 12 outside.[81]
- 1891 175 men were on strike at Valley and many given eviction notices.[82] 32 families evicted.

supported by an article in the *Weekly Courier* in May of 1910: "Fire at Novelty is an Old Blaze."

The Novelty fire lasted longer than the years the mine was open. It became one of the major mine fires of the region. The *Report of the Bureau of Mines* reported, "1898 Fire started in Novelty Mine…. Origin is unknown. Originated in a gob [slag heap], in a portion of the mine which was abandoned two years ago. The fire is a complete mystery. Sealed with cement fire brick stoppings. Filled with water pumped into the mine."[99] The fire was still burning in 1910. The fire at Novelty (the name Frick Mine is never used in reference to this fire) may still be smoldering.

Most of the miners lived in the eighteen tenement houses erected by Frick and Co. along the river at Broadford.[100] Lumber for the houses was purchased from Hoop Jones and Company.[101] These houses were mostly located facing the Yough down river from the distillery. The mine itself stood on the northwest side of the valley just as it exited the village of Broadford. Its entrance was halfway up the cliff side.

If one looks carefully, it is possible to find the entrances to the mines. Most were imploded. This is an entrance to the Frick Mine located along the hillside to the west of the roadway and Galley Run—possibly the original entrance. There were two of them. There were also additional entrances created after the mine was no longer used by U.S. Steel, but by smaller companies mining for local consumption (author photo, 2016).

The difference between eighty-five workers in 1880 and only thirty-five in 1885 is probably related to the opening of the Rist Mine across the valley. It linked the Morgan, Frick, and Henry Clay into a single unit in 1882 and many of the workers moved to Rist.[102]

    1871   Henry Clay Frick founded the Frick Mine at Broadford.
    1871   George Newmyer (Newmeyer), a prominent landowner and mine operator, built three block houses, a bake oven, and wash house.[103]
    1871   Built 50 11' × 5½' bank ovens charged by three wagons for four days producing 48-hour coke and charged by 3.5 wagons on weekends for 72-hour coke. Eleven carloads of coke were shipped daily to "Milwaukee, Chicago, Salt Lake City, and other points west."[104]

1873	John G. White built ten blocks or double houses and was paid $10,000.[105]
1875	131 persons were employed in the Frick and Henry Clay mines combined: 50 were miners (at $1.50 a day) and 50 were coke drawers ($1.80). The remainder held a number of jobs including 10 outside laborers ($1.25), 2 inside laborers ($1.50), 4 outside mechanics ($1.75), 4 outside mule drivers ($1.40), 7 inside mule drivers ($1.40), 2 weigh masters ($1.65), and 2 mining overseers ($1.80).[106]
1876	Two drift entrances, upper linked to the Morgan Mine, just next door.[107]
1885	Two upper and 2 lower entrances to Frick Mine. The upper worked by 11 miners and 2 boys and the lower by 20 miners and 1 boy.[108]
1885	Superintendent was Robert Ramsay and mine boss was John Keck.
1890	Of the 50 acres of coal land, most was mined out.[109]
1891	May 9 evictions began at the Broadford area. Deputy A.W. Stanton was struck by one of the flying missiles.[110]
1892–3	None of ovens working.
1894–5	All ovens in blast.
1910	Number of ovens is 105. Mine reopened.[111]
1913	Off the *Courier* oven list.
1918	Abandoned again.[112]
1919	Rented to Samuel Wiggins for the sum of $250 a year.[113]
1921	Conveyed to "Samuel Wiggins, per letter of Gordon and Smith, dated June 8, 1921."[114]
1922	Frick Mine was abandoned once again.
1950	Jim Wiggins operated the mine. They sold custom coal at $5.00 a ton.[115]
1959	Twenty homes built and only two still standing in 1959.[116]

Incidents and Events

On Monday, March 20, 1876, Frick and Co. took over the company store at Broadford from local merchant E.H. Reid. The company *Daybook* said, "Commenced store business here this day. Bought out stock, fixtures, etc., from E.H. Reid at invoice prices and 10% added. Amount in all, $5,418.95, and gave my personal notes for same."[117] This was a number of years after Frick instituted company scrip. Thomas Lynch, who would go on to be second in command to Frick, began working as a clerk in the store at Broadford. The building was still standing in 2012 and gone in 2015.

"While Frederick Keck, mine boss for the H.C. Frick Coke Company at its Henry Clay works, near Broadford, was returning from Connellsville to his home, Thursday night last, he was struck by the B. & O. express train east and so badly injured that he died a few hours later. He was a most competent man for the position he held, was about 43 years old and leaves a family. Leonard Keck, the Greensburg merchant, and Martin Keck, of Kecksburg, are brothers of the deceased. Later reports state that foul play is suspected."[118] John Keck, perhaps a brother, remained as mine boss at Frick Mine all his life.[119]

"When William Mullen, the superintendent of all the Frick company's works from Broadford to Summit, served eviction notices on the strikers who live on "Dutch Hill" the women notified him that they intended to return the compliment by tendering him a serenade. The polite server of writs was so tickled over the promised honor that he said he would set up a quarter of a barrel of beer if the ladies kept their word, and they did it to the letter. The serenade took place at the Union Supply Company's Broadford store, Thursday evening, and the parade which preceded and followed it had no parallel in the region.

The German matrons formed at their homes on the hill and marched down the road to the little town at the foot, where a big crowd of shouting men and boys fell in and accompanied the procession to the store. First came a slender lover of kraut who kept an old accordion in full operation on one of Strauss' heaviest compositions. She was followed by a motherly-looking old soul who kept only the marching time on a tenor drum. Following these were a whole brigade of tin pan and bucket beaters, and as the rear guard swept a 250 pounder who, with a face as solemn as death, bore aloft an old table cloth banner tied to a pole.

Three pieces, two imported and one domestic, were murdered in cold blood in front of the store and then the spokeswoman advanced and asked for the disappointed superintendent who had been compelled to take in the music by telephone from Summit, where he was at the time guarding a party of Italian "blacklegs." The musicians, however, got their beer for which Store Manager Johnny Miller advanced the money.[120]

"Have you traveled between Scottdale and Broadford? If you have and when all the ovens were burning in all their splendor you would be surprised with the gloomy forsaken appearance that meets the eye to-day. Nothing disturbs the solitary silence of idleness except the activity at Summit and Franklin. The houses are nearly all empty and they present a desolate sight. Blackened by the smoke of years, broken windows, scarcely any signs of ventilation, truly the once prosperous, lively thriving villages are now but the dead remains of what they were a few months ago. Here and there a canvas tent over which the stars and stripes boldly floats are indications that the homeless are sheltered beneath their folds. What is the cause of all this change? Strike! When you reach Broadford you emerge from the silent city of idleness and on the banks of the Yough, the smoke issuing from the ovens at Sterling and Jackson reminded one of olden times."[121]

Henry Clay Mine (Broadford)

Frick built the Henry Clay Mine from scratch. Unlike the Frick Mine, there is evidence of various constructions. A man named John Bixler opened the pit mouth, securing it with twenty posts. John Wilhelm was contracted to build the beehive coke ovens. For ten ovens, he was paid $1980.00. In all, he built seventy of the ovens at this time. When they cleared the land for the ovens, they used horses to trample the ground flat.[122] Zachariah T. Henry worked with or for Wilhelm.[123] When the ovens were completed, L.M. Herrington pulled the first coke from the ovens. He later became Superintendent of Schools for Fayette County.[124]

Like the Frick Mine, this mine also had name issues. In an earlier image, we saw the name Broadford Mines. That stood for both the Frick and the Henry Clay. But the name seems to have stuck to the Henry Clay. Then in 1919 a new name was discovered: Old Slope.[125] It appeared in the obituary for Henry Clay Frick in the *Daily Courier*. No other reference to Old Slope has been found except for the photo on the next page. A slope mine is a mine with an entrance that slopes down into the mine. One would be hard pressed to assume that Slope Mine was the name of the mine when it is constantly identified as the Henry Clay Mine.

Frick immediately began shipping coke next door to the Morgan Mine which, it is

The Henry Clay tipple and slope entrance as seen from the top. The mine was cut into the hillside with the entrance sloping down into the mine (foreground). Coal was placed into wagons drawn by mules up the slope into the tipple. From the tipple it was dropped into larry cars that ran along a bank of coke ovens, where the coal was dropped in. Once fired, the coke was pulled from the ovens and loaded into railroad cars for shipment ("Slope Mine," Connellsville Coke, H.C. Frick Coke Company, Pittsburgh, PA, c. 1883. Helen Clay Frick Foundation Archives [AIS 2002 06], Henry Clay Frick Business Records, 1862–1987, Box 523, Folder 1, Archives Service Center, University of Pittsburgh, p. 8).

presumed, was shipped out to industrial customers. The *Day Book* mentions weekly shipments to Morgan Mines through 1871–72. One finds this occasionally in the ledgers, that Frick either shipped to local mines or paid local mining companies for receiving such orders. It is assumed they helped fulfill orders. An example can be found in the Frick *Journal* on April 18, 1878, when Frick paid Markle, Sherrick & Co., Markle & Co., and J.W. Overholt for carloads of coke.[126]

Ultimately, the Henry Clay Mine included 143.9 acres of surface land and 127.121 acres of coal. It stretched from the B&O tracks along the Yough up the hillside to and including what would become the Broadford Road leading to Broadford from Route 119. The one surface exception was the Rist Cemetery of under an acre on the ridge overlooking the river.

- 1871 Founding date of the Henry Clay Mine was never in question: 1871.
- 1882 Annual report of the Commonwealth of Pennsylvania gave the Henry Clay a bad air report.[127]
- 1886 During strike: February 8, shots were fired at the Henry Clay.
  - Peter Soisson, the yard boss, was beaten.

- Tipple, engine house, and a few railroad cars on the B&O track were set on fire.
- Dozen men trapped in the tipple.
- Sheriff and 25 deputies were dispatched to bring back order.[128]

1888 Six years later, there was a positive air report because a new twelve-foot fan was placed in operation.[129]

1888 Orders were slow, and Frick took the down time to dismantle 100 original beehive coke ovens and build 120 new ones.[130]

1888 Edward Hughes helped build the coke ovens at Henry Clay in 1870–1 and helped tear them down in 1888. "Don Meredith of Mt. Pleasant rebuilt the 100 ovens."[131]

1889 Thomas Lynch was the general superintendent at Henry Clay. His mining boss was Thomas Kane.[132]

1891 80 eviction notices sent to Broadford.[133]

1918 "Remaining Henry Clay Tract was conveyed to Martin Fazenbaker on March 12, 1918."

1930 Henry Clay had been abandoned.

Incidents and Events

"The miners employed in the Henry Clay mines at Broad Ford are very much excited over the appearance of a man in the mines carrying a dark lantern. He has been seen a number of times and acts in a peculiar manner. He will suddenly appear and open his lantern in the face of a miner, then close his light and disappear as suddenly as he came. Several attempts to capture him have failed. A number of the more timid miners and drivers will not enter the mine."[134]

During the strike of 1891, some evicted miners lived in canvas tents, in schoolhouses, or with friends. One group went to live at the German Hall on the hill overlooking Broadford. That is probably the old Rist Schoolhouse, no longer standing. The *Scottdale Independent* notes: "The building is 40 × 60 ft., and is one story high. There are ten families quartered here—fifty six persons in all. Ten fathers, ten mothers, twenty-four children and twelve boarders. Twenty-two beds stand in rows around the hall. The tables are arranged in the center, and to all appearances, it is camp life in its reality. Four stoves are used to do the cooking, and are placed in a shed on the outside. The interior and entire surroundings have a clean and neat appearance, much more so than normally expected under such conditions. The women keep busy looking after their booths, as it seems more like, and the peace and harmony of the children, which range from the smallest little tot to the half grown youth. All are as merry as a 'June party,' and seem far from being the depressed downhearted outcasts they are expected to be.

Visitors daily flock to the hall to see what life after 'eviction' is like, and are kindly treated. German Hall in the future, will be spoken of as a place of much interest, and will long be remembered by some of its present occupants."[135]

The Henry Clay Mine had its own fire. It began in 1897 in an area of the mine that had been closed a number of years earlier. The Bureau of Mines report speculated, "it must have been caused by spontaneous combustion, the first occurrence of the kind in this region."[136] It was stopped by creating brick barriers, five of them, and filling the area with water.

"The Fayette County Board of Commissioners has received court approval to abandon and close an old bridge across the Youghiogheny River at Broad Ford in Connellsville Twp. President Judge Eustace H. Bane approved the closing and removal of the bridge once used by railroads but since 1946 maintained by the county and used only by pedestrians. The commissioners pointed out in a petition to the court that the need for the bridge for pedestrian traffic no longer exists."[137]

After much controversy, the P.R.R. became provoked and spitefully built the Southwest Branch to the west of Mount Pleasant, instead of passing through the town…. Later the Pittsburgh and Connellsville Railroad was asked to come to Mount Pleasant … a joint meeting of officials and citizens was held in the Baptist Church. In the meantime the stock of the Pittsburgh and Connellsville Railroad was absorbed by the B&O, then creeping west from Wheeling, and under this company the railroad to Mount Pleasant was constructed (1871). The ire of the PRR however was aroused and they managed to gain possession of the road by artifice. All the engines of the B&O were ordered across the Broadford bridge and then it was burned. This forced traffic on the road to be hauled by the PRR by way of the Southwest Branch.[138] (No source has been found to confirm this statement.)

Summit Mine (Owensdale)

The Summit Mine is located to the left of the Broadford Road as it enters Owensdale from Broadford. As with all the other mines in this study, the founding and ownership in

The Summit Mine entrance is typical of Frick mines. Not all mines had such entrances. The sides and entrances had to be fortified for fear of the hillside collapsing. When the mines were closed for good, the entrances were imploded ("Summit Mine," Connellsville Coke, H.C. Frick Coke Company, Pittsburgh, PA, c. 1883. Helen Clay Frick Foundation Archives [AIS 2002 06], Henry Clay Frick Business Records, 1862–1987, Box 523, Folder 1, Archives Service Center, University of Pittsburgh, p. 5).

early days are filled with confusion (see dates below). They may all be right. Jackson Shallenberger was a local man whose family still lives in the Broadford area. Cochran is from the famous James Cochran family that started mining and coking in the region and established a grand home at Dawson now known as Linden Hall. The Keister family are another long-standing family in the coal field. They had at least 3 mines in and around the Morgan Valley: Home, Clinton, and Summit. Their papers are at the Coal and Coke Heritage Center at the Penn State Fayette Campus.

The *Industrial Statistics* of the following year added more details, stating that the mine received its name because "the railroad track falls both ways," thus it was at the summit of Morgan Valley. There was a lot of activity at Summit during the bitter strike of 1891. It was the first mine that the Frick company tried to restart in the Morgan Valley. By mid-April, twenty-eight men reported to work. It was nine weeks before the mine was working. It started under armed guard. To keep the mine working, Frick sent twenty-six Italians imported explicitly to work in the mines during the strike.[139] They were to move into the homes of the evicted miners.[140]

1872   Upper Tyrone Township supervisor's web site maintains that in 1872 Jackson Shallenberger constructed the mine that he called Owensdale.[141]

1873   *Uniontown Evening Standard* insisted that Cochran & Keister opened Summit Mine.[142]

1875   *Industrial Statistics* of Pennsylvania agreed with HAER that the first operators were Hurst, Moore & Company.[143]

1876   The mine was taken over by James Cochran & Co., was located on the west side of the valley three miles from Broadford, and had two drift openings.[144]

1878   HAER, using Frick stats, recorded it was opened by Hurst, Moore & Company in 1874 (and taken over by Frick Co. in 1880).[145]

1879   Forty-four people were employed at Summit: 20 miners, 20 outside laborers, 1 outside mechanic, 1 outside mule driver, 1 inside mule driver, and 1 mining overseer. At 230 acres, it had the highest acreage of coal land in the valley.[146]

1879   H. C. Frick Coke Company in December of 1879 bought one-fourth interest in Summit Coke works. The other three-fourths was owned by Henry Ferguson (Frick's partner), and Cochran and Keister. The sale included 102 coke ovens.[147]

1879   There were 101 bank ovens 11½' × 6' in size and produced sixty-six cars weekly which were shipped by Morgan & Co. practically next door. Seventy-five men employed.[148]

1880   The entire mine was sold to the Frick enterprise in early February of 1880.[149]

1880   Ninety-six men employed in the mine, 20 new tenements were built, and a new branch of the Southwest Railroad was constructed. Forty-one new beehive coke ovens were built, bringing the total to 142, where it would remain until near the end.[150]

1881   Thomas Lynch was general superintendent and B.P. Howell the mining engineer.

1884   Mining boss at Summit was J. Moody, while in 1885 Robert Ramsey was the super and J. Moody continued as mining boss.[151]

1891 Italians imported during strike to work at Summit are living in Soup House at Morgan Station.[152]

1891 Next came the importation of Negroes. "110 of them would be given employment at Rist slope, Broadford, and about 100 at Summit and adjoining plants."[153]

1892 The name "was changed June 10, 1892, to that of Summit Mines."[154]

1895 The great storm deluged railroad tracks, the mines submerged and at Summit the B&O bridge was washed out.[155]

1897 Frick bought even more coal land around the Summit Mine. The company paid $200 an acre to Soloman Keister on December 16, 1897, to be deeded to the Youghiogheny Water Company with coal deeded to H.C. Frick Coke Company[156]

1898 The ovens were never in full blast. They were, however, well maintained with good ventilation and drainage supervised by foreman John Noland.[157]

1905 Joseph Bryner, Edward Maritta, and Henry Hetzel bought three acres of coal near Summit Mines from a local farmer.[158]

1909 Summit ovens started up again with coal from another mine in a different district and only about 25 to 30 ovens would be fired.[159]

1943 John Roth of Scottdale began to reclaim coke from refuse dumps. Summit Mine was his headquarters. The best coke was shipped.[160]

1959 In all, 38 tenements were built at Summit, and as of 1959, only six remained.[161]

1960 By 1910, most of the Morgan Valley was mined out. Summit was listed as closed. The community still had a population of 288, but by 1960 only 52 remained.[162]

Incidents and Events

The strike of 1894 was cruel and life-changing. The actions of the Slavs and Huns, who were starving, brought the owners to the conclusion that they must go. In turn, Negroes and Italians were being brought into the region. It created chaos again.

On June 25, the *Dispatch* reported that the Negroes ordered to break the strike by a number of companies had arrived: "Two carloads of new men were shipped into the north end of the coke region to-day. One car went to the Standard and the other to the Summit plant of the Frick Coke Company. The Cambria Iron Company, it is learned to-day, will have 200 negros brought to its Morrell plant, and the McClure Company will have 160 at its Lemont plant."[163]

Battles took place in several towns in the Morgan Valley. On July 11, 1894, they reached the Summit Mine.[164] The *Post* reported a firsthand account of the incident. One of the strikers maintained that the Negroes and officials at the mine caused the problem:

"Well, that day we were marching along the road, past the Summit plant to Scottdale. I and another man were at the head of the procession, and back of us marching in good order were 2,500 strikers, divided into companies. The procession was strung out for a long distance, but all was quiet. That I know, for I had turned and had just given an order, which was heard by the sixth company back. Suddenly there was a crackle of firearms, and as I looked I saw the negroes and deputies firing at the procession from behind the cars. Several of our men were wounded."[165]

White Mine (Globe)

A mere ⁴⁄₁₀ of a mile up Broadford Road from Morgan Mine is the White Mine. The underground portion lies under the road and to the right, but the tipple and entrance stood to the left of the road where the junkyard now stands. The coke ovens, in three rows, were located in the valley beyond or at the edge of the junkyard this side of the railroad tracks. They were either covered over or removed and nothing is visible. Directly across the tracks from the White ovens were the 97 Foundry ovens. Once again, the origin of the mine is difficult to trace.

- 1873 Built by Charles Armstrong under the name of Globe Mine.[166]
- 1875 2 drift entrances, 25 miners, 2 outside laborers, 1 outside mechanic, 2 outside mule drivers, 2 inside mule drivers, 1 weight master, 1 super, 1 mining overseer, and 12 coke drawers.[167]
- 1875 79 bank ovens of 11' × 6' size charged with 3 wagons of coal, which filled 38 freight cars with coke and was shipped west. Forty-five men were working at the time.[168]
- 1877 Purchased by A.A. Hutchinson & Brothers.
- 1878 80 ovens and Centennial Medal for the quality of the coke produced because "it brings more per bushel in Cincinnati than any other."[169]
- 1878 Superintendent at that time was Charles Cunningham and the mining boss was Robert Cowan.[170]
- 1880 148 ovens. Bad ventilation report blamed on the mining boss.[171]
- 1881 Frick acquired the Globe and paid $225,000.[172]
- 1881 Changed the name to White Mine in honor of Superintendent John M. White.[173]
- 1887 52 new beehive coke ovens were added to the line at White.[174]
- 1891 Mine boss John Grambly (Grumley). Inspectors reported that "whitewashing" of safety holes (so miners could see them in the dark) was "better observed here than any other mine in the region."[175]
- 1896–1898 White was managed by three different foremen: in order, they were Terrence Donnelly, William Miner, and Jacob Houser.[176]
- 1930 Closed in 1919, as of January 1, 1930, still being written so it was still owned by the Frick company.
- 1953 Coal from the White Mine was for sale on the local market by C.B. Pletcher.[177]
- 1959 28 tenements were built at White. As of 1959, zero remained.[178]
- 1960 In 1910 the population was 162; by 1960 it was zero.[179]

Incidents and Events

By 1879 Hutchison ran into Frick, and they ended up in court. Hutchinson put a pipeline from his Globe Mine south to the river along the railroad tracks. It cut through the Frick company property and was removed because it was thought to be illegal. They went to court. The Frick company lost.[180] A year later the Frick company constructed a water course from the lower "workings of the White mines, through to the Valley mines, for the purpose of draining the latter mines." The process was supervised by Grambly (who would later work for the McClure Coke Company's Mullen Mine). It ran for over a mile and penetrated the No. 2 heading of Valley Mine. It was intended to form a natural drain for the Valley Mine to the north of White.[181]

This particular drain is somewhat spectacular and there should be some evidence of it today. It was supervised by Chief Engineer J.H. Paddock. The work began at both ends of the drain with 1,623 feet dug from White and 1,790 from Valley. Everything went well except at one point along the Valley drain. It was too deep, and a second smaller drain had to be dug to eliminate that water. That one was 500 feet long and 8 feet wide.[182]

Tip Top Mine

Tip Top was a drift mine with two entrances sitting in a small, deep valley along Jacobs Creek in the upper reaches of Morgan Valley. The ovens were located along the western side of the creek and remnants still exist. Accessibility is difficult, even today. The coal land was 65 acres.[183] Today, as with most mine entrances where tipples once stood, the entry, imploded years ago to protect it, can be distinguished.

The *Journal* of the newly formed H.C. Frick Coke Company reported the acquisition of "two-thirds interest in the Tinstman and Armstrong property (Tip Top Coke Works) situated in Tyrone Township, Fayette Co., Pa, the other one-third being the property of Daniel R. Davidson. The entire property consists of fifty-six coke ovens with the real estate, buildings, coal rights, tools, mules, pit cars, and all the appurtenances for the manufacture of coke. The two-thirds is valued at $50,600."[184]

Tip Top Mine was located down in a deep valley along the railroad tracks. It is far more primitive-looking than the Summit mine (postcard).

As with all the mines in Morgan Valley, the great storm of February 1910 put the mine out of business. Tip Top is in a deep ravine, and the deluge poured into the mine from every opening. Every miner was forced to bail water and try to keep the water out of the mine.[185] In December of the same year, the same newspaper wrote, "With this plant, on the 'dead list' are the Summit, Eagle, Foundry and Novelty [Frick] plants and within the space of a few years they will be joined by the valley's remaining plants."[186]

But Tip Top would not die. Logan Rush had worked at the Union Supply Company for Frick and would go on to be the Register and Recorder of Fayette County and later County Commissioner. Rush founded Rush Coal Company with offices in Connellsville and was a partner with W.E. Rice in the Tyrone Coal Company. Both of these companies were created because of the increased need for coal production brought about by the war in Europe, which would soon become World War I.[187]

1874   Charles H. Armstrong & Son built 41 ovens one-mile northwest of Summit Mine.[188]
1875   The *Pittsburgh Daily Commercial* said Charles H. Armstrong built fifty ovens along the Southwestern Railroad in 1875.
1875   Second Geological Survey of 1875 maintained Tip Top was only a half mile from Summit Mine and had only 12 bank ovens in existence with 73 on the way.[189]
1878   Enman, following the Frick stats, gives the date as 1878.[190]
1878   Tip Top was leased by H.C. Frick & Co. and had a drift opening and 32 men employed.[191]
1879   In the Frick company *Journal* dated January 17, 1879, the mine was purchased from J.B. Young, Trustee. Both Ellis and HAER support the purchase date, but HAER's founding date is 1878.[192]
1882   Tip Top had bad ventilation; men working "beyond the air." Mining boss, Mr. McCleary.[193]
1889   Engine house and boiler house were destroyed by fire.[194]
1890   Four pounds of rock powder exploded prematurely and badly burned miner Ned Sweeny.[195]
1905   121 ovens, the number since the mine was opened, were joined by 200 more.
1909   Tipple erected and a new entry opened to take out outlying coal, called crop coal.[196]
1911   Only 100 mine cars of crop coal were mined at Tip Top and the mine worked only a week.[197]
1911   Frick company lists Tip Top as closed.[198]
1915   Logan Rush bought the remaining coal and built yet another tipple, this time directly over the ovens.[199]
1920   S.C. Whipkey got both surface and lease rights for crop coal in the 1920s.
1960   In 1910, 24 people were listed as living at Tip Top. By 1960, no one was living there.[200]

Rist Mine

Rist was a consolidation effort. It combined the underground coal of a number of mines: Henry Clay, Frick, Eagle and Morgan. This eliminated many duplicate services like office work, water supplies, and more. It did not eliminate the various coke ovens which remained on the *Courier* list under their former names. The 1885 *Industrial Statistics* reported that Rist was opened in 1884 (others say 1882). It goes on to report that Rist had a slope opening.[201]

After one turns the bend at Broadford to head up the Morgan Valley on the current Broadford Road, the Rist Mine entrance is on the right about ¹⁄₁₀ of a mile beyond the current buildings. It runs up the valley at the edge of the Broadford Road. At one time the tipple crossed the road, for the Frick coke ovens used by the Rist Mine were on the left side of the road. A huge 7-foot-diameter, 62½-foot-deep shaft was built to ventilate the mine, which employed forty-one men, three boys, and eleven others. To convey the coal to the ovens, Morris Ramsay constructed a bridge.[202]

It is not easy to find the original mine entrances to any of these mines. They underwent too many changes. Many were imploded. Others were reworked and redesigned. Some were eliminated altogether and strip mined. Today, if one looks hard, one can see the Rist entrance. It was simply closed and blown in. It caved.

By the 1890s, Rist still had a double entry and a slope. Throughout the state inspector reports, the mine was found to be in good condition and the air in good order. In the late 1890s, Charles Winingroth was the mine foreman.[203]

Rist Mine was developed late for the Morgan Valley. The 1914 special centennial edition of the *Connellsville Courier* has it listed as having one hundred ovens, but it was never on the paper's weekly list, which was begun in 1888 and continued well into the 1930s.[204] It had a 7.5-foot-high Pittsburgh Seam and was able to yield 11.25 tons of coal per acre.

In 1884 the *Connellsville Weekly Courier* reported that a tipple was being built at Morgan Station by C.N. Stauk (?) and Brother of Greensburg. It was designed to span the railroad tracks and "is erected for the development of the coal on the opposite side of the valley from the Frick ovens."[205] This is probably the tipple erected at Rist.

In 1917, the huge Rist tipple caught fire. At that time, eighty men were working at the plant, and it was estimated that only two months' supply of coal was yet to be mined before the mine was depleted. The *Connellsville Daily Courier* reported that a small spark fell into the bin of the tipple and caught it on fire. It could not be saved, but the boiler house and engine room were. It was never rebuilt.[206] The Frick company listed the mine as closed the same year.

In 2016, the pillars of the tipple could still be found to the left side of the Broadford Road at Rist. The only coke ovens still in existence in this part of the valley are at Henry Clay Mine along the B&O at Broadford.

Rist did not have its own housing or any other mine-related items. It was completely serviced by facilities already in place at Broadford.

McClure Coke Company

The original study of the early coal mines of Henry Clay Frick began in Bridgeport, just outside of Mount Pleasant in Westmoreland County, where it investigated four Frick company mines. They were not founded by Frick, and before they became a part of the Frick company, they were absorbed into the McClure Coke Company. They are Star, Buckeye, Hazlett, and Mullen. While the investigation of the various strikes in the region continued, additional mines owned by McClure and absorbed by the Frick company became part of our narrative: Bessemer and Alverton (Donnelly, Mayfield, and Union). All play a role

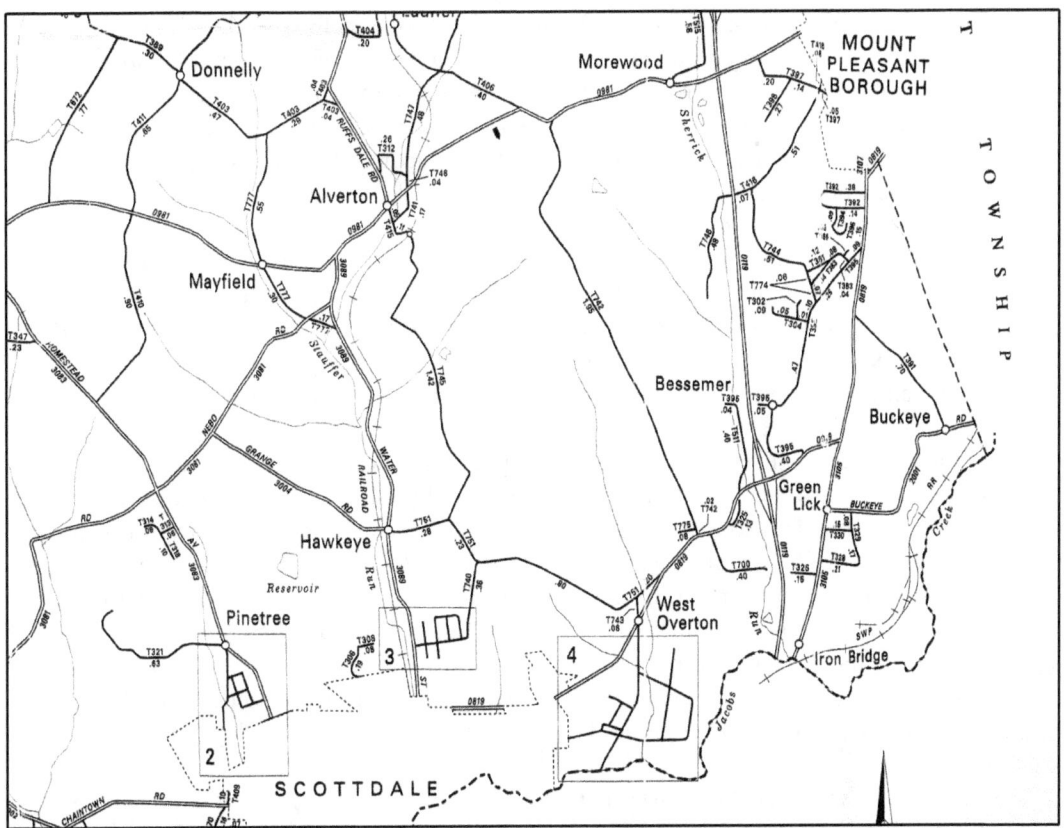

The mines around Mount Pleasant do not run in a straight line but are scattered about. Star, Hazlett, and Mullen mines are not seen on this East Huntingdon Township map, but they are to the east of Buckeye in Mount Pleasant Township (East Huntingdon Second Class Township Map, Westmoreland County, Pennsylvania Department of Transportation, Bureau of Planning and Research, Geographic Information Division, Municipal Code 64 206).

in our research. Additional mines owned by McClure that became Frick properties but are not a part of our narrative are: Coalbrook, Diamond, Enterprise, Lemont 1 and 2, Painter, and Rising Sun.

To complicate matters, once the study delved deeper into the various strikes from 1875 to 1894, more Frick company mines came into play. In fact, they dominated the strike narrative beyond the Morgan Valley and Bridgeport mines because they were bigger, had developed company housing, and contained more immigrants. These regional mines included those in the independently formed Southwest Coal and Coke Company and Southwest Connellsville Coal and Coke Company. These mines also belonged to Frick. Unlike all the others they did not belong to the H.C. Frick Coke Company. But they became too important to the narrative not to be included. So Standard, Morewood, and Alice are also given limited review below.

The Company

The McClure Coke Company has a complicated history with a number of owners and mines. It began with E.W. McClure and Gilbert T. Rafferty in 1872.[207] The name McClure

& Company began around 1878 when Rafferty, Charles Donnelly, and B.H. Rubie formed a partnership. It was merged into another partnership between Rafferty and Donnelly and the combination became the McClure Coke Company. Other men became involved and a court trial was necessary to resolve who owned what and in what amount. The men of McClure did exactly what Henry Clay Frick did: they acquired properties and grew into a bona fide and important company. They acquired the Buckeye and Star mines from the A.C. Cochran Coke Company in 1890.[208]

The road was not always smooth and the men were not all honest. For whatever reason, in 1881 Boyle bought out Hazlett for $75,000, and within the year partnered with Gilbert T. Rafferty to become the Boyle & Rafferty Coal Co. According to the *Connellsville Courier*, Gilbert F. Rafferty (middle initial often confused in sources) already owned half of the Boyle and Hazlett franchise, and when Boyle bought out Hazlett, Boyle became an equal partner with Rafferty.[209]

Rafferty was not liked in "cokedom." Newspapers were often very direct and critical. In 1885 the state determined that mining companies could not own the local company stores and they were required to divest themselves. (Most, like the Frick company, just formed another company.)[210] Rafferty was quoted in the *Scottdale Independent*: "Our employees and those at every mine in the Connellsville region, are Hungarians and other foreigners. They had been laborers working at $1 and $1.25 per day. Now they earn $2 and $2.50. We pay every month, and without the store the men would receive more money than they ever had in their lives at the same time. They are unable to resist the temptation to go on a spree, that is, the majority of them. The result is they sober up a few days later without a cent...."[211]

The 1888 edition of the *Courier* named Charles Donnelly as president; W.J. McTighe as secretary and treasurer; John P. Brennan as general manager; and Charles Donnelly, Gilbert T. Rafferty and B.H. Rubie members of the board of directors.[212] Like those of the Schoonmaker company, the McClure offices were in Everson under the supervision of the general superintendent J.P. Brennen. They, too, were located in the telegraph and train dispatcher's tower, which burned to the ground in early November of 1890. The *Courier* reported "the tower, with most of its contents and the J.M. Schoonmaker Coke Co's office were in ashes."[213] The Pittsburgh offices were at Smithfield and Sixth in what was then the German National Bank building.[214]

The Frick company acquired the holdings of the McClure Coke Company in 1895. At that time, it had fourteen mines. Those not mentioned above have no significant voice in our study. Discussions about the purchase began in 1889. They are a prime example of just how purchases were often made. Nothing ruthless here. First, Frick assessed properties and their successes and reports to Carnegie:

> Quite as anxious as you that we control all the Connellsville Coke and think we will eventually do so but financially and other reasons render it quite impossible to do so at once. Don't think we have made any mistake so far. Have purchased good properties at low prices and on such terms as we can under almost any circumstances take care of the payments. I do not feel disposed, however, (and I don't think you do) to see our Company rush in and buy the McClure Coke Company at such a price as they are now holding their property.
>
> Under almost any condition they cannot expect to get more and <u>will not</u> be able to get more, if as much. Rainey and all of them will come to us in good time. Until we do secure all of them, I think we have it in our power to manage so as to keep them from getting any encouragement from Railroad Companies not to sell out to us.[215]

What an insight into the mind and confidence of Henry Clay Frick. He had things under control. As in the past, when things became impossible or the owners were simply fed up, they sold out and Frick was willing to buy. A few months later he wrote Carnegie:

> McClure Coke Company, a few days ago, sent a party to me to ascertain whether we would not buy them out. In brief, they claim to have about 4,000 acres of coal; 1251 acres of surface; 1371 ovens, for which they want about $3,350,000,000 [sic]. I told their representative, if they would cut those figures in two, there might be a good chance of dealing.
>
> To give you an idea of their notion of values, as compared with what we paid Schoonmaker: They ask for their United and Dentral [sic; Central] stock $490,000,000. We paid Schoonmaker about $170,000. I will discuss this, however, with you when I see you in New York.[216]

Two years later in 1891, the McClure Company was once again a topic of discussion between Frick and Carnegie. The industry had just undergone a major strike that devastated all the companies but hit McClure hard as their mines and miners were deeply involved in the conflicts. This was a major reason that most companies sold out to the Frick company. The pattern of selling to Frick in the past seemed to be discussed over the state of the industry and the unions.

> The McClure people are in pretty bad shape financially, and the more I investigate their property the less attractive it is. The partners desiring to sell did not say that they would accept $960 per acre, but said they would accept that price, provided they could reserve certain surface land, and we would agree to pay six per cent. (6%) interest on deferred payments. This gave me an opportunity of calling the negotiations off for the present. At the same time I said to Mr. Donnelly that he better purchase their interests. In that event, we would be willing to put all of our property in at a valuation of $950 an acre, less our indebtedness, he to put all the McClure property in at the rate of $950 an acre, less their indebtedness; we would take our percentage in the McClure Company and give him his percentage in the Frick Company.[217]

Negotiations continued through to 1895. The deal was essentially the same, with Donnelly negotiating and receiving a special offer for himself, as outlined above. On October 21, Frick sent the following to Carnegie:

> Agreement executed for purchase of McClure Coke Company; had cash payment reduced to $100,000,000, from $250,000,000, and also retained in our hands twice the amount mentioned in agreement you read until coal acreage is determined. It is hoped we can keep this purchase quiet until some other matters now pending are closed.[218]

Star Mine

The Star Mine began small, struggled, and eventually was absorbed into the surrounding mines. Even its origin is difficult to trace. The Star and the Stauffer mines were one and the same. Although it never appeared on the *Report of the Operation and Output of the Coke Ovens of the Connellsville Region* (neither did the Star), the Stauffer Mine was a legitimate small operation at Bridgeport. (There are several Bridgeports in Pennsylvania. This one is attached to Mount Pleasant along Shupe Run. Another became a part of Brownsville along the Monongahela River and was a major boatbuilding center. There is a third on the Schuylkill River in Montgomery County.) The Star probably opened sometime in the early 1870s, was owned and operated by J.F. Stauffer & Co. (some sources say J.R. Stouffer), which had two other nearby mines that *were* on the Connellsville mine list. Local residents remember that the Star had one drift entrance located to the left of Weinman Road. Its tipple practically spanned the road, and its beehive coke ovens ran north along Shupe Run. Its few patch houses were further up Weinman across Shupe Run on the east bank.

As for the fate of the Star Mine, its coke ovens continued to operate for some time. Although the name Weinman is used often in this region and there were Weinman mines as early as the 1890s, it is unlikely that the Star became one of the Weinman (sometimes spelled Wienman) mines prior to the 20th century. However, the property in Bridgeport was heavily worked by the Weinman family and currently belongs to them.

Today the mine is closed, yet linked underground to Buckeye, Hazlett, and Standard. They are all flooded. The Star coke ovens are buried. Many of the miners lived in Bridgeport, but there were a few patch houses at Star. Today there remains a single patch house. It is not habitable because the basement is flooded.

1871		Most sources maintain that it was built by a local man named B.F. Coughanour.[219]
1875		Owned and operated by J.F. Stauffer & Co.[220]
1875		20 beehive 11.5' × 6' bank ovens, each 3 or 4 wagons to charge, and made 13 railcars or 8,125 bushels of coal weekly. It maintained 12 men who worked there and the coal was shipped to the west.[221]
1882		Purchased and joined to Buckeye Mine by the Cochran & Ewing Company.[222]
1886		It transitioned into the A.C. Cochran Coal & Coke Company.
1895		Purchased by H.C. Frick Company from McClure.
1930s		Owed by the Weinman family, who sold coke to U.S. Steel well into the 1950s.[223]

Incidents and Events

From the first strike to the last, the men and boys of the Bridgeport area were involved. When they tried for better wages in 1875, the *Mount Pleasant Dawn* reported, "Boyle and Hazlet [sic] offered their men thirty-three cents per wagon, if they would work on Wednesday...." The owners of the Bessemer Mine nearby stated: "We will positively not pay more than 30 cents per wagon for mining, and, unless our men go to work before we lose some of our contracts, we will then pay only such prices, and run so much of our works as may be convenient. Signed: Sherrick & Markle."[224]

"Mr. Donnelly of the firm of Rafferty & Donnelly paid his men a visit on the 16th inst. at Bridgeport. He called the committee together and made them a proposition to return to work on the 21st and to work two or three days and then ask for a sliding scale, and that he would sign one which would be satisfactory. It must have pleased some of the men for he had hardly finished speaking when some one asked him for some money for beer, which he readily gave—sufficient to purchase 16 gallons. Every day since then there has been a great deal of beer drinking engaged in by men who have been living off the commissary since the second week of the strike."[225]

Buckeye Mine

The Buckeye began as a small mine on the west bank of Shupe Run. As the industry grew, so did Buckeye. It operated with two entrances: a drift and a slope. It wasn't long before it was joined to the Star Mine nearby and became the dominant mine. Today little remains of the Buckeye Mine. There is one patch house, another home along the former rail

The Buckeye tipple, as built by A.C. Cochran in 1882. Buckeye was the biggest of the early mines built around Mount Pleasant, which also included Star, Hazlett, and Mullen ("Buckeye Mine in 1882," Westmoreland–Fayette Historical Society (Box # P16. Folder #16 10 20), West Overton Village and Museums, Scottdale, Pennsylvania).

tracks, now on the Coal & Coke Trail that some say was the superintendent's home (others say was a bakery), a string of coke ovens sometimes visible from the Coal & Coke Trail, and a gob pile (slag dump).

- 1872 Buckeye Mine was built by the Cochran & Ewing Company.[226]
- 1875 60 beehive bank ovens of 10.5' × 5' in size required 100 bushels of coal fired for either 48 or 72 hours. They filled 38 railroad cars weekly and the coke was shipped west. Only 36 men handled the work.[227]
- 1882 Buckeye employed 110 men and had 136 beehive coke ovens.[228]
- 1885 Only forty-seven employees were working.[229]
- 1886 A.C. Cochran Coal & Coke Company employed 48 miners and 58 coke workers, with 122 ovens working.[230]
- 1890 Ventilation in the Buckeye mine poor.[231]
- 1891 A new engine house was erected at Buckeye.[232]
- 1895 Sold to H.C. Frick Coke Company. 248 men and boys employed at Buckeye with 160 beehive ovens.[233]
- 1899 A new tipple was added at Buckeye.
- 1905 Increased the coke ovens at Buckeye to 306.[234]
- 1910 Expanded larry car system 2 miles from the Buckeye via Star Mine to the Hazlett Mine.

1917 Closed.
1918 During World War I, 300 coke ovens were operating at Buckeye in 1918.[235]

Incidents and Events

On Christmas Eve of 1891, a miner wrote a letter to the editor of the *Scottdale Herald*: "Allow me space to place some of our bosses in a true light before the people. Here at Buckeye we have a superintendent and boss who want to ignore the scale made by the operators and try to get men to work for less than what the operators have already given. An effort was made here to get outside men to go to do inside work for outside laborer's wages, and they set up the claim that there was no scale governing inside and outside laborer's wages. Now for the information of these bosses I will state that the companies in their scale get inside labor at $1.65 and outside labor at $1.35. Quite a difference isn't it. WORKMAN."[236]

Hazlett Mines (1&2)

There were two mines with slope entrances named Hazlett on either side of the B&O Railroad (formerly Mt. Pleasant Broadford) in the village of Bridgeport. Hazlett was on the east side. Hazlett 2 was on the west side and purchased by Boyle & Hazlett at a sheriff's sale from the estate of John Myers.[237] Myers's investment of over $100,000 hit hard times with the Panic of 1873.

John D. Boyle and Samuel Hazlett were speculators from Washington, Pennsylvania, who are often credited with building the first coke ovens in Westmoreland County. Evidence does not support that claim. Myers deserves the credit. Among much evidence is a hospital stay in 1905 that was reported in the *Connellsville Weekly Courier* under the title "A Coke Pioneer: John Myers Who Built First Ovens in Westmoreland."[238]

Boyle & Hazlett were ruthless, and much of the antagonism against Henry Clay Frick should go to men like them. The 1876 *Mount Pleasant Dawn* reported, "All the miners in this section of 'cokedom' who were out on a strike last week have gone to work at 25 cents per wagon, the price paid before the strike. Messrs Boyle & Hazlett compelled their men to dig four wagons free to recompense them for the expense incurred by the strike."[239]

In 1882 they began producing 24-hour coke. This was an important milestone in coking history. The industry began by making 72-hour coke for foundry furnaces. Slowly they improved to 48-hour coke and finally 24-hour coke. It saved valuable time. Many only made 72-hour coke on weekends when they were closed on Sunday.[240]

By the turn of the century, the mine owners at Bridgeport began to see the end of the road as the problems mounted. The 261 beehive coke ovens needed to be rebuilt. Nearly half of them had structural problems, but only 150 ovens were rebuilt and in operation.[241]

Today one of the mine entrances is not sealed, for the flood from the interior has formed a small contaminated lake over the entrance. The few coke ovens remaining are on the west and not visible from the Coal & Coke Trail, for the trail bends to the east just before. It is unfortunate, for the ovens are the most important historic artifact at Bridgeport. They need to remain there and be preserved. Not restored; just preserved. They are important to the heritage of the Connellsville Coke Region but may not be the original Myers ovens. Archeologists must find the answer. Hazlett is currently private property.

1872 John Myers (Meyers, Moyers) erected a mine at Bridgeport with a company store, 20 buildings, and 100–150 coke ovens.[242]

1873 Hazlett 1 was built by Boyle & Hazlett on the east side of the railroad.

1875 Boyle & Hazlett Coal Co. bought the Myers property with the ovens, store, and buildings for $33,050 at sheriff's sale held by the First National Bank.[243]

1876 171 beehive coke ovens, 125 men filled 20 rail cars a day.[244]

1876 The ovens were 11⅓ × 6 feet and charged with three to four wagons of coal making 48 and 72-hour coke shipped to Chicago.[245]

1879 Boyle and Hazlett built 100 more ovens and accepted more orders than they could handle.

1880 Sued for failing to deliver 11 railroad cars of coke a day to Missouri Furnace Co. of St. Louis.[246]

1882 Began making 24-hour coke.

1885 Rafferty & Donnelly Coal & Coke Co. bought half interest in Hazlett. Only 84 people employed.[247]

1891 Hazlett Mine connected to Scottdale Water Company alleviating constant need for water.[248]

1893 Hazlett and Mullen mines were working.[249]

1895 H.C. Frick Coke Co. bought Hazlett Mines and leased them to McClure until 1900–03.

1896 Hazlett shaft was turned into a pumping station.[250]

1897–1899 Hazlett off *Connellsville Courier Report of the Operation and Output of the Coke Ovens of the Connellsville Region* list.

1900 Hazlett was back on the *Courier* list for McClure with 150 ovens.

1905–10 Hazlett was off the *Connellsville Courier Report of the Operation and Output of the Coke Ovens of the Connellsville Region* list, this time for good.

1911 Old fire reared its head at Hazlett.

1915 Reopened, but only to mine. It shipped the coal.[251]

1936 Mount Pleasant borough sought to use one of the openings of the mine for sewage disposal.[252]

Incidents and Events

In 1878 a group of reporters, including one from the *Pittsburgh Post*, were given a tour of coal mines along the Mount Pleasant Broadford Railroad. Among the many wonders they saw were fossils in the Hazlett Mine shown to them by the pit boss, an Englishman named Devlin. The author, J.C., does not tell us which of our Hazlett mines, but his description is of some cataclysmic event probably at the dawn of time. "He showed me great trees, which by the mysterious process that had made all the coal, were turned into almost pure charcoal, preserving their shape, the roots, and slightest wrinkles on the bark. Some of these trees are four feet in diameter. Devlin has had the diggers uncover many of them carefully. "In one place would be patches of small plants like the clover, another, great swaths of rushes or coarse prairie grass stretching across the mine as if they had been cut down at one sweep of the scythe. The large trees seem to have been of pithy nature and something like the palmetto in appearance; the bark does not resemble that on any of the trees which now grow in this locality. The trees have all fallen in one direction, the storm or convulsion which cast them down, came from the northeast, as the trees all lie southwest from their roots...." They are in the Pittsburgh Coal Seam so they must be at least 302 million years old.[253]

Mullen (Mullin) Mine

The Mullen Mine is located across Jacob's Creek from Bridgeport. It was built east of Shupe Run and serviced by the Baltimore and Ohio Railroad. W.D. Mullen was a Mount Pleasant man who lived at the corner of Main and Mullen in the borough. He also operated a livery stable and was the director of the First National Bank. Along with J.A. Strickler, Joseph Stoner, and B.F. Coughanour, he founded the Mullen Mine. Some reports state that the Mullen (Mullin) Mine was not built until around 1876. Today it is evident that Mullen was heavily strip mined. It went through an extensive reclamation project in the 1970s.

- 1872 *The Historical Data of the H.C. Frick Coke Company's Plants* reports founding date.
- 1874–5 60 beehive bank ovens measuring 11' × 5.5' each charged 3.5 to 4 wagon loads of 48 and 72-hour coke and shipped thirty-six cars or 22,500 bushels weekly. Only thirty-five men were employed.[254]
- 1885 Mullen Mine replaced its animals with machines.[255]
- 1887 McClure & Co. bought Mullen for $110,000.[256]
- 1895 McClure sold out to the Frick company.
- 1896 Frick company stopped the pumps that were pumping out water 24 hours a day and drained the water naturally.
- 1901 Frick began mining. Mullen had eighty-two beehive coke ovens (often idle).[257]
- 1909 Eight years later, the mine was flooded and sealed.
- 1910 Off the *Connellsville Courier Report of the Operation and Output of the Coke Ovens of the Connellsville Region* list.

Bessemer Mine

Bessemer is a common name, and in addition to the one in question, there were two mines by that name near Masontown in Greene County: a Bessemer Company producing pig iron for the iron trade, and a Bessemer Coke Company. Why so many uses for the name Bessemer? Sir Henry Bessemer was an Englishman who invented a cheaper method of manufacturing steel from pig iron in 1856. From that invention came the Bessemer converter, which was one of the inventions that led to the Industrial Revolution. Later his convertor was replaced by the open-hearth furnace. This Bessemer Mine was in the Mount Pleasant area around Route 819 and Bessemer Road. It was four miles north of Scottdale along Sherrick Run.

As with many of the mines, Bessemer had problems with its seals. It suffered from cave-ins. Bessemer lies, in part, under current Route 819, often called the Mount Pleasant–Scottdale Road. In 1938, the mine collapsed under the road, causing the road to buckle all across its width.[258] Although it was immediately repaired, it happened again in less than a month. By that time a Good Roads Association had been created, but the repairs were not quickly done. This time the state mandated the H.C. Frick Coke Company repair the road. They were given ten days. They did not repair it.

By June, a new request was issued by Secretary of Good Roads, Arthur McCloy.[259] By the end of the month the cave-in was filled with stone. It left 75 feet of roadway unpaved and it remained that way until 1940.[260] A year later the cave-in happened again.[261] The problem persisted, and in 1948 five seals were created at Bessemer.[262]

In 1970 there were fire hazards at Bessemer. At this point the mines were owned by Larry Capana. It seems the property was being used as a garbage dump by nearby residents and the garbage was catching fire. The township had been called to the mine several times to extinguish the fires. A meeting was held including Capana and the Pennsylvania Department of Mines. It was agreed that these openings were to be sealed and Capana would seal them.[263]

Today there is nothing left of the Bessemer Mine. The area where it once stood is now approached by the Bessemer Road just south of Mount Pleasant along Route 819. Passing the YMCA, the road reaches the edge of 119 in the area of the Holiday Inn. All that area was part of the Bessemer complex.

- 1875 Sherrick and Markle owned Bessemer in 1875.[264]
- 1878 Frick archives state that it was founded in 1878.
- 1879 First block of beehive ovens completed (considered the best in the region).[265]
- 1881 C.P. Markle & Sons opened a second Bessemer coke mine.[266]
- 1881-2 Bessemer Mine had six openings: two drifts, one that joined it to the Rising Sun Mine beside it, and three more. Fifty men and two young boys were working in the mine in 1882.[267]
- 1883 It was sold at auction with Schoonmaker, Frick, and McClure bidding. The sale included "a tipple, 20 frame houses, a large frame store building, railroad sidings, 170 ovens, 173 acres of coal and 160 acres of surface." McClure won the bid.[268]
- 1885 Both Bessemer mines were supervised by J.J. Maloney with John Narey as mine boss. Both had drift openings, and 45 persons served both mines.[269]
- 1887 A serious drought in the region. Bessemer depended on pit water until, along with Alice Mine, it received water from the Frick company pipelines.[270]
- 1888 1st *Report of the Operation and Output of the Coke Ovens of the Connellsville Region* in the *Courier* reported a single Bessemer mine and showed under 100 ovens.
- 1899 Bessemer had 278 coke ovens.
- 1906 100 ovens were listed throughout most of the year and they were all out of blast.
- 1907 Off the list completely.
- 1937 Slated to be sealed. Work was stopped. That put 267 WPA workers out of work and brought a temporary end to sealing efforts in the region.[271]

Alverton Mine

Originally called Stonerville, the town was established around 1800. The name was changed to Stoner when a post office was created in 1877 and changed again to Alverton

It is not clear which of the three Alverton mines this image represents (Eureka Coal Collection, courtesy James Steeley).

in 1892 by the Pennsylvania Railroad.[272] Today Alverton remains the name of the town. It straddles Route 981 after it passes Mount Pleasant, descends to Morewood, and climbs up and well beyond the hill once called Fort Defiance.

The biggest problem with dealing with Alverton is that sources do not distinguish between Alverton 1, 2, or 3, and therefore facts are often distorted. The mines at Alverton consist of Donnelly 1, opened by Donnelly and Dillinger Company in 1878, which became Alverton 1; Donnelly 2, opened by the McClure Coke Company, which became Alverton 2; and the Mayfield Mine, which became Alverton 3. Here is the truth as far as I can figure it.

Alverton 1 (Donnelly 1)

1878 Erected by Donnelly and Dillinger with a slope opening.
1882 Donnelly and Dillinger erected 200 coke ovens at their mine.[273]
1899 March 1, Samuel Dillinger *et al.* sold ⅖ interest in this mine to the McClure Coke Company.
1894 Pumphouse was blown up during strike. Records do not clarify which mine.[274]
1898 Foundry and machine shop were erected at Alverton.[275] Records do not clarify which mine.
1901 Alverton 1 had 252 coke ovens while Alverton 2 had 104.
1923 Leased to W.H. Pletcher, and its superintendent was A.O. Keck.[276]

Alverton 2

Both No. 1 and No. 2 were listed on the *Report of the Operation and Output of the Coke Ovens of the Connellsville District* for December 8, 1899. One had 254 ovens and two had 104; both were in full blast. No. 3, Mayfield, was not listed at all under either name.[277] But No. 2 is seldom mentioned in other reports.

1888 Listed as belonging to Gilbert T. Rafferty *et al.* or McClure: 39 acres with 35.881 coal and 3.44 barren of coal.

1890 Alverton 2's mining boss was Andrew Neish.[278]
1902 It was still listed as Alverton No. 2.

Alverton 3

The Mayfield Mine became Alverton No. 3. The life of Alverton No. 3 after its prime is one of the best stories of the Connellsville district. Its ovens kept firing until well into the 1980s. Trying to find a way to reduce the pollution of the beehives, Oliver K. Painter hired James E. MacDonald of Latrobe, and they created the MacDonald Smokeless Sole-Heated Non-Recovery Coke Oven. Painter built and operated eight of these ovens at Alverton.[279] But the Environmental Protection Agency was adamant. It wanted all the coke ovens in the United States closed for good.

1890 Connected to Alverton 2 and fifty new ovens were built. The mine boss was Peter Glenn.[280]
1912 Stoner Coal Company was chartered. Its owners: A.C. Stickel, Robert Norris, and F.M. Richey.[281]
1918 All the ovens were shut down for good, and coal was mined and shipped from the Alverton Mines.[282]
1950 Alverton No. 3 became the Alverton Coke Company leased by Oliver K. Painter.
1971 State sued Painter for pollution and tried to close his forty operating ovens.[283]
1982 June 14, 1982, the United States ordered the closing of all existing coke ovens in the country. The last still operating were the ovens at Alverton 3. They received special permission to fire up one of the four remaining ovens during the Scottdale Coal and Coke Festival and then shut down for good allowing all to fall to ruin.

The Southwests

The Southwest Connellsville Coke Company was chartered in April of 1892 with H.C. Frick, F.W. Haskell, H.A. Gray, W.R. Stirling, and J.L. Yale as directors.[284] Robert Ramsay, Jr., was appointed superintendent of the Southwest Coal & Coke Company Nos. 3 and 4 and made his office at Tarrs.[285] Confused? There is nothing more confusing than to try to sort out the differences between the Southwest Coal and Coke Company and the Southwest Connellsville Coal and Coke Company (unless it is to sort out the Alverton mines). Mines held by each of the Southwests varied from year to year. Some changed names. Others changed companies. No two sources list the same mines belonging to the two companies. For example, the HABS/HAER study, reporting on an in-house Frick company report, lists Southwest 1 as Morewood, 2 as Alice, 3 as Red Top, and 4 as American.[286] The *Journal* lists Morewood, Alice, Alverton, and Tarrs.

Our concern is about the mines that played a major role in the strike narrative. Those are Morewood, Alice, and Standard. Those are the mines discussed below. The two Southwest companies, their achievements and their grandeur, need a book of their own (and years of study). Two of them, Morewood and Standard, were the biggest and best mines in the world at the turn of the nineteenth century.

Morewood (Southwest No. 1)

Prior to the arrival of Standard, Morewood was the largest coal and coke mine in the United States, if not the world. Morewood was built by Henry Clay Frick and J.M. Schoonmaker around 1879 (or, depending on the source, 1878). Frick did not make it a part of the H.C. Frick Coal and Coke Company. By 1885 it was part of the Southwest Coal & Coke Company, and in 1901 the Southwest Connellsville Coke Company with Frick involved. In both instances, it was known as Southwest No. 1. It did not join the H.C. Frick Coal and Coke Company until it became a part of the newly formed United States Steel in 1903. From its beginning, it was linked to the Illinois Steel Company, another holding of H.C. Frick. Morewood sent all its coke to that company. This was also true of the Alice Mine just above it on Fort Defiance.

Morewood, Alice, and Standard dominated the strike events for decades as told in the chapters on strikes. It was at Morewood that the Hungarian women would go into the coke yards with their husbands helping them get the work done faster so they would earn more money.[287] It was at Morewood that men were killed in a confrontation between miners and police that became known as the Morewood Massacre.

It closed its doors in 1934. The following year, the Pennsylvania Railroad sought permission to dismantle a number of spur lines in coal country including the Morewood Branch, sometimes called the June Bug Line, from Morewood to Scottdale in Westmoreland County.[288]

When Morewood closed in 1934, the *Courier* stated, "The whistle at the plant was blown in the morning for the last time. It was sound at 6 o'clock and kept going until steam died down at 6:45." Today the mine area is all reclaimed—the new Route 119 ran right through its heart. The Pennsylvania marker that commemorates the massacre is on Route 981 just above the lake, which is probably drainage from the mine below ("Morewood Mine Worked Out; One of Region's First," *Daily Courier*, August 11, 1934, p. 1).

1878   Built and contained two shafts known as A and B, 200 ovens, and 1,000 acres of coal land.[289]

1888   Morewood was listed as Southwest No. 1 on 1st Connellsville list and had 470 ovens in full blast.[290]

1892   There were 620 ovens, with 618 in blast.[291]

1892   Morewood mines had two mine bosses, 311 miners, 5 miner boys, 30 driers and runners, 12 door boys, 2 outside foremen, 11 blacksmiths and carpenters, 15 engineers and firemen, 283 cokers and yardmen, and 50 horses and mules.

1899   Morewood was still growing as more ovens and fifty new houses were erected at both Tarrs and Morewood and an office building and stable at Morewood.[292]

1934   Morewood was closed for good by U.S. Steel.

1934   Leased to John Mitchell of Mount Pleasant.[293] Closed the plant in August of the same year.

1948   Two shafts at Morewood slated to be sealed by the Pennsylvania Department of Mines.[294]

1950   Work did not commence until July of 1950: both shafts at Morewood, one 107 feet deep and the other 96 feet deep, were sealed.[295]

Alice (Southwest No. 2)

Although some sources say Alice was opened in 1882, the *Legislative Documents* state it was opened in 1880 by James M. Schoonmaker, one of four of his works. It had a slope entry, a tipple, 200 coke ovens, and a number of houses.[296] Schoonmaker named it in honor of his wife.[297] It was not the only Alice Mine in the region, so confusion is possible. That same year the *Courier* reported it was haunted: The ghost of a deceased woman walked abroad at the midnight hour.[298]

In June of 1887 the pump house at Alice was set on fire and completely destroyed.[299] When the first issue of the *Report of the Operation and Output of the Coke Ovens of the Connellsville Region* began in 1888, Alice was listed as Southwest No. 2 and had 68 ovens in full blast.[300]

Alice Mine on Fort Defiance. There is nothing at all on the hillside today to show that Alice Mine stood there. The mine cascaded down the hillside above the Morewood Mine (Alice Mine, Eureka Photo Collection, courtesy James Steeley).

Despite the 1888 date, Alice was purchased by the Southwest Coal & Coke Company in January of 1890 and given the name Southwest No 2. That name had originally been held by another mine, which was then consolidated with the current No. 3 (you figure it out).[301] In 1892 there were 254 ovens.[302] In 1893 the inspector of mines found Alice in "healthful condition," but noted that water from the nearby Union Mine broke into Alice, "washing out the road-beds and flooding the dip workings for a few days." The mining boss at the time was George Santimyer.[303]

Standard

A.A. Hutchinson and Brothers created Standard No. 1 in 1878. They built 150 houses, a company store and 509 beehive ovens. When the first issue of the *Report of the Operation and Output of the Coke Ovens of the Connellsville Region* began in 1888, Standard was listed separately, and it had zero ovens at the time.[304] On the coke oven list, Standard was listed as belonging to H.C. Frick, while Alice and Morewood, as 2 and 1, were listed as Southwest Coal and Coke. On all the coke oven lists through the years, Standard was always listed separately and never listed as belonging to either Southwest.

Carmen Peter DiCiccio maintains Frick bought the mine in 1883.[305] It is an interesting story. Hutchinson joined Frick on a European trip, and as it was coming to an end, he lamented that he wished to continue his journey. Frick made him an offer. He accepted and went off to Asia while Frick came home with Standard in his pocket.

In 1891 the Frick company introduced electric lights into its coal mines. The contract was given to Westinghouse Electric and Manufacturing Company, another southwestern Pennsylvania industrial giant. Each mine was independently lit with lamps along the main underground passages, the tipple, engine house, and other buildings.[306] At that time there were 4500 acres of land and 400 of it was already mined out (495). The ovens were

Section of the Fowler map of Mount Pleasant showing Standard mine coke ovens and rows of patch houses. There were three mines at Standard: Standard, Standard Shaft, and Standard No. 3. The town of Standard still stands, along with some of the mine buildings. Several have received a Pennsylvania marker, but the town and entire complex are not on the National Register of Historic Places, as there were too many changes to the buildings over the years (Thaddeus Fowler, *Map of Mount Pleasant, Westmoreland County, Pennsylvania*, T.M. Fowler and James B. Moyer Publishers, 1900).

12-foot-high beehives with 20 seven-ton larrys, and five locomotives (replacing the mules) built by the H.K. Porter & Co. of Pittsburgh.[307]

In 1892 Standard had 905 ovens.[308] Contrary to myth, Standard never had 999 coke ovens, a portion acquired from the Duncan Brothers. That distinction belonged to the Star Junction Mine along Route 51. The story behind the myth is that if a company had 1000 ovens there was an added tax. In 1894 H.C. Frick Coal and Coke Company paid $1,190 road tax for Standard Mine (plus more for all the other mines).[309]

There is no doubt that Standard was the biggest and best mine in the world. Every newspaper, every coal journal said so. In tribute to that tradition, in 1893 the Frick Company sent a replica off to the World's Fair. Like its mine, it was "the biggest and best in the world." Frick chose Robert Ramsey to create the replica:

> Work began around March of 1892 right on the grounds of Standard Shaft No. 2. It would take six men a year to complete the entire replica. It was an amazing accomplishment. No expense was spared. No corners cut. First they had to contour the land to resemble the topography of the area. Then they lay in the buildings, the rails, and all the items related to the site. In the end it cost the company $12,000 to produce....
>
> In addition to the shaft, the cast iron coke ovens, the wooden tipple, the tracks, and the rolling stock of various kinds, the model included all the buildings of the mine: the boiler house, the blacksmith, carpenter, and machine shops, and a few wooden worker's homes with front porches, interior furniture, and backyard gardens.
>
> Most of the men working on the replica had a specialization. The rams that pushed the cars onto and off of the hole in the tipple where they would discharge the coke into the awaiting railroad cars were built by James Wilson. The construction of the wooden items like the tipple, the rail ties, the wagons, and the houses was left to David Patterson and his assistants Samuel Bungard, Elmer Billings, and George Walters. Billings and Walters made the bin and pit wagons too. The painters were Charley Fletcher, John Shindle, James Cox, and Bert Bobbs. Their work included turning the solid red facades of several building into bricks. Patterson and Bungard would take the replica to Chicago and reassemble the model at the fair.
>
> The Chicago World's Fair came to an end in 1893. When the time came to pack up the exhibits and take them home, Frick wrote to his General Manager Thomas Lynch, "…I would not want the Chicago exhibit disturbed at all, even the models of the individual cars, until I have a full talk with you on the subject. My idea is to keep it intact, store it away somewhere, and use it for some future exhibition."[310] In November the answer came, "I have decided to have our World's Fair exhibit removed to Exhibition building in this city, as it will be of great interest to many of our customers, when they happen to be in this city and avoid the necessity of them taking a trip to the coke region to see the operation of coke making."
>
> And that is where it remained through 1894, 1895, and the Western Pennsylvania Exposition of 1898.
>
> After that the replica, or some of its parts, may have been exhibited in various fairs and expositions but eventually bits and pieces were placed in personal collections. For years one of the cars was in the window of a bank in Uniontown.[311]

Standard and its patch are not on the National Register of Historic Places. The dozens of houses along Route 819 and High Street still stand. Several of the mine buildings do too. They, thank goodness, have a historic marker. Unfortunately, the long line of coke ovens was dismantled long after it should have been acknowledged by the community, the county, and the state that they were historically important.

Chapter Notes

Introduction
1. Carmen Peter DiCiccio, *Bituminous Coal and Coke Resources of Pennsylvania 1740–1945*, National Register of Historic Places Continuation, November 9, 1993.

Chapter 1
1. William E. Edmunds, *Coal in Pennsylvania* (2nd ed.), Pennsylvania Geological Survey, Fourth Series, Educational Series 7, Harrisburg, 2002, p. 2.
2. "The Connellsville Coke Region," *The Engineering Magazine: An International Review* 20 (October 1900 to March 1901): pp. 17–40, p. 27.
3. George Thurston, *Pittsburgh and Allegheny in the Centennial Year*, Pittsburgh: Anderson, 1876, p. 104.
4. *Connellsville Coke*, H.C. Frick Co. Pittsburgh Pa, 1890, Helen Clay Frick Foundation Archives (AIS 2002 06), Henry Clay Frick Business Records, 1862–1987, Box 523, Folder 1, Archives Service Center, University of Pittsburgh, p. 1.
5. B.F. Hoffacker, "Pittsburgh Coal in Fayette County," *Uniontown Morning Herald*, August 18, 1926, p. 4.
6. Jared Sparks, "Journal of George Washington written during an expedition along the Ohio and Kanawha Rivers," *The Writings of George Washington*, Vol. 2, Boston: Charles Tappan, 1847, pp. 516–534. http://www.wvculture.org/history/settlement/washingtonjournal1770.html.
7. "Written Historical and Descriptive Data," *Connellsville Coal and Coke Region*, HAER, No. PA-283, p. 15.
8. Ibid., p. 12.
9. "Early Coke Making," *Daily Courier*, March 25, 1881, p. 1.
10. "Railroad History of Fayette County," http://pghbridges.com/articles/railroads/RRhistory_fayette3.htm.
11. "Broadford to Westmoreland," http://pghbridges.com/articles/railroads/RRhistory_fayette3.htm.
12. "Written Historical and Descriptive Data," *Connellsville Coal and Coke Region*, HAER, No. PA-283, p. 100.
13. "Coal and Coke," *Mt. Pleasant Journal*, August 7, 1893. Scrapbook, May 27, 1893, to February 2, 1894, Helen Clay Frick Foundation Archives (AIS 2002 06), Henry Clay Frick Business Records, 1862, Box 503, Volume 16, Archives Service Center, University of Pittsburgh, p. 8.
14. "Big Frick Shops," *Weekly Courier*, October 2, 1905; *Scottdale 100 Years*, Scottdale Centennial Association, Inc., Scottdale, 1974, p. 9.
15. R.J. Tormay, *A History of Area Mines*, Westmoreland–Fayette Historical Society (Box # 16, Folder # A5), West Overton Village and Museums. Scottdale, Pennsylvania. p. 12.
16. "Deluge: 18 Hours of Rain and 12 Hours of Flood...," *Courier*, August 24, 1888, p. 1.
17. "Two Miners Rescued from Flooded Frick Mine at Broad Ford," *Daily Courier*, August 20, 1912, p. 1.
18. "Flood-Stricken Families Ask for Help from Red Cross," *Uniontown Evening Standard*, October 19, 1954, p. 8.
19. "A Good Outlook for Coke," *Scottdale Independent*, September 28, 1893, p. 1.
20. "Written Historical and Descriptive Data," *Connellsville Coal and Coke Region*, HAER, No. PA-283, p. 61.
21. Arthur A. Socolow, et al., *Coal Resources of Pennsylvania*, Information Circular 88, Pennsylvania Geological Survey, 4th Series, Harrisburg, 1980, pp. 7, 24. Image too.
22. "Who is a Coal-Miner?" *Coal Mines & Coal Miners*, www.workerseducation.org/crutch/phamphlets/coal/coal_5.html.
23. Owen R. Lovejoy, "Child Labor in the Soft Coal Mines," *Annals of the American Academy of Political and Social Science* 29, Child Labor (January 1907): pp. 26–34.
24. "Local Flash," *Mount Pleasant Dawn*, April 19, 1876, p. 3.
25. This story was told to me by Bill Hare of Mount Pleasant, whose father worked at the Carpentertown Mine.
26. Aaron Marcavitch, *Folklore in Southwestern Pennsylvania Bituminous Coal Mining*, http://www.marcavitch.com/research/hppgc/mining/coalfolk.htm, p. 7.
27. Ibid., p. 11.
28. Carmen Peter DiCiccio, *Bituminous Coal and Coke Resources of Pennsylvania 1740–1945*, National Register of Historic Places Continuation, November 9, 1993, p. 35.
29. Ibid., pp. 136–9.
30. "Connellsville Coke," *Weekly Courier*, March 11, 1881, p. 1.
31. DiCiccio, p. 147.
32. John A. Enman, "The Relationship of Coal Mining and Coke Making to the Distribution of Population Agglomerations in the Connellsville (Pennsylvania)

Beehive Coke Region," Ph.D. dissertation, University of Pittsburgh, 1962, p. 281.

33. DiCiccio, p. 147.

34. "By-Product Ovens Surpass Beehive as Coke Producers, Shown by Records of 1921," *Weekly Courier*, March 30, 1822, p. 3.

35. "By-Product Ovens Need Coal, Frick Blows Out Beehives," *Daily Courier*, February 8, 1940, p. 1.

36. Dennis F. Brestensky, *The Early Coke Worker*, Connellsville: Connellsville Printing Company, 1994, p. 1.

37. "Strikers Gain Ground," *Mount Pleasant Journal*, May 1, 1894. Scrapbook, April 16 to May 12, 1894. Helen Clay Frick Foundation Archives (AIS 2002 06). Henry Clay Frick Business Records, 1862–1987 Box 505, Volume 18, Archives Service Center, University of Pittsburgh, p. 107.

38. DiCiccio, p. 280.

39. Ibid., p. 290.

40. Ibid., p. 284.

Chapter 2

1. Guide to the Henry Clay Frick Business Records, 1862–1987, Series XXV. Westmoreland–Fayette Historical Society, 1906–1987. Historical Background, https://digital.library.pitt.edu/islandora/object/pitt%3AUS-PPiU-ais200206/viewer.

2. West Overton Museums, http://www.fay-west.com/westoverton/.

3. Martha Frick Symington Sanger, *Henry Clay Frick: An Intimate Portrait*, New York: Abbeville Press, 1998, pp. 49–50.

4. Ibid., p. 34.

5. George Harvey, *Henry Clay Frick: The Man*, New York: Charles Scribner's Sons, 1928, p. 23.

6. John W. Oliver, *Henry Clay Frick: Pioneer-patriot and Philanthropist 1849–1949*, address delivered at Westmoreland–Fayette County Historical Society, June 18, 1949, p. 9.

7. "Local Flashes," *Mount Pleasant Dawn*, May 24, 1876, p. 3.

8. "H.C. Frick to be Laid at Rest in Pittsburgh Thursday," *Daily Courier*, December 3, 1919, p. 1.

9. Extracts from Day Book, Overholt, Frick & Co, March 10, 1871 to June 20, 1871, Helen Clay Frick Foundation Archives (AIS 2002 06), Henry Clay Frick Business Records, 1862–1987, Box 523, Folder 6, Archives Service Center, University of Pittsburgh.

10. "Local Flashes," *Mount Pleasant Dawn*, April 26, 1876, p. 2.

11. *Connellsville Coke, H.C. Frick Co. Pittsburgh Pa, 1890*, Helen Clay Frick Foundation Archives (AIS 2002 06), Henry Clay Frick Business Records, 1862–1987, Box 523, Folder 1, Archives Service Center, University of Pittsburgh, p. 32.

12. "Tintsman Sells Morgan," *Mount Pleasant Dawn*, March 22, 1876, p. 3.

13. *Connellsville Coke, H.C. Frick Co. Pittsburgh Pa, 1890*, Helen Clay Frick Foundation Archives (AIS 2002 06), Henry Clay Frick Business Records, 1862–1987, Box 523, Folder 1, Archives Service Center, University of Pittsburgh, p. 21.

14. Excerpt from Journals and Daybooks. Journal of H.C. Frick and Company, March 1878–May 31, 1880, December 31, 1878, Helen Clay Frick Foundation Archives (AIS 2002 06), Henry Clay Frick Business Records, 1862–1987, Box 523, Folder 10, Archives Service Center, University of Pittsburgh, p. 1.

15. Guide to the Henry Clay Frick Business Records, 1862–1987, https://digital.library.pitt.edu/islandora/object/pitt%3AUS-PPiU-ais200206/viewer.

16. Excerpt from Journals and Daybooks. Journal of H.C. Frick and Company, March 1878– May 31, 1880, December 31, 1878, Helen Clay Frick Foundation Archives (AIS 2002 06), Henry Clay Frick Business Records, 1862–1987, Box 523, Folder 10, Archives Service Center, University of Pittsburgh, p. 1.

17. Thanks to Ron Baraff, Director of Historic Resources and Facilities at Rivers of Steel, for some of this information.

18. "Written History and Descriptive Data," *Connellsville Coal and Coke Region*, HAER No. PA-283, pp. 75–77.

19. "Will Open New York Office," *Mount Pleasant Journal*, December 29, 1891, p. 104.

20. Digital History Project: Henry Clay Frick, United States Steel Corporation, June 15, 2012, http://www.digitalhistoryproject.com/2012/96/henry-clay-frick-united-states-steel.html.

21. "Frick Superintendent's Office Moving to Uniontown in April," *Morning Herald*, March 29, 1939, p. 1.

22. "Coke Men Crushed," *Penny Press*, June 11, 1887, Scrapbook, March 22, 1884, to August 18, 1887, Helen Clay Frick Foundation Archives (AIS 2002 06), Henry Clay Frick Business Records, 1862–1987, Box 488, Volume 1, Archives Service Center, University of Pittsburgh, p. 73.

23. William S. Dietrich II, "Henry Clay Frick: Blood Pact," *Pittsburgh Quarterly*, Spring 2009, http://www.pittsburghquarterly.com/index.php/Historic-profiles/article-template/Print.html, p. 4.

24. Ibid., pp. 6–7.

25. "Frick's Retirement," *Daily Courier*, December 8, 1899, p. 12.

26. The bullet point of events was adapted from Sanger, pp. 180–183.

27. Ken O'Neal, "Fayette County and Surrounding Country Coal Mines," Fayette County Genealogy Project, http://www.pagenweb.org/~fayette/coal/coal_mines.html.

28. DiCiccio, p. 3.

29. Ibid., pp. 327–8.

30. "Coal and Coke," *Mount Pleasant Journal*, September 6, 1892, p. 2.

31. "Mount Pleasant Rotary Unveils Frick Memorial," *Daily Courier*, November 21, 1930, p. 1.

32. Interview, Joe Eckman, March 17, 2016, Mount Pleasant Glass Museum Meeting; "Mining Practices of the H. C. Frick Coke Co.," *Mines and Minerals*, August, 1904, p. 43; Douglas A. Fisher, *Steel Serves the Nation, 1901 to 1951*, U.S. Steel Corp, 1951, p. 79.

33. "The Morewood Killings," *Mount Pleasant Journal*, April 14, 1891, p. 2.

34. "Unlucky 13th," *Mount Pleasant Journal*, May 12, 1891, p. 1.

35. "The Coke War Not Yet Over," *Reading Times*, April 12, 1894, p. 1.
36. "Little Chance," *Mount Pleasant Journal*, May 5, 1891, p. 1.
37. "Unlucky 13th," p. 1.
38. "May End Strike," *Pittsburgh Press*, April 7, 1910, p. 3.
39. Muriel Earley Sheppard, *Cloud by Day*, Chapel Hill: University of North Carolina Press, 1947, pp. 77–8.
40. "Frick Buys Coal Closing Busy Day," *Pittsburgh Daily Post*, March 13, 1914, p. 2; "H.C. Frick Buys Coal Acreage in Greene for $6,000,000," *Morning Herald*, February 28, 1914, p. 1.
41. "The Harrowing Hun," *Weekly Courier*, January 29, 1886, p. 1.
42. "Coke Making Good Gains," *Scottdale Independent*, October 5, 1893, Scrapbook, May 27, 1893, to February 2, 1894. Box 503, Volume 16, Henry Clay Frick Business Records, 1862–1987, AIS 2002.06, Archives Service Center, University of Pittsburgh, pp. 88–89.
43. "The Coke Trade Gaining," *Scottdale Independent*, November 30, 1893, Scrapbook, May 27, 1893 to February 2, 1894, Box 503, Volume 16, Henry Clay Frick Business Records, 1862–1987, AIS 2002.06, Archives Service Center, University of Pittsburgh, pp. 133–4.
44. "A Justifiable Strike," *Pittsburgh Times*, December 11, 1893, p. 1.
45. "Organization Favored," *Commercial Gazette*, March 22, 1894, p. 6.
46. Kim Leonard, *Henry Clay Frick: Respected and Hated*, December 16, 2007. http://triblive.com/x/pittsburghtrib/news/s_543031.html.
47. *Connellsville Coal and Coke Region*, HAER No. PA-283, p. 66. By mid-century, Lynch's letter was attributed to Henry Clay Frick in Douglas A. Fisher's *Steel Serves the Nation, 1901–1951: The Fifty-Year Story of United States Steel*.
48. "Enthroned a King," *Pittsburgh Dispatch*, August 28, 1889, p. 3.
49. "The Connellsville Coke Regions: Their past, present, and future," *Weekly Courier*, Special Historical and Statistical Number, May, 1914, p. 7.
50. Stephen Gooddale, "Safety the First Consideration," *The Colorado School of Mines Magazine* 1, No. 12 (September 1911): pp. 6–9.
51. Harold L. Nickerson, "Industrial Safety," Association of Governmental Officials in Industry of the United States and Canada, Eighteenth Annual Convention, Boston, MA, May 18–22, 1931; Bulletin of the United States Bureau of Labor Statistics, No. 563, Washington DC: Government Printing Office, 1932, p. 119.
52. "Familiar Faces in the Mining Industry: Henry C. Frick," *The Colliery Engineer* 12 (December 1891), Scrapbook, October 2, 1891, to February 27, 1892, Helen Clay Frick Foundation Archives (AIS 2002 06), Henry Clay Frick Business Records, 1862–1987, Box 496, Volume 9, Archives Service Center, University of Pittsburgh, p. 86.
53. "Condition of Mines: H.C. Frick Coke Company," *Report of the Department of Mines of Pennsylvania*, Part II, Bituminous, 1907, p. 498; "Coal and Coke News: Bituminous Pittsburgh (Frick Award)," *Coal Age*, September 28, 1912, Vol. 2, July 1 to December 31, 1912. New York: Hill Publishing Co., 1912, p. 443.
54. "Centralization of Industrial Control and Operation of Philanthropic Foundations," Senate Documents, Vol. 26, Industrial Relations: Final Report and Testimony submitted to Congress by the Commission on Industrial Relations created by the act of August 21, 1912, Vol. 8, Washington DC: Government Printing Office, 1916, p. 7478.
55. "Coal and Coke News," *Coal Age*, p. 443.
56. *Frick & Co. Dollar Bill*, Helen Clay Frick Foundation Archives (AIS 2002 06), Henry Clay Frick Business Records, 1862–1987, Box 523, Folder 1, Archives Service Center, University of Pittsburgh.
57. "The Harrowing Hun," p. 1.
58. "Written History and Descriptive Data." *Connellsville Coal and Coke Region*. HAER No. PA-283. HAER, pp. 65–66.
59. "Helping Needy Cokers," *Rural Free Press*, July 17, 1893, November 17, 1893, May 27, 1893, to February 2, 1894, Helen Clay Frick Foundation Archives (AIS 2002 06), Henry Clay Frick Business Records, 1862–1987, Box 503, Volume 16, Archives Service Center, University of Pittsburgh, p. 112.
60. "Frick Company Farm Land for Food Planting," *Daily Courier*, May 5, 1917, p. 1.
61. "Mr. Frick's Bequests," *Science Magazine*, December 12, 1919, p. 539.
62. Cassandra Vivian, *Hidden History of the Laurel Highlands*, Charleston: The History Press, 2014, p. 107.
63. "Church Gets Big Check," *Daily Courier*, June 28, 1909, p. 1.
64. Quentin R. Skrabec, Jr., *Henry Clay Frick, The Life of the Perfect Capitalist*, Jefferson, NC: McFarland, 2010, p. 174.
65. Ibid., p. 177.
66. Mr. Stevens's records related to this book are found at Pennsylvania State Archives: http://www.phmc.state.pa.us/bah/dam/mg/sd/m149sd.htm.
67. *Frick vrs. Stevens*, Common Pleas Court of Cumberland County, Pennsylvania, May 25, 1967, https://www.leagle.com/decision/19674943padampc2d6148.
68. Kurt Shaw, "Frick Legacy: Book Examines Life of Industrialist's Daughter," *Pittsburgh Tribune Review*, October 28, 2007, http://triblive.com/x/pittsburghtrib/focus/s_534193.html.

Chapter 3

1. DiCiccio, p. 84.
2. "The Harrowing Hun," p. 1.
3. "First Foreigners in Coke Region," *Daily Courier*, December 14, 1910, p. 12.
4. "An Appeal to American Working Men," *Scottdale Independent*, June 18, 1884, p. 2.
5. "Foreign Laborers," *Scottdale Independent*, December 12, 1885, p. 1.
6. "The Coke Region Hun," *Weekly Courier*, March 22, 1889, p. 1.
7. "Alien Labor Taxation," *Pittsburgh Dispatch*, March 28,

1889, p. 1; "Prohibition Passes," *Weekly Courier*, February 1, 1889, p. 1.

8. Foreign Miner Taxes: http://immigrationtounitedstates.org/506-foreign-miner-taxes.html.

9. *Report of the Select Committee on Immigration and Naturalization and Testimony Taken by the Committee on Immigration of the Senate and the Select Committee on Immigration and Naturalization of the House of Representatives under Concurrent Resolution of March 12, 1890*, Reported to the House by Mr. Owen, of Indiana, January 15, 1891, Washington, DC: Government Printing Office, 1891, pp. ii, v, vii.

10. https://en.wikipedia.org/wiki/Immigration_Restriction_League.

11. "Contract Labor System," *Encyclopedia of Immigration*, September 27, 2011, http://immigration-online.org/448-contract-labor-system.html.

12. John R. Commons, *et al.*, *A Documentary History of American Industrial Society*, Vol. 9, Labor Movement, Cleveland: The Arthur H. Clark Company, 1910, p. 74.

13. *American Emigrant Company*, New York [s.n. 1865], pp. 12–14.

14. "How the Huns Get Here," *Scottdale Independent*, June 18, 1884, p. 2.

15. DiCiccio, p. 97.

16. Andrew A. Marchbin, "Hungarian Activities in Western Pennsylvania," *Western Pennsylvania Historical Society* 23, No. 3 (September 1940): pp. 163–174.

17. Stephen Shumeyko, "Progress of Ukrainians in America," *The Ukrainian Weekly*, October 6, 1933, http://www.ukrweekly.com/old/archive/1933/013303.shtml.

18. For in-depth information about Slovaks and Carpatho-Rusyns, see the Slovak and Carpatho-Rusyn Genealogy Research Pages at http://www.iarelative.com/slovakia.htm.

19. DiCiccio, p. 153.

20. "Friday, February 20, 1880," *Daily Courier*, March 3, 1929, p. 5.

21. Waclaw Kruszka, *A History of Poles in America to 1908*, Part 3: *Poles in the Eastern and Southern States*, Washington, DC: The Catholic University of America Press, 1998, p. 161.

22. Edward Ifkovic, "Croatian Americans," https://www.everyculture.com/multi/Bu-Dr/Croatian-Americans.html#ixzz5UIelxX00.

23. Paul Peirce, "Last Call: Yukon Croatian Club to close for good Friday," Tribune Review, May 29, 2018, https://triblive.com/local/westmoreland/13690771-74/last-call-friday-at-yukon-croatian-club.

24. "Little Lithuania USA Schuylkill County Pa." *Draugas News*. https://www.draugas.org/news/little-lithuania-usa-schuylkill-county-pa/.

25. "Fleeing from domestic famine in the late 1800's: Hordes of Lithuanians came to Pennsylvania to Work in Coal Mines," http://vilnews.com/2012-04-12858.

26. Global True Lithuania Encyclopedia of Lithuanian Heritage Worldwide. http://global.truelithuania.com/pennsylvania-usa-108/.

27. For an interactive map of Lithuanian sites, see the Pennsylvania Map of Lithuanian Sites at http://map.truelithuania.com/en/pennsylvania-map-of-lithuanian-sites/.

28. Mercedes Sowko Crispin, *The Carpatho-Rusyn Immigrant of Pennsylvania Steel Mills 1880–1920*, p. 21. http://humboldtdspace.calstate.edu/bitstream/handle/2148/53/Crispin.pdf;jsessionid=107041A2D5E8D281BDB9384460823F4A.server1?sequence=1.

29. Cassandra Vivian, *Monessen: A Typical Steel Country Town*, Making of America Series. Charleston: Arcadia Publishing, 2002, p. 28.

30. John W. Jordan and James Hadden, *Genealogical and Personal History of Fayette County Pennsylvania*, Vol. 3, New York: Lewis Historical Publishing Company, 1912, p. 650.

31. Rita Moonsammy, *Final Report Steel Industry Heritage Corporation Ethnographic Survey Fayette County Component*, November 21, 1992, p. 38. https://www.riversofsteel.com/_uploads/files/fayette-final-report.pdf.

32. "The Harrowing Hun," p. 1.

33. Ibid.

34. Edwin, Fenton, "Italians in the Labor Movement," *Pennsylvania History: A Journal of Mid-Atlantic Studies* 26, No. 2 (1959): pp. 133–148. JSTOR, www.jstor.org/stable/27769876.

35. Herbert G. Gutman, "The Buena Vista Affair," *Pennsylvania Magazine*, July 1964, pp. 251–293.

36. "Small Town Life: A Tale of Two Towers," *Uniontown Herald-Standard*, December 13, 2015, https://www.heraldstandard.com/community_life/small_town_life/small-town-life-a-tale-of-two-towers/article_d8c5f326-2ada-58e9-ac21-049bc1669f09.html.

37. "The Coke Region, Comments Upon the Wages Paid the Employees, the Pluck-Me," October 8, 1888, Scrapbook, August 19, 1887, to November 2, 1888, Helen Clay Frick Foundation Archives (AIS 2002 06), Henry Clay Frick Business Records, 1862–1987, Box 489. Archives Service Center, University of Pittsburgh, p. 173.

38. *Coal and Coke Resource Analysis*, America's Industrial Heritage Project, United States Department of the Interior, National Park Service, November, 1992, p. 45. Despite this criticism, AIHP is an excellent resource on many levels and a good place to receive background. It began in the 1980s and has improved each year, serving the public well.

39. Cassandra Vivian, *The Overseer's Family*, Monessen: Trade Routes Enterprises, 2002, p. 34.

40. "Wretched Abodes," *Pittsburgh Post-Gazette*, April 17, 1897, p. 1.

41. Enman, 'Relationship of Coal Mining," pp. 273–4.

42. Jett Lauck, "The Bituminous Coal Miner and Coke Worker of Western Pennsylvania," *The Survey* 26, April–September 1911, New York: The Charity Organization Society, April 1, 1911, pp. 34–51. Lauck's papers are at the University of Virginia Library Manuscript Division.

43. *United States Steel Corporation Hearings before the Committee on Investigation of United States Steel Corporation*, House of Representatives, Wednesday,

February 14, 1912, Washington, DC: Government Printing Office, 1912, p. 3282.
44. "Around About," *Keystone Courier*, July 23, 1880, p. 3.
45. Enman, "Relationship of Coal Mining and Coke Making," p. 342.
46. Evelyn A. Hovanec, *Common Lives of Uncommon Strength: The Women of the Coal and Coke Era of Southwestern Pennsylvania 1880-1970*, Dunbar, PA: Patch/Work Voices Publishing, 2001, p. 19. There is no way of knowing the date of the events in this story.
47. John J. Stoffey, "Memories of a Coal Cracker," https://www.mcall.com/opinion/white/mc-bw-coal-cracker-20170128-story.html.
48. Eileen Mount Joy, *A Woman's Day: Work and Anxiety*, Special Collection and University Archives, Indiana University of Pennsylvania, 2007-8. https://www.iup.edu/archives/coal/people-lives-stories/a-woman-s-day--work-and-anxiety/.
49. Ibid.
50. Ole S. Johnson, *The Industrial Store: Its History, Operations and Economic Significance*, School of Business Administration, University of Georgia, 1952, pp. 11-15.
51. DiCiccio, p. 175.
52. Lauck, p. 38.
53. "Fayette Facts," *Weekly Courier*, February 1, 1884, p. 4.
54. Moonsammy, p. 8.
55. *Connellsville Coal & Coke*, HAER, No. PA-28, pp. 63-64.
56. Union Supply Company Photograph, Westmoreland-Fayette Historical Society (Box P25, Folder #4176), West Overton Village and Museums. Scottdale, Pennsylvania.
57. Joy, *A Woman's Day*.
58. "A Miner's Story," *The Independent*, 1902. ehistory, Ohio State University, Department of History, https://ehistory.osu.edu/exhibitions/gildedage/content/MinersStory.
59. *Coal and Coke Resource Analysis*, p. 50.
60. John A. Enman, "Coal Company Store Prices Questioned: A Case Study of the Union Supply Company," 1905-1906, *Pennsylvania History* 41, No. 1 (January 1974): p. 60.
61. Enman, "Relationship of Coal Mining," p. 61.
62. "Centralization of Industrial Control and Operation of Philanthropic Foundations," Senate Documents, Vol. 26; Industrial Relations: *Final Report and Testimony submitted to Congress by the Commission on Industrial Relations created by the act of August 21, 1912*, Vol. 8, Washington, DC: Government Printing Office, 1916, pp. 7478, 7486-87. Tarbell, an investigative reporter who brought down Standard Oil and broke monopolies in the U.S., talks at length to the Senate committee on Frick company mines, their stores, their houses and more, painting a positive impression of the company.
63. *Coal and Coke Resource Analysis*, p. 50.
64. Johnson, p. 33.
65. "James B. Morgan," *Pittsburgh Post-Gazette*, August 8, 1915, p. 2.
66. Price V. Fishback, "Did Coal Miners 'Owe Their Souls to the Company Store'? Theory and Evidence from the Early 1900s," *The Journal of Economic History* 46, No. 4 (December 1986): pp.1011-1029. See also: Report of the U.S. Coal Commission, Washington, DC, 1925, part 3.
67. H.C. Frick Coke Company Record, Subseries 3: Administrative Records 1871-1921, Box 523, Folder 6, Excerpts from Journals and Daybooks 1871-1876, Henry Clay Frick Foundation Archives (AIS 2002 06), Henry Clay Frick Business Records, 1862-1967, pp. 9, 15.
68. *History of Wages in the United States from Colonial Times to 1928*, Bulletin of the United States Bureau of Labor Statistics, No. 604, United States Department of Labor, Washington, DC: Government Printing Office, 1934, pp. 154-332.
69. United States Steel Corporation Hearings before the Committee of Investigation of United States Steel Corporation, House of Representatives, February 14, 1912, Washington, DC: Government Printing Office, 1912, p. 3672.
70. https://www.thebalance.com/capitalism-characteristics-examples-pros-cons-3305588.
71. "Notes on Labor, 1875-1900," http://claver.gprep.org/sjochs/labor.htm.
72. *Coal and Coke Resource Analysis*, p. 52.
73. https://www.dli.pa.gov/Individuals/Workers-Compensation/publications/Pages/WC%20Act/WC-Act-Landing-Page.aspx.
74. "Accident Relief Fund Established," *Pittsburgh Daily Post*, June 11, 1910, p. 1.
75. "Minor Coal and Coke Notes, *Weekly Courier*, January 28, 1887, p. 1.
76. T.T. O'Malley, *Adventures in the Mines, Perils Underground*, Akron: The Werner Printing and Litho Company, 1891, pp. 350-377.
77. "Furniture Loss of Widow Made Good by Frick Company," *Daily Courier*, October 18, 1912, p. 1.
78. Wasyl Halich, *Notes and Documents: Ukrainians in Western Pennsylvania*, Historical Society of Western Pennsylvania, 1935, pp. 139-146.

Chapter 4

1. Carroll D. Wright, "An Historical Sketch of the Knights of Labor," *The Quarterly Journal of Economics* 1, No. 2 (January 1887): pp. 137-168.
2. James Dougherty, "A Reference Guide to Resources on Coal Mining and Associated Materials in the Central/Western Pennsylvania Region. Knights of Labor Locals in America's Industrial Heritage Counties." From: Johnathan Garlock, *Guide to The Local Assemblies of the Knights of Labor*, Westport: Greenwood Press. 1982.
3. Jörg Rössel, "Industrial Structure, Union Strategy, and Strike Activity in American Bituminous Coal Mining, 1881-1894," *Social Science History* 26, No. 1 (Spring 2002): pp. 1-32.
4. Wright, pp. 137-168.
5. Jesse S. Robinson, *The Amalgamated Association of Iron, Steel and Tin Workers*, Johns Hopkins University Studies in Historical and Political Science, Baltimore: The Johns Hopkins Press, 1920, p. 9.

6. "A Scale or a Strike," *Weekly Courier*, February 1, 1889, p. 1.
7. "The Coke Region Troubles," *Pittsburgh Daily Post*, November 26, 1886, p. 1.
8. Pinkerton's National Detective Agency Records, http://rs5.loc.gov/service/mss/eadxmlmss/eadpdfmss/2003/ms003007.pdf.
9. Judith McDonough, "Worker Solidarity, Judicial Oppression, and Police Repression in the Westmoreland County, Pennsylvania Coal Miner's Strike, 1910–11," *Pennsylvania History* 64, No. 3 (Summer 1997): pp. 384–406. See also: Harrison and Kellogg, "The Westmoreland Strike," *The Survey*, December 1910, p. 351; and *The Shame of Pennsylvania*, ACLU, 1928.
10. N.B. Critchfield, "The History of Mount Pleasant," *Mount Pleasant Dawn*, August 23, 1876, p. 1. Critchfield was an important citizen of Mount Pleasant who was a minister, a trustee of the Institute, a principal and then superintendent of the school district, Secretary of Agriculture of Pennsylvania, and Senator of the 36th District of Pennsylvania. He also served as superintendent of the U.S. Christian Commission during the Civil War. http://royalmutts.blogspot.com/2010/01/nb-critchfield.html.
11. Critchfield, p. 1.
12. *Pettingill's Newspaper Directory*, New York: S.M. Pettingill Co., 1878, p. 71.
13. John N. Boucher, *History of Westmoreland County*, Volume 2, New York: The Lewis Publishing Company, 1906, pp. 124–5.
14. *Pettingill's Newspaper Directory*, p. 77.
15. John M. Gresham, *Biographical and Portrait Cyclopedia of Fayette County*, 1889, p. 233.
16. "Scottdale, Everson—separated by creek—share mining past," *TribLive*, March 24, 2015. http://triblive.com/news/westmoreland/7765527-74/scottdale-built-everson.
17. "Meeting of Coke Manufacturers," *Mount Pleasant Dawn*, August 12, 1875, p. 2.
18. Kenneth Warren, "Like the Midnight Sun—the Leisenring Venture in the Connellsville Coke Region, 1880–1889," *Pittsburgh History*, Historical Society of Western Pennsylvania, Spring 1995, pp. 35–45.
19. "A Strike Among the Miners," *Mount Pleasant Dawn*, May 6, 1875, p. 1.
20. "Scottdale: Daring Escape Miner's Procession," *Mount Pleasant Dawn*, May 13, 1875, p. 2.
21. "Miners on the War Path," *Mount Pleasant Dawn*, May 13, 1875, p. 3.
22. John Newton Boucher, "John A. Stevenson," *Old and New Westmoreland*, Vol. 3, New York: The American Historical Society, Inc., 1918, pp. 399–400.
23. "Short Stops," *Mount Pleasant Dawn*, May 20, 1875, p. 3.
24. "Short Stops," *Mount Pleasant Dawn*, June 3, 1875, p. 3.
25. No title, *Mount Pleasant Dawn*, September 2, 1875, p. 2.
26. "Local Flash," *Mount Pleasant Dawn*, May 10, 1876, p. 3. Frick gave himself a salary about double that of his workers. See Chapter Three: The Workers and their World.
27. "The Financial Outlook for Mount Pleasant," *Mount Pleasant Dawn*, July 19, 1876, p. 2.
28. "Short Stops," *Mount Pleasant Dawn*, May 27, 1875, p. 3.
29. "Short Stops," *Mount Pleasant Dawn*, June 3, 1875, p. 3.
30. "A Scale or a Strike," *Weekly Courier*, February 1, 1889, p. 1.
31. Ibid.
32. "The Strike in the Coke Regions," *Pittsburgh Daily Post*, March 26, 1879, p. 4.
33. Ibid.
34. "Coke Region Strikers," *Pittsburgh Daily Post*, April 11, 1879, p. 1.
35. "The Strike in the Coke Region," *Pittsburgh Commercial Gazette*, April 12, 1879, p. 1. Newspapers.com lists this reference under the *Post-Gazette*.
36. "Coke Region Strikers," *Pittsburgh Daily Post*, April 18, 1879, p. 4.
37. "Dissatisfied Miners," *The Tennessean*, March 4, 1881, p. 1.
38. "Trouble in the Coke Region," *Pittsburgh Post-Gazette*, June 3, 1881, p. 4.
39. "The Diggers and Drawers," *Weekly Courier*, June 3, 1881, p. 4.
40. "Coal and Coke," *Weekly Courier*, June 10, 1881, p. 1.
41. "The Coke Region Strike," *Pittsburgh Daily Post*, June 16, 1881, p. 4.
42. Ibid.
43. "Coke and Iron," *Pittsburgh Commercial Gazette*, June 17, 1881, p. 4.
44. Ibid.
45. "Coal and Coke: Strike Over," *Weekly Courier*, July 1, 1881, p. 1.
46. "Meeting of the Miners," *Weekly Courier*, July 15, 1881, p. 1.
47. Ibid.
48. "Hordes of Huns," *Mount Pleasant Journal*, January 19, 1886, p. 1.
49. "A Reign of Terror," *Pittsburgh Daily Post*, January 21, 1886, p. 1.
50. James Dunwoody Brownson DeBow. *Statistical View of the United States...*, United States Census Office, 7th Census, Volume 850. Washington: Beverley Tucker, Senate Printer, 1854, p. 370.
51. "Hordes of Huns," p. 1.
52. "Will Ask Higher Wages," *Weekly Courier*, January 15, 1886, p. 1.
53. Peter Wise of Scottdale was an important voice in the early strikes in the Connellsville coke region. The newspapers acknowledged his command of languages. By 1905 Peter Wise had left the region and was operating a hotel in Avenmore. *Weekly Courier*, July 15, 1905, p. 1.
54. "Hostile Huns," *Mount Pleasant Journal*, January 26, 1886, p. 1.
55. "Splinters from the Strike," *Mount Pleasant Journal*, February 9, 1886, p. 1. The name Fort Defiance had been elusive until this article was found. The hill where these events took place is on Route 981 and overlooks Route 119, which was originally a portion of the Catawba Trail, and Route 31, originally Glade's Path. So it was assumed the name was in reference to the hill as a safe haven for colonials. But obviously it was not. It was named for the miners defying the operators in 1886.
56. "From Shop and Mill," *Saint Paul Globe*, June 27, 1886, p. 12.
57. "Coke Region Anarchists,"

Scottdale Independent, July 17, 1886, p. 3.
58. "Organize the Huns," *Pittsburgh Dispatch*, January 31, 1890, p. 5.
59. "Beaten by the Strikers," *Pittsburgh Daily Post*, January 27, 1886, p. 1.
60. "The Harrowing Hun," p. 1.
61. George Dallas Albert, *History of the County of Westmoreland*, Philadelphia: L.H. Everts & Co., 1882, p. 408.
62. The web site of the Pennsylvania Annual Reports on Mining Activities only has an Anthracite report of 1886: http://www.coalmininghistorypa.org/.
63. "The Strike Goes On," *Scottdale Independent*, January 13, 1886, p. 1.
64. "The Great Strike," *Scottdale Independent*, January 23, 1886, p. 1.
65. "Firmly United," *Scottdale Independent*, January 30, 1886, p. 2.
66. "The Strike Still On," *Weekly Courier*, February 5, 1886, p. 1.
67. "A Humane Sheriff Refuses to Evict Strikers During the Blizzard," *Philadelphia Inquirer*, February 6, 1886, p. 5.
68. "Coke Miners Returning, *The Times*, February 4, 1886, p. 3.
69. "The Strike Still On," p. 1.
70. "Coke Region Troubles," *The Times*, February 12, 1886, p. 1.
71. "The Strike Settled," *Keystone Courier*, February 26, 1886, p. 1.
72. "The Strikers Win," *Scottdale Independent*, February 27, 1886, p. 1.

Chapter 5

1. "Our Coke Ovens Idle," *Weekly Courier*, May 6, 1887, p. 1.
2. "A Big Federation," *Mount Pleasant Journal*, January 18, 1887, p. 1.
3. "The Offer Refused," *Mount Pleasant Journal*, February 8, 1887, p. 1.
4. "Editorial Notes," *Mount Pleasant Journal*, February 22, 1887, p. 1.
5. "Morewood Haulers Strike," *Mount Pleasant Journal*, February 22, 1887, p. 1.
6. "Left to Arbitration," *Mount Pleasant Journal*, March 1, 1887, p. 1.
7. "Coal and Coke," *Mount Pleasant Journal*, March 1, 1887, p. 1.
8. "Price of Coke Advanced," *Mount Pleasant Journal*, February 1, 1887, p. 1.
9. Ibid.
10. "Up Goes Coke," *Scottdale Independent*, February 5, 1887, p. 3.
11. "On the Wage Question," *Mount Pleasant Journal*, February 22, 1887, p. 1.
12. "The Coke Arbitration," *Mount Pleasant Journal*, March 15, 1887, p. 1.
13. "Trouble Among the Miners," *Mount Pleasant Journal*, March 22, 1887, p. 1.
14. "Arbitration Begun," *Mount Pleasant Journal*, April 5, 1887, p. 1.
15. Ibid.
16. "The Coke Workers Out," *Scottdale Independent*, May 6, 1887, p. 1.
17. "No Break in the Strike," *Weekly Courier*, May 13, 1887, p. 1.
18. Ibid.
19. "Coke Strike Still On," *Mount Pleasant Journal*, May 17, 1887, p. 1.
20. "Stauffers," *Scottdale Independent*, May 20, 1887, p. 1.
21. "Coke Strike Continues," *Mount Pleasant Journal*, May 24, 1887, p. 1.
22. "Four Weeks of Strike," *Mount Pleasant Journal*, May 31, 1887, p. 1.
23. "Iron Men Interfered," *Weekly Courier*, May 27, 1887, p. 2.
24. "Work or Strike, Which," *Mount Pleasant Journal*, June 7, 1887, p. 1.
25. Ibid.
26. "The Coke Strike: Steel Makers Cause a Change," *Commercial Telegraph*, June 11, 1887, Scrapbook, March 22, 1884, to August 18, 1887, Helen Clay Frick Foundation Archives (AIS 2002 06), Henry Clay Frick Business Records, 1862–1987, Box 488, Volume 1, Archives Service Center, University of Pittsburgh, p. 72; "Editorial Notes," *Mount Pleasant Journal*, February 22, 1887, p. 1.
27. "H.C. Frick Resignation," May 13, 1887"; "H.C. Frick Resignation, June 7, 1887"; "Accompanying Letter, June 7, 1887," Correspondence 1883–1919, Andrew Carnegie, 1883–1912, Folder 2, Henry Clay Frick Business Records, 1862–1987, AIS.2002.06, Archives Service Center, University of Pittsburgh.
28. "The Coke Strike," *American Manufacturer*, June 17, 1887, Scrapbook, March 22, 1884, to August 18, 1887, Box 488, Volume 1, Helen Clay Frick Foundation Archives (AIS 2002 06), Henry Clay Frick Business Records, 1862–1987, Archives Service Center, University of Pittsburgh, p. 81.
29. "The Coke Strike and its Lessons," *American Manufacturer*, July 1, 1887, Scrapbook, March 22, 1884, to August 18, 1887, Box 488, Volume 1, Helen Clay Frick Foundation Archives (AIS 2002 06), Henry Clay Frick Business Records, 1862–1987, Archives Service Center, University of Pittsburgh, p. 97.
30. "Pinkerton on Hand," *Commercial Gazette*, July 6, 1887, p. 8.
31. "An Ominous War Cloud," *Weekly Courier*, July 8 1887, p. 1.
32. "The Line Solid," *Scottdale Independent*," July 8, 1887, p. 1.
33. Ibid.
34. "To the Bitter End," *Mount Pleasant Journal*, July 12, 1887, p, 1.
35. DiCiccio, p. 100.
36. "Powderly Speaks," *Scottdale Independent*, July 22, 1887, p. 1.
37. "An Ominous War Cloud," p. 1.
38. "Declared Off," *Scottdale Independent*, July 22, 1887, p. 1.
39. "Not All At Work," *Scottdale Independent*, July 29, 1887, p. 1.
40. "The Iron Clad," *Scottdale Independent*, July 7, 1887, p. 2.
41. Christopher Hanes, *The Rise and Fall of the Sliding Scale or Why Wages Aren't Indexed to Product Prices*, November 2003.
42. "Signed at Last," *Scottdale Independent*, August 26, 1887, p. 2.
43. "Scale Offered by Syndicate and Producers," *Scottdale Independent*, September 9, 1887, p. 4.
44. "Different Opinions," *Mount Pleasant Journal*, September 13, 1887, p. 1.

45. "No Scale Signed as Yet," *Mount Pleasant Journal*, September 27, 1887, p. 1.
46. "No Coke Syndicate Yet," *Mount Pleasant Journal*, December 6, 1887, p. 1.
47. "Coke Strike a Fizzle," *Mount Pleasant Journal*, February 12, 1898, p. 1.
48. "It Looks to be General," *Mount Pleasant Journal*, August 6, 1889, p. 1.
49. "The Horrible Huns," *orrible huns Weekly Courier*, August 16, 1889, p. 1.
50. "The Hungarian Raids," *Weekly Courier*, August 23, 1889, p. 1.
51. "Two Gigantic Coke Deals," *Mount Pleasant Journal*, September 3, 1889, p. 1.
52. "The Great Gobbler," *Weekly Courier*, August 30, 1889, p. 1.

Chapter 6

1. Kenneth Warren, *Wealth, Waste, and Alienation: Growth and Decline in the Connellsville Coke Industry*, Pittsburgh: University of Pittsburgh Press, 2001, p. 77.
2. "The Industrial Wars of the Connellsville Coke Region," *Daily Courier Centennial History*, June 20, 1976, p. D-4.
3. "Conference on Strike," *Mount Pleasant Journal*, January 27, 1891, p. 1.
4. Ibid.
5. "Is Not Settled Yet," *Pittsburg Dispatch*, February 3, 1891, p. 5.
6. "Called a Suspension," *Mount Pleasant Journal*, February 10, 1891, p. 1.
7. "Editorial Notes," *Mount Pleasant Journal*, February 10, 1891, p. 1.
8. "The Coke Strikers Endeavor to Compel the Rainey Men to Join Their Forces," *The Dispatch*, February 24, 1891, p. 6.
9. "Miners Still Out," *The Dispatch*, March 3, 1891, p. 6. It must be noted that although Schoonmaker sold his properties, during the strike of 1891, he continued to participate in discussions with unions.
10. Ibid.
11. "The Miners are Firm," *The Dispatch*, March 20, 1891, p. 5.

12. Forcing the Coke Strike," *Pittsburgh Times*. March 26, 1891, Scrapbook, February 15 to April 3, 1891. Helen Clay Frick Foundation Archives (AIS 2002 06), Henry Clay Frick Business Records, 1862–1987, Box 496, Volume 9, Archives Service Center, University of Pittsburgh, p. 119.
13. "Strike Broken," *Courier*, March 7, 1891, Scrapbook, February 15 to April 3, 1891, Helen Clay Frick Foundation Archives (AIS 2002 06), Henry Clay Frick Business Records, 1862–1987, Box 496, Volume 9, Archives Service Center, University of Pittsburgh, p. 126; "Ends in Riot," *Mount Pleasant Journal*, March 31, 1891, p. 1.
14. "Ends in Riot," p. 1.
15. "Tumult Through the Region," *Pittsburg Times*, March 28, 1891, Scrapbook, Helen Clay Frick Foundation Archives (AIS 2002 06), Henry Clay Frick Business Records, 1862–1987, Box 496, Volume 9, Archives Service Center, University of Pittsburgh, p. 132.
16. "Ends in Riot," p. 1.
17. Ibid.
18. "Shot Down," *Weekly Courier*, April 3, 1891, p. 1.
19. Ibid.
20. Ibid.
21. "Bloodshed at the Morewood Works," *Chronicle Telegraph*, April 2, 1891, p. 1.
22. "Riot and Bloodshed," *Mount Pleasant Journal*, April 7, 1891, p. 1.
23. Ibid.
24. "The Coke Strike," *Annual Report of the Secretary of Internal Affairs of the Commonwealth of Pennsylvania*, Part 3, Industrial Statistics, Vol. 19, 1891, Harrisburg: Edwin K. Meyers State Printer, 1892, pp. 2D–13D, pp. D8–9.
25. "Soldiers on Guard," *Weekly Courier*, April 10, 1891, p. 1.
26. "Riot and Bloodshed," p. 1.
27. Ibid.
28. *Mount Pleasant Journal*, April 14, 1891, p. 1. Paper torn; title not visible.
29. Ibid.
30. "Eviction Notices," *Chronicle Telegraph*, April 8, 1891, Scrapbook, April 3 to 18, 1891, Helen

Clay Frick Foundation Archives (AIS 2002 06), Henry Clay Frick Business Records, 1862–1987, Box 496, Volume 9, Archives Service Center, University of Pittsburgh, p. 89.
31. "May be Settled," *Chronicle Telegraph*, April 9, 1891, Scrapbook, April 3 to 18, 1891, Helen Clay Frick Foundation Archives (AIS 2002 06), Henry Clay Frick Business Records, 1862–1987, Box 496, Volume 9, Archives Service Center, University of Pittsburgh, p. 106.
32. *Mount Pleasant Journal*, April 14, 1891, p. 1.
33. Ibid.
34. "All Quiet Now," *Mount Pleasant Journal*, April 21, 1891, p. 1.
35. "Same Old Story," *Mount Pleasant Journal*, April 28, 1891, p. 1.
36. "All Quiet Now," p. 1.
37. Ibid.
38. "Little Chance," *Mount Pleasant Journal*, May 5, 1891, p. 1.
39. Ibid.
40. "All Quiet Now," p. 1.
41. "Eviction Notices Not Feared," *Greensburg Daily Record*, April 9, 1891, Scrapbook, April 3 to 18, 1891, Helen Clay Frick Foundation Archives (AIS 2002 06), Henry Clay Frick Business Records, 1862–1987, Box 496, Volume 9, Archives Service Center, University of Pittsburgh, p. 154.
42. "The Strike Collapsing," *Reading Times*, April 15, 1891, p. 1.
43. "Coal and Coke," *Mount Pleasant Journal*, July 21, 1892, p. 2.
44. "Italian Laborers," *Commercial Gazette*, April 17, 1891, p. 6.
45. "Foreign Workmen Being Brought into the Coke Region to Help Break the Strike," *Pittsburg Leader*, April 16, 1891, Scrapbook, April 3 to 18, 1891, Helen Clay Frick Foundation Archives (AIS 2002 06), Henry Clay Frick Business Records, 1862–1987, Box 496, Volume 9, Archives Service Center, University of Pittsburgh, p. 169.
46. "Troops Recalled," *Greensburg Daily Record*, April 17, 1891.

Scrapbook, April 3 to 18, 1891, Helen Clay Frick Foundation Archives (AIS 2002 06), Henry Clay Frick Business Records, 1862–1987, Box 496, Volume 9, Archives Service Center, University of Pittsburgh, pp. 178–9.

47. "Gone to Jury," *Pittsburgh Leader*, April 17, 1891. Scrapbook, April 3 to 18, 1891, Helen Clay Frick Foundation Archives (AIS 2002 06), Henry Clay Frick Business Records, 1862–1987, Box 496, Volume 9, Archives Service Center, University of Pittsburgh, pp. 180–81.

48. "Evicting all the Leaders," *Commercial Gazette*, April 18, 1891, Scrapbook, April 3 to 18, 1891, Helen Clay Frick Foundation Archives (AIS 2002 06), Henry Clay Frick Business Records 1862–1987, Box 496, Volume 9, Archives Service Center, University of Pittsburgh, p. 189.

49. "Rioting," *Chronicle Telegraph*, April 18, 1891. Scrapbook, April 3 to 18, 1891, Helen Clay Frick Foundation Archives (AIS 2002 06), Henry Clay Frick Business Records, 1862–1987, Box 496, Volume 9, Archives Service Center, University of Pittsburgh, p. 189.

50. "Cokers Use Dynamite," *Pittsburg Leader*, April 18, 1891. Scrapbook, April 18 to May 20, 1891, Helen Clay Frick Foundation Archives (AIS 2002 06), Henry Clay Frick Business Records, 1862–1987, Box 496, Volume 9, Archives Service Center, University of Pittsburgh, p. 4.

51. "Made the Earth Tremble," *Pittsburgh Dispatch*, April 19, 1891, p. 1.

52. "Quiet in the Coke Region," *Pittsburg Times*, April 21, 1891. Scrapbook, April 18 to May 20, 1891, Helen Clay Frick Foundation Archives (AIS 2002 06), Henry Clay Frick Business Records, 1862–1967, Box 496, Volume 9, Archives Service Center, University of Pittsburgh, pp. 23–4.

53. "A Riot at Adelaide," *Pittsburgh Leader*, April 22, 1891. Scrapbook, April 18 to May 20, 1891, Helen Clay Frick Foundation Archives (AIS 2002 06), Henry Clay Frick Business Records, 1862–1987, Box 496, Volume 9, Archives Service Center, University of Pittsburgh, p. 31.

54. "Wild Work at Leisenring," *Pittsburg Times*, April 24, 1891. Scrapbook, April 18 to May 20, 1891, Helen Clay Frick Foundation Archives (AIS 2002 06), Henry Clay Frick Business Records, 1862–1987, Box 496, Volume 9, Archives Service Center, University of Pittsburgh, pp. 48–9.

55. "Same Old Story," p. 1.

56. "The Fiery Hun," *Weekly Courier*, April 24, 1891, p. 1.

57. "Little Chance," p. 1.

58. "Unlucky 13th," p. 1.

59. "Convention at Scottdale," Weekly *Courier*, April 17, 1891, p. 1.

60. "Women in a Midnight Raid," *The Post*, April 15, 1891, p. 1.

61. "Ten Are Convicted," *Mount Pleasant Journal*, May 19, 1891, p. 1.

62. Records for the Huntingdon Reformatory can be found at: http://www.phmc.pa.gov/Archives/Research-Online/Pages/Prison-Records.aspx.

63. "Ten Are Convicted," p. 1.

64. "Loar and his Men Free," *Mount Pleasant Journal*, May 26, 1891, p. 1.

65. Ibid.

66. Ibid.

67. "The Coke Strike Ended," *Mount Pleasant Journal*, May 26, 1891, p. 1.

68. "Editorial Notes: Another Lesson in Strikes," *Mount Pleasant Journal*, May 26, 1891, p. 1.

Chapter 7

1. Muriel Earley Sheppard, *Cloud by Day*, Chapel Hill: University of North Carolina Press, 1947, p. 44.

2. "The Great Coal Strike," *The Cyclopedic Review of Current History*, Vol. 4, Colombian Annual, 894, Buffalo: Garretson Cox and Co, 1895, p. 295.

3. *Panic of 1893*. https://en.wikipedia.org/wiki/Panic_of_1893.

4. Slovak Colonization Society, www.loc.govrreuropeanimskslovakia.html; http://www.slovakiaonline.com/2014/09/14/slovaks-america-slovaks-in-america/.

5. "Cutting on Coke," *Commercial Gazette*, September 13, 1893, p. 3.

6. "Coke Making Good Gains," *Scottdale Independent*, October 5, 1893. Scrapbook, May 27, 1893, to February 2, 1894. Helen Clay Frick Foundation Archives (AIS 2002 06), Henry Clay Frick Business Records, 1862–1987, Box 503, Volume 16, Archives Service Center, University of Pittsburgh, pp. 88–89.

7. "Helping Needy Cokers," p. 112.

8. "The Coke Trade Gaining," *Scottdale Independent*, November 30, 1893, Scrapbook, May 27, 1893, to February 2, 1894, Box 503, Volume 16, Henry Clay Frick Business Records, 1862–1987, AIS 2002.06, Archives Service Center, University of Pittsburgh, pp. 133–4.

9. Ibid.

10. "The Wages of Coke Workers," *Courier*, December 15, 1893, p. 1.

11. "Ninety-Cent Coke a Fact," *Courier*, January 12, 1894, p. 1.

12. "The Frick Wage Scale," *Courier*, January 19, 1894, p. 1.

13. "Frick's New Coke Scale," *Pittsburgh Times*, January 15, 1894, Scrapbook, May 27, 1893, to February 2, 1894, Helen Clay Frick Foundation Archives (AIS 2002 06), Henry Clay Frick Business Records, 1862–1987, Box 503, Volume 16, Archives Service Center, University of Pittsburgh, p. 181.

14. "Ninety-Cent Coke A Fact," p. 1.

15. "The Industrial Situation," *Courier*, February 2, 1894, p. 1.

16. E.F. Duffy, "A Very Sad Story," *Pittsburgh Daily Post*, May 29, 1894, p. 1.

17. "Claim 4,000 Members," *Pittsburg Leader*, March 20, 1894. Scrapbook, February 1 to April 15, 1894. Box 504, Volume 17, Henry Clay Frick Business Records, 1862–1987, AIS 2002.06, Archives Service Center, University of Pittsburgh, p. 70.

18. "Coke News," *Scottdale Independent*, March 29, 1894, p. 1.

19. "The Cokers Organize,"

Mount Pleasant Journal, March 27, 1894, p. 1.
20. "Organization Favored," *Commercial Gazette*, March 22, 1894, p. 6.
21. "May Refuse a Conference," *Pittsburgh Post*, March 23, 1894, Scrapbook, February 1 to April 15, 1894, Helen Clay Frick Foundation Archives (AIS 2002 06), Henry Clay Frick Business Records, 1862–1987, Box 504, Volume 17, Archives Service Center, University of Pittsburgh, p. 71.
22. "Closing Their Furnaces," *The Post*, March 29, 1894, p. 1.
23. Ibid.
24. "Ordered to Strike," *The Dispatch*, March 30, 1894, p. 1.
25. "Riotous Slavs," *Pittsburgh Press*, April 2, 1894, p. 1.
26. "Paddock Killed," *Scottdale Independent*, April 5, 1894, p. 1.
27. "Coke Strike is Brought to a Crisis," *The Dispatch*, April 5, 1894. Scrapbook, February 2 to April 15, 1894. Helen Clay Frick Foundation Archives (AIS 2002 06), Henry Clay Frick Business Records, 1862–1987, Box 504, Volume 17, Archives Service Center, University of Pittsburgh, pp. 105–06.
28. "Paddock's Companion," *The Dispatch*, April 5, 1891, p. 1.
29. "Coke Region Topography," *Pittsburgh Press*, March 3, 1893, p. 3.
30. "The Coke Region on Paper," *Mount Pleasant Journal*, March 7, 1893. Scrapbook, January 27 to August 3, 1893, Helen Clay Frick Foundation Archives (AIS 2002 06), Henry Clay Frick Business Records, Box 502, Volume 15, Archives Service Center, University of Pittsburgh, pp. 40–42.
31. "Pursuit of Rioters." Unknown newspaper, April 4, 1894, Scrapbook, February 1 to April 15, 1894, Helen Clay Frick Foundation Archives (AIS 2002 06), Henry Clay Frick Business Records, 1862–1987, Box 504, Volume 17, Archives Service Center, University of Pittsburgh, pp. 107–08.
32. "Coke Strike is Brought to a Crisis," *The Dispatch*, April 5, 1894, Scrapbook February 2 to April 15, 1894, Helen Clay Frick Foundation Archives (AIS 2002 06), Henry Clay Frick Business Records, 1862–1987, Box 504, Volume 17, Archives Service Center, University of Pittsburgh, pp. 105–6.
33. "A Girl Saw Paddock Killed, The [sic] Testifies That He Jumped From a Tipple," *Pittsburgh Press*, June 7, 1894, p. 3.
34. "Paddock Murder Trial," *Pittsburgh Press*, June 4, 1894, p. 4.
35. "Hussar Found Guilty," *Pittsburgh Press*, June 8, 1895, p. 1.
36. "Furin Found Guilty," *The News Standard*, June 14, 1894, p. 1.
37. "Barrett is Confident," *Mount Pleasant Journal*, June 26, 1894, p. 1.
38. "Five Lives Go Out," *The Dispatch*, April 4, 1894, pp. 1–2.
39. "Peace with Arms," *The Post*, April 6, 1894, Scrapbook, February 1 to April 15, 1894, Helen Clay Frick Foundation Archives (AIS 2002 06), Henry Clay Frick Business Records, 1862–1987, Box 504, Volume 17, Archives Service Center, University of Pittsburgh, p. 133.
40. "The Strike General," *Scottdale Rural Free Press*, April 27, 1894, Scrapbook, April 16 to May 20, Helen Clay Frick Foundation Archives (AIS 2002 06), Henry Clay Frick Business Records, 1862–1987, Box 505, Volume 18, Archives Service Center, University of Pittsburgh, p. 84.
41. "Evictions at Port Royal," *Pittsburgh Leader*, June 25, 1894, Scrapbook, June 23 to October 12, 1894, Helen Clay Frick Foundation Archives (AIS 2002 06), Henry Clay Frick Business Records 1862–1987, Box 505, Volume 18, Archives Service Center, University of Pittsburgh, p. 11.
42. John B. Baskin, "Earn Only $1.05 A Day," *The Post*, July 30, 1894, p. 1.
43. John B. Baskin, "Among the Homeless," *The Post*, August 4, 1894, Scrapbook, June 23 to October 12, 1894. Helen Clay Frick Foundation Archives (AIS 2002 06), Henry Clay Frick Business Records, 1862–1987, Box 505, Volume 18, Archives Service Center, University of Pittsburgh, pp. 97–98.
44. "The Industrial Wars of the Connellsville Coke Region," *Daily Courier Bicentennial Edition*, June 25, 1976, p. D-4.
45. *Written Historical and Descriptive Data Reduced Copies of Drawings*, Connellsville Coal & Coke Region HAER No. Pa-283, Historical American Engineering Record, National Park Service, Appendix E: New Companies Absorbed by Frick, pp. 111.

Chapter 8

1. *Mine Sealing in Southwestern Pennsylvania During the Great Depression*, Uniontown: Pennsylvania Department of Transportation, 2014, p. 7.
2. C.H. McConnell, *et al.*, *Operation Scarlift—Mine Drainage Abatement*, Preprint 2770, p. 6.
3. Nicholas Casner, "Acid Water: A History of Coal Mine Pollution in Western Pennsylvania, 1880–1950," Ph.D. dissertation, Carnegie Mellon University, 1994, p. 84.
4. "End of Pollution Seems in Sight," *Coal and Coke Operators* 13, No. 8 (August 1915): p. 621–3.
5. See also Casner, Chapter 5: "The Pennsylvania Railroad and the Progression of Pollution Law," pp. 95–119.
6. Casner, pp. 125–27.
7. "State Supreme Court Rules Against Draining Mine Water into Indian Creek," *Daily Courier*, September 29, 1924, p. 1.
8. "Would Stop Mining of Coal in Little Developed Areas to Protect Water Supply," *Daily Courier*, July 2, 1926, p. 10.
9. "Laboratory Experiments Show Sealing of Mines Will Reduce Stream Pollution," *Daily Courier*, April 23, 1930, p. 10.
10. National Industrial Recovery Act, Wikipedia. http://en.wikipedia.org/wiki/National_industrial_Recovery_act.
11. "More Help Needed on Abandoned Mine Survey in West PA," *Daily Courier*, January 11, 1934, pp. 1, 6.
12. "Mine Sealing Gets Under Way This Week; One Near Reidmore Marks Beginning," *Daily Courier*, January 7, 1936, p. 1.
13. "Report Progress in Mine Sealing Work in State, *Daily Courier*, May 11, 1936, p. 7.

14. "Sewage Problems of Mine Sealing," *Daily Courier*, May 29, 1936, p. 4.

15. "Over 3,000 Abandoned Coal Mines Being Sealed by State with WPA Funds," *Daily Courier*, February 12, 1937, p. 13.

16. "Operators to Be Held Liable for Damage From Cave-ins of Coal Mines," *Daily Courier*, April 14, 1939, p. 1. For subsidence go to: www.pamsi.org.

17. "Mine Sealing in State Will Take 10 Years," *Daily Courier*, August 30, 1937, p. 8.

18. *Mine Sealing in Southwestern Pennsylvania During the Great Depression*, p. 48.

19. "Mine Sealing Now Required by State Law," *Daily Courier*, July 2, 1947, p. 1.

20. "Elimination of Pollution of Youghiogheny River Early Objective of Drive to Seal Abandoned Mines," *Daily Courier*, August 26, 1948, p. 1.

21. "State to Seal Abandoned Mines Along Jacobs Creek," *Daily Courier*, January 24, 1948, p. 1.

22. "Abandoned Mines Will Be Sealed in Fayette, State Engineers Seek Location of Openings," *Daily Courier*, July 22, 1949, p 1.

23. Ibid. Despite numerous phone calls to Ebensburg, the office maintains they have no details on the location of mine openings.

24. "Begin Sealing of Shafts at Abandoned Plants," *Daily Courier*, July 14, 1950, p. 1.

25. *Inactive and Abandoned Underground Mines*, Office of Water and Hazardous Materials, Washington DC: United States Environmental Protection Agency, June, 1975, p. 45.

26. *Youghiogheny River Basin Mine Drainage Pollution Abatement Project*, Operation Scarlift Project No. SL-103. Gibbs and Hill, Inc., September 1972, p. VI-1 and VI-2.

27. "Mine Fire Danger in German Twp. Studied by State," *Daily Courier*, July 22, 1970, p. 2.

28. Youghiogheny River Basin Mine Drainage Pollution Abatement Project, Operation Scarlift Project No. SL-103. Gibbs and Hill, Inc., September 1972, V-2.

29. Ibid., p. II-4.

30. Redstone Creek Watershed, Mine Drainage Pollution Abatement Survey, Project No. 141-2, GEO Project 73043, 1977, p. 67-68.

31. Ibid., pp. D-8-9.

32. WPCAMR has offices in Greensburg. It is always seeking new members. Contact phone/fax: 724 832–3625; email: info@wpcamr.org. http://www.wpcamr.org/

33. *Comprehensive Plan for Abandoned Mine Reclamation*, Pennsylvania Department of Environmental Protection, http://www1.portal.state.pa.us/portal/server.pt?open=514&objID=588910&mode=2.

34. *Abandoned Mine Reclamation in Pennsylvania*, Pennsylvania Organization for Watersheds and Rivers, pp. 4, 9–10.

35. David Kubarek, "Researchers team up to tackle state's acid mine drainage problem," http://news.psu.edu/story/505679/2018/02/21/research/researchers-team-tackle-state%E2%80%99s-acid-mine-drainage-problem, 1–5.

36. AMD and Art Project, 1996–2005. https://amdandart.info/signage.html.

37. "Pennsylvania Allocates More Than $20 Million For Water Quality Projects," www.lancasterfarming.com/unpublished/pennsylvania-alloctes-mnore0thab-million-for-water-quality-projects/article.

Appendix

1. Enman, "Relationship of Coal Mining," p. 137.

2. *Annual Report of the Secretary of State of the Commonwealth of Pennsylvania*, Part III, Industrial Statistics, Vol. VII, 1879–80, Harrisburg: Lane S. Hart, 1881, p. 27.

3. Franklin Ellis, *History of Fayette County, Pennsylvania with Biographical Sketches of many of the Pioneers and Prominent Men*, Philadelphia: L.H. Everts & Co., 1882, p. 802.

4. Extract from Store Day Book and Journal, *H. Clay Frick*. Broad Ford, March 20, 1876, to April 23, 1881, Helen Clay Frick Foundation Archives (AIS 2002 06), Henry Clay Frick Business Records, 1862–1987, Box 523, Folder 9, December 14, 1877, Archives Service Center, University of Pittsburgh.

5. *Annual Report of the Secretary of Internal Affairs of the Commonwealth of Pennsylvania*, Part III, Industrial Statistics, Vol. V, 1876–7, Harrisburg: Lane S. Hart, 1878, p. 247.

6. Albert, p. 548.

7. Ellis, p. 802.

8. Albert, p. 548. The third partner, A.J. Crossland, was from Latrobe, where Morgan & Co. also had mining interests.

9. Enman, "Relationship of Coal Mining," Appendix A, pp. 430-33.

10. Franklin Platt, *Second Geological Survey of Pennsylvania: 1875, Special Report on the Coke Manufacture of the Youghiogheny River Valley in Fayette and Westmoreland Counties, with Geological Notes of the Coal and Iron Ore Beds*, Harrisburg: Board of Commissioners, 1876, p. 49.

11. Ibid., p. 76.

12. "Local Flashes," *Mount Pleasant Dawn*, March 22, 1876, p. 2.

13. *Annual Report of the Secretary of Internal Affairs of the Commonwealth of Pennsylvania*, Part III, Industrial Statistics, Vol. V, 1876–7, Harrisburg: B.F. Meyers, 1878, p. 122.

14. "James B. Morgan," *Pittsburgh Post-Gazette*, August 8, 1915, p. 2.

15. Extract from Store Day Book and Journal, *H. Clay Frick.*, Broad Ford, March 20, 1876, to April 23, 1881, Helen Clay Frick Foundation Archives (AIS 2002 06), Henry Clay Frick Business Records, 1862–1987, Box 523, Folder 9, December 14, 1877, Archives Service Center, University of Pittsburgh.

16. "The *Courier* Man in the Coke Field," *Weekly Courier*, August 13, 1880, p. 1.

17. "The Cokers' Strike," *Pittsburg Post-Gazette*, June 17, 1881, p. 4.

18. *Reports of the Inspectors of Coal Mines of PA for the Year 1896*. Harrisburg: Clarence M Busch, State Printer, 1897, p. 423.

19. *Report of the Bureau of Mines, Dept. of Internal Affairs of*

Pa, 1897, Wm. Stanley Ray, State Printer, 1898, p. 470.

20. "The Morgan Store Has Been Closed; Ovens Banked," *Daily Courier*, May 25, 1910, p. 1.

21. "Abandoned Morgan Works Fired Again; Coal from Novelty," *Daily Courier*, January 21, 1920, p. 1.

22. Ad, *Uniontown Evening Standard*, January 4, 1954, p. 12.

23. Ad, *Daily Courier*, November 19, 1946, p. 8.

24. Redstone Creek Watershed, Mine Drainage Pollution Abatement Survey, Project No. 141-2, GEO Project 73043, 1977, Appendix D, pp. D-8-9.

25. Interview, Joe Eckman, March 17, 2016.

26. "Beaten by the Strikers," *Pittsburgh Daily Post*, January 27, 1886, p. 1.

27. "Outrage at Morgan," *Weekly Courier*, January 29, 1886, p. 1.

28. "The Horrible Huns," *Weekly Courier*, Aug 16, 1889, p. 1.

29. "The Talk of Two Towns," *Courier*, November 6, 1891, p. 5.

30. "Hunger is Pressing Hard," *Pittsburg Times*, May 18, 1891. Scrapbook, April 18 to May 20, 1891, Helen Clay Frick Foundation Archives (AIS 2002 06), Henry Clay Frick Business Records, 1862–1987, Box 497, Volume 10, Archives Service Center, University of Pittsburgh, pp. 194–95.

31. "Leaped into a Coke Oven," *Pittsburgh Post-Gazette*, April 24, 1900, p. 4.

32. *Annual Report of the Secretary of Internal Affairs of the Commonwealth of Pennsylvania*, Part III, Industrial Statistics, Vol. V, 1876-7, Harrisburg: Lane S. Hart, 1878, p. 248.

33. "Condition of the Coal Mines," *Pittsburgh Post*, March 30, 1878, p. 6.

34. *Annual Report of the Secretary of State of the Commonwealth of Pennsylvania*, Part III, Industrial Statistics, Vol. VII, 1879–80, Harrisburg: Lane S. Hart, 1881, p. 27.

35. Ellis, p. 802.

36. *Evening Standard*, February 10, 1958, p. 73.

37. "Excerpts from Journals and Daybooks," 1878–1880, *From Journal of H.C. Frick and Company March 1878—May 31, 1880*, December 31, 1878 (AIS 2002 06), Box 523, Folder 10, p. 1–2.

38. *Annual Report of the Secretary of Internal Affairs of the Commonwealth of Pennsylvania*, Part III, Industrial Statistics, Vol. IX, 1880–81, Harrisburg: Lane S. Hart, 1882, p. 418-19.

39. *Annual Report of the Secretary of Internal Affairs of the Commonwealth of Pennsylvania*, Part III, Industrial Statistics, Vol. XV, 1887, Harrisburg: E.K. Meyers, 1888, p. 6m.

40. "Coke Works Shut Down," *Commercial Gazette*, March 11, 1889, Scrapbook, November 1, 1888, to August 18, 1889, Helen Clay Frick Foundation Archives (AIS 2002 06), Henry Clay Frick Business Records, 1862–1987, Box 490. Volume 3, Archives Service Center, University of Pittsburgh, p. 98.

41. *Reports of the Inspectors of Mines of the Anthracite and Bituminous Coal Regions of Pennsylvania for the Year 1890*, Harrisburg: Edwin K. Meyers, State Printer, 1891, p. 381.

42. "The Slavs Must Go," *Pittsburgh Times*, June 27, 1894, Scrapbook, June 23 to October 12, 1894, Helen Clay Frick Foundation Archives (AIS 2002 06), Henry Clay Frick Business Records, 1862–1987, Box 505, Volume 18, Archives Service Center, University of Pittsburgh, p. 18.

43. "The Old Eagle Coke Plant is to Resume," *Daily Courier*, September 7, 1909, p. 1.

44. Enman, "Relationship of Coal Mining," Appendix E, p. 451.

45. "Refuses to Yield," *Daily Courier*, July 18, 1917, p. 1.

46. "Corrado-Schenck Coal Co.," *Weekly Courier*, February 28, 1918, p. 10.

47. "AMD site US60 in Uniontown Syncline, 1998–2000," Carnegie Mellon University, http://www.ce.cmu.edu/~acidmine/sites/siteUS60.htm.

48. "A New Record," *Daily Courier*, August 8, 1917, p. 1; "Refuses to Yield," *Daily Courier*, July 18, 1917, p. 1.

49. "Classes in Citizenship," *Daily Courier*, December 23, 1916, p. 1.

50. "Corrado-Schenck Coal Co.," p. 10.

51. "Corrado Interests are now Operating 1,001 Coke Ovens at 14 Plants in the Connellsville and West Virginia Regions" *Daily Courier*, February 10, 1926, p. 1.

52. "Frick Plant Leased by Mr. Corrado," *Uniontown Morning Herald*, May 29, 1933, p. 9.

53. John Lane began speculating in coal in the 1850s. After his partnership with Strickler, he worked with A.S.M. Morgan, Laughlin & Company, and finally with H.C. Frick, where he worked at the Tyrone Mines. He died in 1904. J.A. Strickler created the J.A. Strickler Coke Company and opened several mines in Westmoreland County, including one near Calumet (Hecla?), which shipped coal to Duluth, Wisconsin.

54. Ellis, p. 802.

55. Platt, p. 45.

56. "From Journal of H.C. Frick and Company, March 1878 to May 31, 1880," *Excerpts from Journals and Daybooks, 1878–1880* (AIS 2002 06), Henry Clay Frick Business Records, 1862–1987, Box 523, Folder 10, Archives Service Center, University of Pittsburgh, p. 1.

57. "*Courier* Man in the Coal Field," p. 1.

58. "Reports of the Mine Inspectors of the Bituminous Coal Fields," Legislative Document No. 7, First, Second, and Fifth districts in *Annual Report of the Secretary of the Internal Affairs of the Commonwealth of Pennsylvania*, Part III, Industrial Statistics, Vol. XI, 1982-83, 7a-153a, p. 132a.

59. *Annual Report of the Secretary of State of the Commonwealth of Pennsylvania*, Part III, Industrial Statistics, Vol. VII, 1879–80, Harrisburg: Lane S. Hart, 1881, p. 27.

60. *Annual Report of the Secretary of Internal Affairs of the Commonwealth of Pennsylvania*, Part III, Industrial Statistics, Vol. XV, 1887, Harrisburg: E.K. Meyers, 1888, p. 6m.

61. *Reports of the Inspectors of Mines of the Anthracite and Bituminous Coal Regions of PA for the Year 1890*, Harrisburg: Edwin K. Meyers, State Printer, 1891, p. 381.

62. *Reports of the Inspectors of*

Mines of the Anthracite and Bituminous Coal Regions of PA for the Year 1891, Harrisburg: Edwin K Meyers, State Printer, 1892, p. 395.

63. *Reports of the Inspectors of Coal Mines of PA for the Year 1896*. Harrisburg: Clarence M. Busch, State Printer, 1897, p. 531.

64. *Report of the Bureau of Mines Dept of Internal Affairs of Pennsylvania, 1897*, Wm. Stanley Ray, State Printer, 1898, p. 470.

65. "Coke Ovens of the Connellsville Region," *Weekly Courier*, July 21, 1905, p. 2. Title was changed from "Our Fiery Ovens."

66. "The Coke Strike Ended," *Mount Pleasant Journal*, May 26, 1891, p. 1.

67. *Annual Report of the Secretary of State of the Commonwealth of Pennsylvania*, Part III, Industrial Statistics, Vol. VII, 1879–80, Harrisburg: Lane S. Hart, 1881, p. 27.

68. Image, "The Connellsville Coke Region," *The Engineering Magazine: An International Review* 20 (October 1900 to March 1901): pp. 17–40.

69. "A Big Deal in Coal," *Mount Pleasant Journal*, December 13, 1882, p. 1.

70. "Mine Oven and Mill," *Weekly Courier*, March 2, 1883, p. 1.

71. *Annual Report of the Secretary of Internal Affairs of the Commonwealth of Pennsylvania*, Part III, Industrial Statistics, Vol. VI, 1977–78, Harrisburg: Lane S. Hart, 1979, p. 46.

72. Ellis, p. 802.

73. *Annual Report of the Secretary of Internal Affairs of the Commonwealth of Pennsylvania*, Part III, Industrial Statistics, Vol. V, 1876-7, Harrisburg: Lane S. Hart, 1878, p. 248.

74. Platt, p. 46.

75. Journal of H.C. Frick and Company, May 17, 1878, March 1878 to May 31, 1880, Excerpts from Journal and Daybooks, 1878–1880 (AIS 2002 06), Box 523, Folder 10, Archives Service Center, University of Pittsburgh.

76. *Annual Report of the Secretary of Internal Affairs of the Commonwealth of Pennsylvania*, Part III, Industrial Statistics, Vol. V, 1876–7, Harrisburg: Lane S. Hart, 1878, p. 248.

77. *Connellsville Coke, H.C. Frick Co. Pittsburgh Pa, 1890*, Helen Clay Frick Foundation Archives (AIS 2002 06), Henry Clay Frick Business Records, 1862–1987, Box 523, Folder 1, Archives Service Center, University of Pittsburgh, p. 42.

78. "Around About," *Keystone Courier*, April 30, 1880, p. 3.

79. "The Cokers' Strike," *Pittsburgh Post-Gazette*, June, 17, 1881, p. 4.

80. "Coal and Coke," *Weekly Courier*, September 15, 1882, p. 1.

81. *Annual Report of the Secretary of Internal Affairs of the Commonwealth of Pennsylvania*, Part III, Industrial Statistics, Vol. XIII, 1885, Harrisburg: E.K. Meyers, 1886, p. 151B-152B.

82. "Depending Upon Italians," *The Post*, May 2, 1891, p. 1.

83. "Resort to Arson," *Pittsburgh Press*, July 12, 1894, p. 1.

84. "Dynamite Tried Again," *The Dispatch*, August 3, 1894. Scrapbook, June 23 to October 12, 1894, Helen Clay Frick Foundation Archives (AIS 2002 06), Henry Clay Frick Business Records, 1862–1987, Box 505, Volume 18, Archives Service Center, University of Pittsburgh, p. 92.

85. "Fire Still Burns," *Daily Courier*, January 11, 1907, p. 1.

86. "The Morgan Valley," *Daily Courier*, November 17, 1910, p. 1.

87. Enman, "Relationship of Coal Mining," Appendix E, p. 452.

88. "Operators are Given till June 1 to Complete Tunnel," *Daily Courier*, December 1, 1926, p. 1.

89. "A Chapter of Accidents," *Weekly Courier*, January 4, 1889, p. 1.

90. "Gompers Here," *Scottdale Evening Herald*, May 14–18, 1891. Scrapbook, April 18 to May 20, 1891, Helen Clay Frick Foundation Archives (AIS 2002 06), Henry Clay Frick Business Records, 1862–1987, Box 497, Volume 10, Archives Service Center, University of Pittsburgh, p. 185.

91. "In Jackson's Hall," *Scottdale Herald*, May, 1891. Scrapbook, April 18 to May 20, 1891, Helen Clay Frick Foundation Archives (AIS 2002 06), Henry Clay Frick Business Records, 1862-1987, Box 497, Volume 10, Archives Service Center, University of Pittsburgh, p. 185.

92. "There is No Let Up," *Scottdale Evening Herald*, May 19, 1891. Scrapbook, April 18 to May 20, 1891, Helen Clay Frick Foundation Archives (AIS 2002 06), Henry Clay Frick Business Records, 1862–1987, Box 497, Volume 10, Archives Service Center, University of Pittsburgh, p. 198–99.

93. "Bloody Riot at Lemont," *Pittsburg Press*, June 11, 1894, p. 4.

94. "By Mine Car Inside," *Report of the Department of Mines of Pennsylvania Bituminous Region, 1903*, Wm. Stanley Ray: State Printer of Pennsylvania, 1904, p. 683.

95. "Santa Uses Auto," *Pittsburgh Daily Post*, December 26, 1908, p. 8.

96. *Extract from Store Day Book and Journal, H. Clay Frick., Broad Ford*, March 20, 1876 to April 23, 1881, December 14, 1877, Helen Clay Frick Foundation Archives (AIS 2002 06), Henry Clay Frick Business Records, 1862–1987, Box 523, Folder 9, Archives Service Center, University of Pittsburgh.

97. Tyrone Plant Long Abandoned in Blast," *Weekly Courier*, October 6, 1905, p. 9.

98. "H.C. Frick to be Laid at Rest in Pittsburgh Thursday; Wanted to be Buried There," *Daily Courier*, December 3, 1919, p. 1.

99. *Report of the Bureau of Mines of the Department of Internal Affairs of Pennsylvania including Reports of Mine Inspectors*, Wm. Stanley Ray, State Printer of Pennsylvania, 1898, p. 468.

100. Ellis, *History of Fayette County*, p. 414.

101. *Extracts from Day Book of Overholt, Frick & Co*, March 10, 1871, to June 20, 1871, March 29, 1871, Helen Clay Frick Foundation Archives (AIS 2002 06), Henry Clay Frick Business Records, 1862–1987, Box 523, Folder 6, Archives Service Center, University of Pittsburgh.

102. Enman, p. 160.

103. *Extracts from Day Book of Overholt, Frick & Co*, March 10, 1871, to June 20, 1871, November 15, 1871, Helen Clay Frick Foundation Archives (AIS 2002

06), Henry Clay Frick Business Records, 1862–1987, Box 523, Folder 6, Archives Service Center, University of Pittsburgh, p. 14.

104. Platt, p. 48.

105. *Extracts from Journals and Day Books 1871 to 1876*, April 1, 1873, Helen Clay Frick Foundation Archives (AIS 2002 06), Henry Clay Frick Business Records, 1862–1987, Box 523, Folder 6, Archives Service Center, University of Pittsburgh, p. 26.

106. *Annual Report of the Secretary of Internal Affairs of the Commonwealth of Pennsylvania*, Part III, Industrial Statistics, Vol. IV, 1875–76, Harrisburg: B.F. Meyers, 1877, p. 282.

107. *Annual Report of the Secretary of Internal Affairs of the Commonwealth of Pennsylvania*, Part III, Industrial Statistics, Vol. VI, 1877–78, Harrisburg: Lane S. Hart, 1879, p. 45.

108. *Annual Report of the Secretary of Internal Affairs of the Commonwealth of Pennsylvania*, Part III, Industrial Statistics, Vol. XIII, Harrisburg: E.K. Meyers, State Printer, 1885, p. 150b. Children were often used in the mines. According to one report, 175 to 200 boys under 16 worked in local mines. They would get doctor's excuses to be excused from school for disability and then enter the mines. See Owen R. Lovejoy, "Child Labor in the Soft Coal Mines," *Annals of Political and Social Science* 29, Child Labor (January 1907): pp. 26–34.

109. *Annual Report of the Secretary of State of the Commonwealth of Pennsylvania*, Part III, Industrial Statistics, Vol. VII, 1879–80, Harrisburg: Lane S. Hart, 1881, p. 27.

110. "Sheriff's Officers Strike," *Labor Tribune*, May 9, 1891. Scrapbook, April 18 to May 20, 1891, Helen Clay Frick Foundation Archives (AIS 2002 06), Henry Clay Frick Business Records, 1862–1987, Scrapbook Series, Box 496, Volume 9, Archives Service Center, University of Pittsburgh, p. 152.

111. "Morgan Valley Being Revived," *Weekly Courier*, March 10, 1910, p. 1.

112. "Novelty Fire Still Burning," *Weekly Courier*, February 28, 1918, p. 1; *Report of the Bureau of Mines of the Department of Internal Affairs of Pennsylvania including Reports of Mine Inspectors*, Wm. Stanley Ray, State Printer of Pennsylvania, 1898, p. 468.

113. Letter, December 31, 1919, p. 372. Westmoreland-Fayette Historical Society (Box 536, Folder #), West Overton Village and Museums, Scottdale, Pennsylvania.

114. Letter, December 31, 1921. p. 373. Westmoreland-Fayette Historical Society (Box # 536, Folder #), West Overton Village and Museums, Scottdale, Pennsylvania.

115. Interview, George Wettgen, March 17, 2016, and January 15, 2017.

116. Enman, Appendix D, p. 444.

117. *Excerpts from Journals and Daybooks, March 20, 1876, to April 23, 1881*, March 20, 1876, Helen Clay Frick Foundation Archives (AIS 2002 06), Henry Clay Frick Business Records, 1862–1987, Box 523, Folder 9, Archives Service Center, University of Pittsburgh. Also reported in "Local Flashes," *Mount Pleasant Dawn*, March 22, 1876, p. 3.

118. "Huns with Scurvy," *Mount Pleasant Journal*, June 23, 1891, p. 1.

119. "John Keck, Frick Veteran Succumbs to Brief Illness," *Daily Courier*, April 28, 1914, p. 1.

120. "All Quiet Now," *Mount Pleasant Journal*, April 21, 1891, p. 1.

121. "Scenes on the Road," *Scottdale Herald*, May 14, 1891. Scrapbook, April 18 to May 20, 1891, Helen Clay Frick Foundation Archives (AIS 2002 06), Henry Clay Frick Business Records, 1862–1987, Box 497, Volume 10, Archives Service Center, University of Pittsburgh, p. 184.

122. *Extracts from Day Book Overholt, Frick & Company*, March 10, 1871, to June 20, 1871, Helen Clay Frick Foundation Archives (AIS 2002 06), Henry Clay Frick Business Records, 1862–1987, Box 523, Folder 6, Archives Service Center, University of Pittsburgh, pp. 3, 6, 10, 13.

123. "Zachariah T. Henry Dies; Helped Build First Frick Coke Plant at Broad Ford," *Daily Courier*, April 2, 1927, p. 1.

124. "Sidelights," *Daily Courier*, January 19, 1939, p. 4.

125. "H.C. Frick to be Laid at Rest in Pittsburgh Thursday, p. 1.

126. *Journal of H. C. Frick and Company, March 1, 1878–January 20, 1881*, Excerpts from Journals and Daybooks, 1878–1880, Helen Clay Frick Foundation Archives (AIS 2002 06), Henry Clay Frick Business Records, 1862–1987, Box 534, Archives Service Center, University of Pittsburgh, April 18, 1878.

127. "Reports of the Mine Inspectors of the Bituminous Coal Fields," Legislative Document No. 7, First, Second, and Fifth districts in *Annual Report of the Secretary of the Internal Affairs of the Commonwealth of Pennsylvania*, Part III, Industrial Statistics, Vol. XI, 1982–83, p. 7a-153a, 132a.

128. "Coke Region Troubles," *Harrisburg Daily Independent*, February 8, 1886, p. 1.

129. "Henry Clay," *Annual Report of the Secretary of Internal Affairs of the Commonwealth of Pennsylvania*, Part III, Industrial Statistics, Vol. XV, 1887, Harrisburg: E.K. Meyers, 1888, p. 82.

130. "The Coke Trade's Birth: Tearing Down of the Old Henry Clay Works," *Penny Press*, April 7, 1888. Scrapbook, August 19, 1887 to November 2, 1888, Helen Clay Frick Foundation Archives (AIS 2002 06), Henry Clay Frick Business Records, 1862, Box 489, Volume 2, Archives Service Center, University of Pittsburgh, p. 100.

131. Ibid.

132. *Reports of the Inspectors of Mines of the Anthracite and Bituminous for the year 1888*, Harrisburg: Edwin K. Meyers, State Printer, 1889, p. 333.

133. "Evicting all the Leaders," *Commercial Gazette*, April 18, 1891. Scrapbook, April 3 to 18, 1891, Helen Clay Frick Foundation Archives (AIS 2002 06), Henry Clay Frick Business Records, 1862–1987, Box 496, Volume 9, Archives Service Center, University of Pittsburgh, p. 189.

134. "A Ghost in the Mine," *Keystone Courier*, February 11, 1887, p. 1.

135. "Now in the Fourteenth Week," *Scottdale Independent*, May 14, 1891. Scrapbook, April 18 to May 20, 1891, Helen Clay Frick Foundation Archives (AIS 2002 06), Henry Clay Frick Business Records, 1862-1987, Box 497, Volume 10, Archives Service Center, University of Pittsburgh, pp. 186-7.

136. *Report of the Bureau of Mines, Dept. of Internal Affairs of Pa, 1897*, Harrisburg: Wm. Stanley Ray, State Printer of Pa, 1898, p. 468.

137. "Bridge Closed at Broad Ford," *Herald Standard*, March 27, 1963, p. 19.

138. *A Town that Grew at the Crossroad*, Sesquicentennial Edition Reprint, Mount Pleasant Area Historic Preservation Committee, 1995, pp. 26-7.

139. "Foreign Workmen," *Pittsburgh Leader*, April 16, 1891, Scrapbook, April 3 to 18, 1891, Helen Clay Frick Foundation Archives (AIS 2002 06), Henry Clay Frick Business Records, 1862-1987, Box 496, Volume 9, Archives Service Center, University of Pittsburgh, p. 169.

140. "Italian Laborers," *Commercial Gazette*, April 17, 1891, p. 6.

141. Upper Tyrone Township Homepage: http://uppertyronetwp.org/?page_id=4. The information came straight out of *Nelson's Biographical Dictionary and Historical Reference Book of Fayette County*, Vol. 1, p. 469.

142. *Evening Standard*, February 10, 1958, p. 73.

143. *Annual Report of the Secretary of Internal Affairs of the Commonwealth of Pennsylvania*, Part III, Industrial Statistics, Vol. IV, 1875-6, Harrisburg: B.F. Meyers, 1877, p. 288.

144. *Annual Report of the Secretary of Internal Affairs of the Commonwealth of Pennsylvania*, Part III, Industrial Statistics, Vol. V, 1876-7, Harrisburg: Lane S. Hart, 1878, p. 248.

145. *Historic American Engineering Record (HABS/HAER): Connellsville Coal & Coke Region, Fayette County, Pennsylvania. (1994)*, America's Industrial Heritage Project (AIHP). HAER No. PA-283, National Park Service, Department of the Interior, Washington, DC, No PA 283, p. 164.

146. *Annual Report of the Secretary of State of the Commonwealth of Pennsylvania*, Part III, Industrial Statistics, Vol. VII, 1879-80, Harrisburg: Lane S. Hart, 1881, p. 27.

147. Excerpts from Journals and Daybooks, 1879-1881, From *Journal of H.C. Frick Company, December 1879 to March 31, 1881*, Box 523, Folder 11.

148. Platt, p. 50.

149. "Coal, Coke, Steel in This District; First Furnace," *Evening Standard*, February 10, 1958, p. 73.

150. "The *Courier* Man in the Coke Field," p. 1.

151. *Annual Report of the Secretary of Internal Affairs of the Commonwealth of Pennsylvania*, Part III, Industrial Statistics, Vol. X, 1881-82, Harrisburg: Lane S. Hart, 1883, p. 16a; *Annual Report of the Secretary of Internal Affairs of the Commonwealth of Pennsylvania*, Part III, Industrial Statistics, Vol. XII, 1884, Harrisburg: Lane S. Hart, 1885, 150a.

152. "Trouble to Follow," *The Dispatch*, April 20, 1891, p. 1.

153. "Awaiting Orders," *Commercial Gazette*, April 20, 1891, p. 1.

154. Upper Tyrone Township Homepage.

155. "Fayette County Storm Swept," *News Standard*, July 25, 1895, p. 1.

156. Frick, H.C. (1897, December 16) Letter to Solomon Keister, Westmoreland-Fayette Historical Society (Box P24, Folder 5), West Overton Village and Museums, Scottdale, Pennsylvania.

157. *Report of the Bureau of Mines Dept. of Internal Affairs of Pa 1897*, Wm. Stanley Ray, State Printer of PA, 1898, p. 470.

158. "Bought Coking Coal," *Daily Courier*, April 22, 1902, p. 1.

159. "Old Summit Opened," *Daily Courier*, July 16, 1909, p. 5.

160. "Scottdale Contractor Will Reclaim Coke from Refuse Dumps in County," *Daily Courier*, December 7, 1943, p. 1.

161. Enman, "Relationship of Coal Mining," Appendix D, p. 447.

162. Idid., Appendix E, p. 452.2

163. "Coke Strike Breaking Up," *The Dispatch*, June 25, 1894. Scrapbook, June 23 to October 13, 1894. Helen Clay Frick Foundation Archives (AIS 2002 06), Henry Clay Frick Business Records, 1862-1987, Box 508, Volume 21, Archives Service Center, University of Pittsburgh, pp. 8-9.

164. "A Riot at Summit," *Pittsburgh Times*, July 12, 1894. Scrapbook, June 23 to October 12, 1894, Helen Clay Frick Foundation Archives (AIS 2002 06), Henry Clay Frick Business Records, 1862-1987, Box 508, Volume 21, Archives Service Center, University of Pittsburgh, p. 57.

165. "The Slav's Character," *The Post*, August 6, 1894. Scrapbook, June 23 to October 12, 1894, Helen Clay Frick Foundation Archives (AIS 2002 06), Henry Clay Frick Business Records, 1862-1987, Box 508, Volume 21, Archives Service Center, University of Pittsburgh, p. 98.

166. *Annual Report of the Secretary of Internal Affairs of the Commonwealth of Pennsylvania*, Part III, Industrial Statistics, Vol. V, 1876-7, Harrisburg: Lane S. Hart, 1878, p. 247.

167. Ibid., p. 123, 247.

168. Platt, p. 49.

169. "In the Coke Regions: The Coke Burning Around Broad Ford," *Pittsburg Weekly Post*, April 6, 1878, p. 7.

170. *Annual Report of the Secretary of Internal Affairs of the Commonwealth of Pennsylvania*, Part III, Industrial Statistics, Vol. VI, 1877-78, Harrisburg: Lane S. Hart, 1879, p. 61.

171. "The *Courier* Man in the Coke Field," p. 1; *Annual Report of the Secretary of Internal Affairs of the Commonwealth of Pennsylvania*, Part III, Industrial Statistics, Vol. IX, 1880-81, Harrisburg: Lane S. Hart, 1882, p. 418.

172. "Surrounding Sections," *Weekly Courier*, January 21, 1881, p. 3.

173. "Coal and Coke," *Weekly Courier*, July 15, 1881, p. 1.

174. "Coal and Coke Notes," *Weekly Courier*, June 3, 1887, p. 1.

175. *Reports of the Inspectors of Mines of the Anthracite and Bituminous Coal Regions of PA for the*

Year 1891, Harrisburg: Edwin K. Meyers, State Printer 1892, p. 398.

176. *Reports of the Inspectors of Mines of the Anthracite and Bituminous Coal Regions of PA for the Year 1891*, Harrisburg: Edwin K Meyers, State Printer, 1892, p. 398.

177. "FOR SALE," *Daily Courier*, November 24, 1953, p. 17.

178. Enman, "Relationship of Coal Mining," Appendix D, p. 447.

179. Ibid., Appendix E, p. 453.

180. "Legal Strife Among Coke Men," *Pittsburgh Post-Gazette*, July 10, 1879, p. 4.

181. "Coke News," *Scottdale Independent*, February 18, 1892, p. 1.

182. "The Valley Watercourse," *Courier*, March 11, 1892, p. 2.

183. *Annual Report of the Secretary of State of the Commonwealth of Pennsylvania*, Part III, Industrial Statistics, Vol. VII, 1879–80, Harrisburg: Lane S. Hart, 1881, p. 27.

184. *Excerpts from Journals and Daybooks*, 1879–1881, Box 523, Folder 11, p. 3.

185. "Tip Top Mine Shut Down by Water," *Daily Courier*, February 24, 1910, p. 1.

186. "Old Tip Top Mine has its Last Run," *Weekly Courier*, December 21, 1911, p. 8; *Weekly Courier*, December 18, 1911, p. 1.

187. "Connellsville Operators Active in Local and Other Fields," *Weekly Courier*, February 28, 1918, p. 11.

188. *Pittsburgh Daily Commercial*, October 16, 1875, p. 4.

189. Platt, p. 50.

190. Enman, "Relationship of Coal," Appendix A, p. 431.

191. *Annual Report of the Secretary of Internal Affairs of the Commonwealth of Pennsylvania*, Part III, Industrial Statistics, Vol. VI, Harrisburg: Lane Hart, 1879, p. 48. Charles H. Armstrong immigrated to the U.S. from Ireland in 1838. He tried a number of industries in Pittsburgh before he established coal mines along the Youghiogheny River. The company maintained offices in Pittsburgh at Liberty Avenue.

192. Ellis, p. 802; *Excerpts from Journals and Daybooks*, 1879–1881, Box 523, Folder 11, p. 3.

193. "Reports of the Mine Inspectors of the Bituminous Coal Fields," Legislative Document No. 7, First, Second, and Fifth districts in *Annual Report of the Secretary of the Internal Affairs of the Commonwealth of Pennsylvania*, Part III, Industrial Statistics, Vol. XI, 1882–83, p. 7a-153a, 132–33a.

194. "Fire at Tip Top Coke Works," *Commercial Gazette*, July 22, 1889, p. 4.

195. "Explosion in a Mine," *Pittsburgh Dispatch*, March 29, 1890, p. 5.

196. "Mail Route Changed for Summit Office," *Daily Courier*, November 4, 1909, p. 5.

197. "Crop Opening at Tip Top," *Weekly Courier*, January 5, 1911, p. 2.

198. "Owensdale," *Daily Courier*, October 5, 1911, p. 5.

199. "The Rejuvenation of Owensdale as a Coke Town," *Daily Courier*, November 9, 1915, p. 9.

200. Enman, "Relationship of Coal," Appendix E, p. 452.

201. *Report of the Secretary of Internal Affairs of the Commonwealth of Pennsylvania*, Part III, Industrial Statistics, Vol. XIII, 1885, Harrisburg: E.K. Meyers, 1886, p. 150b.

202. Ibid.

203. *Report of the Bureau of Mines Department of Internal Affairs of Pa, 1898*, Harrisburg: Wm. Stanley Ray, State Printer, 1899, p. 502.

204. "The Connellsville Coke Regions Their Past, Present and Future: Coke Works of the Connellsville Region; Ovens and Operating Companies," Special Historical and Statistical Number, *Weekly Courier*, May 1914, p. 2.

205. "Coal and Coke Notes," *Weekly Courier*, July 18, 1884, p. 1.

206. "Rist Tipple Fire May Mean Closing Down of Plant," *Daily Courier*, March 2, 1917, p. 1.

207. *Written Historical and Descriptive Data Reduced Copies of Drawings*, p. 168.

208. "A Big Coke Deal," *Daily Post*, September 19, 1890, p. 2.

209. "Changes in Coke Firm," *Keystone Courier*, February 4, 1881, p. 1.

210. *Legislative Documents, Comprising the Department and Other Reports Made to the Senate and House of Representatives of PA*, Vol. 4, Bituminous, 1880, Harrisburg: Lane S. Hart, State Printer. 1881, p. 199.

211. "Miners, Attention: What a Coke Operator Thinks of his Slaves—The Miners of the Connellsville Coke Region," *Scottdale Independent*, April 15, 1885, pp. 1, 6.

212. "The Coke Trade: Coke Cinders," *Courier*, June 8, 1888, p. 2.

213. "Flames at Everson," *Weekly Courier*, November 7, 1890, p. 1.

214. "McClure Coke Company Ad," Scrapbook, February 26 to July 15 1892, Helen Clay Frick Foundation Archives (AIS 2002 06), Henry Clay Frick Business Records, 1862–1987, Box 500, Volume 13, Archives Service Center, University of Pittsburgh, p. 142.

215. "Writing to Carnegie in New York, Frick discusses Connellsville Coal purchase of properties, employees, and Drexel and Morgan and Company," October 21, 1889, Folder 11, Henry Clay Business Records, 1862–1987, Archives Service Center, University of Pittsburgh.

216. "Frick discusses the purchase of the Davis Coal property and negotiations to buy out McClure Coke Company," December 9, 1889, Folder 14, Henry Clay Business Records, 1862–1987, Archives Service Center, University of Pittsburgh.

217. "Frick received Carnegie's telegram, and he thinks that the McClure property is less desirable because of the bad financial status of the partners. Frick also writes on the Pittsburgh & Western bonds and practices at Homestead," June 10, 1891, Volume 6, Henry Clay Frick Papers, Series VIII: Letterpress Copybooks, 1881–1923, The Frick Collection/Frick Art Reference Library Archives, New York.

218. "Carnegie writes on the finalized agreement of the McClure Coke Company purchase. Frick hopes the deal will be kept quiet until the matters that are pending are closed," October 21 1895, Scrapbook, Volume 11, Henry Clay Frick Business Records.

219. "The Works at Bridge-

port: Description of the Mullen, Boyle, Buckeye, and Star Mines," *Keystone Courier*, March 24, 1882, p. 1.
220. Platt, p. 54.
221. Ibid.
222. "Industrial Items," *Miner's Record*, 1882, p. 2.
223. Interview with John Weinman, 2015.
224. "A Strike Among the Miners," *Mount Pleasant Dawn*, May 6, 1875, p. 2.
225. "Stauffers," *Scottdale Independent*, July 22, 1887, p. 4.
226. *Annual Report of the Secretary of Internal Affairs of the Commonwealth of Pennsylvania*, Part III, Industrial Statistics, Vol. V, 1876-7, Harrisburg: Land S. Hart, 1878, p. 250; *Historical Data H.C. Frick Coke Company's Plants*, H.C. Frick Coke Co. The former lists 1873 as the opening and the latter lists 1872. Several secondary sources give different dates for the founding of these mines, including 1871.
227. Platt, p. 54.
228. "The Works at Bridgeport," p. 1.
229. "Reports of the Mine Inspectors of the Bituminous Coal Fields," Legislative Document No. 6, First, Second, and Fifth districts in *Annual Report of the Secretary of the Internal Affairs of the Commonwealth of Pennsylvania*, Part III, Industrial Statistics, 1885, Vol. XIII, 1886, 1b-308b, 41b.
230. Edward K. Muller, et al., *Westmoreland County, Pennsylvania: An Inventory of Historic American Buildings Survey/Historic American Engineering Record* (HABS/HaER), America's Industrial Heritage Project (AIHP), Washington D.C.: National Park Service, U.S. Department of the Interior, *1994*, p. 40.
231. "Reports of the Mine Inspectors of the Bituminous Coal Fields," p. 315.
232. "Coke News," *Scottdale Independent*, April 13, 1893, p. 1.
233. *Written Historical and Descriptive Data Reduced Copies of Drawings*, p. 40.
234. "List of Coke Ovens in The Connellsville District," *Weekly Courier*, February 28, 1918, p. 2.
235. Ibid..
236. "The Coke Trade," *Scottdale Herald*, December 24, 1891, Scrapbook, October 2, 1891, to February 27, 1892, Helen Clay Frick Foundation Archives (AIS 2002 06), Henry Clay Frick Business Records, 1862, Box 489, Volume 2, Archives Service Center, University of Pittsburgh, p. 92.
237. "Coke Works Sold," *Mount Pleasant Dawn*, April 15, 1875, p. 3.
238. "A Coke Pioneer: John Myers Who Built First Ovens in Westmoreland," *Weekly Courier*, July 20, 1905, p. 6.
239. *Mount Pleasant Dawn*, May 15, 1875, p. 3.
240. "Making Coke in Shorter Time," *Pittsburgh Daily Post*, February 2, 1900, p. 2.
241. "Cokers and Coking," *Weekly Courier*, February 9, 1900, p. 2.
242. *Annual Report of the Secretary of Internal Affairs of the Commonwealth of Pennsylvania*, Part III, Industrial Statistics, Vol. V, 1876-7, Harrisburg: Land S. Hart, B.F. Meyers, 1878, p. 250.
243. "Coke Works Sold," p. 3.
244. *Historic American Engineering Record* (HABS/HaER). America's Industrial Heritage Project (AIHP). Washington, DC: National Park Service, U.S. Department of the Interior, 1994, p. 40.
245. Platt, p. 54.
246. "$600,000 Damages Wanted," *Keystone Courier*, February 6, 1880, p. 1.
247. "Reports of the Mine Inspectors of the Bituminous Coal Fields," Legislative Document No. 6, First, Second, and Fifth districts in *Annual Report of the Secretary of the Internal Affairs of the Commonwealth of Pennsylvania*, Part III, Industrial Statistics, 1885, Vol. XIII, 1886, 1b-308b, 45b.
248. "Connellsville Region Coke Notes," *Courier*, December 18, 1891, p. 2.
249. *Reports of the Inspectors of Coal Mines of Pennsylvania 1893*, Harrisburg: State Printer of Pennsylvania, 1894, p. 487.
250. *Reports of the Inspectors of Coal Mines of Pennsylvania 1896*, Harrisburg: State Printer of Pennsylvania, 1897, p. 532.
251. "Coal and Coke," *Mount Pleasant Journal*, December 21, 1915, p. 1.
252. "Would Turn Sewage into Abandoned Mine," *Daily Courier*, July 7–8, 1936, p. 2.
253. J.C., "In the Coke Fields, Connellsville Coke on the Mt. Pleasant Branch, Interesting Fossil Remains in Coal Mines," *Pittsburgh Post*, April 20, 1878, p. 3.
254. Platt, p. 54.
255. *Historic American Engineering Record* (HABS/HaER), p. 51.
256. "Coal and Coke Notes," *Weekly Courier*, June 10, 1887, p. 1.
257. "Blast Furnaces Banked," *Daily Courier*, November 15, 1901, p. 2.
258. "Mt. Pleasant Road Closed by Mine Fall," *Daily Courier*, April 18, 1938, p. 7.
259. "No Repairs on Blocked Road," *Daily Courier*, June 21, 1938, p. 5.
260. "Bessemer Road Being Improved," *Daily Courier*, September 28, 1940, p. 5.
261. "Mine Heading Caves in Under Bessemer Road," *Daily Courier*, January 12, 1941, p. 6.
262. "Elimination of Pollution of Youghiogheny River is Early Objective of Drive to Seal Abandoned Mines," *Daily Courier*, August 26, 1948, p. 1.
263. "Old Mine Hazards Aired at Meeting with Owners," *Daily Courier*, August 22, 1970, p. 13.
264. "A Strike Among the Miners," *Mount Pleasant Dawn*, May 6, 1875, p. 1–3.
265. "Notices," *Keystone Courier*, November 14, 1879, p. 3.
266. *Legislative Documents, Comprising the Department and Other Reports Made to the Senate and House of Representatives of PA*, Vol. 4, Bituminous, 1880, Harrisburg: Lane S. Hart, State Printer, 1881, p. 291.
267. "Report of the Mine Inspectors of the Bituminous Coal Fields," Legislative Document No. 7, First, Second, and Fifth districts in *Annual Report of the Secretary of the Internal Affairs of the Commonwealth of Pennsylvania*, Part III, Industrial Statistics, Vol. XI, 1882-83, 208, 44a.
268. "Bessemer Sold," *Mount Pleasant Journal*, December 11, 1883, p. 1.
269. "Report of the Mine

Inspectors of the Bituminous Coal Fields," Legislative Document No. 6, First, Second, and Fifth districts in *Annual Report of the Secretary of the Internal Affairs of the Commonwealth of Pennsylvania*, Part III, Industrial Statistics, Vol. XIII, 1886, 1b 308b, 41b.

270. "Effects of the Drouth [sic]," *Keystone Courier*, November 11, 1887, p. 1.

271. "Mine Sealing Halted as Funds Give Out," *Daily Courier*, January 21, 1937, p. 7.

272. "Legacy: A compendium of Southwestern Pennsylvania community histories," *Sunday Tribune-Review*, July 9, 1989, tabloid insert, p. 25.

273. "Coal Coke &c.," *Miner's Record*, July 27, 1882.

274. "Miners Continue to do Violence," *New York Times*, June 15, 1894, https://www.nytimes.com/1894/06/15/archives/miners-continue-to-do-violence-pump-house-blown-up-with-dynamite.html.

275. "Cokers and Coking," *Courier*, October 7, 1898, p. 2.

276. *Historical and Statistical Information by H.C. Frick Mines 1882–1976*. USX Corporation records, 1840–1983, Box 39, Folder 10, vol. 1, CCHC1, March 19, 2014. Coal and Coke Heritage Center at Penn State Fayette, the Eberly Campus.

277. "Report of the Operation and Output of the Coke Ovens of the Connellsville District," *Weekly Courier*, December 8, 1899, p. 4.

278. *Reports of the Inspectors of Mines of the Anthracite and Bituminous Coal Regions of Pennsylvania, for the year 1890*, Harrisburg: Edwin N. Myers, State Printer, 1891, p. 315.

279. *Historic American Engineering Record (HABS/HAER): Alverton Coke Works, Westmoreland, Pennsylvania* (1990), America's Industrial Heritage Project (AIHP), HAER No. PA-288, National Park Service, Department of the Interior, Washington, DC.

280. *Reports of the Inspectors of Mines of the Anthracite and Bituminous Coal Regions of Pennsylvania, for the year 1890*, p. 315.

281. "Stoner Coal Company Chartered," *Weekly Courier*, September 12, 1912, p. 2.

282. "Prizes Awarded for Gardens and Lawns at Frick Coke Plants," *Weekly Courier*, August 1, 1918, p. 3.

283. "File Suit To Close Coke Ovens," *Valley Independent*, February 12, 1971, p. 5.

284. "Coal and Coke," *Mount Pleasant Journal*, April 12, 1892, p. 1.

285. "Coal and Coke," *Mount Pleasant Journal*, July 7, 1892, p. 1.

286. *Written Historical and Descriptive Data Reduced Copies of Drawings*, p. 163.

287. "Coal and Coke," *Keystone Courier*, March 24, 1882, p. 1.

288. "Pennsylvania Seeks to Abandon Branches in Fay-West Region," *Daily Courier*, June 13, 1935, p. 8.

289. "Largest Coke Works in the United States," *Coal Trade Journal*, April 28, 1880, p. 263.

290. "Report of the Operation and Output of the Coke Ovens of the Connellsville Region," *Courier*, August 3, 1888, p. 2.

291. "Report of the Operation and Output of the Coke Ovens of the Connellsville Region," *Courier*, March 18, 1892, p. 2.

292. "A Big Year's Business," *Courier*, January 18, 1899, p. 2.

293. "Morewood Mine is Leased by Frick; Operations Begun," *Daily Courier*, April 19, 1934, p. 5.

294. "Elimination of Pollution of Youghiogheny River is Early Objective of Driver to Seal Abandoned Mines," *Daily Courier*, August 26, 1948, p. 1.

295. "Begin Sealing of Shafts at Abandoned Plants," *Daily Courier*, July 14, 1950, p. 1.

296. *Legislative Documents, Comprising the Department and Other Reports Made to the Senate and House of Representatives of PA*, Vol. 4, Bituminous, 1880, Harrisburg: Lane S. Hart, State Printer, 1881, p. 291.

297. John M. Gresham, *Biographical and Portrait Cyclopedia of Fayette County*, 1889, p. 601.

298. "Coal and Coke," *Keystone Courier*, March 24, 1882, p. 1.

299. "The Fire-Bug Abroad," *Keystone Courier*, June 24, 1887, p. 1.

300. "Report of the Operation and Output of the Coke Ovens of the Connellsville Region," *Courier*, August 3, 1888, p. 2.

301. Untitled article, *Weekly Courier*, January 10, 1890, Scrapbook, August 19, 1889, to February 16, 1890, Helen Clay Frick Foundation Archives (AIS 2002 06), Henry Clay Frick Business Records, 1862–1987, Box 491, Volume 4, Archives Service Center, University of Pittsburgh, p. 84.

302. "Report of the Operation and Output of the Coke Ovens of the Connellsville Region," *Courier*, March 18, 1892, p. 2.

303. *Reports of the Inspectors of Mines of the Anthracite and Bituminous Coal Region of Pennsylvania for the Year 1892*, Harrisburg: Edwin E. Meyers, State Printer, 1893, p. 301.

304. "Report of the Operation and Output of the Coke Ovens of the Connellsville Region," *Courier*, August 3, 1888, p. 2.

305. DiCiccio, p. 193.

306. "Electric Lighting in Coal Mines," *The Electrical Age*, New York, October 17, 1891, p. 19.

307. "The Standard Works of the H.C. Frick Coke Company," *American Manufacture and Iron World* 48 (June 19, 1891): pp. 495–504.

308. "Report of the Operation and Output of the Coke Ovens of the Connellsville Region," *Courier*, March 18, 1892, p. 2.

309. "Coal and Coke," *Mount Pleasant Journal*, February 6, 1894, p. 1.

310. "Letter from H.C. Frick to Thomas Lynch," October 4, 1893, Helen Clay Frick Collection, AIS.2002.06, Series XIII, H.C. Frick Coke Company, 1871–1921, Box 517, Vol. 5, Letterpress Copy Book 5, February 9, 1893–June 17, 1895, p. 118.

311. Vivian, *Hidden History of the Laurel Highlands*, pp. 44–50.

Bibliography

Abandoned Mine Reclamation in Pennsylvania. Pennsylvania Organization for Watersheds and Rivers, pp. 4, 9–10.

"Abandoned Mines Will Be Sealed in Fayette, State Engineers Seek Location of Openings." *Daily Courier.* July 22, 1949, p 1.

"Abandoned Morgan Works Fired Again; Coal from Novelty." *Daily Courier.* January 21, 1920, p. 1.

"Accident Relief Fund Established." *Pittsburgh Daily Post.* June 11, 1910, p. 1.

"After the Company Store." *Mount Pleasant Journal.* February 13, 1894, p. 1.

"After Two Years Fire in Mullin Mine Breaks Out." *Daily Courier.* January 14, 1911, p. 1.

Albert, George Dallas. *History of the County of Westmoreland.* Philadelphia: L.H. Everts and Co., 1882.

Alice Mine. Eureka Photo Collection. Courtesy of James Steeley.

"Alien Labor Taxation." *Pittsburgh Dispatch.* March 28, 1889, p. 1.

"All Quiet Now." *Mount Pleasant Journal.* April 21, 1891, p. 1.

Alverton Mine. Eureka Coal Collection. Courtesy of James Steeley.

Alverton 1 Underground Map. RGGS Land & Minerals. 1888.

AMD and Art Project, 1996–2005. https://amdandart.info/signage.html.

"AMD site US60 in Uniontown Syncline, 1998–2000." Carnegie Mellon University, http://www.ce.cmu.edu/~acidmine/sites/siteUS60.htm.

"American Emigrant Company." *Baltimore Daily Commercial.* October 18, 1865, p. 4.

American Emigrant Company. New York [s.n. 1865], pp. 12–14.

"Anarchy's Red Flag." *Pittsburgh Dispatch.* April 21, 1891, p. 1.

Annual Report of the Secretary of Internal Affairs of the Commonwealth of Pennsylvania. Part III. Industrial Statistics. Vol. IV. 1875–76. Harrisburg: B.F. Meyers, 1877.

Annual Report of the Secretary of Internal Affairs of the Commonwealth of Pennsylvania. Part III. Industrial Statistics. Vol. VI. 1877–78. Harrisburg: Lane S. Hart, 1879.

Annual Report of the Secretary of Internal Affairs of the Commonwealth of Pennsylvania. Part III. Industrial Statistics. Vol. VII. 1879–80. Harrisburg: Lane S. Hart, 1881.

Annual Report of the Secretary of Internal Affairs of the Commonwealth of Pennsylvania. Part III. Industrial Statistics. Vol. IX. 1880–81. Harrisburg: Lane S. Hart, 1882.

Annual Report of the Secretary of Internal Affairs of the Commonwealth of Pennsylvania. Part III. Industrial Statistics. Vol. XIII. Harrisburg: E.K. Meyers, 1885.

Annual Report of the Secretary of Internal Affairs of the Commonwealth of Pennsylvania. Part III. Industrial Statistics. Vol. XIV. 1886. Harrisburg: E.K. Meyers. 1886.

Annual Report of the Secretary of Internal Affairs of the Commonwealth of Pennsylvania. Part III. Industrial Statistics. Vol. XV. 1887. Harrisburg: E.K. Meyers, 1888.

Annual Report of the Secretary of Internal Affairs of the Commonwealth of Pennsylvania. Part III. Industrial Statistics. Vol XXXVII. 1909. Harrisburg: C.E. Aughinbaugh, 1910.

"An Appeal to American Working Men." *Scottdale Independent.* June 18, 1884, p. 2.

"Arbitration Begun." *Mount Pleasant Journal.* April 5, 1887, p. 1.

"Around About." *Keystone Courier.* April 30, 1880, p. 3.

"Around About." *Keystone Courier.* July 23, 1880, p. 3.

"As a Steady Runner." *Mount Pleasant Journal.* April 24, 1893. Scrapbook. January 27 to August 3, 1893. Helen Clay Frick Foundation Archives. (AIS 2002 06). Henry Clay Frick Business Records, 1862–1987. Box 502. Vol. 15. Archives Service Center. University of Pittsburgh, p. 116.

"Awaiting Orders." *Commercial Gazette.* April 20, 1891. Scrapbook. April 18 to May 20, 1891. Henry Clay Frick Foundation Archives. (AIS 2002 06). Henry Clay Frick Business Records, 1862–1987. Scrapbook Series. Box 497. Volume 10. Archives Service Center. University of Pittsburgh, pp. 10–11.

"Barrett is Confident." *Mount Pleasant Journal.* June 26, 1894, p. 1.

Baskin, John B. "Among the Homeless." *The Post.* August 4, 1894. Scrapbook. June 23 to October 12, 1894. Box 505. Volume 18. Henry Clay Frick Business Records, 1862–1987. AIS 2002.06. Archives Service Center. University of Pittsburgh, pp. 97–98.

_____. "Earn Only $1.05 a Day." *The Post*. July 30, 1894, p. 1.
"Bayonet Rule for Slav and Hun." *New York Herald*. May 3, 1891, p. 13.
"Beaten by the Strikers." *Pittsburgh Daily Post*. January 27, 1886, p. 1.
"Begin Sealing of Shafts at Abandoned Plants." *Daily Courier*. July 14, 1950, p. 1.
"Bessemer Road Being Improved." *Daily Courier*. September 28, 1940, p. 5.
"Bessemer Sold." *Mount Pleasant Journal*. December 11, 1883, p. 1.
"A Big Coke Combine." *Mount Pleasant Journal*. June 7, 1892. Scrapbook. February 26 to July 15, 1892. Henry Clay Frick Foundation Archives. (AIS 2002 06). Henry Clay Frick Business Records, 1862–1987. Scrapbook Series. Box 500. Volume 13. Archives Service Center. University of Pittsburgh, p. 157.
"A Big Coke Deal." *Daily Post*. September 19, 1890, p. 2.
"A Big Deal in Coal." *Mount Pleasant Journal*. December 13, 1882, p. 1.
"A Big Federation." *Mount Pleasant Journal*. January 18, 1887, p. 1.
"Big Frick Shops." *Weekly Courier*. October 2, 1905, p. 1.
"A Big Year's Business." *Courier*. January 18, 1899, p. 2.
"Bits of Bituminous Coal News." *Weekly Courier*, March 30, 1888, p. 1.
"Blast Furnaces Banked." *Daily Courier*. November 15, 1901, p. 2.
"Bloodshed at the Morewood Works." *Chronicle Telegraph*. April 2, 1891, p. 1.
"Bloody Riot at Lemont." *Pittsburg Press*. June 11, 1894, p. 4.
Boucher, John Newton. "John A. Stevenson." *Old and New Westmoreland*. Vol. 3. New York: The American Historical Society, Inc., 1918, pp. 399–400.
"Bought Coking Coal." *Daily Courier*. April 22, 1902, p. 1.
"Bought Kenton sorrel horse 6 yrs old in May from H.F. Buckner, Lexington, Ky." *Mount Pleasant Dawn*. May 24, 1876, p. 3.
Brestensky, Dennis F. *The Early Coke Worker*. Connellsville: Connellsville Printing Company, 1994.
"Bridge Closed at Broad Ford." *Herald Standard*. March 27, 1963, p. 19.
Broad Ford Mines Billhead 1870. Helen Clay Frick Foundation Archives. (AIS 2002 06). Henry Clay Frick Business Records, 1862–1987. Box 523. Folder 1. Archives Service Center. University of Pittsburgh.
Broadford Station. 3955. Westmoreland-Fayette Historical Society (Box # 25. Folder #2 076). West Overton Village and Museums. Scottdale, Pennsylvania.
"Broadford to Westmoreland." http://pghbridges.com/articles/railroads/RRhistory_fayette3.htm.
Buckeye Mine in 1882 photo, Westmoreland-Fayette Historical Society. (Box # P16. Folder #16 10 20). West Overton Village and Museums. Scottdale, Pennsylvania.
"Bummers Burned in Coke Ovens." *Harrisburg Daily Independent*. October 8, 1878, p. 1.
"By Mine Car Inside." *Report of the Department of Mines of Pennsylvania Bituminous Region, 1903*. Wm. Stanley Ray: State Printer of Pennsylvania, 1904.
"By-Product Ovens Need Coal, Frick Blows Out Beehives." *Daily Courier*. February 8, 1940, p. 1.
"By-Product Ovens Surpass Beehive as Coke Producers, Shown by Records of 1921." *Weekly Courier*. March 30, 1822, p. 3.
"Called a Suspension." *Mount Pleasant Journal*. February 10, 1891, p. 1.
"Carnegie writes on the finalized agreement of the McClure Coke Company purchase. Frick hopes the deal will be kept quiet until the matters that are pending are closed." October 21 1895, Scrapbook, Volume 11, Henry Clay Business Records. AIS 2002.06. Archives Service Center. University of Pittsburgh.
Casner, Nicholas. "Acid Water: A History of Coal Mine Pollution in Western Pennsylvania, 1880–1950." Ph.D. dissertation. Carnegie Mellon University, 1994.
"Centralization of Industrial Control and Operation of Philanthropic Foundations." Senate Documents. Vol 26, Industrial Relations: Final Report and Testimony submitted to Congress by the Commission on Industrial Relations created by the act of August 21, 1912. Vol. VIII, Washington DC: Government Printing Office, 1916.
"Changes in Coke Firm." *Keystone Courier*. February 4, 1881, p. 1.
"A Chapter of Accidents." *Weekly Courier*. January 4, 1889, p. 1.
"Church Gets Big Check." *Daily Courier*. June 28, 1909, p. 1.
"Claim 4,000 Members." *Pittsburg Leader*. March 20, 1894. Scrapbook. February 1 to April 15, 1894. Henry Clay Frick Business Records, 1862–1987. Box 504. Volume 17. AIS 2002.06. Archives Service Center. University of Pittsburgh, p. 70.
"Classes in Citizenship." *Daily Courier*. December 23, 1916, p. 1.
"Closing Their Furnaces." *The Post*. March 29, 1894, p. 1.
"Coal and Coke." *Commercial Gazette*. May 8, 1892. Scrapbook. February 26 to July 15, 1892. Henry Clay Frick Foundation Archives. (AIS 2002 06). Henry Clay Frick Business Records, 1862–1987. Box 500. Volume 13. Archives Service Center. University of Pittsburgh, p. 101.
"Coal and Coke." *Keystone Courier*. March 24, 1882, p. 1.
"Coal and Coke." *Mount Pleasant Journal*. November 24, 1891, p. 1.
"Coal and Coke." *Mount Pleasant Journal*. April 12, 1892, p. 1.
"Coal and Coke." *Mount Pleasant Journal*. July 7, 1892, p. 1.
"Coal and Coke." *Mount Pleasant Journal*. July 21, 1892, p. 2.

"Coal and Coke." *Mount Pleasant Journal.* September 6, 1892, p. 2.

"Coal and Coke." *The Journal (sic),* Mt Pleasant. August 7, 1893, p. 1.

"Coal and Coke." *Mount Pleasant Journal.* October 24, 1883, p. 1.

"Coal and Coke." *Mount Pleasant Journal.* March 1, 1887, p. 1.

"Coal and Coke." *Mount Pleasant Journal.* February 6, 1894, p. 1.

"Coal and Coke." *Mount Pleasant Journal.* April 12, 1911, p. 1.

"Coal and Coke." *Mount Pleasant Journal.* April 19, 1911, p. 1.

"Coal and Coke." *Mount Pleasant Journal.* December 21, 1915, p. 1.

"Coal and Coke." *Weekly Courier.* June 10, 1881, p. 1.

"Coal and Coke." *Weekly Courier.* July 15, 1881, p. 1.

"Coal and Coke News: Bituminous Pittsburgh (Frick Award)." *Coal Age.* September 28, 1912. Vol. II. July 1 to December 31, 1912. New York: Hill Publishing Co., 1912, p. 443.

"Coal and Coke Notes." *Weekly Courier.* July 18, 1884, p. 1.

"Coal and Coke Notes." *Weekly Courier.* June 3, 1887, p. 1.

"Coal and Coke Notes." *Weekly Courier.* June 10, 1887, p. 1.

Coal and Coke Resource Analysis. America's Industrial Heritage Project, United States Department of the Interior, National Park Service, November, 1992, p. 45.

"Coal and Coke: Strike Over." *Weekly Courier.* July 1, 1881, p. 1.

"Coal, Coke, Steel in This District: First Furnace." *Evening Standard.* February 10, 1958, p. 73.

"Coke and Iron." *Pittsburg Commercial Gazette.* June 17, 1881, p. 4.

"The Coke Arbitration." *Mount Pleasant Journal.* March 15, 1887, p. 1.

"The Coke King." *Pittsburgh Daily Post.* December 20, 1878, p. 3.

"Coke Making Good Gains." *Scottdale Independent.* October 5, 1893. Scrapbook. May 27, 1893, to February 2, 1894. Box 503. Volume 16. Henry Clay Frick Business Records, 1862-1987. AIS 2002.06. Archives Service Center. University of Pittsburgh, pp. 88–89.

"Coke Men Crushed." *Penny Press.* June 11, 1887. Scrapbook. March 22, 1884-August 18, 1887. Helen Clay Frick Foundation Archives. (AIS 2002 06) Henry Clay Frick Business Records, 1862-1987. Box 488. Volume 1. Archives Service Center. University of Pittsburgh, p. 73.

"Coke Miners Returning. *The Times.* February 4, 1886, p. 3.

"Coke News." *Scottdale Independent.* April 13, 1893, p. 1.

"Coke News." *Scottdale Independent.* Feb 18, 1892, p. 1.

"Coke News," *Scottdale Independent.* March 29, 1894, p. 1.

"Coke News." *Scottdale Independent.* March 29, 1894, p. 1.

"Coke News." *Scottdale Independent.* July 5, 1894, p. 1.

"Coke Ovens of the Connellsville Region." *Weekly Courier.* July 21, 1905, p. 2.

"A Coke Pioneer: John Myers Who Built First Ovens in Westmoreland." *Weekly Courier.* July 20, 1905, p. 6.

"Coke Region Anarchists." *Scottdale Independent.* July 17, 1886, p. 3.

"The Coke Region, Comments Upon the Wages Paid the Employees, the Pluck-Me." October 8, 1888. Scrapbook, August 19, 1887–November 2, 1888, Helen Clay Frick Foundation Archives (AIS 2002 06), Henry Clay Frick Business Records, 1862-1987, Box 489. Archives Service Center, University of Pittsburgh, p. 173.

"The Coke Region Hun." *Weekly Courier.* March 22, 1889, p. 1.

"Coke Region Labor Matters." *Courier.* October 11, 1889, p. 1.

"A Coke Region Leader." *Pittsburgh Post.* June 20, 1887, Scrapbook. March 22, 1884–August 18, 1887. Henry Clay Frick Foundation Archives. (AIS 2002 06). Henry Clay Frick Business Records, 1862-1987. Box 488. Volume 1. Archives Service Center. University of Pittsburgh, p. 82.

"The Coke Region on Paper." *Mount Pleasant Journal.* March 7, 1893. Scrapbook. January 27 to August 3, 1893. Helen Clay Frick Foundation Archives. (AIS 2002 06). Henry Clay Frick Business Records, 1862-1987. Scrapbook Series. Box 502. Volume 15. Archives Service Center. University of Pittsburgh, pp. 40–42.

"The Coke Region Strike." *Pittsburgh Daily Post.* June 16, 1881, p. 4.

"Coke Region Strikers." *Pittsburgh Daily Post.* April 11, 1879, p. 1.

"Coke Region Topography." *Pittsburgh Press.* March 3, 1893. Scrapbook. January 27 to August 3, 1893. Helen Clay Frick Foundation Archives. (AIS 2002 06). Henry Clay Frick Business Records, 1862-1987. Scrapbook Series. Box 502. Volume 15. Archives Service Center. University of Pittsburgh, p. 40.

"Coke Region Troubles." *Harrisburg Daily Independent.* February 8, 1886, p. 1.

"Coke Region Troubles." *The Times.* February 12, 1886, p. 1.

"The Coke Region Troubles." *Pittsburgh Daily Post.* November 26, 1886, p. 1.

"The Coke Strike." *American Manufacturer.* June 17, 1887. Scrapbook. March 22, 1884, to August 18, 1887. Helen Clay Frick Foundation Archives (AIS 2002 06). Henry Clay Frick Business Records, 1862-1987. Box 488. Volume 1. Archives Service Center. University of Pittsburgh, p. 81.

"The Coke Strike." *Annual Report of the Secretary of Internal Affairs of the Commonwealth of Pennsylvania.* Part III. Industrial Statistics. Vol. XIX. 1891. Harrisburg: Edwin K. Meyers State Printer, 1892, pp. D2–D13, pp. D12–D13.

"Coke Strike a Fizzle." *Mount Pleasant Journal.* February 12, 1898, p. 1.

"The Coke Strike and its Lessons." American Manufacturer. July 1, 1887. Scrapbook. March 22,

1884, to August 18, 1887. Helen Clay Frick Foundation Archives. (AIS 2002 06). Henry Clay Frick Business Records, 1862–1987. Box 488. Volume 1. Archives Service Center. University of Pittsburgh, p. 97.

"Coke Strike Breaking Up." *The Dispatch*. June 25, 1894. Scrapbook. June 23 to October 13, 1894. Box 508. Volume 21. Henry Clay Frick Business Records, 1862–1987. AIS 2002.06. Archives Service Center. University of Pittsburgh, pp. 8–9.

"Coke Strike Continues." *Mount Pleasant Journal*. May 24, 1887, p. 1.

"The Coke Strike Ended." *Mount Pleasant Journal*. May 26, 1891, p. 1.

"Coke Strike is Brought to a Crisis." *The Dispatch*. April 5, 1894. Scrapbook. February 2 to April 15, 1894. Henry Clay Frick Foundation Archives. AIS 2002.0. Henry Clay Frick Business Records, 1862–1987. Box 504. Volume 17. Archives Service Center. University of Pittsburgh, pp. 105–6.

"The Coke Strike: Steel Makers Cause a Change." *Commercial Telegraph*. June 11, 1887. Scrapbook. March 22, 1884, to August 18, 1887. Helen Clay Frick Foundation Archives (AIS 2002 06). Henry Clay Frick Business Records, 1862–1987. Box 488. Volume 1. Archives Service Center, University of Pittsburgh, p. 72.

"Coke Strike Still On." *Mount Pleasant Journal*. May 17, 1887, p. 1.

"The Coke Strikers Endeavor to Compel the Rainey Men to Join Their Forces." *The Dispatch*. February 24, 1891, p. 6.

"The Coke Trade." *Scottdale Herald*. December 24, 1891. Scrapbook. October 2 1891 to February 27, 1892. Henry Clay Frick Foundation Archives. (AIS 2002 06). Henry Clay Frick Business Records, 1862. Scrapbook Series. Box 489. Volume 2. Archives Service Center. University of Pittsburgh, p. 92.

"The Coke Trade." *Weekly Courier*. May 28, 1880, p. 3.

"The Coke Trade: Coke Cinders." *Courier*. June 8, 1888, p. 2.

"The Coke Trade Gaining." *Scottdale Independent*. November 30, 1893. Scrapbook. May 27, 1893, to February 2, 1894. Box 503. Volume 16, pp. 133–4. Henry Clay Frick Business Records, 1862–1987. AIS 2002.06. Archives Service Center. University of Pittsburgh.

"The Coke Trade's Birth: Tearing Down of the Old Henry Clay Works." *Penny Press*. April 7, 1888. Scrapbook. August 19, 1887, to November 2, 1888. Helen Clay Frick Foundation Archives. (AIS 2002 06). Henry Clay Frick Business Records, 1862–1987. Box 489. Volume 2. Archives Service Center. University of Pittsburgh, p. 100.

"The Coke War Not Yet Over." *The Reading Times*. April 12, 1894, p. 1.

"The Coke Workers Out." *Scottdale Independent*. May 6, 1887, p. 1.

"Coke Works Sold." *Mount Pleasant Dawn*. April 15, 1875, p. 3.

"Cokers and Coking." *Weekly Courier*. February 9, 1900, p. 2.

"Cokers and Coking." *Weekly Courier*. October 7, 1898, p. 2.

"The Cokers Organize." *Mount Pleasant Journal*. March 27, 1894, p. 1.

"The Cokers' Strike." *Pittsburg Post-Gazette*. June 17, 1881, p. 4.

"Cokers Use Dynamite." *Pittsburg Leader*. April 18, 1891. Scrapbook. April 18 to May 20, 1891. Helen Clay Frick Foundation Archives. (AIS 2002 06). Henry Clay Frick Business Records, 1862–1987. Scrapbook Series. Box 496. Volume 9. Archives Service Center. University of Pittsburgh, p. 4.

Commons, John R., et al. *A Documentary History of American Industrial Society*. Vol. IX. Labor Movement. Cleveland: The Arthur H. Clark Company, 1910.

"Company Store Robbed." *Weekly Courier*. August 12, 1892, p. 1.

Comprehensive Plan for Abandoned Mine Reclamation. Pennsylvania Department of Environmental Protection. http://www1.portal.state.pa.us/portal/server.pt?open=514&obJID=588910&mode=2.

"Concerning Alverton Mine Fire Proposal Scrapped by Court." *Evening Standard*. March 11, 1975, p. 25.

"Condition of Mines: H.C. Frick Coke Company." *Report of the Department of Mines of Pennsylvania*, Part II: Bituminous, 1907, p. 498.

"Condition of the Coal Mines." *Pittsburgh Post*. March 30, 1878, p. 6.

"Conference on Strike." *Mount Pleasant Journal*. January 27, 1891, p. 1.

"Connellsville Coke." *Weekly Courier*. March 11, 1881, p. 1.

Connellsville Coke, H.C. Frick Coke Company. Pittsburgh, c. 1883. Helen Clay Frick Foundation Archives (AIS 2002 06), Henry Clay Frick Business Records, 1862–1987, Box 523, Folder 1. Archives Service Center, University of Pittsburgh, p. 5.

Connellsville Coke, H.C. Frick Coke Company. Pittsburgh, c. 1883. Helen Clay Frick Foundation Archives. (AIS 2002 06). Henry Clay Frick Business Records, 1862–1987. Box 523. Folder 1. Archives Service Center. University of Pittsburgh, p. 8.

Connellsville Coke, H.C. Frick Company. Pittsburgh, 1890. Helen Clay Frick Foundation Archives. (AIS 2002 06). Henry Clay Frick Business Records, 1862–1987. Box 523. Folder 1. Archives Service Center. University of Pittsburgh, p. 42.

"The Connellsville Coke Region." *The Engineering Magazine: An International Review* 20 (October 1900 to March 1901): pp. 17–40.

"The Connellsville Coke Regions: Their Past, Present, And Future." *Weekly Courier*. Special Historical and Statistical Number. May 1914.

"Connellsville Operators Active in Local and Other Fields." *Weekly Courier*. February 28, 1918, p. 11.

"Connellsville Region Coke Notes." *Courier*. December 18, 1891, p. 2.

"Contract Labor System." *Encyclopedia of Immigration*. September 27, 2011.

"Convention at Scottdale." *Weekly Courier*. April 17, 1891, p. 1.

"Corrado Interests are now Operating 1,001 Coke Ovens at 14 Plants in the Connellsville and West Virginia Regions." *Daily Courier*. February 10, 1926, p. 1.

"Corrado-Schenck Coal Co." *Weekly Courier*. February 28, 1918, p. 10.

"The *Courier* Man in the Coke Field." *Weekly Courier*, August 13, 1880, p. 3.

"Crime and Punishment." *Pittsburgh Press*. March 22, 1894, p. 9.

"The Crisis at Hand: The Experience of One Hungarian." *Pittsburgh Dispatch*. April 6, 1891, p. 6.

Crispin, Mercedes Sowko. "The Carpatho-Rusyn Immigrant of Pennsylvania Steel Mills 1880–1920." http://humboldtdspace.calstate.edu/bitstream/handle/2148/53/Crispin.pdf;jsessionid=107041A2D5E8D281BDB9384460823F4A.server1?sequence=1.

Critchfield, N.B. "The History of Mount Pleasant." *Mount Pleasant Dawn*. August 23, 1876, p. 1.

"Crop Opening at Tip Top." *Weekly Courier*. January 5, 1911, p. 2.

"Cutting on Coke." *Commercial Gazette*. September 13, 1893, p. 3.

DeBow, James Dunwoody Brownson. *Statistical View of the United States....* United States Census Office. 7th Census. Volume 850. Washington: Beverley Tucker, Senate Printer, 1854, p. 370.

"Declared Off." *Scottdale Independent*. July 22, 1887, p. 1.

"Deluge: 18 Hours of Rain and 12 Hours of Flood..." *Courier*. August 24, 1888, p. 1.

The Demographic Statistical Atlas of the United States. https://statisticalatlas.com/county/Pennsylvania/Fayette-County/Ancestry. https://statisticalatlas.com/county/Pennsylvania/Westmoreland-County/Ancestry.

"Depending Upon Italians." *The Post*. May 2, 1891, p. 1.

DiCiccio, Carmen Peter. *Bituminous Coal and Coke Resources of Pennsylvania 1740–1945*. National Register of Historic Places Continuation. November 9, 1993.

Dietrich, William S. II. "Henry Clay Frick: Blood Pact," *Pittsburgh Quarterly*, Spring 2009. http://www.pittsburghquarterly.com/index.php/Historic-profiles/article-template/Print.html, p. 4.

"Different Opinions." *Mount Pleasant Journal*. September 13, 1887, p. 1.

"The Diggers and Drawers." *Weekly Courier*. June 3, 1881, p. 4.

Digital History Project: Henry Clay Frick. United States Steel Corporation. June 15, 2012. http://www.digitalhistoryproject.com/2012/96/henry-clay-frick-united-states-steel.html.

"Dissatisfied Miners." *The Tennessean*. March 4, 1881, p. 1.

Dougherty, James. "A Reference Guide to Resources on Coal Mining and Associated Materials in the Central/Western Pennsylvania Region. Knights of Labor Locals in America's Industrial Heritage Counties." From: Johnathan Garlock. *Guide to The Local Assemblies of the Knights of Labor*. Westport: Greenwood Press. 1982.

Duffy, E.F. "A Very Sad Story." *Pittsburgh Daily Post*. May 29, 1894, p. 1.

"Dynamite Tried Again." *The Dispatch*. August 3, 1894. Scrapbook. June 23 to October 12, 1894. Helen Clay Frick Foundation Archives. (AIS 2002 06). Henry Clay Frick Business Records, 1862–1987. Box 505. Volume 18. Archives Service Center. University of Pittsburgh, p. 92.

"Early Coke Making." *The Daily Courier*. March 25, 1881, p. 1.

"Early Coke Making: How Morgan Began," *Weekly Courier*, March 25, 1881, p. 1.

East Huntingdon Second Class Township Map. Westmoreland County. Pennsylvania Department of Transportation. Bureau of Planning and Research, Geographic Information Division. Municipal Code 64 206.

Eckman, Joe. Interview. March 17, 2016. Mount Pleasant Glass Museum Meeting.

"Editorial Notes." *Mount Pleasant Journal*. February 22, 1887, p. 1.

"Editorial Notes." *Mount Pleasant Journal*. February 10, 1891, p. 1.

"Editorial Notes: Another Lesson in Strikes." *Mount Pleasant Journal*. May 26, 1891, p. 1.

Edmunds, William E. *Coal in Pennsylvania* (2nd ed.). Harrisburg: Pennsylvania Geological Survey. Fourth Series. Educational Series 7, 2002.

"Effects of the Drouth [sic]." *Keystone Courier*. November 11, 1887, p. 1.

"Electric Lighting in Coal Mines." *The Electrical Age*. New York. October 17, 1891, p. 19.

"Elimination of Pollution of Youghiogheny River is Early Objective of Drive to Seal Abandoned Mines." *Daily Courier*. August 26, 1948, p. 1.

Ellis, Franklin. *History of Fayette County, Pennsylvania with Biographical Sketches of many of the Pioneers and Prominent Men*. Philadelphia: L.H. Everts & Co., 1882.

"End of Pollution Seems in Sight." *Coal and Coke Operators* 13, No. 8 (August 1915): pp. 621–3.

"Ends in Riot." *Mount Pleasant Journal*. March 31, 1891, p. 1.

Enman, John Aubrey. "Coal Company Store Prices Questioned: A Case Study of the Union Supply Company 1905–1906." *Pennsylvania History* 41, No. 1 (January 1974).

_____. "The Relationship of Coal Mining and Coke Making to the Distribution of Population Agglomerations in the Connellsville (Pennsylvania) Beehive Coke Region." Unpublished Ph.D. dissertation. Pittsburgh, PA: University of Pittsburgh Library, 1962.

"Enthroned a King." *Pittsburgh Dispatch*. August 28, 1889, p. 3.

Evans, Walker. High Street. Standard. WPA Farm Security Administration. 1935.

"Evicting all the Leaders." *Commercial Gazette*. April 18, 1891, p. 7.

"Eviction Notices." *Chronicle Telegraph*. April 8, 1891. Scrapbook. April 3–18, 1891. Henry Clay Frick Foundation Archives (AIS 2002 06). Henry Clay Frick Business Records, 1862–1987. Box 496. Volume 9. Archives Service Center. University of Pittsburgh, p. 89.

"Eviction Notices Not Feared." *Greensburg Daily Record*. April 9, 1891. Scrapbook. April 3–18, 1891. Henry Clay Frick Foundation Archives (AIS 2002 06). Henry Clay Frick Business Records, 1862–1987. Box 496. Volume 9. Archives Service Center. University of Pittsburgh, p. 154.

"Evictions at Port Royal." *Pittsburg Leader*. June 25, 1894. Scrapbook. June 23 to October 12, 1894. Henry Clay Frick Foundation Archives (AIS 2002 06). Henry Clay Frick Business Records, 1862–1987. Box 505. Volume 18. Archives Service Center. University of Pittsburgh, p. 11.

"Evictions Comparatively Peaceful." May 1891. Scrapbook. April 18 to May 20, 1891. Henry Clay Frick Foundation Archives (AIS 2002 06). Henry Clay Frick Business Records, 1862–1987. Box 496. Volume 9. Archives Service Center. University of Pittsburgh, p. 156.

"Excerpts from Journals and Daybooks." March 20, 1876, to April 23, 1881. March 20, 1876. Henry Clay Frick Foundation Archives (AIS 2002 06). Henry Clay Frick Business Records, 1862–1987. Box 523. Folder 9. Archives Service Center. University of Pittsburgh.

"Excerpts from Journals and Daybooks." 1878–1880. From *Journal of H.C. Frick and Company March 1878–May 31, 1880*. December 31, 1878. Henry Clay Frick Foundation Archives (AIS 2002 06). Henry Clay Frick Business Records, 1862–1987 Box 523. Folder 10, pp. 1–2.

"Excerpts from Journals and Daybooks." 1879–1881. From *Journal of H.C. Frick and Company. March 1878–May 31, 1880*. Henry Clay Frick Foundation Archives (AIS 2002 06). Henry Clay Frick Business Records, 1862–1987. Box 523. Folder 11, p. 2.

"Explosion in a Mine." *Pittsburg Dispatch*. March 29, 1890, p. 5.

Extract from H.C. Frick Company Ledger. "Estate of H. C. Frick (240 6), Estate of E.M. Ferguson (98 6)." December 31, 1921. September 1894–December 1921. Helen Clay Frick Foundation Archives (AIS 2002 06). Henry Clay Frick Business Records, 1862–1987. Box 536. Folder 6. Archives Service Center. University of Pittsburgh, p. 374.

Extract from Store Day Book and Journal, H. Clay Frick. Broad Ford. March 20, 1876 to April 23, 1881. Henry Clay Frick Foundation Archives (AIS 2002 06). Henry Clay Frick Business Records, 1862–1987. Box 523. Folder 9. December 14, 1877. Archives Service Center. University of Pittsburgh.

"Extracts from Day Book, Overholt, Frick & Co, March 10, 1871 to June 20, 1871." Henry Clay Frick Foundation Archives (AIS 2002 06). Henry Clay Frick Business Records, 1862–1987. Box 523. Folder 6. Archives Service Center. University of Pittsburgh.

"Familiar Faces in the Mining Industry: Henry C. Frick." *The Colliery Engineer* 12 (December 1891). October 2, 1891 to February 27, 1892. Helen Clay Frick Foundation Archives (AIS 2002 06). Henry Clay Frick Business Records, 1862–1987. Box 496, Volume 9. Archives Service Center, University of Pittsburgh, p. 86.

"Fayette County Storm Swept." *News Standard*. July 25, 1895, p. 1.

"Fayette Facts." *Weekly Courier*. February 1, 1884, p. 4.

Fenton, Edwin. "Italians In the Labor Movement." *Pennsylvania History: A Journal of Mid-Atlantic Studies* 26, No. 2 (1959): pp. 133–148. JSTOR, www.jstor.org/stable/27769876.

"The Fiery Hun." *Weekly Courier*. April 24, 1891, p. 1.

"The Fight with the Mob." *Commercial Gazette*. April 3, 1891, p. 1.

"File Suit To Close Coke Ovens." *Valley Independent*. February 12, 1971, p. 5.

"The Financial Outlook for Mount Pleasant." *Mount Pleasant Dawn*. July 19, 1876, p. 2.

"Fire at Frick Farm." *Daily Courier*. April 25, 1935, p. 5.

"Fire at Novelty." *Daily Courier*. May 21, 1910, p. 6.

"Fire at Tip Top Coke Works." *Commercial Gazette*. July 22, 1889, p. 4.

"The Fire-Bug Abroad." *Keystone Courier*. June 24, 1887, p. 1.

"Fire Still Burns." *Daily Courier*. January 11, 1907, p. 1.

"Firmly United." *Scottdale Independent*. January 30, 1886, p. 2.

"First Foreigners in Coke Region." *Daily Courier*. December 14, 1910, p. 12.

Fishback, Price V. "Did Coal Miners 'Owe Their Souls to the Company Store'? Theory and Evidence from the Early 1900s." *The Journal of Economic History* 46, No. 4 (December 1986): pp. 1011–1029.

Fisher, Douglas A. *Steel Serves the Nation, 1901 to 1951*. US Steel Corp., 1951.

"Five Lives Go Out." *The Dispatch*, April 4, 1894, pp. 1–2.

"Fleeing from domestic famine in the late 1800's: Hordes of Lithuanians came to Pennsylvania to Work in Coal Mines." http://vilnews.com/2012-04-12858

Fleming, George T. *History of Pittsburgh and Environs, from Prehistory to the Beginning of the American Revolution*. Vol. 3. New York: American Historical Society, 1922.

"FOR SALE." *Daily Courier*. November 24, 1953, p. 17.

"Forcing the Coke Strike." *Pittsburg Times*. March 26, 1891. February 15 to April 3, 1891. Henry Clay Frick Foundation Archives (AIS 2002 06). Henry Clay Frick Business Records, 1862–1987. Box 496. Volume 9. Archives Service Center. University of Pittsburgh, p. 119.

"Foreign Laborers." *Scottdale Independent.* December 12, 1885, p. 1.

Foreign Miner Taxes. http://immigrationtounited states.org/506-foreign-miner-taxes.html.

"Foreign Workmen." *Pittsburg Leader.* April 16, 1891. Scrapbook. April 3–18 1891. Helen Clay Frick Foundation Archives (AIS 2002 06). Henry Clay Frick Business Records, 1862–1987. Box 496. Volume 9. Archives Service Center. University of Pittsburgh, p. 169.

"Four Weeks of Strike. *Mount Pleasant Journal.* May 31, 1887, p. 1.

Fowler, Thaddeus. Map of Mount Pleasant, Westmoreland County, Pennsylvania. T.M. Fowler and James B. Moyer, Publishers, 1900.

Frank Leslie's Illustrated Newspaper 21, January to June 1886. New York: "Frank Leslie Pub. House. February 6, 1886, p. 408.

Frick & Co. Dollar Bill. Helen Clay Frick Foundation Archives (AIS 2002 06). Henry Clay Frick Business Records, 1862–1987. Box 523. Folder 1. Archives Service Center. University of Pittsburgh.

"Frick Buys Coal Closing Busy Day." *Pittsburgh Daily Post.* March 13, 1914, p. 2.

"Frick Buys McClure." *Pittsburgh Post-Gazette.* November 4, 1895, p. 2.

"Frick Company Farm Land for Food Planting." *Daily Courier.* May 5, 1917, p. 1.

"Frick Company Originated the Slogan of 'Safety First.'" *Coal and Coke Operator.* July 1916, p. 97.

"Frick discusses the purchase of the Davis Coal property and negotiations to buy out McClure Coke Company." December 9, 1889. Folder 14. Henry Clay Business Records. 1862–1987. Archives Service Center. University of Pittsburgh.

Frick Family Albums and Scrapbooks (PS-50). The Frick Collection/Frick Art Reference Library Archives, p. 42.

Frick, H.C. Letter to Solomon Keister. December 16, 1897. Westmoreland–Fayette Historical Society. Box P24. Folder 5. West Overton Village and Museums. Scottdale, Pennsylvania.

"Frick Plant Leased by Mr. Corrado." *Uniontown Morning Herald.* May 29, 1933, p. 9.

"Frick received Carnegie's telegram, and he thinks that the McClure property is less desirable because of the bad financial status of the partners. Frick also writes on the Pittsburgh & Western bonds and practices at Homestead." June 10, 1891. Volume 6. Henry Clay Frick Papers, Series VIII: Letterpress Copybooks, 1881–1923. The Frick Collection/Frick Art Reference Library Archives, New York.

"Frick Superintendent's Office Moving to Uniontown in April." *Morning Herald.* March 29, 1939, p. 1.

Frick Topography Map, RGGS Land & Minerals, 1915.

Frick vrs. Stevens. Common Pleas Court of Cumberland County, Pennsylvania. May 25, 1967. https://www.leagle.com/decision/19674943p adampc2d6148.

"The Frick Wage Scale." *Courier.* January 19, 1894, p. 1.

"Frick's New Coke Scale." *Pittsburg Times.* January 15, 1894. May 27, 1893, to February 2, 1894. Henry Clay Frick Foundation Archives (AIS 2002 06). Henry Clay Frick Business Records, 1862–1987. Box 503. Volume 16. Archives Service Center. University of Pittsburgh, p. 181.

"Frick's Retirement." *Daily Courier.* December 8, 1899, p. 12.

"From Journal of H.C. Frick and Company, March 1878–May 31 1880." Excerpts from Journals and Daybooks. 1878–1880 (AIS 2002 06). Henry Clay Frick Business Records, 1862–1987. Box 523. Folder 10. Archives Service Center, University of Pittsburgh, p. 1.

"From Shop and Mill." *Saint Paul Globe.* June 27, 1886, p. 12.

Front Page. *Pittsburg Dispatch.* April 4, 1891, p. 1.

"Furin Found Guilty." *News Standard.* June 14, 1894, p. 1.

"Furniture Loss of Widow Made Good by Frick Company." *Daily Courier.* October 18, 1912, p. 1.

Galley, Henrietta, and J.O. Arnold. *History of the Galley Family with Local and Old-Time Sketches in the Yough Region.* Philadelphia: Philadelphia Printing and Publishing Co., 1906.

Gates, John K. *The Beehive Coke Years: A Pictorial History of Those Times.* Uniontown: John K. Gates, 1990, p. 28.

George, Henry. "Labor in Pennsylvania." *The North American Review* 143, No. 357 (August 1886): pp. 165–182. http//www.jstor.org/stable/25101088.

"A Ghost in the Mine." *Keystone Courier.* February 11, 1887, p. 1.

Global True Lithuania Encyclopedia of Lithuanian Heritage Worldwide. http://global.truelithuania.com/pennsylvania-usa-108/.

"Gompers Here." *Scottdale Evening Herald.* May 14–18, 1891. April 18 to May 20 1891. Henry Clay Frick Foundation Archives (AIS 2002 06). Henry Clay Frick Business Records, 1862–1987. Box 497. Volume 10. Archives Service Center. University of Pittsburgh, p. 185.

"Gone to Jury." *Pittsburgh Leader.* April 17, 1891. April 3–18, 1891. Helen Clay Frick Foundation Archives (AIS 2002 06). Henry Clay Frick Business Records, 1862–1987. Box 496. Volume 9. Archives Service Center. University of Pittsburgh, pp. 180–81.

"A Good Outlook for Coke." *Scottdale Independent.* September 28, 1893, p. 1.

Gooddale, Stephen. "Safety the First Consideration." *The Colorado School of Mines Magazine* 1, No 12 (September 1911): pp. 6–9.

"Gould Coal Company." *Daily Courier.* November 19, 1946, p. 8.

"The Great Coal Strike." *The Cyclopedic Review of Current History.* Vol. 4. Colombian Annual. 894. Buffalo: Garretson Cox and Co., 1895, p. 295.

"Great Gobbler, The." *Weekly Courier.* August 30, 1889, p. 1.

"The Great Strike." *Scottdale Independent.* January 23, 1886, p. 1.

Gresham, John M. *Biographical and Portrait Cyclopedia of Fayette County.* 1889, p. 601.

Guide to the Henry Clay Frick Business Records, 1862–1987, Series XXV. Westmoreland-Fayette Historical Society, 1906–1987. Historical Background. https://digital.library.pitt.edu/islandora/object/pitt%3AUS-PPiU-ais200206/viewer.

Gutman, Herbert G. "The Buena Vista Affair." *Pennsylvania Magazine* (July 1964): pp. 251–293.

"H.C. Frick Buys Coal Acreage in Greene for $6,000,000." *Morning Herald.* February 28, 1914, p. 1.

H.C. Frick Coke Company Record. Subseries 3: Administrative Records 1871–1921. Box 523. Folder 6. Excerpts from Journals and Daybooks 1871–1876, pp. 9, 15.

H.C. Frick Coke Company. RGGS Mine Map, Sheet 000B Buckeye [map]. 1910. 1:1200. "RGGS Mine Map Collection." Posted: December 5, 2012. Pennsylvania Department of Environmental Protection and Penn State University's Pennsylvania Mine Map Atlas.

"H.C. Frick Resignation, May 13, 1887," "H.C. Frick Resignation, June 7, 1887," and "Accompanying Letter, June 7, 1887, Correspondence 1883–1919, Andrew Carnegie, 1883–1912, Folder 2. Henry Clay Frick Business Records, 1862–1987 (AIS 2002 06). Archives Service Center. University of Pittsburgh.

"H.C. Frick to be Laid at Rest in Pittsburgh Thursday: Wanted to be Buried There." *Daily Courier.* December 3, 1919, p. 1.

Halich, Wasyl. *Notes and Documents: Ukrainians in Western Pennsylvania.* Historical Society of Western Pennsylvania, 1935, pp. 139–146.

Hanes, Christopher. *The Rise and Fall of the Sliding Scale, or Why Wages Aren't Indexed to Product Prices.* November 2003.

"The Harrowing Hun." *Weekly Courier.* January 29, 1886, p. 1.

Harvey, George. *Henry Clay Frick: The Man.* New York: Charles Scribner's Sons, 1928.

Heinrich, Keith. "Mine Sealing: A Little-Known Legacy of the New Deal." April 19, 2017. https://pahistoricpreservation.com/mine-sealing-little-known-legacy-the-new-deal/.

"Helping Needy Cokers." *Rural Free Press.* July 17, 1893. November 17, 1893. May 27, 1893, to February 2, 1894. Henry Clay Frick Foundation Archives (AIS 2002 06). Henry Clay Frick Business Records, 1862–1987. Box 503. Volume 16. Archives Service Center. University of Pittsburgh, p. 112.

Historic American Engineering Record. C. Donnelly & Dillinger. McClure Coke Company. H.C. Frick Coke Company & Painter. O.K. (1968).

Historic American Engineering Record (HABS/HAER): Town of Standard, Westmoreland, Pennsylvania. (1991). America's Industrial Heritage Project (AIHP). HAER No. PA-290. National Park Service. Department of the Interior. Washington, DC.

Historical and Statistical Information by H.C. Frick Mines 1882–1976. USX Corporation records 1840–1983. Box 39. Folder 10, vol. 1. CCHC1. March 19, 2014. Coal and Coke Heritage Center at Penn State Fayette. The Eberly Campus.

History of Wages in the United States from Colonial Times to 1928. Bulletin of the United States Bureau of Labor Statistics. No. 604. United States Department of Labor. Washington: Government Printing Office, 1934, pp. 154–332.

Hoffacker, B.F. "Pittsburgh Coal in Fayette County." *Uniontown Morning Herald.* August 18, 1926, p. 4.

"Hordes of Huns." *Mount Pleasant Journal.* January 19, 1886, p. 1.

"The Horrible Huns." *Weekly Courier.* August 16, 1889, p. 1.

"Hostile Huns." *Mount Pleasant Journal.* January 26, 1886, p. 1.

"House Coal." *Evening Standard,* January 4, 1954, p. 12.

Hovanec, Evelyn A. *Common Lives of Uncommon Strength: The Women of the Coal and Coke Era of Southwestern Pennsylvania 1880–1970.* Dunbar, PA: Patch/Work Voices Publishing, 2001.

"How the Huns Get Here." *Scottdale Independent.* June 18, 1884, p. 2.

"A Humane Sheriff Refuses to Evict Strikers During the Blizzard." *Philadelphia Inquirer.* February 6, 1886, p. 5.

"The Hun Must Stay." *Courier.* October 31, 1890, p. 1.

"Huns with Scurvy." *Mount Pleasant Journal.* June 23, 1891, p. 1.

"The Hungarian Raids." *Weekly Courier.* August 23, 1889, p. 1.

"Hunger is Pressing Hard." *Pittsburgh Times.* May 18, 1891. April 18 to May 20, 1891. Helen Clay Frick Foundation Archives (AIS 2002 06). Henry Clay Frick Business Records, 1862–1987. Box 497. Volume 10. Archives Service Center. University of Pittsburgh, pp. 194–95.

"Hussar Found Guilty." *Pittsburgh Press.* June 8, 1895, p. 1.

Ifkovic, Edward. "Croatian Americans." https://www.everyculture.com/multi/Bu-Dr/Croatian-Americans.html#ixzz5UIelxX00.

Image adapted from RGGS Land & Minerals *100 031.* RGGS Land & Minerals. ftp://data1.commons.psu.edu/pub/minemaps/Map_Repository/Other_Collections/RGGS_Collection/Archive_TIFF_Images/.

Images. *Philadelphia Times.* Scrapbook. April 18 to May 20 1891. Helen Clay Frick Foundation Archives. (AIS 2002 06). Henry Clay Frick Business Records, 1862. Scrapbook Series. Box 497. Volume 10, p. 123. Archives Service Center. University of Pittsburgh.

"In Jackson's Hall." *Scottdale Herald.* May, 14, 1891. Scrapbook. April 18 to May 20, 1891. Henry Clay Frick Foundation Archives (AIS 2002 06). Henry Clay Frick Business Records, 1862–1987. Box 497. Volume 10. Archives Service Center. University of Pittsburgh, p. 185.

Inactive and Abandoned Underground Mines. Office

of Water and Hazardous Materials. Washington, DC: United States Environmental Protection Agency. June, 1975, p. 45.

"Industrial Items." *Miner's Record*. 1882, p. 2.

"The Industrial Situation." *Courier*. February 2, 1894, p. 1.

"The Industrial Wars of the Connellsville Coke Region." *Daily Courier Bicentennial Edition*. June 25, 1976, p. D-4.

"The Iron Clad." *Scottdale Independent*. July 7, 1887, p. 2.

"Iron Men Interfered." *Weekly Courier*. May 27, 1887, p. 2.

"Is Not Settled Yet." *Pittsburg Dispatch*. February 3, 1891, p. 5.

"Isometric Beehive Coke Oven Measured Drawing." *Historic American Engineering Record (HABS/HAER): Connellsville Coal & Coke Region, Fayette County, Pennsylvania*. (1994). America's Industrial Heritage Project (AIHP). HAER No. PA-283. National Park Service. Department of the Interior. Washington, DC.

"It Looks to be General." *Mount Pleasant Journal*. August 6, 1889, p. 1.

"Italian Laborers." *Commercial Gazette*. April 17, 1891, p. 6.

"The Italians Scared." *Courier*. June 29, 1894. June 23 to October 12, 1894. Helen Clay Frick Foundation Archives (AIS 2002 06). Henry Clay Frick Business Records, 1862–1987. Box 505. Volume 18. Archives Service Center. University of Pittsburgh, p. 30.

J.C. "In the Coke Fields. Connellsville Coke on the Mt. Pleasant Branch. Interesting Fossil Remains in Coal Mines." *Pittsburgh Post*. April 20, 1878, p. 3.

"James B. Morgan." *Pittsburgh Post-Gazette*. August 8, 1915, p. 2.

"John Keck, Frick Veteran Succumbs to Brief Illness." *Daily Courier*. April 28, 1914, p. 1.

Johnson, Ole S. *The Industrial Store: Its History, Operations and Economic Significance*. School of Business Administration. University of Georgia, 1952.

Jordan, John W., and James Hadden. *Genealogical and Personal History of Fayette County Pennsylvania*. Vol. 3. New York: Lewis Historical Publishing Company, 1912.

"A Justifiable Strike." *Pittsburgh Times*. December 11, 1893, p. 1.

Keister to Frick. Letter. June 1, 1889, and November 6, 1889 (WOB53A094). Westmoreland-Fayette Historical Society (Box P24, Folder 5). West Overton Village and Museums. Scottdale, Pennsylvania.

"Kerfoot No Drawing Card." *The Post*. December 30, 1891, p. 1.

Kruszka, Waclaw. *A History of Poles in America to 1908, Part 3: Poles in the Eastern and Southern States*. Washington, DC: The Catholic University of America Press, 1998.

Kubarek, David. "Researchers team up to tackle state's acid mine drainage problem." http://news.psu.edu/story/505679/2018/02/21/research/researchers-team-tackle-state%E2%80%99s-acid-mine-drainage-problem, pp. 1–5.

"Labor Abuses." *Pittsburgh Post*. June 29, 1894, p. 1.

"The Labor World." *Scottdale Independent*. June 17, 1885, p. 1.

"Laboratory Experiments Show Sealing of Mines Will Reduce Stream Pollution." *Daily Courier*. April 23, 1930, p. 10.

"Largest Coke Works in the United States." *Coal Trade Journal*. April 28, 1880, p. 263.

Lauck, Jeff. "The Bituminous Coal Miner and Coke Worker of Western Pennsylvania." *The Survey* 26 (April 1891 to September 1891). New York: The Charity Organization Society. April 1, 1911.

"Leaped into a Coke Oven." *Pittsburgh Post-Gazette*. April 24, 1900, p. 4.

"Left to Arbitration." *Mount Pleasant Journal*. March 1, 1887, p. 1.

"Legacy: A compendium of Southwestern Pennsylvania community histories." *Sunday Tribune-Review*. July 9, 1989, tabloid insert, p. 25.

"Legal Strife Among Coke Men." *Pittsburgh Post-Gazette*. July 10, 1879, p. 4.

Legislative Documents, Comprising the Department and Other Reports Made to the Senate and House of Representatives of PA, Vol. 4. Bituminous. 1880. Harrisburg: Lane S Hart. State Printer, 1881.

Leonard, Kim. *Henry Clay Frick: Respected and Hated*. December 16, 2007. http://triblive.com/x/pittsburghtrib/news/s_543031.html.

Letter. December 31, 1919, p. 372. Westmoreland-Fayette Historical Society (Box 536. Folder #). West Overton Village and Museums. Scottdale, Pennsylvania.

Letter. December 31, 1921, p. 373. Westmoreland-Fayette Historical Society (Box 536. Folder #). West Overton Village and Museums. Scottdale, Pennsylvania.

"Letters by Night Mail." *Pittsburgh Post*. June 29, 1894, p. 4.

"The Line Solid." *Scottdale Independent*. July 8, 1887, p. 1.

"Lishko Surrenders." *Pittsburg Leader*. April 15, 1891, p. 1.

"List of Coke Ovens in the Connellsville District." *Weekly Courier*. February 28, 1918, p. 2.

List of Notices Served on Strikers May 1 to be out May 5, 1894. 1894 060. Westmoreland-Fayette Historical Society (Box 15B, Folder 01). West Overton Village and Museums. Scottdale, Pennsylvania.

"Little Chance." *Mount Pleasant Journal*. May 5, 1891, p. 1.

"Little Lithuania USA Schuylkill County Pa." *Draugas News*. https://www.draugas.org/news/little-lithuania-usa-schuylkill-county-pa/.

"Living in a Cow House." *Pittsburg Times*. May 18, 1891. Scrapbook, April 18 to May 20, 1891. Henry Clay Frick Foundation Archives (AIS 2002 06). Henry Clay Frick Business Records, 1862–1987. Box 497. Volume 10. Archives Service Center. University of Pittsburgh, pp. 194–95.

"Lloyd Gowatski, Flywheel Victim. Dies of Injuries." *Daily Courier.* May 18, 1937, p. 1.

"Loar and his Men Free." *Mount Pleasant Journal.* May 26, 1891, p. 1.

"Local Fire Fighters Save the Big Tipple at Valley." *Daily Courier.* September 10, 1909, p. 1.

"Local Flash." *Mount Pleasant Dawn.* April 19, 1876, p. 3.

"Local Flash." *Mount Pleasant Dawn.* May 10, 1876, p. 3.

"Local Flashes." *Mount Pleasant Dawn.* March 22, 1876, p. 3.

"Local Flashes," *Mount Pleasant Dawn.* April 26, 1876, p. 2.

"Local Flashes," *Mount Pleasant Dawn.* May 24, 1876, p. 3.

Lovejoy, Owen R. "Child Labor in the Soft Coal Mines." *Annals of the American Academy of Political and Social Science* 29. Child Labor (January 1907): pp. 26–34.

McClure Coke Company Ad. Scrapbook. February 26 to July 15 1892. Helen Clay Frick Foundation Archives (AIS 2002 06). Henry Clay Frick Business Records, 1862–1987. Box 500. Volume 13. Archives Service Center. University of Pittsburgh, p. 142.

McConnell, C.H., et al. Operation Scarlift—Mine Drainage Abatement. Preprint 2770.

McDonough, Judith. "Worker Solidarity, Judicial Oppression, and Police Repression in the Westmoreland County. Pennsylvania Coal Miner's Strike, 1910–11." *Pennsylvania History* 64, No. 3 (Summer 1997): pp. 384–406.

"Made the Earth Tremble." *Pittsburgh Dispatch.* April 19, 1891, p. 1.

"Mail Route Changed for Summit Office." *Daily Courier.* November 4, 1909, p. 5.

"Making Coke in Shorter Time." *Pittsburgh Daily Post.* February 2, 1900, p. 2.

"Mance, Mike. Old Industry of Southwestern Pennsylvania" at http://coalandcoke.blogspot.com/2013/02/boyle-hazlett-coke-works-bridgeport.html.

Marcavitch, Aaron. "Folklore in Southwestern Pennsylvania Bituminous Coal Mining." http://www.marcavitch.com/research/hppgc/mining/coalfolk.htm.

Marchbin, Andrew A. *Hungarian Activities in Western Pennsylvania.* Western Pennsylvania Historical Society 23, No. 3 (September 1940): pp. 163–174.

"May be Settled." *Chronicle Telegraph.* April 9, 1891. April 3–18, 1891. Helen Clay Frick Foundation Archives (AIS 2002 06). Henry Clay Frick Business Records, 1862–1987. Box 496. Volume 9. Archives Service Center. University of Pittsburgh, p. 106.

"May End Strike." *Pittsburgh Press.* April 7, 1910, p. 3.

"May Refuse a Conference." *Pittsburgh Post.* March 23, 1894. February 1 to April 15, 1894. Henry Clay Frick Foundation Archives (AIS 2002 06). Henry Clay Frick Business Records, 1862–1987. Box 504. Volume 17. Archives Service Center. University of Pittsburgh, p. 71.

"Max Samuels Dead." *Pittsburgh Press.* March 16, 1895, p. 1.

"Meeting of Coke Manufacturers." *Mount Pleasant Dawn.* August 12, 1875, p. 2.

"Meeting of the Miners." *Weekly Courier.* July 15, 1881, p. 1.

"Mine Fire Danger in German Twp. Studied by State." *Daily Courier.* July 22, 1970, p. 2.

"Mine Heading Caves in Under Bessemer Road." *Daily Courier.* January 12, 1941, p. 6.

"Mine Oven and Mill." *Weekly Courier.* March 2, 1883, p. 1.

"Mine Sealing Gets Under Way This Week; One Near Reidmore Marks Beginning." *Daily Courier.* January 7, 1936, p. 1.

Mine Sealing in Southwestern Pennsylvania During the Great Depression. Uniontown: Pennsylvania Department of Transportation. 2014.

"Mine Sealing in State will Take 10 Years." *Daily Courier.* August 30, 1937, p. 8.

"The Miners are Firm." *The Dispatch.* March 20, 1891, p. 5.

"Miners, Attention: What a Coke Operator Thinks of his Slaves—The Miners of the Connellsville Coke Region." *Scottdale Independent.* April 15, 1885, pp. 1, 6.

"Miners Continue to do Violence." *New York Times.* June 15, 1894. https://www.nytimes.com/1894/06/15/archives/miners-continue-to-do-violence-pump-house-blown-up-with-dynamite.html.

"Miners on the War Path." *Mount Pleasant Dawn.* May 13, 1875, p. 3.

"Miners Still Out." *The Dispatch.* March 3, 1891, p. 6.

"A Miner's Story." *The Independent.* 1902. ehistory, Ohio State University, Department of History. https://ehistory.osu.edu/exhibitions/gildedage/content/MinersStory.

"Mining Practices of the H.C. Frick Coke Co." *Mines and Minerals.* August, 1904, p. 43.

"Minor Coal and Coke Notes." *Weekly Courier.* January 28, 1887, p. 1.

"Mr. Frick's Bequests." *Science Magazine.* December 12, 1919, p. 539.

Modelski, Andrew M. *Railroad Maps of North America: The First 100 Years.* Washington: Library of Congress, 1984, p. 139.

Moonsammy, Rita. *Final Report Steel Industry Heritage Corporation Ethnographic Survey Fayette County Component.* November 21, 1992.

"More Help Needed on Abandoned Mine Survey in West PA." *Daily Courier.* January 11, 1934, pp. 1, 6.

"Morewood Company Store." Eureka Fuel Company, Fayette County, Pa. and the South-West Connellsville Coke Company, Westmoreland County, PA. June 1901.

"Morewood Haulers Strike." *Mount Pleasant Journal.* February 22, 1887, p. 1.

"The Morewood Killings." *Mount Pleasant Journal.* April 14, 1891, p. 2.

"Morewood Mine is Leased by Frick; Operations Begun." *Daily Courier*. April 19, 1934, p. 5.

Morewood Mine postcard.

"Morewood Mine Worked Out; One of Region's First." *Daily Courier*. August 11, 1934, p. 1.

"The Morgan Store Has Been Closed; Ovens Banked." *Daily Courier*. May 25, 1910, p. 1.

"The Morgan Valley." *Daily Courier*. November 17, 1910, p. 1.

"Morgan Valley Being Revived." *Weekly Courier*. March 10, 1910, p. 1.

Mount Joy, Eileen. *A Woman's Day: Work and Anxiety*. Special Collection and University Archives, Indiana University of Pennsylvania. 2007–8. https://www.iup.edu/archives/coal/people-lives-stories/a-woman-s-day--work-and-anxiety/.

"Mt. Pleasant and Broad Ford Railroad Company. Report for the Year ending September 30, 1888." *Annual Report of the Secretary of Internal Affairs of the Commonwealth of Pennsylvania. Part IV: Railroad Canal, Navigation, Telegraph, and Telephone Companies for the Year 1888*. Harrisburg: E. K. Meyers. 1889, pp. 530–534.

Mount Pleasant Dawn. May 15, 1875, p. 3.

Mount Pleasant Dawn, April 26, 1876, p. 2.

Mount Pleasant Journal, April 14, 1891, p. 1. (Paper torn; title of article not visible.)

"Mt. Pleasant Road Closed by Mine Fall." *Daily Courier*. Monday April 18, 1938, p. 7.

"Mount Pleasant Rotary Unveils Frick Memorial." *Daily Courier*. November 21, 1930, p. 1.

Muller, Edward K, *et al. Westmoreland County, Pennsylvania: An Inventory of Historic American Buildings Survey/ Historic American Engineering Record* (HABS/HaER). America's Industrial Heritage Project (AIHP). Washington, DC: National Park Service. U.S. Department of the Interior, 1994.

Mulroney, M. *A Legacy of Coal: The Coal Company Towns of Southwestern Pennsylvania*. HABS/HAER. Washington, D.C.: NPS. 1989.

"Murder of Engineer Paddock, The." *Pittsburg Press*, April 5, 1894, p. 1.

"A Mutual Starve-Out." *The Times*. February 10, 1886, p. 1.

National Industrial Recovery Act. Wikipedia. http://en.wikipedia.org/wiki/National_industrial_Recovery_act.

"A New Record." *Daily Courier*. August 8, 1917, p. 1.

Nickerson, Harold L. "Industrial Safety." Association of Governmental Officials in Industry of the United States and Canada." Eighteenth Annual Convention Boston, Mass. May 18–22, 1931. Bulletin of the United States Bureau of Labor Statistics. No. 563. Washington, DC: Government Printing Office, 1932.

"Ninety-Cent Coke a Fact." *Courier*. January 12, 1894, p. 1.

"No Break in the Strike." *Weekly Courier*. May 13, 1887, p. 1.

"No Coke Syndicate Yet." *Mount Pleasant Journal*. December 6, 1887, p. 1.

"No Repairs on Blocked Road." *Daily Courier*. June 21, 1938, p. 5.

"No Scale Signed as Yet." *Mount Pleasant Journal*. September 27, 1887, p. 1.

"Not All at Work." *Scottdale Independent*. July 29, 1887, p. 1.

"Not Places Enough." *Mount Pleasant Journal*. June 2, 1891, p. 1.

"Not Yet Out of Danger." *Mount Pleasant Journal*. March 13, 1894. February 1 to April 15, 1894. Henry Clay Frick Foundation Archives (AIS 2002 06). Henry Clay Frick Business Records, 1862–1987. Box 504. Volume 17. Archive Service Center. University of Pittsburgh, p. 64.

"Notice to Employees." Thomas Lynch Misc. Letters and Documents (1889–1891). DOC December 26, 1889. University of Pittsburgh at Greensburg. UPG Archives RG 82.1.

"Notices." *Keystone Courier*. November 14, 1879, p. 3.

"Novelty Fire Still Burning." *Weekly Courier*. February 28, 1918, p. 1.

"Now in the Fourteenth Week." *Scottdale Independent*. May 14, 1891. April 18 to May 20, 1891. Henry Helen Clay Frick Foundation Archives (AIS 2002 06). Henry Clay Frick Business Records, 1862–1987. Box 497. Volume 10. Archives Service Center. University of Pittsburgh, pp. 186–7.

"The Offer Refused." *Mount Pleasant Journal*. February 8, 1887, p. 1.

"The Old Eagle Coke Plant is to Resume." *Daily Courier*. September 7, 1909, p. 1.

"Old Mine Hazards Aired at Meeting with Owners." *Daily Courier*. August 22, 1970, p. 13.

"Old Summit Opened." *Daily Courier*. July 16, 1909, p. 5.

"Old Tip Top Mine has its Last Run." *Weekly Courier*. December 18, 1911, p. 1; December 21, 1911, p. 8.

Oliver, John W. Oliver. *Henry Clay Frick: Pioneer-patriot and Philanthropist 1849–1949*. Address delivered at Westmoreland-Fayette County Historical Society, June 18, 1949.

O'Malley, T.T. *Adventures in the Mines: Perils Underground*. Akron: The Werner Printing and Litho Company, 1891, pp. 350–377.

"An Ominous War Cloud." *Weekly Courier*. July 8, 1887, p. 1.

O'Neal, Ken. "Fayette County and Surrounding Country Coal Mines." *Fayette County Genealogy Project*. http://www.pagenweb.org/~fayette/coal/coal_mines.html.

"On the Wage Question." *Mount Pleasant Journal*. February 22, 1887, p. 1.

"On the Warpath." *Pittsburg Press*. April 23, 1891, p. 1.

"One Mine Tramway to Haul Eagle Coal." *Daily Courier*. October 8, 1909, p. 1.

"Operators are Given till June 1 to Complete Tunnel." *Daily Courier*. December 1, 1926, p. 1.

"Operators to Be Held Liable for Damage from Cave-ins of Coal Mines." *Daily Courier*. April 14, 1939, p. 1.

"Ordered to Strike." *The Dispatch*. March 30, 1894, p. 1.

"Organization Favored." *Commercial Gazette*. March 22, 1894, p. 6.

"Organizational News." *Scottdale Independent*. February 21, 1890. Scrapbook. February 18 to August 27, 1890. Henry Clay Frick Foundation Archives (AIS 2002 06). Henry Clay Frick Business Records, 1862–1987. Box 492. Volume 5. Archive Service Center, p. 12.

"Organize the Huns." *Pittsburgh Dispatch*. January 31, 1890, p. 5.

"Our Coke Ovens Idle." *Weekly Courier*. May 6, 1887, p. 1.

"Our Fiery Ovens." *Weekly Courier*. January 25, 1889, p. 2.

"Outrage at Morgan." *Weekly Courier*. January 29, 1886, p. 1.

Oven Repair Form 067. Westmoreland–Fayette Historical Society (Box 15, Folder D 05). West Overton Village and Museums. Scottdale, Pennsylvania.

"Over 3,000 Abandoned Coal Mines Being Sealed by State with WPA Funds." *Daily Courier*. February 12, 1937, p. 13.

"Owensdale." *Daily Courier*. October 5, 1911, p. 5.

"Owensdale." *Daily Courier*. April 13, 1912, p. 1.

"Paddock Killed." *Scottdale Independent*. April 5, 1894, p. 1.

"Paddock Murder Trial." *Pittsburgh Press*. June 4, 1894, p. 4.

"Paddock's Companion." *The Dispatch*. April 5, 1891, p. 1.

Panic of 1893. https://en.wikipedia.org/wiki/Panic_of_1893.

"A Passive Volcano." *Pittsburgh Dispatch*. April 4, 1891, p. 1.

Paul, James W. "Report on the Sealing of Abandoned Coal Mines in Pennsylvania under Federal C.W.A. Project, 1934." Typescript. C.W.A. Pittsburgh, Pennsylvania.

"Peace with Arms." *The Post*. April 6, 1894. Scrapbook. February 1 to April 15, 1894. Henry Clay Frick Foundation Archives (AIS 2002 06). Henry Clay Frick Business Records, 1862–1987. Box 504. Volume 17. Archives Service Center. University of Pittsburgh, p. 133.

Peirce, Paul. "Last Call: Yukon Croatian Club to close for good Friday." *Tribune Review*. May 29, 2018. https://triblive.com/local/westmoreland/13690771-74/last-call-friday-at-yukon-croatian-club.

"Pennsylvania Allocates More Than $20 Million For Water Quality Projects." www.lancasterfarming.com/unpublished/pennsylvania-alloctes-mnore0thab-million-for-water-quality-projects/article.

Pennsylvania Map of Lithuanian Sites. http://map.truelithuania.com/en/pennsylvania-map-of-lithuanian-sites/.

"Pennsylvania Seeks to Abandon Branches in Fay-West Region." *Daily Courier*. June 13, 1935, p. 8.

Pettingill's Newspaper Directory. New York: S.M. Pettingill Co., 1878.

"Petty Strikes in the Region." *Weekly Courier*. December 17, 1886, p. 1.

"Pinkerton on Hand." *Commercial Gazette*. July 6, 1887, p. 8.

Pinkerton's National Detective Agency Records. http://rs5.loc.gov/service/mss/eadxmlmss/eadpdfmss/2003/ms003007.pdf.

"A Pioneer Coke Producer." *Courier*. March 16, 1894, p. 1.

"Pittsburg Leader." *Slovensky Hlas (Slavonic Voice)*, June 28, 1894, p. 1.

"Pittsburgh Trade Report." *The Coal Trade Journal*. June 15, 1887. Scrapbook, March 22, 1884, to August 18, 1887. Helen Clay Frick Foundation Archives (AIS 2002 06). Henry Clay Frick Business Records, 1862–1987. Box 488. Volume 1. Archives Service Center. University of Pittsburgh, p. 81.

Platt, Franklin. *Second Geological Survey of Pennsylvania 1875 Special Report of the Coke Manufacture of the Youghiogheny River Valley in Fayette and Westmoreland County with Geological Notes of the Coal and Iron Ore Beds*. Harrisburg: Board of Commissioners, 1876.

"Powderly Speaks." *Scottdale Independent*. July 22, 1887, p. 1.

Price List of Goods Sold at the Valley Store (H.C. Frick & Co.) Compared to Other Stores." *Legislative Documents Comprising the Department and Other Reports made to the Senate and House of Representatives of PA*, Vol. 4. Bituminous. 1880. Harrisburg: Lane S. Hart, State Printer, 1881, p. 199.

"Price of Coke Advanced." *Mount Pleasant Journal*. February 1, 1887, p. 1.

"Prizes Awarded for Gardens and Lawns at Frick Coke Plants." *Weekly Courier*. August 1, 1918, p. 3.

"Prohibition Passes." *Weekly Courier*. February 1, 1889, p. 1.

"Pure Connellsville Coke Ad." *Pittsburgh Daily Post*. March 28, 1879, p. 2.

"Pursuit of Rioters." *Commercial Gazette*. April 4, 1894. Scrapbook. February 1 to April 15, 1894. Henry Clay Frick Foundation Archives (AIS 2002 06). Henry Clay Frick Business Records, 1862–1987. Box 504. Volume 17. Archives Service Center. University of Pittsburgh, pp. 107–08.

"Quiet in the Coke Region." *Pittsburg Times*. April 21, 1891. Scrapbook. April 18 to May 20, 1891. Henry Clay Frick Business Records, 1862–1987. Helen Clay Frick Foundation Archives (AIS 2002 06). Box 496. Volume 9. Archives Service Center. University of Pittsburgh, pp. 23–4.

"Railroad History of Fayette County." http://pghbridges.com/articles/railroads/RRhistory_fayette3.htm.

"Rainey Buys Union." *Weekly Courier*. December 31. 1897, p. 1.

Receipt of J.O. Tinstman. Westmoreland-Fayette Historical Society (Box 2 P16. Folder B10). West Overton Village and Museums. Scottdale, Pennsylvania.

Redstone Creek Watershed, Mine Drainage Pollution Abatement Survey. Project No. 141–2. GEO Project 73043. 1977, pp. 67–68.

"Refuses to Yield." *Daily Courier*. July 18, 1917, p. 1.

Clay Frick Business Records, 1862–1967. Box 496. Volume 9. Archives Service Center. University of Pittsburgh, p. 126.
"The Strike Collapsing." *Reading Times*. April 15, 1891, p. 1.
"The Strike General." *Scottdale Rural Free Press*. April 27, 1894. Scrapbook. April 16 to May 20. Helen Clay Frick Foundation Archives. (AIS 2002 06). Henry Clay Frick Business Records, 1862–1987. Box 505. Volume 18. Archives Service Center. University of Pittsburgh, p. 84.
"The Strike Goes On." *Scottdale Independent*. January 13, 1886, p. 1.
"The Strike in the Coke Region." *Pittsburgh Commercial Gazette*. April 12, 1879, p. 1.
"Strike in the Coke Region." *Pittsburgh Daily Post*. March 26, 1879, p. 4.
"The Strike in the Coke Regions." *Pittsburgh Daily Post*. June 18, 1881, p. 4.
"Strike Pending." *Pittsburgh Press*. July 22, 1889, p. 7.
"Strike Prices Boom 'Snow Bird' Coal Pits." *Gazette Times*. August 6, 1922, p. 35.
"The Strike Settled." *Keystone Courier*. February 26, 1886, p. 1.
"The Strike Situation." *Weekly Courier*. May 20, 1887, p. 1.
"The Strike Still On." *Weekly Courier*. February 5, 1886, p. 1.
"Strikers Gain Ground." *Mount Pleasant Journal*. May 1, 1894. Scrapbook. April 16 to May 12, 1894. Henry Clay Frick Foundation Archives (AIS 2002 06). Henry Clay Frick Business Records, 1862–1987. Box 505. Volume 18. Archives Service Center. University of Pittsburgh, p. 107.
"The Strikers Win." *Scottdale Independent*. February 27, 1886, p. 1.
"Summit Evicted Miners." *Pittsburgh Times*. Scrapbook. April 18 to May 20, 1891. Helen Clay Frick Foundation Archives (AIS 2002 06). Henry Clay Frick Business Records, 1862–1987. Box 497. Vol. 10. 1891, p. 123.
"Surrounding Sections." *Weekly Courier*. January 21, 1881, p. 3.
"The Talk of the Town." *Weekly Courier*. May 22, 1891, p. 5.
"The Talk of Two Towns." *Courier*. November 6, 1891, p. 5.
"Ten Are Convicted." *Mount Pleasant Journal*. May 19, 1891, p. 1.
"There is No Let Up." *Scottdale Evening Herald*. May 19, 1891. Scrapbook. April 18 to May 20, 1891. Helen Clay Frick Foundation Archives (AIS 2002 06). Henry Clay Frick Business Records, 1862–1987. Box 497. Volume 10. Archives Service Center. University of Pittsburgh, pp. 198–99.
"Three New Demands." *Weekly Courier*. November 14, 1890, p. 1.
Thurston, George. *Pittsburgh and Allegheny in the Centennial Year*. Pittsburgh: Anderson, 1876.
"Tintsman Sells Morgan." *Mount Pleasant Dawn*. March 22, 1876, p. 3.
Tip Top Mine postcard.
"Tip Top Mine Shut Down by Water." *Daily Courier*. February 24, 1910, p. 1.
"To the Bitter End." *Mount Pleasant Journal*. July 12, 1887, p, 1.
Tormay, R.J. *A History of Area Mines*. Westmoreland–Fayette Historical Society (Box # 16, Folder # A5), West Overton Village and Museums. Scottdale, Pennsylvania, p. 12.
A Town That Grew at the Crossroad. Sesquicentennial Edition Reprint. Mount Pleasant Area Historic Preservation Committee. 1995, pp. 26–7.
"Trade Growing Slacker." *Courier*. July 11, 1890, p. 2.
"Troops Recalled." *Greensburg Daily Record*. April 17, 1891. Scrapbook. April 3–18, 1891. Helen Clay Frick Foundation Archives (AIS 2002 06). Henry Clay Frick Business Records, 1862–1987. Box 496. Volume 9. Archives Service Center. University of Pittsburgh, pp. 178–9.
"Trouble Among the Miners." *Mount Pleasant Journal*. March 22, 1887, p. 1.
"Trouble in the Coke Region." *Pittsburgh Post-Gazette*. June 3, 1881, p. 4.
"Trouble to Follow." *The Dispatch*. April 20, 1891, p. 1.
"Tumult Through the Region." *Pittsburg Times*. March 28, 1891. Scrapbook. February 15 to April 3, 1891. Helen Clay Frick Foundation Archives (AIS 2002 06). Henry Clay Frick Business Records, 1862–1987. Box 496. Volume 9. Archives Service Center. University of Pittsburgh, p. 132.
"Two Frick Plants Resume." *Pittsburgh Leader*. May 1, 1894. Scrapbook. April 16 to May 20, 1894. Helen Clay Frick Foundation Archives (AIS 2002 06). Henry Clay Frick Business Records, 1862–1987. Box 505. Volume 18. Archives Service Center. University of Pittsburgh, pp. 109–10.
"Two Gigantic Coke Deals." *Mount Pleasant Journal*. September 3, 1889, p. 1.
"Two Miners Rescued from Flooded Frick Mine at Broad Ford." *Daily Courier*. August 20, 1912, p. 1.
"Tyrone Plant Long Abandoned in Blast." *Weekly Courier*. October 6, 1905, p. 9.
Uniontown Genius of Liberty. December 18, 1890. Scrapbook. December 12, 1890, to February 14, 1891. Helen Clay Frick Foundation Archives (AIS 2002 06). Henry Clay Frick Business Records, 1862–1987. Box 494. Volume 7. Archives Service Center. University of Pittsburgh, p. 19.
United States Steel Corporation Hearings before the Committee on Investigation of United States Steel Corporation. House of Representatives. Wednesday, February 14, 1912. Washington, DC: Government Printing Office, 1912, p. 3282.
"Unlucky 13th." *Mount Pleasant Journal*. May 12, 1891, p. 1.
"Up Goes Coke." *Scottdale Independent*. February 5, 1887, p. 3.
Upper Tyrone Township Homepage: http://uppertyronetwp.org/?page_id=4. The information came straight out of *Nelson's Biographical Dictionary and Historical Reference Book of Fayette County*, Vol. 1, p. 469.
"The Valley Watercourse." *Courier*. March 11, 1892, p. 2.

"A Very Mysterious Death." *Weekly Courier.* March 22, 1895, p. 1.

Virtual Museum of Coal Mining in Western Pennsylvania. http://patheoldminer.rootsweb.ancestry.com/.

Vivian, Cassandra. *Hidden History of the Laurel Highlands.* Chapter: "A Frick Observatory and a Brashear Telescope," pp. 107–09. Charleston: The History Press, 2014.

_____. *Monessen: A Typical Steel Country Town.* Making of America Series. Charleston: Arcadia Publishing, 2002.

_____. *The Overseer's Family.* Monessen: Trade Routes Enterprises, 2002.

"The Wages of Coke Workers." *Courier.* December 15, 1893, p. 1.

"Wanted Wives." *Daily Courier.* March 23, 1900, p. 1.

Warren, Kenneth. "Like the Midnight Sun—the Leisenring Venture in the Connellsville Coke Region. 1880–1889." *Pittsburgh History.* Historical Society of Western Pennsylvania. Spring 1995, pp. 35–45.

_____. *Wealth, Waste, and Alienation: Growth and Decline in the Connellsville Coke Industry.* Pittsburgh: University of Pittsburgh Press, 2001.

"Water Companies." Connellsville Coal & Coke Region. HAER, No. PA-283, p. 61.

Weinman, John. Interview. 2015.

Western Pennsylvania Coalition for Abandoned Mine Reclamation. *Project Gob Pile Final Project Report*, 2001. http://www.amrclearinghouse.org/Sub/landreclamation/ProjectGobPile/.

"Westmoreland Mine Sealing Work Resumes." *Daily Courier.* May 11, 1937, p. 8.

Wettgen, George. Interview. March 17, 2016, and January 15, 2017.

"Where the Strikers Gathered Early Yesterday Morning." *Pittsburg Leader.* April 3, 1891. Scrapbook. February 15 to April 3, 1891. Helen Clay Frick Foundation Archives (AIS 2002 06). Henry Clay Frick Business Records, 1862–1987. Box 496. Volume 9. Archives Service Center. University of Pittsburgh, p. 178.

"Whipkey with Union Trust Co." *Daily Courier.* December 28, 1925, p. 1.

"White Mine Closed." *Daily Courier.* February 8, 1919, p. 1.

"Who is a Coal-Miner?" *Coal Mines & Coal Miners.* www.workerseducation.org/crutch/phamphlets/coal/coal_5.html.

"Wild Work at Leisenring." *Pittsburg Times.* April 24, 1891. Scrapbook. April 18 to May 20, 1891. Helen Clay Frick Foundation Archives (AIS 2002 06). Henry Clay Frick Business Records, 1862–1987. Box 496. Volume 9. Archives Service Center. University of Pittsburgh, pp. 48–9.

"Will Ask Higher Wages." *Weekly Courier.* January 15, 1886, p. 1.

"Will Open New York Office." *Mount Pleasant Journal.* December 29, 1891, p. 104.

"Women at Coke Works." *Weekly Courier.* October 8, 1886, p. 3.

"Women in a Midnight Raid." *The Post.* April 15, 1891, p. 1.

"Work or Strike, Which." *Mount Pleasant Journal.* June 7, 1887, p. 1.

"The Works at Bridgeport: Description of the Mullen, Boyle, Buckeye, and Star Mines." *Keystone Courier*, March 24, 1882, p. 1.

Works Progress Administration, U.S. Government. *WPA Mine Map. Connellsville Sheet 6, Pittsburgh Coal Seam* [map]. 1934.1:14,4000. "*Works Progress Act Mine Map Collection.*" Posted: 21 February 2013. Pennsylvania Department of Environmental Protection and Penn State University's Pennsylvania Mine Map Atlas. ftp://data1.commons.psu.edu/pub/minemaps/Map_Repository/Other_Collections/WPA_Maps/WPA_Connellsville_Sht_6_PGH.zip (23 March 2015).

_____. WPA Project No. 4483. *Connellsville Sheet 8. Pittsburgh Coal Seam* [map]. 1934.1:14,4000.

"Would Stop Mining of Coal in Little Developed Areas to Protect Water Supply." *Daily Courier.* July 2, 1926, p. 10.

"Would Turn Sewage into Abandoned Mine." *Daily Courier.* July 7–8, 1936, p. 2.

"Wretched Abodes." *Pittsburgh Post-Gazette.* April 17, 1897, p. 1.

Wright, Carroll D. "An Historical Sketch of the Knights of Labor." *The Quarterly Journal of Economics* 1, No. 2 (January 1887): pp. 137–168.

"Writing to Carnegie in New York, Frick discusses Connellsville Coal purchase of properties, employees, and Drexel and Morgan and Company." October 21, 1889. Folder 11. Henry Clay Frick Business Records, 1862–1987. Archives Service Center, University of Pittsburgh.

Written Historical and Descriptive Data Reduced Copies of Drawings. Connellsville Coal & Coke Region HAER No. Pa-283. Historical American Engineering Record. National Park Service, p. 168.

"Written History and Descriptive Data." *Connellsville Coal and Coke Region.* HAER No. PA-283.

Youghiogheny River Basin Mine Drainage Pollution Abatement Project. Operation Scarlift. Project No. SL-103. Gibbs and Hill, Inc. September 1972, pp. VI-1 and VI-2.

"Zachariah T. Henry Dies; Helped Build First Frick Coke Plant at Broad Ford." *Daily Courier.* April 2, 1927, p. 1.

Index

A.A. Hutchison & Bros. 159, 176; sells to Frick 159-160
Abandoned Mine Lands 136-138
A.C. Cochran Coke Company (A.C. Cochran & Co.) 91, 164, 166
Acid Mine Drainage (AMD) 134
Act to Encourage Immigration 43
Adelaide camp of evicted miners 130
Adelaide Mine 12, 45, 116; sealings 136-138; strikers marching 129
Agan, James 111-114
Albert, George Dallas 85
ALCOA 38
Alice Mine (Southwest No 2) 7, 9, 22, 46, 49, 57; history 175-176; march to 104-108; meetings 96-97, 98, 100; sold to Frick 101; strikers arrive 78-79
Allegheny Observatory of Pittsburgh 38
Allen, Kenneth 126
Alsop, Daniel 143
Alverton (Stonerville) 69, 78-79, 110; march on Morewood 105-108
Alverton Coke Company 173
Alverton Mine (I, II, III) 7, 9, 17, 18, 22; history, incidents and events 171-173; sealings 136-138
Amalgamated Association of Iron and Steel Workers (at Homestead) 25-27, 30, 74, 80, 88, 98; negotiating strike of 1889 89-92; origins 63-64
AMD and Art 138
American Emigrant Company 6, 43-44
American Manufacturer 95
American Mining Congress 134
Americans strike of 1891 102-103
Ammon, Frank A. 128
An Appeal to American Working Men 41
anarchists 101
Anchor Mine 22
Anderson, Senator George H. 132
Anderson, J.T. 112-114
Andrjejewski, Mrs. 61
Angus, Joseph 109
anthracite 9, 47

Armstrong, Charles 27, 48, 97, 159
Armstrong Station 48
Asian Barred Zone 43
Associated Brotherhood of Iron and Steel Heaters, Rollers, and Roughers of the United States 63
Austro-Hungarian Empire 45
Austro-Hungarians *see* immigrants

Baer, Grant 109
Bailey, James M. 90
Baldwin, James 111-114, 118-119
Ball, H.L. 102-103
Balogh, Jim 92
Baltimore and Ohio Railroad Company (B&O Railroad) 11, 21, 59, 69; strikers marching 129
bananas 15
Bane, Eustace H. 156
Barkley, W.F. 80, 109
barn boss 14
Barnhart, J.A. 22
Barrett, Jerry 112
Barrett, Michael 30; Morewood trials 111-114, 118-119
Basco, Frank 92
Baskin, John B. 130
Baughman, Agnes 110
Beacom, James S. 111-114, 118-119
Beaver, Governor James 95-94
Beehive Coke Oven 15-17, 20
Beerbower, R.C. 61
Belgium 16
Bellair Nail Works 91
Belle Vernon 10
Bellstein, William 92
benefits, for workers 60-61
Benjoe, Andrew (Bon Jac) 92
Bentz, August 112
Berger, Harry 107; Morewood trial 111-114
Berger Jesse 119
Berkman, Alexander 27
Berlin Museum of Safety 35
Bessemer, Henry 170
Bessemer Mine 7, 9, 22, 87, 97, 99, 100; history, incidents and events 170-171; march to 104-105; seals 135; strikers marching 129
Biasco, Michael 92

Bituminous Coal and Coke Resources of Pennsylvania 1740-1945 5
Bituminous Coal Mine Drainage Board 134
The Bituminous Coal Miner and Coke Worker of Western Pennsylvania 52-53
Bixler, John 153
Black Leg 69
Blashko, Andy (and wife) 117
Bliss, A.W. 88, 90
boatbuilding 10
Body, Christ 101
Boyle, John D. 70, 164
Boyle & Hazlett 15; on wages 69-70, 73, 164, 169
Boyle & Rafferty Coal Co. 164
Braddock Road Chapter of the DAR 67
Braddock's army 10
Brashear, John 38
Brashear Refractor Telescope 38
Breiner, Joe 77
Brendlinger, John 111-112
Brennen, J.P. 96, 164; strike of 1891 meeting 102-103
Bridgeport 18, 20, 78, 97
Brinker, M.S. 109
Broadford (Broad Ford) 9, 10, 11, 12, 17, 19-20, 25, 44, 46, 49, 57, 65, 69, 124; arrests 126-127; evictions 87-88, 116-117; shooting 85-86; strikers marching 129; 141
Broadford Mines 22, 104
Brophy, Dick 79
Brown, Carey 111-114, 119
Brown, Norman 107
Brown, W.H. 72
Brown & Co. 69, 72
Brownsville 10, 38
Bryne, J.R. (John) 67, 90
Buckeye Mine 7, 9, 22, 91, 98; history, incidents and events 166-168; strikers marching 129
Buckley, Harry 111-114, 118-119
Buena Vista Affair 48, 97
Buffington 58
Bunker Hill 80
Bureau of Mines 134, 141
Burns, Richard (Dick) 107; Morewood trial 111-114, 119

213

Index

Buskey, Mrs. 109
Buskey, Peter 109
Busko, Marshal 109
By-Product Oven 16
Byrnes Hall 123

California 10
Call (Coll), Hugh 124–128
Calumet 45, 46, 47, 48, 100
Cambria Iron Company 33, 122
Campbell, Frank 100
Campbell, George W. 42
Campbell, James 10
Campbell, John 112
Campbell Bill (1889) 42
Canada 69
canary 14
Capana, Larry 171
Carbaugh, George 107; Morewood trial 111–114
Carboniferous Period 9
Cardale 47
Carnegie, Andrew 6, 7, 66, 89, 93–98, 142; and Frick 22–25
Carnegie Building 22, 38
Carnegie Mellon University 136–138
Carnegie, Phipps & Co. 93
Carnegie Steel 25, 31, 142
Carnes, Steve 111–114
Carpentertown Mine 15, 17
Case, Joseph 143
Castle Garden 6, 44, 73
Central Mine 30, 98, 112; march to 104–108; strikers marching 129
Centralia 12
Centralization of Industrial Control and Operation of Philanthropic Foundations 35
Charles H. Armstrong & Son 161
Charlotte Mine 98
Chicago 91
Chicago and Northwestern Railway Company 60
Chicago World's Fair 126
children in mine 14
Chinese *see* immigrants
Church of God 46
Cincinnati 10
City Deposit Bank 60
Civil War 43, 63, 64
Clairton 16
Clark, J.H. 65
Clawson, Sheriff 104–105, 108–109; Morewood trial 111–114
Clay Coke Company 142, 150
Clean Streams Law 135
Cleveland 91
Cleveland, Grover 43, 118
Clingerman, W.H. 22
Clinton Mine 98
Cloud by Day 32, 121
Coal and Coke 8–18
Coal and Coke Heitage Center 157
Coal and Iron Police 6, 64, 80, 92, 96, 100
Coal Commission Report of 1922 59

Coal Mines & Coal Miners 14
Coalbrook Mine 99
Cochran, A.C. 88
Cochran, James 10
Cochran, John F. 70
Cochran, Mordecai 10
Cochran & Ewing Company 166
Cochran & Keister 157
Cochrans 27, 28, 33, 66, 72
Coke Country Chronicle 63, 71
Coleman, William 118–119
Colliery Engineer 34
Collins, Daniel 110
Collins, John 110
Collins, Wilson 105
Columbus, Ohio 90
Commer, Steve 100
Commercial Gazette 126–127
company stores: history 56–59; pricing 36–37
Comprehensive Plan for Abandoned Mine Reclamation 136–138
Congress 43
Connellsville 12, 13, 16, 17, 23, 25, 29, 30, 32, 33, 34, 35, 36, 45, 46, 48, 61, 73, 78, 89, 92, 99, 100, 102, 104, 121, 130
Connellsville Canteen 2
Connellsville Coal Basin 9
Connellsville Coke 21
Connellsville Coke and Iron 22, 68
Connellsville Coke Producers Association 68; strike of 1886 meeting 88
Connellsville Coke Region 1, 15, 64
Connellsville Courier 1, 16, 24, 30, 38, 67, 91; arrests 100; strike settled 88
Connellsville Daily Courier 41, 46, 67, 71; abandoned mines 135
Connellsville Keystone Courier 53, 67
Connellsville Tribune 67
Connellsville Weekly Courier 41, 67, 73, 105; compares Frick wages 122–123; "The Harrowing Hun" 81–85; "The Horrible Huns" 99–100; mines sold to Frick 101; Morewood funerals 108; weekly mine reports 141–177
Connor, James 146
Consolidation Coal Company 28
Contract Labor Law 42–43
Cook, John 92
Cooper, M.A. 69–71
Cooper, Officer 77
Corrado, Gaetano 146
Corrado-Schenck Coal Company (Corrado Coal Company) 143, 145, 146
Cossacks 65
Costello, John 89
Cottage Hospital of Connellsville 37
Coughanour, B.F. 166
Coulehan, Thomas 143
Cowan, Robert 159
C.P. Markle and Sons 146, 171

Crabtree 46, 47
Crawford 10
Crichton, Andrew 134
Croatian Fraternal Union Lodge 47
Croatians *see* immigrants
Crossland, A.J. 65
Crow, James 102–103
Cunningham, Charles 159
Cunningham, W.J. 110

Daily Courier see *Connellsville Courier*
Dank, John 112
Darby, Daniel 123
Darr Mine 12
Davidson, D.R. (Daniel) 65, 98, 143, 160
Davidson Mine 35, 61; death of Paddock 124–128
Davis, L.R. 123, 128
Davis, L.S. (Lewis) 107, 123; Morewood trial 111–114, 119
Dawson 10, 103, 104, 105, 141
Dayton, J.M. 99
DeHaven, Frank 103
Deieber 117–118
DeLeon (socialist) 117
Dellegati, Harry 103
Dellinger, Samuel 11
Democrat 43
Denk, Owen 118
Department of Mines 141
Dexter Mine 97, 98
DiCiccio, Carmen Peter 5, 28, 176
Did Coal Miners "Owe Their Souls to the Company Store"? 59
Dillinger, D.L. 70 88
Dillinger, Samuel 172
Disman, Michael 30, 88, 102–103, 112, 123
Donnelly, Charles 78, 164
Donnelly, E.B. 146
Donnelly, Terrence 159
Donnelly and Dillinger Company 172
Donnelly Mine 9, 79, 97; march on Morewood 105–108; *see also* Alverton
Dorm, William 109
Dorsett, Charles 80
Dravo, Captain 42
drift entrance 13
Duffy, E.F. 123
Dunbar 17, 47, 81, 99
Dunbar Furnace Company 16, 34
Dungan, A.C. 99
Dungler, Joseph 97

Eagle Mine 7, 9, 41, 45, 48, 69, 72, 98, 104; history, incidents and events 145–146
Eagle Street 69
East End House 112
Eastman, Mike 100
Eckard, James 126–128
Eckles, Frank 112
Edenborn 45

Educational Fund Commission Pittsburgh 37
Eggers (Ager) 115
Eicher, Justice 111–114, 118–119
Eisaman, John E. 119
Ellis, Franklin 142, 145, 146, 148, 161
Ellis Island 43
Engineering Magazine 9
England 56
Enman, John 17, 49, 52, 54, 57–58, 141–142, 161 Europe 41; overpricing 36
Environmental Protection Agency 173
Europe 65, 142
Evans, Walker 55
Everson 11, 18, 30, 45, 46, 72, 76, 88, 141; negotiation 90–91; strikers marching 129
eviction(s) 87–88, 111–112, 114, 155; strike of 1894 129–131
Ewing, Judge 128

Fairchance 45, 46, 47, 89, 97, 104, 116
Fairdull, John 100
Fayette City 10
Fayette County Board of Commissioners 156
Fayette Monitor 67
Fazenbaker, Martin 155
Fenton, Edwin 48
Ferguson, E.M. 21, 93, 142
Ferguson, Henry 157
Ferguson, Walter 93
Ferguson Mine 22
Fietcher, Thomas 110
fire 12, 132; at Frick Mine 151
fire boss 14, 35, 146
Fishback, Price V. 59
Fisher, John 103
flood 12
folklore in the mines 15
Fort Defiance 79–80, 98, 99
Fort Frick 26
Fort Hill Mine 22, 92, 103
Forty Martyrs Church 46
fossils in Hazlett Mine 169–170
Foundry Mine 7, 9, 22, 72, 98, 104
Fountain Mine 22
Fox, W. 67
France 56
Franklin, Benjamin 64
Franks, Scott 99
Frazier, A.P. 89
Frey, Charles 118–119
Frick, Helen Clay 19, 37, 38–40, 71, 93–98
Frick, Henry Clay 1, 2, 3, 5, 12, 28–37, 57, 101, 123; best housing 52–53; buying McClure 164–165; buys from Hutchison 159–160; calls in Pinkertons 117; and Carnegie 22–25, 93–98, 164; early life 19; hatred of 19; in Homestead Strike 25–27; misinformation 50–54; Morewood Massacre viewpoint 109–110; organizing 20; resigns 94; shot 27; strike of 1886 78, 88; wealth 37, 44
Frick, Martha 27
Frick & Co. 21, 70
Frick Building 22, 38
Frick Coke Company 33, 35
"Frick dollar" 59
Frick Mine 7, 9, 21, 98; history, incidents and events 150–153
Frick Park observatory and telescope 37–38
Fry, S.B. 119
Furen, Mike 127–128

Galley Run 10, 20, 136
Ganskey, Martin 80
Garmbly (Grumley), John 159
Garshbar, M. 77
Gary, Elbert H. 25
Gay, Constable 111–114
Germans *see* immigrants
Germany 56
Ghost Town Trail 138
Gibson, Leo T. 134
Gilbert, Harry 107, 119
glassmaking 10
Globe Mine *see* White Mine
Goering Bill 134
golabki 49
Golden Era of King Coal, Queen Coke and Princess Steel 1880–1920 28
Good Roads Association 171
Gotler, Mike 77
Gould Coal Company 143
Grace Mine 22; strikers marching 128
Grand Opera House 104
Great Allegheny Passage 11
Greek Catholic 45, 47
Greenlick Junction 92
Greensburg 37, 78, 80, 89, 104, 135
Greensburg Tribune Review 34
Gregg, District Attorney 111–114, 119
Gregor, Jo 100
Gregor, Martin 150
Grimm, T.S. 112
Gulf Oil 38

HABS/HAER *see* Historic American Engineering Record
Hailes, John 118–119
Halich, Wasyl 61
Halsinger, E.B. 67
halupki 49
Hann, Miles 107, 119
Hann, Miley 111–114, 119
Hanney, William 109
Hansil, A. 77
Harbaugh, John 119
Hardy, John 109
Harris, Pres. 90
Harrisburg 42
Harshman, Joseph 99
Hart, John 112–114
Hartigan, John 77
Harvard 37

Harvey, George 19
Hastings, Adj. Gen. 96
Haverstick, A.C. 67
Hawk, Lew K. 119
Hawkins, Col. A.L. 108–109
Hay, William 102–103
Hayes, M.L. 150
Hayes, S.J. 67
Hazleton 45
Hazlett 73
Hazlett Mine 7, 9, 15, 22, 45, 69, 78, 91, 96
H.C. Frick Coke Company 6, 7, 11, 16, 17, 21, 34, 93–98, 107; buys out competitors 22, 101; company stores 36–37, 41, 46, 56–59; death of Paddock 124–128; evictions 116; maintains sliding scale 121–122; position 118; property records 141–177; safety 32–37, 61; scrip 59–60; strike of 1891 102–103; wages 32–33, 60–61, 69
Head (lawyer) 111–114, 118–119
Hecla Mine 100
Helm, John 92
Henry, Zachariah T. 153
Henry Clay Mine 7, 9, 21, 72; history, incidents and events 152–156; seals 136; shooting during strike of 86, 85–86
Herrington, L.M. 153
Hibernian 69
Hickman Run 141
Hidden History of the Laurel Highlands 37
Hill Farm Mine 12, 34
Hillman Library 67
Historic American Engineering Record (HABS/HAER) 55, 131, 145, 146, 148, 157, 161
Historical Data H.C. Frick Coke Company Plants 146, 170
A History of Area Mines 11
History of the County of Westmoreland 85
Hitchman, J.J. 109
Hitchman, William J. 11
H.K. Porter & Co. 177
Hocking Valley, Ohio 80
Holly, Albert 109
Home Mine 72, 98
home remedies 56
Homestead 6, 30, 64, 102, 121; strike of 1892 25–27, 29
Hooper (pit boss) 105
horses 15
Hostetter Connellsville Coke Company 33, 102–103
Houser, Jacob 159
Howard, Henry 112
Hughes, Edward 155
Humphries, W.T. 102–103
Hungarians *see* immigrants
Hungary Row 79, 87
Hunter, Josiah 119
Hurst, Moore & Company 157
Hussar, John 127–128
Hutchison A.A. 21

Index

Illinois Central Railroad 64
Illinois Steel Company 21, 94
Immigrant Act 43
immigrants 6, 41–60; African Americans 48; Austro-Hungarians 45, 74 Belgians 46; Carpatho-Rusyns (Ruthenians, Rusyns) 45, 47–48; Chinese 43; Croatians 41, 47, 49; Hungarians (Huns) 30, 32, 42, 44, 48, 76, 80, 82, 84–85, 86, 87, 92, 99–100, 102–103, 105, 121, 126–127, 130; German 41, 44, 70, 72, 77, 80, 102–103; Irish 41, 44–45; Italians 31, 41, 48, 102–103, 130; Lithuanians 47; Magyars 41; Poles (Polish) 41, 45, 46–47; Romanians 45; Scottish 41; Slovaks (Slavs) 41, 45–46, 102–103, 116, 130; Ukrainians (Russniaks) 45, 61–62; Welsh 41
Immigration Restriction League 43
Incox, Frank 100
Industrial Age 41
Industrial Revolution 44
International Exposition of Hygiene at Dresden, Germany 35
Interstate Commerce Commission 90
Irish *see* immigrants
Iron and Steel Roll Hands Union 63
Iron Clad Agreement 24
Italians *see* immigrants
Italians in the Labor Movement 48

Jackson, James 74
Jackson, John B. 90
Jacobs Creek 9, 10, 12, 69, 135, 136–138
James, Thomas P. 89
James Cochran, Sons & Company 33, 122, 157; *see also* Cochran
Jamestown 45
Jarrett, John 90
J.F. Stauffer & Co. 165
J.H. Rumbaugh field 114
Jimtown Mine 22, 92, 97, 105; sold to Frick 101
J.M. Schoonmaker Coke Company 101, 164
John, Viq 92
Johnson, Ole 58
Johnston, Jake 80
Jonas (socialist) 117–118
Jones and Laughlin Steel Company 33, 122
Jordan, James 109
Jordan, J.B. 11
J.W. Moore Company 34, 101

Kane, Thomas 155
Kantz, A.B. 109
Keck, Frederick 152
Keck, John 152
Keck, Leonard 152
Keck, Martin 152
Keighley, Thomas W. 136
Keister, B.F. 88

Keister, Officer Armel 76
Keister, Soloman 158
Keller, George 112–114
Keller, Phillip 22
Kelley (officer) 76
Kelley, William 92, 100
Kennedy, Orran W. 22
Kerfoot, Master Workman 102–103
Kerr, John 119
Keystone Courier see Connellsville Courier
King, Mathias 112–114
Kitchman, John 77
Kittanning 111
Kline, Lawrence 103
Klondike 9, 47
Kneass, Strickland 65
Knights of Labor 27, 61, 72, 74, 78, 80, 96–97, 98; fighting for power 63–64; Morewood trials 118–119; negotiations strike of 1887 89–92
Komm, Karl 92
Kosciuszko Club 46
Kowalshik, John 77
Kowalshik, P. 77
Kyle Mine 104, 115, 116

Labor Tribune 92
Lake, Col. 70
Lamb, Robert 109
Lambling, Father 79–80, 108, 118
Lane, James 111–114, 118–119
Larimer, William M. 119
larry cars 14, 15
Latrobe 9, 119, 134
Lauck, Jett 52–53
Leisenring 45, 47
Leisenring Mines 22, 36, 96–97, 103, 115, 116, 117, 128
Leith Mine 46, 47, 87, 98, 105, 115
Lemont (Furnace) 11, 46
Lemont Mine 98, 146
Lesko, Steve 100
The Life of the Perfect Capitalist 38
Ligonier township 119
Limpus, Lowell 28
Lincoln, Abraham 64
Linden, Captain 96
Lindsay, R.H. 128
Lindway, Mike 112
Loar, J.A. 104, 105–108, 111–114, 119, 112–114, 115, 119
Lodge, Henry Cabot 43
Logan, Barney 92
Logan, James E. 11
Lynch, Thomas 32–35, 72, 94, 107; attack on Leith 105; Frick wages higher 92; on Hungarians 48, 59; on Morewood Massacre 110; overcharging 36, 41; strike of 1886 meeting 88; strike of 1891 meeting 102–103; on strikers 81–82
Lyndon, Julius 92
Lytle, Justice 92

MacBride-Dexter, Dr. Edith 135
MacDonald, James E. 173

MacDonald Smokeless Sole-Heated Non-Recovery Coke Oven 173
Madonna of Czestochowa Catholic Church 47
Magyar, Mike 92
Magyars *see* immigrants
Maloney, J.J. 171
Mammoth Mine 45, 46, 97, 104; disaster 12, 34, 35, 61, 81; evictions 130; strikers marching 100–101
management, miners and unions 20, 25–27, 63
Marchand, H.C. 65
marching, miners 69, 76–78, 79, 100; demands 102, 103; Morewood 105–108; strikers 128–129
Marenko, John 100
Markle, C.C. 65
Markle, C.P. 11, 69
Markle, Sherrick & Co. 145, 154
Marshall, Tom 119, 128
Martin, R.L. 88
Mason, Samuel 128
Matos, Antun 47
May, Ben 77–80
Mayfield Mine 9, 79, 97; march on Morewood 105–108
McBride, John 90, 102–103
McCabe, John 79
McCaleb, J.D. 107, 111–114
McCarthy, John 118–119
McCausland's Hall 119
McClain, John 80
McClan, John 118
McCleary (mine boss) 161
McClelland, Adj. Gen. 30, 64
McCloy, Arthur 171
McClure, E.W. 163–164
McClure Coke Company 7, 11, 22, 33, 36, 71, 96, 98, 101, 104; attack on 78–79; history, incidents and events 162–173; overcharging 36, 66; strike of 1891 meeting 102–103; strikers marching 128; syndicate 68; wages 122
McConnell, Deputy 105–108, 112–114
McCormick, Provance 10
McCormick, Sheriff 103, 117
McCurdy, Mr. 67
McDonnell, Martin 92
McDonon 111–114
McDonough, Michael 118–119
McDonough, Pat 118–119
McEnery family 115
McGinty, Thomas 135
McGuire, James 102–103
McGurgan, Frank 150
McIndoe, John 109
McIndoe, Mary 109
McKenna, Patrick 88
McNulty, John 102–103
M'Creighton, J.M. 65
McSloy, John 92, 103, 127–128
McTighe, W.J. 164
M'Cullough, Welty 65
Meason, Isaac 10
Meiliga, George 112

Index

Mellon Institute for Industrial Research 135
Mellon National Bank 60
Mellons 38, 66
Mencovish, Peter 100
Mennonite 19, 44
Menoher (pit boss) 78
Mentzer (beaten boy) 79
Mercy Hospital 37
Meredith, Don 155
Metz, Alex 118–119
Mezzadria (sharecropping system) 51–52
Middle Ages 1, 36, 37, 50–54, 56–59
Miller, Johnny 153
Miller, Sheriff 96, 100
Mine Drainage Stream Pollution 134
mine seals 134–135
Miner, William 159
miners 20, 23, 63; meetings 78, 80, 87, 102, 116; response to Lynch 83–84; and unions 30–31, 102, 118
Miners and Progressive Union 63
Miners' Association 74
Miners' Hall in Everson 74
Miner's Record 67, 74
Minert, John 146
mines: history, incidents and events 141–177
Mining in a Nutshell 146
Mining, Mathematics Simplified 146
Mississippi Watershed 10
Missouri Furnace Co. 169
Mitchell, John 31, 175
Molly Maguires 45
Mon *see* Monongahela River
Monessen 47–48
Monongahela House 22
Monongahela River 10, 16, 26, 47; sealings 136–138
Moody, J. 157
Mooney, Edward 146
Moore, J.W. 81; sells to Frick 101
Moorhead (lawyer) 111–114, 118–119
Morewood Mine 7, 9, 21–2, 30, 41, 46, 48, 49, 57, 74, 86, 87, 104; evictions 1891 111–112; history, incidents and events 174–175; inquest and trial 110–114; massacre 7, 105–114; protests 76–78; seals 135; strike 96–97, 98–100; strikers marching 128–129
Morgan, A.S.M. 21
Morgan, J.P. 25
Morgan (town) 11, 18, 99, 115; strikers marching 129
Morgan & Company 21
Morgan Mine 7, 9, 20, 22, 59, 72, 98, 100, 118; history, incidents and events 142–145
Morgan Station 11, 74, 87
Morgan Valley 2, 5, 7, 11, 12, 13, 17, 19, 20, 22, 36, 41, 49, 59, 66, 73, 76, 80, 89–91, 97, 116, 117, 130, 141
Morgantown 91
Morrell Mine 98

Moses, Harry M. 22
Mount Braddock 11
Mount Pleasant 2, 7, 9, 10, 12, 15, 17, 19, 20, 25, 44, 45–46, 65, 69, 72, 73, 97, 103; mine sealing 135–136; National Guard 108–109; strike of 1886 76–81; strikers marching 128–129; town traumatized 108
Mount Pleasant and Broadford Railroad 6, 11, 21, 59, 65, 71, 78
Mount Pleasant Dawn 1, 19, 66; early strikes 67–71, 123
Mount Pleasant Historical Society 67
Mount Pleasant Independent 67
Mount Pleasant Journal 1, 2, 11, 30, 67, 135; coroner's inquest 109; "Hostile Huns" 78–81; march on Morewood 105–108; mines sold to Frick 101; more marches 98, 104; Morewood officers trial 119–120; Morewood trial testimonies 109–111, 112–114; Paddock murder 127–128; Pinkertons explained 96; quarreling unions 89; strike of 1886 Hordes of Huns 76–78; strike of 1891 meeting 102–103; violence 91–92
Mount Pleasant Library 2, 67
Mount Pleasant Memorial Hospital 37
Mount Pleasant Rotary Club 29
Mount Pleasant Water Company 12
Mountain Watershed Association 136–138
Moyer Mine 81, 92, 99, 100, 123, 127
mule(s) 15
Mullen (Mullin) Mine 7, 9, 22, 170
Mullin, William 81, 90, 93, 170
Murphy, A.S. 99
Murphy, Elizabeth 112
Musco, Andy 100
Muscovit, Mike 100
Mutchko, Mike 100
Myers (Meyers/Moyers) John 169

Narey, John 171
Nashville Tennessean 73
National Federation of Miners and Mine Laborers of the United States and Territories 63
National Hotel 29, 80, 114
National Industrial Recovery Act 134
National Progressive Union 63, 71–72, 118
National Register of Historic Places 19
National Trade Assembly No. 135 63
National Union Fire Insurance Company 60
Native Americans 10
Need, J. 74
Needham, John 74
Neel, James 11
Neish, Andrew 173
Nelly Mine 103

Neuner, Thomas 92
New Geneva 10
New Orleans 10
New Orleans (steamboat) 10
New York City 37, 48, 70, 72
New York Daily News 28
Newmyer John S. (Newmeyer) 88, 152
Nichol, Elmer 107, 111–114, 119
Nixon, Robert 111–114, 118–119
Noble Order of Knights of Labor of America 63
Nogel, Annie 127
Nolan, John 146, 158
Norris, Robert 173
Novelty Mine *see* Frick Mine

O'Connell (yard boss, Leith) 105
Ohio 102
Ohio River 10
Old Basin 9, 28
Oliphant Mine 97, 104
Oliver Coke and Furnace Company 33, 122
Oliver eviction 130
Oliver Mine 46
O'Neil, Michael 97
Operation Scarlift 136–138
Orient Coal Company 47
Orient Mine 47
Osceola 48
O'Toole, Edward 22
Otto, Jacob 101
Our Lady of Sorrows Slovak Church 46
Overholt, Aaron, and John 150
Overholt, Abraham 19
Overholt, B.F. 65; strike of 1886 meeting 88; strike of 1891 meeting 102–103
Overholt, C.S. 11, 44, 65
Overholt, J.S.R. 20
Overholt, J.W. 154
Overholt Distillery 11
Overholt, Frick & Co. 20–1
Owensdale 18

Paddock, J.H. 7, 124–128, 159
padrone system 51–52
Painter, Israel 11
Painter, Oliver K. 173
Painter Mine 79
Palassio, Antonio 3, 30
Pamphlet Law 2787 135
Panic of 1873 6, 19, 21, 35, 59, 65–66, 142
Panic of 1893 6, 33, 121
Paradise Lake 47
Paratic, John 111–112
Parish of the Transfiguration 46
Parker C.W. 102–103
pasanka 48
patch 49, 51–52, 54
Patroski, John 100
Patterson, (Pattison) Governor Robert 104–105
Paul Mine 22, 103
Pennsville Mine 99, 148

Pennsylvania: Birthplace of a Nation 38
Pennsylvania Bureau of Historic Preservation 28
Pennsylvania Department of Mines 171, 175
Pennsylvania Era 9
Pennsylvania Historical and Museum Commission 38
Pennsylvania Miners' Association 90
Pennsylvania National Guard 25, 29, 64, 104, 114, 108–109, 115, 116, 117, 129–131
Pennsylvania Railroad Company 60, 69
Pennsylvania Railway 11
Pennsylvania Secretary of Health 135
Pennsylvania State Library 67
Pennsylvania State Militia 27
Pennsylvania Supreme Court 133
Pennsylvania Workmen's Compensation Act 61
Penrose, Senator Boise 31
Percy Mine 81
Percy Mining Company 81
Philadelphia 63, 97
Philadelphia and Reading Coal and Iron Company 60
Philadelphia and Reading Railway Company 60
Philadelphia Inquirer 87
philanthropy 37–40
Phillippi, Mike 118–119
Phillips, Henry, Jr. 94
Phillips Mine 17
Pigman, Morris 112–114
Pigots, Mike 100
Pinkerton Detective Agency 6, 25–27, 29, 64, 95–97, 102–103, 117
Pitcairn, Robert 65
Piteur, Steve 100
Pittsburgh 16, 32, 36, 48, 57, 80, 88, 90, 119
Pittsburgh and Allegheny in the Centennial Year 9
Pittsburgh and Connellsville Railroad Company 11, 143, 156
Pittsburgh Commercial Gazette 72–73
Pittsburgh Daily Post 76, 123
Pittsburgh Dispatch 72
Pittsburg(h), McKeesport and Youghiogheny bridge 126
Pittsburgh Press 127
Pittsburgh Seam 10, 13, 16
Pittsburgh Street 69
Pittsburgh, Virginia and Charleston railway 96
Pletcher, W.H. 172
Plumstock Iron Works 10
Poland 47
Polish Poles *see* immigrants
Polko, A. 77
Port Royal Mine 130
Porter, W.N. 67
Porter's Gap 69

Powderly, Master Workman 96–98
Pramiki, John 112
Prebula, Joe 100
Price, Thomas 92
Princeton 37
Promuka, Steve 112
Property Records 141–177
Public Works Administration 134
Pulp and Paper Mills 134
Purity of Waters Act 133

Rae, J.B. 102–103
Rafferty, B.F. 88
Rafferty, Gilbert 71, 163–164
Rafferty & Donnelly Coal & Coke Co. 169
Rainey, W.J. 11, 16, 22, 27, 33, 66, 81, 92–93, 97, 99, 101, 117; strike of 1886 84, 88; strike of 1891 meeting 102–103; sues the unions 103; wages 122
Ramsey, Erskine 29
Ramsey, Morris 30, 76, 78–79, 102–103, 104–105, 107
Ramsey, Robert 30, 79, 152
Ramsey School 37
Reading Company 60
Reading Times 116
rectangular oven 16–17
Redstone Creek Watershed 136–138
Redstone Mine 22, 97; sold to Frick 101
Redtop 112
Reed, David, Jr. 119
Reese, Orrin[e] 111–114, 119
Reid, E.H. 152
Reid, J.M. 88
Report on the Operation and Output of the Coke Ovens of the Connellsville Region 67, 141–177
Republican 42–43, 176
Reyburn, Judge 111–114, 118–119
RGGS Land & Minerals 22, 141–177
Rice, W.E. 161
Richey, F.M. 173
Rinehart, Mart 111–114, 118–119
Rinehart, Ward 118–119
Rinehart, William 118–119
Ringler, Nora 110
Rist, Joseph 20–1
Rist Mine 9, 20; history, incidents and events 161–162; sealings 136–138
Robbins, Joseph 144
Rock, Jesse 112–114
Rollison, Helen 54
Roman Catholic 45
Rooks, Joseph 80
Rosser (superintendent, Leith) 105
Roth, John 158
Rowbaker, John 109
Rubie, B.H. 90, 164
Rural Free Press 36
Rush, Logan 161
Rush Coal Company 161
Rusty (the mule) 15

Sable, John 146
safety 34–36
Safety First 34
Saggie, Michael 85–86
St. Cyril and Methodius 47
St. Florin Church 46
St. John the Baptist Byzantine Catholic Church 45, 48
St. John the Baptist Roman Catholic Cemetery, Scottdale 108
St. John the Divine Russian Orthodox Church 47–48
St. Joseph's Polish Catholic Church 46
St. Paul Coal Company 21
St. Peter's Episcopal Church 38
St. Peter's Slovak Lutheran Church 46
St. Stanislaus Church 47
St. Stephen Byzantine Catholic Church 48
St. Vincent's Irish Catholic Church 45
Sanger, Martha Frick Symington 19
Sanitary Water Board 133–134
sarma 49
Scaife, Oliver P. 90
Schamberg, Max 33, 80–81, 86
Schenck, H.E. 146
Schenck, W.P. 146
Schoonmaker Col. J.M. 22, 66, 68, 71, 79, 90, 92–93, 98; sells to Frick 101; strike of 1886 meeting 88; strike of 1891 meeting 102–103
Schoonmaker, J.S. 101, 102–103
Schoonmaker, S.L. 22, 71, 72, 79, 90–91; 101
Schrader, John 111–112
Schuylkill 47, 64
Schwab, Charles 25
Science Magazine 37
Sclava, Steve 118–119
Scottdale 7, 18, 19, 22, 47, 69, 70, 78, 80, 89, 90–91, 102, 104, 111, 118, 135, 141
Scottdale Herald 67
Scottdale House 70
Scottdale Independent 1, 32, 41, 44, 67, 88, 91, 97, 122; death of Paddock 124–125; strike of 1886 85–87
Scottdale Independent Observer 67
Scottdale Rural Free Press 67
Scottdale Tribune 67
Scots *see* immigrants
Scranton 96
scrip 6, 28–29, 36, 59–60
sealing *see* individual mines
Seeman, Edward 107, 111–114
Semet-Solvay Company 16
Sen, Frank 111–112
shaft entrance 13
Shallenberger, Jackson 157
Shallenberger, Lloyd 19
Shaw Coal Company 21
Shawley, Mrs. 112–114
Sheebock, John 110
Sheiebell, Michael 97

Index

Shenango Valley 91
Sheppard, Muriel Earley 32, 121
Sherrick, A.H. 88
Sherrick, Christopher 11, 69
Sherrick, Peter 70
Sherrick Coal & Coke Company 22
Sherrick Run 136–138
Shields, John 12, 67
Shirer, Thomas 110
Shoaf Mine 17
Shorthill, James 113–114
Shosky, Andy 100
Shrader, Daniel 109, 112
Shrader, Harry 119
Shrader, John 119
Shrum, Robert 119
Shrum, William 99
Shulak, N. 80
Shupe, Daniel 11
Shupe, David 109
Shupe Run 20
Shupe's mill 112
Skera, Peter 112
Skrabec, Quentin, Jr. 38
Slangina, George 80
Slater, Al 77
Slater (superintendent) 77
sliding scale 68, 71–72, 97–98; broken 121–122; offered 103–104; union proposal 123–124
Sligra, Mike 112
slope entrance 13
Slovak Citizens Club 46
Slovak Colonization Society 121
Slovakia 47
Slovaks *see* immigrants
Smeigle, Rev 108
Smith, Stany 100
Smithton 48, 130
Snyder, H.P. 67
Socialist Labor Party of America 118
Socialists 88, 117–118
Soisson, Peter 154
Solvay Soda Ash Works 16
Southwest (Connellsville) Coal and Coke Company 76, 78, 94, 101, 107, 163; eviction notice 112; history, incidents and events 173–176; strikers marching 129
Southwest No 1. *see* Morewood Mine
Southwest No. 2 *see* Alice Mine
Southwest No. 3 *see* Alverton Mine
Southwest No. 4 *see* Tarrs Mine
Southwest Pennsylvania Railway Company 11
Speigle (attorney) 118–119
Spencer, C.H. 22
Standard Mine 7, 9, 21–2, 30, 46, 49, 57, 76, 78, 87, 89, 91, 98, 100; history 176–177; march to 104–105; plight of evicted miners 130–131
Standard Oil 35, 59
Stannix, Andy 80
Stannix, George 80
Stannix, Stefan (Steve) 78–80

Star (Stauffer) Mine 7, 9, 22, 91; history, incidents and events 165–166
Star Junction Mine 177
Stauffer (Stouffer), Joseph R. 11, 65, 88, 97, 102–103
Stauffer Run sealings 136–138
Steel, J.R. 119
Stentz, D.P. 67
Sterling, Sheriff 87
Sterling Mine 22; sold to Frick 101
Stevens, Sylvester K. 38
Stevenson, John 67, 70
Stewart, Sheriff 78–79, 87
Stewart Mine 98
Stickel, A.C. 173
Stickleback 88
Stillwagon, Charles 144
Stoner, Mrs. Jerry 112–114
Stoner Coal Company 173
Stonerville *see* Alverton
Stouffer, J.T. 69
Strickler, Hiram B. 67
Strickler, J.A. 88
Strickler and Lane 146
strikes 6–7; 1875 68–70; 1875 to 1886 63–88; 1875 to 1879 7, 66; 1876 70–71; 1879 71–73; 1881 73–74; 1886 7, 66, 74–88; 1887 7, 66, 89–98; 1889 7, 66, 98–101; 1891 7, 66, 102–120; 1894 7, 66, 121–131
Struckey, John 100
Stuch coke drawer (Leith) 105
Summit Mine 7, 9, 11, 73, 74; evictions 87, 98, 116; history, incidents and events 156–158; meeting 116; strikers marching 129
The Survey 57
Sweeney, Ned 161
Sweeney, Robert 118
Syndicate (Coke Syndicate) 68, 88–90 93, 98

Taggart, J.K. 88, 90
Tannery Waste Disposal Committee of Pennsylvania 134
Tarbell, Ida 35, 59
Tarrs Mine 22, 57, 98; march to 104–108
Taylor (bookkeeper, Leith) 105
Taylor, George 109
Taylor, John 10
Thaw, William 33
Thompson, George 88
Thompson, J.V. 32
Thurston, George 9
Tinstman, A.O. 11, 20–1, 65, 71
Tip Top Mine 7, 9, 22, 72, 74, 98, 104; history, incidents and events 160–161; sealings 136–138
tipple 13, 14
Tomosko, John 100
Trauger 46, 47
Tribune Press 67
Trinity Building, New York 22
Trinity Church 69
Trotter Mine 35; damaged 115; evictions 87, 92

Trotter Water Company 12
Truca, Michael 92
Tuzak, John 80
Tyrone Coal Company 161

Ukraine 47
Ukrainians *see* immigrants
Ulery, William 119
Union Insurance Company 60
Union Mine 9
Union Pacific Railroad Company 60
Union Savings Bank 38
Union Supply Company 30, 32, 36, 56–58; Christmas cheer 150; helping families 121–122
Union Trust Company of Pittsburgh 60
Uniondale 98
Unions 20, 23, 63, 72, 89
Uniontown 11, 17, 22, 32, 45, 47, 72, 73, 78, 81, 89, 99, 100, 104, 115, 116, 117, 126, 135–136; hospital 37
United Coal and Coke Company 129
United Mine 46, 100
United Mine Workers (of America) 30, 32, 61, 63–64, 102–104, 121; reform 123
United Presbyterian Church 38
United Sons of Vulcan 63
United States 102
U.S. Emigration Office 43
United States Senate Commission on Industrial Relations 35
United States Senate Committee on Interstate Commerce 28
United States Steel *see* U.S. Steel
U.S. Steel 2, 6, 16, 22, 24, 31–32, 34, 38; company housing 52–53, 60, 142
United States Supreme Court 133
University of Pittsburgh 2, 68

Valley Mine 7, 9, 22, 72, 74, 76, 78; evictions 78; fire 148; history, incidents and events 147–150; strikebreakers 87, 98, 104, 110, 118; strikers marching 129
Valley Station 69
Vancourt, W.O. 136
Van Meter 12
Vintondale Mine 138

wages 33–34, 56–57, 60–61, 69, 71, 122
Walker, Andrew 92
Walker, John 94
Wardell, James 145, 146
Warren, Kenneth 102, 121
Washabaugh, George 19
Washington, George 10
Watchorn, Robert 99; Morewood Massacre viewpoint 109–110; strike of 1891 meeting 102–103
water 12, 132
Wealth, Waste, and Alienation 102
Weddell, Robert 109, 119

Index

Weekly Courier see *Connellsville Courier*
Weigenski, Martain 114
Weigenski, Mrs. 112, 114
weighmaster 14
Weinman 166
Welsh, John 112, 118
Welsh, Joseph 88
Welsh *see* immigrants
West Overton Mine 78, 97
West Overton Village 19, 44, 67, 72
West Virginia 102
Western Pennsylvania Coalition for Abandoned Mine Reclamation 136–138
Westinghouse Electric and Manufacturing Company 176
Westmoreland and Fayette Historical Society 19
Westmoreland Coal and Coke Company 48, 97
Westmoreland Hospital 37
Wetherell, Vint 100
W.H. Blake & Co. 148
Wheeler Mine 92, 98
Whipkey, S.C. 161

White, John (J.M.) 72, 74
White, John G. 152
White Mine (Globe) 7, 9, 12, 17, 41, 48, 98, 104; history, incidents and events 159–160
Whitney Mine 118
Whyle, Superintendent 105
Wiggins, Jim 152
Wiggins, Samuel 143, 152
Wilhelm, John 153
Wilhelm, Sheriff 126–128
Wilkinshaw H.W. 111–114
William Penn Hotel 32, 38
Willson, Alpheus E. 11
Wilson, Harry 107, 111–114, 119
Wilson, Rev. Howard S. 38
Wilson, Woodrow 43
Wilson, Boyle, Playford and Ewing 148
Winchester rifles 96; strikers marching 128
Winingroth, Charles 162
Winjewski, Martin 112
Wise, Peter 74, 78, 80, 105, 108; strike of 1891 meetings 102–103, 104

Woods, John Y. 135
World's Fair of 1893 177
Woshuck, John 100
WPA Farm Security Administration 54
Wyano 46, 48
Wynn Mine 101, 104

Yellow Dogs 65
Yenrack, Josef 105
Yochman, John 89–90
Yough *see* Youghiogheny
Youghioghenian 67
Youghiogheny 9, 10, 11, 12, 19, 21, 45; seals 135, 141
Youghiogheny Water Company 12, 158
Youngstown 98
Yukon 46, 47, 48
Yusco, John 100

Zimmerman, Undertaker 107, 108
Zundel, J.A. (Jacob) 107, 111–114, 119

www.ingramcontent.com/pod-product-compliance
Lightning Source LLC
Chambersburg PA
CBHW080804300426
44114CB00020B/2821